Springer Series on Asian Criminology and Criminal Justice Research

Series editor

The series publishes both theoretical and empirical work along several themes in Asian Criminology, with a focus on research-level monographs and edited volumes. It aims to cover 4 main themes: the elaborations and adaptations of research models and established theories (established mainly by Western scholarship) to Asian contexts; an introduction of innovative concepts, theories and policies originating in Asian societies to Western audiences; and in-depth studies of particular Asian countries, as they reflect local traditions and cultures one hand, and a general understanding of criminal behavior or criminal justice, on the other. It will feature authors from any country of origin doing research about or pertaining to Asian countries.

The series encourages submissions of both quantitative and qualitative research approaches, as well as mixed methods and comparative approaches, with a focus on studies using rigorous methods and presenting new research results. It will be of interest to researchers in criminology and criminal justice, as well as related fields such as sociology, demography and international studies.

More information about this series at http://www.springer.com/series/15738

Jianhong Liu • Setsuo Miyazawa
Editors

Crime and Justice in Contemporary Japan

Springer

Editors
Jianhong Liu
Department of Social Sciences
University of Macau
Taipa, Macau, China

Setsuo Miyazawa
Hastings College of the Law
University of California
San Francisco, CA, USA

ISSN 2522-5545 ISSN 2522-5553 (electronic)
Springer Series on Asian Criminology and Criminal Justice Research
ISBN 978-3-319-69358-3 ISBN 978-3-319-69359-0 (eBook)
https://doi.org/10.1007/978-3-319-69359-0

Library of Congress Control Number: 2017963552

Printed on acid-free paper

This Springer imprint is published by Springer Nature
The registered company is Springer International Publishing AG
The registered company address is: Gewerbestrasse 11, 6330 Cham, Switzerland

Contents

Contributors

Tsuneyuki Abe Graduate School of Arts and Letters, Tohoku University, Sendai, Japan

Laura Bui Department of Social Science, Liverpool Hope University, Liverpool, UK

Marika Dawkins University of Texas Rio Grande Valley, Edinburg, TX, USA

David P. Farrington Institute of Criminology, University of Cambridge, Cambridge, UK

Michael H. Fox Japan Innocence and Death Penalty Information Center, Hyogo University, Kakogawa, Japan

Kyoko Fujino Department of Letters, Arts and Sciences, Waseda University, Tokyo, Japan

Masahiro Fujita Faculty of Sociology, Kansai University, Suita, Osaka, Japan

Camille Gibson Prairie View A&M University, Prairie View, TX, USA

Yutaka Harada Crime Prevention Section, Department of Criminology and Behavioral Sciences, National Research Institute of Police Science, Kashiwa, Japan

Mari Hirayama Faculty of Law, Professor of Criminal Procedure and Crime Policy at Hakuoh University, Tochigi, Japan

Mari Kita University of Hawai'i at Mānoa, Honolulu, HI, USA

Mark A. Levin William S. Richardson School of Law, University of Hawai'i at Mānoa, Honolulu, HI, USA

Jianhong Liu Department of Social Sciences, University of Macau, Taipa, Macao, China

Setsuo Miyazawa Hastings College of the Law, University of California, San Francisco, CA, USA

Takemi Mori Faculty of Human Sciences, Konan Women's University, Kobe, Japan

Takaharu Ohara Self-Reliance Support Facilities, National Musashino Gakuin, Saitama, Japan

Hideo Okamoto Division of Human Life and Environmental Sciences, Nara Women's University, Nara, Japan

Nicola Padfield Institute of Criminology, University of Cambridge, Cambridge, UK

Aki Roberts Department of Sociology, University of Wisconsin-Milwaukee, Milwaukee, WI, USA

Mai Sato School of Law, University of Reading, Reading, UK

Toyoji Saito Emeritus Professor of Konan University, Kobe, Japan

Masahiko Saeki Graduate School of Social Sciences, Chiba University, Chiba, Japan

Yuji Shiroshita Faculty of Law, Hokkaido University, Sapporo, Japan

Yuichiro Tsuji Graduate School of Humanities and Social Science, University of Tsukuba, Tsukuba, Japan

Mitsuaki Ueda Institute of Advanced Research and Education, Doshisha University, Kamigyo-ku, Kyoto, Japan

Eiichiro Watamura Graduate School of Human Sciences, Osaka University, Osaka, Japan

Julius Weitzdörfer Faculty of Law, University of Cambridge, Cambridge, UK

Etsuko Yuhara Department of Social Welfare, Nihon Fukushi University, Okuda, Mihama-cho, Aichi-pref, Chita-gun, Japan

Minoru Yokoyama Kokugakuin University, Tokyo, Japan

Chapter 1
Asian Criminology and Crime and Justice in Japan: An Introduction

Jianhong Liu and Setsuo Miyazawa

Japan is well known for an outstanding fact that its crime rates, particularly the violent crime rates, are the lowest among all industrialized countries. Theories of modernization and social change from Durkheim's time have been repeatedly supported by the facts that almost all the countries experience a rapid rise in crimes along with the process of modernization, industrialization, and large-scaled population migration (e.g., Liu, Zhang, & Messner, 2001a, 2001b; Liu & Messner, 2001). Japan is an outstanding exception (see Tables 1.1 and 1.2). Criminologists naturally ask why, How do we explain this criminological mystery? Prominent Western scholars of comparative criminology explain the importance of understanding crime and justice in Asia. Karstedt (2001) has pointed out that the low crime rates in Asia are a major puzzle. She stated that scholars "look in awe to Asia, and try to solve the enigma of modern, affluent societies with low rates especially of violent crimes" (Karstedt, 2001, p. 285). These observations demonstrate the critical importance of developing criminology in Asia. In recent years, an increasing number of prominent scholars have recognized the importance and contributions of Asian criminology (Agnew, 2015; Belknap, 2015; Braithwaite, 2014, 2015; Carrington, Hogg, & Sozzo, 2015; Messner, 2014, 2015; Sampson, 2015; Thilagaraj & Liu, 2017; Walklate, 2015).

John Braithwaite in his keynote speech in the Sixth Asian Criminological Conference in Osaka on June 27–29, 2014, has made it clear of the role of Asia in developing criminology today:

> Asia and the Pacific embrace the regions of greatest cultural and linguistic diversity in the world. Asia's most important contribution to global criminology is therefore in opening its eyes to completely new ways of seeing, as opposed to adjusting, testing, or revising western

J. Liu (✉)
Department of Social Sciences, University of Macau, Taipa, Macao, China
e-mail: jliu@umac.mo

S. Miyazawa
Hastings College of the Law, University of California, San Francisco, CA, USA

J. Liu, S. Miyazawa (eds.), *Crime and Justice in Contemporary Japan*,
Springer Series on Asian Criminology and Criminal Justice Research,
https://doi.org/10.1007/978-3-319-69359-0_1

Table 1.1 Crime rates per 100,000 population in five industrialized countries in 2014

	Japan	United States	France	Germany	United Kingdom
Assault	21.0	232.1	354.5	155.9	649.1
Kidnapping	0.2	–	4.6	6.2	3.8
Sexual violence	6.8	–	48.3	58.3	136.9
Homicide	0.3	3.9[a]	1.2	0.9	0.9[a]
Total for violence crime	28.3	236	408.6	221.3	790.7
Theft	356.2	1833.9	1970.4	1624.0	2209.0
Robbery	2.4	102.0	177.9	56.4	87.5
Burglary	73.8	541.5	587.3	553.1	716.7
Motor vehicle theft	47.2	215.8	263.7	79.7	132.1
Total for property crime	479.6	2693.2	2999.3	2313.2	3145.3

Source: UNODC (https://data.unodc.org)
Note: The data of kidnapping and sexual violence of the United States is not provided
[a]Data of 2013

> theories in light of eastern experience. Restorative justice innovation provides good examples of how Asian philosophy and practice can enrich western criminal justice in ways that enhance crime control and respect for rights in the west. (Braithwaite, 2015)

> It is the right time in the development of criminology in Asia to move away from an international division of scholarly labor whereby influential theories are developed in the west, while Asia's role is to apply or test those theories in Asian contexts or adapt them to Asian realities. It is time for a new era of criminological theory that was given birth in Asia by Asian scholars. (Braithwaite, 2015)

With the mission to develop Asian criminology, I have discussed key questions of the approach and strategies for developing Asian criminology in several papers and speeches (Liu, 2009a, 2016, 2017a, 2017b; Liu, Travers, & Chang, 2017a, 2017b), In my 2009 paper, "Asian Criminology – Challenges, Opportunities, and Directions" (Liu, 2009a), I stressed that "The paradigm of Asian criminology should consider the diversity of Asia, particularly encouraging the in-depth study of Asian contexts, traditions, and theoretical or practice models, as well as topics that are particularly Asian." (p. 8). I have stressed the importance of an Asian criminological paradigm as an overall program to develop Asian criminology (Liu, 2009a, 2016, 2017a, 2017b). Japan provides an excellent context to develop Asian criminology.

This book demonstrates and is organized around the three major approaches in the Asian criminological paradigm. The first approach is to stress the central importance of analyzing and understanding special features of social and cultural context in generating criminological knowledge (Liu, 2009a; Liu, Jou, & Hebenton, 2013; Liu et al., 2001a, 2001b). The second approach is to adopt the three strategies in developing theoretical knowledge under Asia contexts (Liu, 2016, 2017a, 2017b). The third approach is to emphasize the importance of taking special consideration of the challenges of Asian contexts in generating knowledge in criminal justice policy (Liu, 2014, 2016, 2017a, 2017b). This book includes five sections; the chapters in each section suggest how each of these approaches within the Asian

Table 1.2 Crime rates per 100,000 population in Japan from 2003 to 2014

	2003	2004	2005	2006	2007	2008	2009	2010	2011	2012	2013	2014
Assault	46.2	47.0	47.5	51.1	49.5	47.2	20.9	20.9	20.4	22.1	21.9	21.0
Kidnapping	0.2	0.3	0.2	0.2	0.2	0.1	0.1	0.1	0.1	0.1	0.1	0.2
Sexual violence	9.9	9.0	8.5	8.1	7.4	6.9	6.4	6.6	6.4	6.8	7.1	6.8
Homicide	0.6	0.6	0.5	0.5	0.5	0.5	0.4	0.4	0.3	0.3	0.3	0.3
Theft	–	837.1	727.1	638.1	584.7	566.0	517.3	485.5	458.0	429.5	391.9	356.2
Robbery	–	5.8	4.7	4.0	3.6	3.4	3.6	3.2	2.9	2.9	2.6	2.4
Burglary	263.4	229.2	192.8	161.6	138.1	122.0	116.8	107.4	99.3	90.7	84.5	73.8
Motor vehicle theft	–	146.3	118.8	101.7	90.2	85.3	85.4	77.2	73.9	64.3	57.5	47.2

Source: UNODC (https://data.unodc.org)

criminological paradigm have been adopted by influential Japanese scholars in their research and how they generate knowledge important to criminology in general.

For the first approach, Asian criminological paradigm stresses the central importance of analyzing Asian context in generating important knowledge for criminology. It is foundationally important to examine the special features of the context of the countries (Liu, 2009a). For example, an outstanding feature of Japanese context is the low crime rates. The crime rate of Japan is the lowest among major industrialized countries. Table 1.1 shows the crime rates of major crime types in five industrialized countries in 2014. Japan has lowest rates compared with the other four countries in all the major crime types.

Examining the trend of crime, Japan has also enjoyed a declining crime rate in the last decade. For example, the homicide rate per 100,000 population is from 0.6 in 2003 to 0.3 in 2014 in Japan.

Section 1 of the book titled "Changing Crimes in Japan" extends our general knowledge of lower crime rates to examine in more details how special features of Japanese context influence crimes in Japan, reflecting the general strategy of Asian criminological paradigm. A very special and important feature of the Japanese context is the aging of the population. The first paper "Changes in Crime and Reactions to Crime in Japan Becoming Stagnant with Aging" by Professor Minoru Yokoyama examines the changes in crimes under the contexts of an aging population. The paper analyzes how the demographic change—an aging population in Japan—influences crime rates, through its influence to migration policy and phenomena of immigration.

The second paper is by Mari Kita, the title is "Kin, Crime, and Criminal Justice in Contemporary Japan." This paper addresses a policy issue on the interactions of family members of offenders and suspects with criminal justice system in Japan. The research conducted ethnographic work on 43 individuals to address the suffering and adverse experience of family members of offenders, provided important policy suggestions of providing needed assistance to them, and respected their human rights.

The third paper "Incidents of Homicides or Murder–suicides by Family Caregivers in Japan and Challenges for Prevention" by Professor Etsuko Yuhara further examines the contextual features of aging society by focusing on a special type of crime—murder–suicides by family caregivers.

The fourth paper "The Effect of Disaster Damage on the Occurrence of Crime: A Survey of Residents of Four Prefectures Affected by the Great East Japan Earthquake" is written by Hideo Okamoto and his colleagues. This paper explores the relationship between disaster damage and crime based on an online survey of participants sampled from residents of prefectures which suffered significant damage in the Great East Japan Earthquake of 2011.

The fifth paper is "Revisiting Japan's Postwar Homicide Trend, 1951-2014" by Aki Roberts. This paper is a replication and extension of the 2004 paper's national time series analysis published at *Criminology* by the author, focusing on homicide rates and including data through 2014. The new analysis found statistically significant and positive associations with homicide for poverty, income inequality, and young male population. Results provide further support for the importance of absolute and relative economic stress and population composition as factors in Japan's homicide trend.

These papers demonstrate the central role of analyzing crime under Japanese context and their special features. These analyses provide information that otherwise can't be recognized in Western contexts and generate important knowledge about crime for criminology.

For its second approach, Asian criminological paradigm proposes three strategies to develop criminological concepts and theories in Asia (Liu, 2016, 2017a, 2017b). A central task for Asian criminology is to understand features of the context and how various factors influence crimes and their distributions and by special groups. These strategies correspond to the three stages of development of theories (Liu, 2016, 2017a, 2017b).

The first strategy is to examine the established Western criminology theory under Asian contexts, that is, to apply the theory established in the West, to test its applicability under Asian Contexts, and to evaluate its feasibility and generalizability to a broader scope of Asian contexts.

The second strategy is to transform the theory or theories to a new form under Asian contexts. This involved creating and incorporating new concepts that are more faithful to the social realities of non-Western societies such as Asia (e.g., Liu, 1999, 2004, 2005, 2009b).

The third strategy is to establish distinctively a different theory that is based on the comparative and Asian realities and that answers distinctively important questions that Asian criminology more naturally asks and answers. It analyzes the special features of Asian contexts and conceptual processes to establish new concepts and theories (Braithwaite, 2015; Liu, 2014, 2016).

The second section of the book titled "Testing and Developing theories of Crime and Delinquency" reflects how these strategies are adopted by influential Japanese scholars in their research on developing theories under the context of Japan.

The first paper "Potential Risk Factors for Serious Delinquency in Japan: Findings from Osaka Male Youths" is coauthored by Laura Bui, David P. Farrington, and Mitsuaki Ueda. The paper takes the strategy of testing well-established Western theory to Japan context. The paper tests the applicability of risk factors of juvenile delinquency found in Western criminological research to the Japanese context. The paper reports results of a quantitative research and found that four risk factors have effects similar to those found in Western research and discusses policy implications of their findings.

The second paper in this section is Yutaka Harada's paper, "Laying the Groundwork for Testing the Routine Activity Theory at Micro Level with the Aid of Japanese Satellite Positioning Technology." The paper elaborates the routine activity theory with new methods of data collection and new data collected with application of a state-of-art technology. The research produced interesting theoretical elaborations and produced clear policy implications.

The third paper by Professor Kyoko Fujino, "Analysis of Current Criminals in Japan Based on Typology of Relationships with Others," reflects the third strategy of Asian criminological paradigm to develop new theoretical ideas. The paper proposed a new interesting theoretical typology, based on the idea of a typology of relationships with others. The concepts and typology are based on results of her quantitative research about the relationship between self-control, bonding to conventional world, and delinquency and discuss implications of theories of Gottfredson, Hirschi, and Braithwaite in the context of Japanese society from the perspective of criminal psychology.

For the third approach, Asian criminological paradigm stresses the importance of developing research questions important for Asian contexts, and reflecting the needs of Asian policy, and produces innovative policy ideas and solutions to criminal justice issues and practice. This knowledge is important to extend our understanding crime control and effective society response to crime problems thus expand criminology (Liu, 2016). This book included three sections, the section three to section five, to address different aspects of criminal justice policies in Japan that reflect the various features of Japanese criminal justice innovations and their development. These innovations in many ways differ from the typical Western system and contribute to the crime control and social order, reflect important contributions to criminal justice knowledge, and are important contents of Asian Criminology.

The third section of the book, "Challenges and Trends in Criminal Justice Reform," is designed to report research on the features of Japanese criminal justice practice and policies that reflect the contribution of Japanese context to criminology and criminal justice research in general. The section addresses several specific criminal justice issues that reflect important features of Japanese criminal justice. The attentions are given to acute questions raised in the criminal justice policy and practice debates.

The first paper by Mark Levin is "Considering Japanese Criminal Justice from an Original Position." This work posits that differences in public awareness of race in Japan and the United States are salient and encourages reformers in Japan to contemplate this when strategizing their efforts. To that end, the discourse that deploys John Rawls' veil of ignorance in his *Theory of Justice* into the Japanese public consciousness may provide a fruitful mechanism for improving the efficacy of reform efforts there.

The second paper by Julius Weitzdörfer et al., "Sentencing and Punishment in Japan and England: A Comparative Discussion," discusses the sentencing and punishment in Japan from the comparative perspective. The paper compares England and Wales, as a jurisdiction allowing indefinite imprisonment without chance of parole, with Japan, as a jurisdiction retaining the death penalty. The paper discusses trends in both sentencing regimes and introduces four recent Japanese reforms.

The third paper is "Fire, Coerced Confession, and Wrongful Conviction: A Tale of Two Countries" by Michael H. Fox. This paper compares two fire cases and argues that the criminal justice authorities created crimes and carried out willful prosecutions against innocent suspects. Though unusual in the field of wrongful conviction research, this paper asks and attempts to answer why the arrests occurred. It also asserts that if the fires occurred today, it is unlikely that either the American or Japanese defendants would be convicted. Several reasons are also discussed for this.

The fourth paper is Mai Sato's "From measuring support for the death penalty to justifying its retention: Japanese public opinion surveys on crime and punishment, 1956-2014." The paper addresses a major public policy issue and public opinion on death penalty. Professor Mai Sato is a top authority on the topic and has published her influential book *The Death Penalty in Japan: Will the Public Tolerate Abolition?*

(Sato, 2014). Sato's analyses of the public opinion survey conducted by the Japanese government in 1967 found that the Japanese public would probably have been ready for abolition death penalty around that time, while the data have been interpreted by the Japanese government that the public support their retentionist policy.

The fifth paper is "Crime victims' protection under the free speech law in Japan" by Yuichiro Tsuji. This paper argues that the amount of damage by defamation or privacy infringement in Japan is so small that the publisher might get an article published even in face of potential litigation. It also reviews if recent cases are challenging the market of ideas.

The fourth section "Lay Judges System" addresses a unique innovation of Japanese criminal justice system: lay judge system. The paper in this section discusses various issues involved, showing how Japanese scholars and policy makers develop criminal policy under special Japanese contexts.

The first paper is "The Impact of Previous Sentencing Trends on Lay Judges' Sentencing Decisions" coauthored by Masahiko Saeki and Eiichiro Watamura.

The paper addresses a Japanese innovative criminal justice reform of using lay judges and the effects of such a new system. The paper employs an experimental design to study the justice policy issues. The findings provide scientific research results useful for guiding policy reform.

The second paper is Masahiro Fujita's "To be suspended or not to be? The effects of emotions and personality variables on lay people's judgment of suspension of punishment." This study explores the effects of emotional or other subjective factors on suspending decisions with a questionnaire experiment which is participated by university students. Through analyses of the participants' judgments on a fictitious criminal case, the author investigated the effects of emotional and empathic factors on the judgments of suspension of the accused. At the same time, the author looked into the relationships between the judgments and attitudes toward crime and law and relationships between judgments and empathic personality traits.

The third paper in this section is by Mari Hirayama. The title of the paper is "Future of Criminal Justice Policy for Sex Crime in Japan: The Possible Impacts by the Lay Judge System." The paper considers how special features of Japanese society and the special lay judge system influence the criminal justice policy for sex crime and its future.

This last section is "Juvenile Justice and Support System in Japan" which discusses special features of the juvenile justice system and shows us how special Japanese contexts shape the innovations and effective programs in juvenile justice systems in Japan.

The first paper of this section is "The Juvenile Justice System of Japan: An Overview" by Camille Gibson and Marika Dawkins, which made an overview about the juvenile justice system of Japan, including policies and legislations, patterns in juvenile delinquency, the family court procedures, and family court hearings.

The second paper is by Takaharu Ohara, titled as "Empirical Research on Socio-Cultural Transition in Children in the Children's Self-Reliance Support Facility and the Effect of Support." The paper addresses a very important the Japanese criminal justice practice. In Japan, juvenile delinquents may be committed to either a reformatory under the jurisdiction of the justice ministry or a children's self-reliance support facility under the jurisdiction of the Ministry of Health, Labor, and Welfare.

As staff member of a national children's self-reliance support facility, Ohara analyzes characteristics of juveniles admitted to his facility in 1980 through 2010. This research is continuing, and the findings will have important policy implication.

In sum, Japan has provided an excellent context for developing Asian criminology. The papers published in this book reported much important accomplishment in the study of crime, theoretical efforts, and criminal justice issues that are important in Japan, providing much valuable knowledge in the development of criminology in general.

References

Agnew, R. (2015). Using general strain theory to explain crime in Asian societies. *Asian Journal of Criminology, 10*(2), 131–147.

Belknap, J. (2015, June). The expansion of Asian criminology and how it is advancing criminology research and crime control. In *Keynote speech at 7th ACS annual conference*, Hong Kong.

Braithwaite, J. (2014). Crime in Asia: Toward a better future. *Asian Journal of Criminology, 9*, 65–75.

Braithwaite, J. (2015). Rethinking criminology through radical diversity in Asian reconciliation. *Asian Journal of Criminology, 10*(3), 183–191.

Carrington, K., Hogg, R., & Sozzo, M. (2015). Southern criminology. *British Journal of Criminology, 56*(1), 1–20. https://doi.org/10.1093/bjc/azv083.

Karstedt, S. (2001). Comparing cultures, comparing crime: Challenges, prospects and problems for a global criminology. *Crime, Law and Social Change, 36*(3), 285–308.

Liu, J. (1999). Social capital and covariates of reoffending risk in the Chinese context. *International Criminal Justice Review, 9*, 39–55.

Liu, J. (2004). Social transition and crime in China: An economic motivation thesis. *Australian and New Zealand Journal of Criminology, 37*, 122–138. supplement issue.

Liu, J. (2005). Crime patterns during the market transition in China. *British Journal of Criminology, 45*, 613–633.

Liu, J. (2009a). Asian criminology – Challenges, opportunities and directions. *Asian Journal of Criminology, 4*, 1–9.

Liu, J. (2009b). Re-conceptualizing crime patterns during modernization. In E. W. Plywaczewski (Ed.), *Current problems of the penal law and criminology*. Bialystok: Temida 2 Press.

Liu, J. (2014, June 27–29). Keynote address: Culture and criminal justice – A theory of relational justice. *Presentation at the Sixth Annual Conference of Asian Criminological Society*, Osaka, Japan

Liu, J. (2016). Asian paradigm theory and access to justice. *Journal of Contemporary Criminal Justice, 32*(3), 205–224.

Liu, J. (2017a). The Asian criminological paradigm and how it links global north and south: Combining an extended conceptual toolbox from the north with innovative Asian contexts. *International Journal for Crime, Justice and Social Democracy, 6*(1), 73–87. https://doi.org/10.5204/ijcjsd.v6i1.385.

Liu, J. (2017b). The new Asian paradigm: A relational approach. In J. Liu, M. Travers, & L. Chang (Eds.), *Comparative criminology in Asia*. New York: Springer.

Liu, J., Jou, S., & Hebenton, B. (2013). *Handbook of Asian criminology*. New York: Springer Publishing. ISBN: 978-1-4614-5217-1.

Liu, J., & Messner, S. F. (2001). Modernization and crime trend in China's reform era. In J. Liu, L. Zhang, & S. F. Messner (Eds.), *Crime and social control in a changing China*. Westport: Greenwood Publishing Group Inc..

Liu, J., Travers, M., & Chang, L. (2017a). Introduction to 'Comparative criminology in Asia'. In J. Liu, M. Travers, & L. Chang (Eds.), *Comparative criminology in Asia*. New York: Springer.

Liu, J., Travers, M., & Chang, L. (2017b). Reflecting on comparison: A view from Asia. In J. Liu, M. Travers, & L. Chang (Eds.), *Comparative criminology in Asia*. New York: Springer.

Liu, J., Zhang, L., & Messner, S. F. (2001a). *Crime and social control in a changing China*. Westport: Greenwood Publishing Group Inc.. ISBN: 0-313-31652-X.

Liu, J., Zhang, L., & Messner, S. F. (2001b). Introduction – Impact of market transition: Changing crime and social control in China. In J. Liu, L. Zhang, & S. F. Messner (Eds.), *Crime and social control in a changing China*. Westport: Greenwood Publishing Group Inc..

Messner, S. F. (2014). Social institutions, theory development, and the promise of comparative criminological research. *Asian Journal of Criminology, 9*, 49–63.

Messner, S. F. (2015). When west meets east: Generalizing theory and expanding the conceptual toolkit of criminology. *Asian Journal of Criminology, 10*(2), 117–129.

Sampson, R. J. (2015). Crime and the life course in a changing world: Insights from Chicago and implications for global criminology. *Asian Journal of Criminology, 10*(4), 277–286.

Sato, M. (2014). *The death penalty in Japan: Will the public tolerate abolition?* Weisbaden: Springer VS. ISBN 9783658006778.

Thilagaraj, R., & Liu, J. (2017). Introduction: Restorative justice for a harmonious India. In R. Thilagaraj & J. Liu (Eds.), *Restorative justice in India*. Cham: Springer Publishing.

Walklate, S. (2015, June). Whither criminology: Its global future(s)? In *Keynote presentation to the Asian Criminology Conference*.

Part I
Changing Crimes in Japan

Chapter 2
Changes in Crime and Reactions to Crime in Japan Becoming Stagnant with Aging

Minoru Yokoyama

1 Demographic Analysis on Change into Japanese Stagnant Society

Social problems including the problem of crime can be analyzed demographically. I analyze the change in crimes in Japan on the basis of the framework presented by David Riesman et al. in *The Lonely Crowd* in 1950.

Riesman et al. pointed out that the total population was stable for a long time before the Industrial Revolution owing to the high rate of both birth and death. After the Revolution the population explosion occurred because the rate of death declined owing to improvement of health conditions. However, in advanced Western countries the total population is gradually declining because people begin to enjoy their private life with no child or a few children. Riesman et al. foresaw the occurrence of this demographic change in other countries as the flowing.

> It seems reasonably well established ... that during this period the curve of population growth in the Western countries has shown an S-shape of a particular type (as other countries are drawn more closely into the net of Western civilization, their populations also show a tendency to develop along the lines of this S-shaped curve) (Riesman, Glazer, & Denny, 1973, p. 7).

Japan has followed Western civilization since the Meiji Restoration of 1867. Therefore, we also see population chance in the form of an S-shape as described by Riesman.

Before the Meiji Restoration we saw the bottom horizontal line of the S representing a situation where the total population increases very slowly. In this situation the number of birth roughly equaling the number of death, and both are high. The estimated total population increased slightly from 31,000,000 around 1720 to 34,200,000 in 1868 (Sudo, 2005). Riesman et al. pointed out that it was a society of

M. Yokoyama (✉)
Kokugakuin University, Tokyo, Japan
e-mail: minoruyo@kokugakuin.ac.jp

J. Liu, S. Miyazawa (eds.), *Crime and Justice in Contemporary Japan*, Springer Series on Asian Criminology and Criminal Justice Research,
https://doi.org/10.1007/978-3-319-69359-0_2

high-potential growth with a typical tendency to follow tradition. The social character in such a society is called *traditional-directed.*

With the advance of Western civilization after the Meiji Restoration, Japan became *a society of transitional population growth* in which we find people with the social character of being *inner-directed.* Their conformity is insured by their tendency to acquire an internalized set of goals early in life.

At this stage we witness a "population explosion" caused by the decline in the death rate. The total population reached 59,740,000 in 1925. During the war against China and World War II from 1937 to 1945, Japan was short of manpower. Therefore, our government encouraged people to have as many babies as possible.

At the final stage of the war the total population decreased slightly mainly due to many war deaths in battle and by bombing from US fighters. Soon after the war we witnessed a baby boom.[1] The total population then increased to 83,200,000 in 1950. With an increase in the power of people with the character of *inner-directedness*, Japan succeeded in recovering from damages caused by the war and enjoyed rapid economic growth until 1973 when an oil shock occurred. During 3 years from 1971, we witnessed a second baby boom with 2,091,983 babies born in 1973, the peak of the boom.

However, after 1973 youngsters hesitated to get married. When they did marry, in most cases they did not want to have more than two children. Japan then rushed into a third stage—"incipient population decline"—in which both birth and death are low. At this stage people began to have the social character of being *other-directed.* They lived in a society *dependent on other-direction.*

In spite of the decrease in babies, the total population continued to increase to 127,690,000 in 2004 because of a lengthening of people's life span. After 2004 the total population began to decline. According to the census carried out in October in 2010, the total population decreased for the first time during the 5-year span since 2005. The estimated total population declined to 127,040,000 on September 1 in 2014. If the low birth rate continues, the total population is estimated to decrease to 62,410,000 in 2100. Therefore, in June in 2014 the Japanese government announced a policy to maintain the total population of over 100,000,000 during 50 years into the future. If we fail to realize this policy, Japanese life standard would decline.

Japan is approaching the third stage with rapid advancement of aging. In 1970 total population reached 103,720,000 among which old people of at least 65 years of age amounted to 7.1%. Around 1985 our government foresaw that old people would increase to 21.8% in 2020. However, this forecast was wrong, as the birth rate decreased even more rapidly. In September in 2014 old people aged 65 and over reached 25.9% of the total population. In such a situation crimes committed by old-aged people became a serious social problem in Japan.

On the other hand, children under 15 years of age decreased from 13.8% of the population in 2005 to 12.8% in 2014. Most children are raised under sufficient protection by their parents and adults around them. In such a situation the quality and quantity of juvenile delinquency have changed drastically.

---

[1] During the baby boom from 1947 to 1949, about 8,000,000 babies were born, in which 2,696,638 were born in 1949, the peak of the boom.

2 Change in Juvenile Delinquency After World War II

Soon after World War II, we lived in a situation of absolute poverty, in which juveniles, especially orphans, committed crimes, especially thefts (Yokoyama, 2015, p. 188). I estimate that in a chaotic situation at that time, the quantity and quality of juvenile delinquency were the worst in our history, although we did not see the high crime rate among juveniles in the crime statistics. With the gradual establishment of a system for the policing for juveniles, the police could arrest or guide more juvenile delinquents than previously (Yokoyama, 2010a, p. 154). Then, the rate of juvenile Penal Code offenders caught by the police per population of 1000 juveniles between 10 and 19 years old reached 9.5 in 1951, the first peak of juvenile crimes.

In the early 1960s the baby boomers became teenagers. They often committed violent behavior at their high schools which drew our attention. After graduation from their junior high schools, many juveniles moved to urban areas where there were many good jobs to be found with rapid industrialization.[2] They often lived at the house of an employer or in a dormitory. Some of them who dropped out from their place of work committed crimes.[3] In such a situation the rate of juvenile Penal Code offenders increased to 11.9 in 1964, the second peak of juvenile crimes. At that time many antisocial behaviors were committed by juvenile offenders with a social character of *inner-directedness*. According to Merton's typology of modes of individual adaptation, they seemed to assume the mode of *innovation*[4] (Merton, 1968).

In the early 1980s the second baby boomers became the teenagers. Police carried out a net widening to arrest or guide more and more juvenile delinquents for minor offenses and deviant behaviors (Yokoyama, 1989, p. 47). Then, in 1983 there was a third peak of juvenile Penal Code offenses, in which the rate reached 17.1. In this year the police caught 317,438 juvenile Penal Code offenders, the highest number in history. As mentioned previously, juveniles with a social character of *other-directedness* became prevalent. In addition, with the advancement of equality between sexes, male youngsters became herbivorous-typed persons.[5] Then, many juveniles committed a social delinquency instead of antisocial one. In the early 1990s the second baby boomers became adults. Then, the number of juvenile delinquents

---

[2] During the period of high economic growth, there was an increase in the percentage of entrance to senior high schools after graduation from junior ones. The increase in the percentage was from 51.5% in 1955 to 70.7% in 1965 and to 91.9% in 1975. Although education in a senior high school is not compulsive, most young people have a chance to receive education in a senior high school if they wish.

[3] Boryokudan, a Japanese gangsters' group, succeeded in recruiting many young dropouts as its members (Yokoyama, 2000, p. 3).

[4] Around 1965 there was great cultural emphasis upon success. It invited a prevalence of the mode of *innovation* even among juvenile delinquents through the use of institutionally proscribed but often effective means of attaining the simulacra of success: wealth and power.

[5] Previously, male youngsters behaved violently like a carnivorous animal under the subculture of being proud of masculinity. Owing to the decline of such subculture, they do not attack others by the use of physical violence like an herbivorous animal. They are called "herbivorous-typed persons" in Japan.

decreased gradually until 1995 when the rate of juvenile Penal Code offenders declined to 12.1.

In the late 1990s the mass media reported about the movement of crime victims to demand the imposition of the severer punishment on offenders. As many people sympathized with this movement, the police adopted the tough policy against offenders, especially juvenile delinquents. The Juvenile Law was revised in 2000 toward a partial criminalization (Yokoyama, 2009, p. 670). Under the tough policy backed up by conservative public opinion, the rate of juvenile Penal Code offenders rose to 15.5 in 2003 (Yokoyama, 2007, p. 12).

However, the rate decreased constantly for a decade from 2003. The total number of juveniles caught for a Penal Code offense declined to 101,098 in 2012, when the rate also dropped to 8.5. Since the police maintained a tough policy against juvenile offenders, juvenile offenses seemed to decrease in reality. Why do juvenile offenses, especially violent offenses, decrease?

3 Juvenile Delinquency in Japanese Society with Declining Birth Rate

As most juveniles are raised as one child or two children in their family, they tend to be overprotected and supervised by adults around them, especially their parents.[6] I foresaw 30 years ago that *retreatism*, one of Merton's adaption modes, would increase among Japanese youngsters who are raised with overprotection (Yokoyama, 1986, p. 112).[7] As I foresaw, nowadays the *retreatism-typed* young people increase. We see more and more young people shutting themselves without participating in any positive activity.[8]

Juveniles behaving in the mode of *innovation* and *rebellion* decrease because of effective education against violence that started at the time of the second peak of juvenile crimes.[9] Most juveniles behave according to *conformity* or *ritualism*.[10] They observe laws and rules and behave according to manuals. Especially, those

[6]We still see many juvenile offenders in a juvenile training school who have grown up in the poor protective environment, although their total number decreases.

[7]According to Merton the character of *retreatism* is the retreat from both cultural goals and institutional means.

[8]During the period from 1995 to 2012, the rate of young people between 15 and 34 without going to a school, participating in family affairs, or commuting to a place of work among people between 15 and 34 years old rose double and reached 2.3% (*White Paper on Children and Youngsters in 2013*, p. 37).

[9]The adaption mode of *rebellion* leads persons outside the environing social structure to envisage and seek to bring into being a greatly modified social structure. Young people of this type were participants in a radical students' movement around 1970. Recently, we no longer see this type, because most young people are not interested in social problems and political issues.

[10]The *ritualistic* type of adaption involves the abandoning or scaling down of the cultural goal of pecuniary success and rapid social mobility to the point where aspirations can be satisfied. On the other hand, a person assuming this adaption type continues to abide almost compulsively by institutional norms.

assuming *ritualism* do so without recognizing purposes of laws, rules, and manuals. As those two adoption modes are prevalent, the rate of juveniles satisfying the current life increases.[11] However, they fear about being neglected by others, especially their peers, as a person assuming the character of *other-directedness*.[12] Reflecting the change in the social character of juveniles, juvenile delinquency decreased drastically during the decade after 2003.

The percentage of the total number of juveniles among all non-traffic Penal Code offenders decreased constantly from 41.3% in 2003 to 26.5% in 2012. At present juvenile crime is a small social problem. However, preventive measures for juvenile delinquency are still important because our aged society cannot be maintained in the future without the support of well-raised youngsters.

Under the pressure of a movement by crime victims, Japan's Juvenile Law was revised four times since 2000 to adopt a tough policy against juvenile delinquents. In addition the measures to prevent escape from a facility such as a juvenile prison or a juvenile training school were emphasized (Yokoyama, 2016a, p. 48). However, the educational protective programs, especially programs for education to take the viewpoints of crime victims, have been improved in facilities for juvenile delinquents operated by the Ministry of Justice under the rehabilitation model. In contrast to the crime control model in the United States, we still maintain the welfare model in juvenile justice, although partial criminalization was advanced under the revisions of Juvenile Law.

4 Decrease of Crimes in Conforming Society

Since the breakdown of a bubble economy in 1990, we have had low economic growth. However, we also enjoyed comfortable lives in a society with affluence of goods based on past assets. In addition, the social character of *conformity* or *ritualism* is prevalent. Therefore, crimes decreased during the period from 2003 to 2012. The rate of non-traffic Penal Code offenses known by the police per population of 100,000 declined by half, from 2187 in 2003 to 1084 in 2012 (*White Paper on Crime in 2004*: 3 and *that in 2013*, p. 2). Japan seems to be moving to becoming a society with few crimes in which behavior of over-conformity and over-compliance

[11] According to the results of research of the Ministry of Health, Labor and Welfare to about 3000 young people between 15 and 39 in March in 2013, about 63% of all respondents answered that they were satisfied with their current life (Asahi Shimbun on September 11, 2013). Among all respondents answering it, about 83% of their reasons for their satisfaction were related to private affairs such as their family life and their hobby. This result shows the prevalence of other-directedness, because inner-directed persons find satisfaction in learning and working rather than their private life. On the other hand, only 19% of respondents answered that Japan's future is bright. They cherish anxiousness about the future as persons of the other-directedness type.

[12] The fear spreads in the prevalence of the use of a smartphone, because a person may be neglected by friends if he/she does not write a reply immediately after receiving a mail.

is prevalent.[13] Then, Japanese become more and more intolerant of deviant behavior (Yokoyama, 2017, p. 831). In such a situation the police guide and arrest more and more juveniles for minor offenses and deviant behavior (Yokoyama, 2015, p. 193). As a result Japan may become a stagnant society with low tolerance level against a deviant behavior, in which active creation is suppressed.

Another reason why Japan is becoming a stagnant society is its advancement of aging. Reflecting the phenomenon of aging, crimes committed by old-aged people have increased (Yokoyama, 2014, p. 791). The percentage of offenders aged 60 years old and over increased from 2.5% in 1974 to 12.2% in 2003 (*White Paper on Crime in 2004*, p. 7). During a decade from 2003, the rate of the old-aged offenders of 65 years old and over rose drastically. As crimes committed by old-aged people became a social problem, the Ministry of Justice published *White Paper on Crime in 2008* with a special feature on "The Situation of Highly Old-Aged Criminals and Treatment of Them." In this white paper they began to use a category of those of 65 years old and over as "the highly old-aged," although those of 60 and over had been analyzed as old-aged criminals in the previous white papers on crime. In 2012 the total number of non-traffic Penal Code offenders arrested by the police amounted to 287,386. The percentage of those aged 65 and over 65 increased from 7.8% in 2003 to 16.9% in 2012.[14]

5 Change in Population of Persons Confined in Criminal Facilities

With the adoption of tough policies during a decade from 1992, more and more offenders were confined in criminal facilities such as detention houses and prisons operated by the Ministry of Justice.[15] In 1992 we saw the smallest average daily number of persons confined in all criminal facilities, that is, 44,876, of which 7198 and 37,522 were confined in detention houses and prisons, respectively. As criminalization was carried out in the upsurge of a movement by crime victims since the

[13]The prevalence of such behavior is sociologically analyzed as deviant, as Merton pointed out (1968, p. 236).

[14]The percentages of each age group among all non-traffic Penal Code offenders were 10.0% in the age group of 14 and 15 years old, 8.2% of 16 and 17, 4.7% of 18 and 19, 9.0% of the age group of between 20 and 24, 7.0% of between 25 and 29, 13.7% of between 30 and 39, 13.0% of between 40 and 49, 10.5% of between 50 and 59, 6.9% of between 60 and 64, 5.5% of between 65 and 69, and 11.4% of 70 and over 70.

[15]Before the upsurge of the movement by victim crimes, neighbors sympathized with even an offender having committed some heinous offense under an extenuating condition. For example, they sympathized with a single mother killing a baby in an extremely miserable situation. When such a case occurred, many neighbors petitioned a criminal court to mitigate the punishment imposed on the offender. However, the human tie in the community has become weak. In addition, the tolerance level against offenders is lowered under the influence of the movement by crime victims who emphasize rights of crime victims, especially value of life of a killed person. Therefore, more and more offenders with an extenuating condition are sentenced to the imprisonment without its suspension.

late 1990s, the average daily number of confined persons increased drastically to 77,932 in 2005, of which 11,131 and 65,780 were confined in detention houses and prisons respectively. Then, the percentage of the confined persons per the capacity of all criminal facilities increased from 70.7% in 1992 to 104.0% in 2005.[16] In response to the demand by crime victims, the maximum punishment was increased by the revised Penal Code of 2005. For example, the maximum prison term was raised from 15 years to 20, while the maximum aggravated term was lifted from 20 years to 30. However, with advancement of aging and the prevalence of conformity, people commit heinous or violent crimes more infrequently. Therefore, in spite of the maintenance of a tough policy in criminal justice system, the average daily number of confined persons declined to 62,971 in 2013, of which 6731 and 55,316 stayed in detention houses and prisons, respectively. The percentage of confined persons per the capacity also decreased to 69.6%.

Next, I would like to analyze the change in the prison terms of newly confined persons in a prison. In 1992 the total number of newly confined prisoners amounted to 20,864, of which 29.8% were imprisoned for terms of 1 year and under while 41.0% for 2 years and under, 16.8% for 3 years and under, 8.2% for 5 years and under, and 3.1% for over 5 years. With the advancement of the touch policy, short terms decreased for a decade. In 2005 the total number of newly confined prisoners increased to 32,528, of which 21.6% were for a term of 1 year and under while 35.4% for 2 years and under, 21.8% for 3 years and under, 13.7% for 5 years and under, and 7.6% for over 5 years. Since the enforcement of the revised Penal Code of 2004, the tough policy against offenders has been strengthened. However, the total number of newly confined prisoners decreased to 22,755 in 2012. Then, the percentage of confined people per the capacity of all criminal facilities decreased from 106.5% in 2002 to 82.2% in 2012. The percentage of those imprisoned for 1 year and under decreased to 20.9%, while 37.2% were imprisoned for 2 years and under, 23.4% for 3 years and under, 12.7% for 5 years and under, and 5.7% for over 5 years. The slight decrease in the percentage of prisoners newly imprisoned for over 3 years from 21.3% in 2005 to 18.4% might be due to the recent decrease in heinous and violent offenses with the spread of conformity.

Prisoners are classified into several indexes and sent to a prison according to their index. Main indexes are A-index for prisoners with less criminality and B-index for ones with advanced criminality. Persons imprisoned for long prison terms are categorized as L-index. Previously, prisons for L-index prisoners accommodated those who were imprisoned for 8 years and over. However, these prisons became overcrowded by the accumulation of prisoners as an adverse effect of the extension of the maximum punishment by the revised Penal Code of 2004. For example, previously prisoners with life sentences could be released on parole after serving approximate 18 years. However, they cannot receive release on parole before

[16] Owning to over-crowdedness the percent exceeded 100% in 2005.

30 years under the revised Penal Code of 2004.[17] The accumulation of prisoners in L-index prisons is one reason why the number of old-aged prisoners increases.

The percentage of old-aged prisoners has become higher during the decade from 2003. The percentage of newly confined men of the age group of between 60 and 64 years old increased from 5.1% in 2003 to 7.9% in 2012, and the age group of 65 and over increased from 4.2% to 8.5% for the same period. In case of women the percentage of the former rose from 4.3% to 7.2%, and the latter rose from 5.5% to 12.8%. The treatment of old-aged prisoners becomes a serious problem in prisons, especially in prisons for female offenders.[18]

In Japan almost all prisoners are obliged to work at a prison factory. As the old-aged prisoners increase, the main laborers in the prison factories are members of Boryokudan, a Japanese gangsters' group, and foreigners. It is difficult for the prison to offer suitable jobs to old-aged prisoners.

Prisons are increasingly requested to offer care and medical treatment to the old-aged prisoners. Old-aged prisoners imprisoned for life or for a long time need special care and medical treatment. I saw two old prisoners in wheelchairs at the Kitakyushu Medical Prison. Several other prisoners took care of them as prison jobs, like nurses at a nursing home for the elderly. Such cases will increase in the near future.

Japanese prisons begin to function in ways similar to hospitals and nursing homes for senior persons. Many old-aged prisoners suffer from some disease such as the high blood pressure and diabetes. They are given special treatment such as special meals and lighter jobs. If they are mentally or physically disordered with aging, they are classified as M-index or P-index, respectively. They get special medial cure and care in a medical prison and at a hospital ward in several main prisons.

The costs to take care of the elderly in a prison are higher than those in a non-prison facility for care and medical treatment. Judging from the cost benefits, the old-aged persons who committed minor offenses, and even those who committed serious offenses for the first time under an extenuating condition, should be diverted from criminal procedure at the earlier stage of the criminal justice.[19]

On January 21 in 2013, the Tokyo Public Prosecutor's Office employed a social worker for the first time in Japan to screen cases under a diversion program to refer some cases to agencies for social welfare and facilities for medical treatment without prosecuting to a criminal court. We expect that more public prosecutors' offices will employ a social worker for the purpose of this program. It would be desirable for the police and public prosecutors' office to refer more cases of old-aged offender to agencies for social welfare and facilities for medical treatment in order to offer

[17] Prisoners confined for a long period usually cannot find a person to support them after their release on parole. In addition, they become too old to find a job after returning to a society. Therefore, it becomes difficult for them to be released on parole before the expiration of their prison term. Especially, those with life sentences are destined to be confined until their death. This phenomenon marks a breakdown of treatment in a prison under the rehabilitation model.

[18] Over-crowdedness in prisons for female offenders still continues. The percentage of the offenders per the capacity of the prisons remained 103.4% at the end of 2012. In such a situation female security officers, most of whom are younger than prisoners, have heavy work load.

[19] In the late 1960s the labeling theorists in the United States advocated to divert cases of a minor offense from criminal justice at the earlier stage in order to avoid being strongly stigmatized as a criminal.

aid and services to meet his/her needs. Judging from the labeling perspectives, the old-aged persons who committed an offense for the first time, even a murder caused by difficulty in their family situation, should be confined as little as possible to avoid being stigmatized.[20] If they were confined in a prison, they would identify themselves as prisoners. Even if they were released, they would be stigmatized as ex-prisoners by others in the community.

If persons released from a prison continue to be identified as ex-prisoners, they might give up rehabilitating themselves in the community. Recently, people's tolerance level against offenders has become lower. Therefore, it is very difficult for old-aged ex-prisoners to rehabilitate themselves in the community.

Recently people, especially those working for social welfare services, began to realize that there are many prisoners with physical and mental handicaps and elderly people who cannot rehabilitate themselves without help after release from a prison. Therefore, the Center to Support Settlement of Community Life was formally established in July in 2009 in order to help them. The Ministry of Justice employs a social worker in main prisons. The social worker stationing in main prisons gives counseling to prisoners who need assistance after release. The caseworker in a prison sends information about old-aged prisoners after acquiring their consent to the center to request some aid. The center works as a coordinator. If an ex-prisoner needs accommodation, the center would ask a home for senior persons about whether the home could offer accommodation. We expect further development of the system for old-aged ex-prisoners regarding rehabilitation in the community.

Many old-aged people born before 1949 assume a social character of *inner-directedness*. They identify themselves as previously diligent workers who contributed to the achievement of prosperity in Japan. As such they hesitate to commit crimes even if they become impoverished. However, such psychological resistance against committing a crime will decline owing to the decrease in persons with a character of *inner-directedness*. In the near future the safety nets for seniors such as pensions and medical aid are in decline. Therefore, more and more seniors will commit crimes, especially theft repeatedly in order to have daily necessities. If they are confined in a prison as recidivists, after their release they will commit crimes more easily by assuming their identification as recidivists.[21] In reality the living standard

[20] With advancement of aging we witness increasingly such a case that old-aged persons have to take care of their diseased spouse in a nuclear family. When they become desperate owing to nursing fatigue, they may kill their spouse by the intension of relieving their spouse of pain and anguish or according to the spouse's death wish. In such a case most old-aged murderers have few possibility of committing crime again because of the lack of criminal tendency. However, as I mentioned before, even in such cases more and more offenders are sentenced to the imprisonment without its suspension.

[21] When I visited Yokosuka Prison, I heard about an old-aged prisoner serving for his term of 2 years and a half who was convicted of stealing a packed box lunch twice owing to his impoverishment. For the first stealing he was sentenced to 1-year imprisonment with its suspension for 2 years, as he did not have any criminal career. Soon after being released he was caught for stealing a packed box lunch again. Then, he was sentenced to the aggravated imprisonment of a year and a half as a recidivist. As the suspension of the previous sentence was revoked, he was compelled to serve for 2 years and a half in Yokosuka Prison.

in a prison is higher than in many illegal nursing houses with poor facilities. Therefore, more and more old-aged ex-prisoners will return to a prison by committing a theft of such trifle goods as a packed box lunch and a minor fraud such as eating at a restaurant without money. If we fail to avoid such a vicious cycle, Japan will confront an increase in crimes committed by senior persons.

6 Measures for Maintenance of Manpower

To maintain the current life standard in Japan, we need to maintain manpower. Without new babies, the shortage of manpower would have to be made up by immigrants. However, our government has adopted a policy of extremely limited acceptance of immigrants (Yokoyama, 1999, p. 182). Although many foreigners began to rush into Japan to make money after 1980, the government did not admit them as immigrants. They have been called "visiting foreigners" instead of "immigrants."

The conservative politicians, the Ministry of Justice, and the police tend to regard "visiting foreigners" as potential criminals. They fear that our social order would be greatly damaged if we accepted immigrants, especially those as plain laborers. To examine whether their fear is justified or not, I would like to analyze roughly the change in crimes by visiting foreigners since 1980.

7 Visiting Foreigners and Their Crimes in 1980s

The total number of visiting foreigners gradually increased from 598,061 in 1970 to 1,089,341 in 1979. Visiting foreigners caught for crimes increased from 195 in 1970 to 403 in 1979. Our police worried that more and more international criminals might come to Japan. To cope with international criminal cases, the law to aid international investigation was enacted in 1980.

In 1981 the Immigration Control Law was replaced by the Immigration-Control and Refugee-Recognition Law to accept Vietnamese refugees, although our government did not admit the entry of alien plain laborers (Yokoyama, 1999, p. 182). In the early 1980s Japan became a consumer society in which sexual service was a prosperous business. Around 1983 many alien females began to come to Japan from neighboring Asian countries. First, we saw many females entering Japan from Taiwan and the Philippines with the tourist visas and the visa for show business. Some of them were victims of human trafficking.[22] But, Japanese police did not protect them as victims. If they entered Japan illegally, the police caught them as offenders of a law such as the Immigration-Control and Refugee-Recognition Law and Prostitution Prevention Law (Yokoyama, 2010b, p. 29).

[22] At that time Japan was a target country for human trafficking from neighboring developing countries.

In 1983 our government adopted a policy of accepting more alien students. In 1984 it began to allow foreigners to get the visas for pre-college students by summary procedure. With this visa many Chinese and Koreans rushed to Japan. Many of them engaged in illegal work to make money without going to any school.

In the late 1980s Japan enjoyed prosperity in a bubble economy, in which Japanese youngsters did not want to work in any dangerous, dirty, or hard job. At that time there was a shortage in the labor supply. This shortage was filled by illegal alien laborers coming to Japan with the visa for pre-college students.

In the late 1980s many visiting foreigners succeeded in making money. In such a situation they refrained from committing crimes against Japanese persons. In case they committed a crime, they victimized other foreigners, especially illegal laborers who came from their same mother country, because they knew that these victims would rarely report to the police.

However, crimes committed by visiting foreigners increased gradually with the drastic growth in their total population in the late 1980s. The total number of visiting foreigners arrested for a non-traffic Penal Code offense increased from 390 in 1978 to 3020 in 1988.

In December in 1988 our government decided to check the application documents for the visa for a pre-college student, because most of those applying for this visa did not have any intention to study at a language or professional school. In 1988 the Tokyo Metropolitan Police established the section for international investigation for the first time in Japan.

In December in 1989 the Immigration-Control and Refugee-Recognition Law was revised. Under the revised law people with a Japanese ancestor became qualified to stay in Japan as settlers who can work legally. Another purpose of this law was to strengthen the control of illegal alien entrants and stayers. The law prescribes punishment imposed on persons who employ foreigners illegally and on brokers who introduce a foreigner illegally to an employer.

After the revision of the Immigration-Control and Refugee-Recognition Law, large-sized companies recruited many foreigners with a Japanese ancestor mainly from Brazil and Peru. In 1989 the total number of alien entrants into Japan increased to about 2,986,000, the highest number in our history. Our police published *White Paper on Police in 1990* with a feature article on "Measures for the Police to Cope with the Increase in Alien Laborers."

8 Preventive Measures of Crimes by Visiting Foreigners in 1990s

In *White Paper on Police in 1990*, Japanese police pointed out that Boryokudan was engaged with human trafficking to exploit alien females, especially Thai females. In the summer in 1990, our bubble economy broke down, after which many visiting foreigners especially alien illegal workers lost jobs. Boryokudan helped them illegally to find jobs as plain laborers in factories and at construction sites.

In *White Paper on Police in 1991*, there was a feature article entitled "Change in Crimes at the Borderless Time," in which the crimes by visiting foreigners were analyzed as a kind of crimes committed across the border of a country.

The total number of visiting foreigners arrested for a crime increased drastically from 2978 in 1990 to 4813 in 1991, which might be due to the influence of the serious economic depression that started in the summer of 1990.

In 1990 the police and the Maritime Safety Agency found two cases in which a total of 18 foreigners smuggled themselves in a group into Japan by ship. Such cases of human trafficking from a neighboring country, especially from China increased in the 1990s. During the 3 years after the breakdown of bubble economy, we witnessed a continuous increase in the number of alien illegal entrants into Japan. Many Chinese entered Japan illegally by the arrangement of Snake Head, the Chinese group for human trafficking.

Around 1994 our attention was given to serious crimes committed by an alien-organized criminal group. Members of a Korean group for pickpocketing used sprays and knives to escape from being arrested. Those affiliated with a group coming from Hong Kong such as Triad Society broke into a store by using explosives in order to steal money and precious stones. After the breakdown of the socialist system of the USSR, Russian mafias participated in smuggling drugs and weapons into Japan and transporting used or stolen cars to Russia.

In 1997 the police and the Maritime Safety Agency caught 1369 Chinese for smuggling themselves in a group by ship into Japan. To criminalize illegal entrance of foreigners in a group and the business to assist their illegal entrance, the Immigration-Control and Refugee-Recognition Law was revised, which was enforced in May in 1997. In 1997 the National Police Agency established the office to cope with crimes committed by visiting foreigners. In January in 1998 the police in conjunction with the Immigration Bureau of the Ministry of Justice strengthened the roundup of illegally staying foreigners.

In May in 1998 the G-8 Summit was held in Birmingham, at which cooperation for combating against international crimes was discussed. At that time *White Paper on Police in 1999* had a feature article on "Combat against Crimes across National Border."

Our attention was given to Iranian sellers of illegal drugs in the late 1990s. Iranians arrested for an offense of a drug control law numbered 289 in 1998, 30% of which were caught for trade in an illegal drug. They sold drugs by the use of cellular telephones, by which they succeeded in evading arrest by the police.

Around 1999 stealing was committed in a group by Vietnamese settlers. Some Brazilians with a Japanese ancestor also committed stealing in a group. We began to see the increase in offenses committed by Brazilian youngsters who did not adjust to a Japanese lifestyle.

In 1998 the law to regulate and rationalize business relating to public morals was revised, under which a person with a career of employing alien females illegally was prohibited from participating in such business related to public moral as a nightclub with hostesses or a bar with dark lightning. In addition, those who participated in such business were prohibited from taking a passport from their alien employers. We saw the words "human trafficking" for the first time in *White Paper on Police in 2000*.

Chinese were the main foreigners who smuggled themselves into Japan. In July in 1999 Keizo Obuchi, our prime minister, and Zhu Rongii, the premier of the People's Republic of China, had a meeting, at which they talked about the cooperative regulation of illegal entrance in a group from China into Japan. By the exchange of information with Chinese security police, Japanese police activated the roundup of Chinese criminals, above all, the Snake Head group. By such means the total number of Chinese arrested for illegal entrance in a group decreased drastically from 701 in 1999 to 80 in 2000.

9 Promotion of Coexistence with Foreigners Since 2000

Previously, Japanese people expected foreigners staying in Japan to assimilate into Japanese culture. However, such expectation gradually declined in 1990s, as many Japanese began to live together with foreigners while respecting their own cultural backgrounds and lifestyle. In response to this change, Japanese police advocated the promotion of living together with foreigners for the first time in *White Paper on Police in 2002*. In December in 2002 the police began to promote measures in six prefectures to cope with visiting foreigners, especially the settled foreigners with a Japanese ancestor. The police began to carry out the special activities for crime prevention in the area where many foreigners dowelled. However, it was not until March in 2009 that the National Police Agency issued the notification on promotion of the comprehensive measures for settled foreigners in the community.[23]

In November in 2016 police officers affiliated with 61 police stations in 14 prefectures worked for such settled foreigners as Brazilians, Peruvians, Chinese, Vietnamese, and Filipino. The police carry out such activities as visiting their house together with an interpreter to grasp their family situation and holding a meeting to inform them of traffic rules. Through these activities the police grasp the situation in their residence area, promote the mutual understandings with them, acquire their confidence in police officers, eradicate their fear and their sense of alienation, and make them feel coexistence with Japanese people.

People in neighboring Asian countries, especially in China have enjoyed prosperity since 2000, while the Japanese economy has been stagnant. Therefore, foreigners coming to Japan from these countries to make money illegally have decreased.

The Total Research Institute on Legal Affairs, the Ministry of Justice, published a *White Paper on Crime in 2013* with the feature entitled "Criminal Policy with Globalization." According to this white paper, the total number of alien illegal

---

[23] The purpose of the total measures is to prevent the dwelling area of many foreigners from becoming a hotbed of crimes.

stayers decreased from 298,646 in 1993 to 62,009 in 2013. The number of alien illegal stayers, the so-called potential criminals, has decreased drastically. The total number of visiting foreigners caught for a non-traffic Penal Code offense decreased from 8505 in 2005 to 5260 in 2013. The crimes committed by visiting foreigners become a less serious social problem than in the 1990s.

10 Conclusion

Recently, the numbers of alien illegal entrants and stayers have decreased. Almost all visiting foreigners staying legally for a long time adjust to a Japanese lifestyle. They do not dare to commit crimes as they enjoy a peaceful and comfortable life in Japan. Therefore, conservative Japanese should abandon their idea that visiting foreigners are potential criminals.

As we do not have sufficient manpower, we need to accept immigrants step by step. If many foreigners come to Japan in a rush for a short period, for example, many Korean boat people coming in a rush from North Korea in case its dictatorial regime breaks down, we might have a serious problem of crimes committed by such people. This problem may occur in the near future.

Large-sized companies expand their markets to foreign countries because domestic markets shrink with advancement of aging. Therefore, they become eager to employ alien workers, especially those with professional skills and knowledge. In the response to their demand, our government should change the policy of limited acceptance of alien workers.[24] However, difficulties remain in attracting foreign workers because of cultural differences and language barriers.[25]

Given such a situation, the police and the Ministry of Justice have begun to think about the acceptance of foreigners. In *White Paper on Crimes in 2013*, the Ministry of Justice emphasized the necessity that alien prisoners with qualifications to stay legally in Japan are given special programs to rehabilitate themselves into Japanese society.

Criminologists in other countries, especially neighboring Asian counties, can find many lessons to learn from Japan's experiences.

Declaration of Conflicting Interests The author declared no potential conflicts of interest with respect to the research, authorship, and/or publication of this article.

[24] To make up for shortage of manpower of plain laborers, Japan has used the trainee system since 1981 (Yokoyama, 2016b, p. 3). However, as this system has many problems, we should establish the fundamental policy on immigration without using the term of "visiting foreigners."

[25] By the agreement with the Philippines in 2006 and that with Indonesia in 2007, Japan accepted young people coming from both countries as trainees to master the way to treat patients as a nurse. However, most of them failed to pass the national examination to become a nurse before the expiration of the period for their permitted stay because the examination is carried out in the Japanese language. As a result fewer young people now come from neighboring countries to work as a nurse in Japan which has a shortage of nurses and an increased need for them due to the enormous aged population.

Funding The author received no financial support for the research, authorship, and/or publication of this article.

References

Merton, R. (1968). *Social theory and social structure – 1968 enlarged edition*. New York: The Free Press. The original book was published in 1949.

Riesman, D., Glazer, N., & Denny, R. (1973). *The lonely crowd – A study of the changing American character, Abridged edition with a 1969 preface*. New Haven: Yale University Press. The original book was published in 1950.

Sudo, K. (2005). *Understanding of Japanese population*. http://group.dai-ichi-life.co.jp/dlri/monthly/pdf/0506_9.pdf#search='%E6%B1%9F%E6%88%B8%E6%99%82%E4%BB%A3+%E7%B7%8F%E4%BA%BA%E5%8F%A3'. Retrieved October 10, 2014. Accessed 10 October 2014.

Yokoyama, M. (1986). The Juvenile justice system in Japan. In M. Brusten, J. Graham, N. Herriger, & P. Malinowski (Eds.), *Youth crime, social control and prevention: Theoretical perspectives and policy implications* (pp. 102–113). Pfaffenweiler: Centaurus-Verlagsgesellschaft.

Yokoyama, M. (1989). Net-widening of the juvenile justice system in Japan. *Criminal Justice Review, 14*(1), 43–53.

Yokoyama, M. (1999). Analysis of the crimes by foreigners in Japan. *International Journal of Comparative and Applied Criminal Justice, 23*(2), 181–213. Reprinted in J. D. Freilich & G. R. Newman (Eds.), *Crime and Immigration* (The international library of criminology, criminal justice & penology; second series) USA, Ashgate Publishing Company, 179–211.

Yokoyama, M. (2000). Change in Japanese organized crime and enforcement of the Law to Cope with Boryokudan in 1992. *Kokugakuin Journal of Law and Politics, 38*(3), 1–33.

Yokoyama, M. (2007). Criminalization under conservative public opinion in Japan. *Kokugakuin Journal of Law and Politics, 44*(4), 1–46.

Yokoyama, M. (2009). How has the revised juvenile law functioned since 2001 in Japan? In E. W. Plywaczewski (Ed.), *Current problems of the penal law and the criminology No. 4* (pp. 667–702). Bialystok: Temida 2.

Yokoyama, M. (2010a). Development of guidance activities by police for prevention of Juvenile delinquency in Japan. In C. Roberson, D. K. Das, & J. K. Singer (Eds.), *Police without borders-the fading distinction between local and global* (pp. 151–175). Boca Raton: CRC Press.

Yokoyama, M. (2010b). A legal response measures against human trafficking in Japan. *Women & Criminal Justice, 20*(1–2), 27–39. Routledge.

Yokoyama, M. (2014). Increase in crimes committed in Japan by elderly people and the way they are treated in criminal justice. In E. W. Plywaczewski (Ed.), *Current problems of the penal law and the criminology No. 6* (pp. 790–803). Warszawa: Wydawnictwo C.H. Beck.

Yokoyama, M. (2015). Juvenile justice and Juvenile crime: An overview of Japan. In J. Winterdyk (Ed.), *Juvenile justice systems – International perspectives, models, and trends* (pp. 179–208). Boca Raton: CRC Press.

Yokoyama, M. (2016a). Change in educative treatment in Japanese Juvenile Training School. *Kokugakuin Journal of Law and Politics, 53*(4), 31–65.

Yokoyama, M. (2016b). Is Japanese trainee system the disguised human trafficking? *Kokugakuin Journal of Law and Politics, 53*(4), 1–29.

Yokoyama, M. (2017). Exclusion and inclusion of offenders in Japan with low tolerance. In E. W. Plywaczewski & E. M. Guzik-Makaruk (Eds.), *Current problems of the penal law and the criminology No. 7* (pp. 790–803). Warszawa: Wydawnictwo C.H. Beck.

Chapter 3
Kin, Crime, and Criminal Justice in Contemporary Japan

Mari Kita

1 Introduction

Although Japan's incarceration rate has been declining since 2009, its penal system has taken a punitive turn in the last decade. It has adopted the "get-tough-on-crime" approach and become less focused on rehabilitation due to "a greater sense of public insecurity, economic and social disruption, increased anxieties about foreigners, politicians' emphasis on law and order, and a series of police scandals and notorious crimes" (Johnson, 2007, p. 371). The emergence of a new wave of movement for victims' rights, which has won the support of prosecutors who hold substantial power in the justice system, contributes to this punitive shift as well. Moreover, in May 2009, the much-anticipated lay-judge system was inaugurated in Japan. This newly adopted judicial system allows lay people to join judges not only in fact-finding processes but also in sentencing decisions (Levin & Tice, 2009). A study has found that a salient impact of the lay-judge system is seen in sex-related criminal trials as lay judges have a tendency to impose disproportionately harsher sentences on defendants in sex offense cases than for other crimes (Hirayama, 2012). As Japan heads down the path of "penal populism" (Hamai & Ellis, 2009), now is the crucial time to carefully investigate the full-scale consequences of crime in contemporary Japan.

Despite a growing Western literature on the family members of offenders, much less is known about such people in Japan. Today, Japan continues to enjoy one of the lowest crime rates among the developed democracies. In 2016, a total of 58,497 people were housed in prisons, jails, and detention centers (Ministry of Justice, 2016). Although the number may seem minuscule compared to the correctional population of 6,741,400 persons in the USA (Kaeble & Glaze, 2016), it is estimated that at least 117,000 family members (two family members per prisoner) are affected

M. Kita (✉)
University of Hawai'i at Mānoa, Honolulu, HI, USA
e-mail: marikita@hawaii.edu

J. Liu, S. Miyazawa (eds.), *Crime and Justice in Contemporary Japan*, Springer Series on Asian Criminology and Criminal Justice Research,
https://doi.org/10.1007/978-3-319-69359-0_3

by their kin's confinement. Studies on the collateral consequences of incarceration in the USA and the UK have already found that the family members of prisoners suffer from various financial, psychological, physical, and social repercussions due to their affiliation with incarcerated kin. Some family members reportedly even felt that they were being punished instead of their condemned kin (Beck, Britto, & Andrews, 2009). Similarly, in Japan, the climate that the families of offenders face creates the impression that they are the ones being "punished" by the criminal justice system for their kin's crime. A progressive defense attorney and legal scholar, Koichi Kikuta (2002), writes that "it seems as though Japan's penal system is trying its hardest to remind them that they are the family members of criminals time and time again" (p. 92). Indeed, the families of those who had committed serious offenses in Japan express resentment at being treated as criminals while also admitting feelings of guilt and responsibility for their kin's offenses (Suzuki, 2010).

By using in-depth interviews and participant observation, this ethnographic research seeks to render the best possible image of how the lives of the family members of offenders in Japan are altered from the moment of police encounter to incarceration and reentry. This paper particularly focuses on the interactions between the families and the criminal justice authorities in Japan such as the police officers, defense attorneys, prosecutors, judges, correctional officers, and probation/parole officers. By using the grounded theory approach, this study seeks to generate thick descriptions of the everyday interactions between offenders' kin and various actors in Japan's criminal justice system.

2 Review of the Literature

In the USA and the UK, scholarly views toward the penal system have been largely critical. The US system, which sends a disproportionate number of racial minorities to prison for non-violent drug offenses without any chance of rehabilitation, in particular has been critiqued by numerous social scientists as criminogenic (Wakefield & Wildeman, 2011), disenfranchising (Hirschi et al., 2002; Petersilia, 2003), and racially segregating (Alexander, 2012; Wacquant, 2001). Moreover, an increasing number of both American and British studies have revealed that the consequences of incarceration extend to the kin and intimates of inmates and that such repercussions engender significant economic, health, psychological, and social disruptions in their lives (Braman, 2007; Christian, Mellow, & Thomas, 2006; Comfort, 2003; Condry, 2007; Dressel & Barnhill, 1994; Fishman, 1988; Howarth & Rock, 2000). According to Hagan and Dinovitzer (1999), the most profound collateral consequences of incarceration can be seen on the children of prisoners. Christian (2005) contends that families are caught in a double bind, as their effort to support the prisoner's reentry is hindered by the prison system, which takes away the resources needed to maintain a strong relationship with the incarcerated kin. Comfort (2003, p. 79) argues that women experience *secondary prisonization* and that "women whose kin and intimates are caught in the revolving door of 'corrections' experience restricted rights, diminished resources, social marginalization, and other consequences of penal confinement, even though they are legally innocent and reside outside of the prison's boundaries". Furthermore, a study done by Rose, Clear, and Ryder (2001) shows that incarceration disrupts the social capital of people in the community. The studies of prisoners' families, however, have also revealed benefits of imprisonment, especially the positive impact of providing relief for women and children who had been living with lawbreaking husbands, partners, and fathers (Comfort, 2008; Hagan & Dinovitzer, 1999). Hence, research on the family members of prisoners has assisted Western criminologists in gaining more complex and nuanced understandings of the broader consequences of imprisonment (Sampson, 2011).

In contrast, studies of the Japanese system of crime control and punishment have yet to reach the level of sophistication and rigor achieved in the Western literature of criminal justice (Miyazawa, 1990). Classical studies on Japan's criminal justice system have largely been an attempt by Western scholars to demystify the mechanism of maintaining "safe streets" in such a dense, industrialized, and urbanized society. For instance, in his well-regarded book, Braithwaite (1989) delineates how Japanese society controls crime by separating shame and punishment, one of the most significant characteristics of reintegrative shaming. Contrasting the Japanese police to its American counterpart, Bayley (1991) maintains that Japan's police prod, guide, and alert society in order to lower Japan's crime rate. Other scholars have joined the search for culturally "unique" features of Japanese crime control measures and have pointed to social solidarity as one of the explanations for the low incarceration rate (Johnson, 1996). In more recent studies, however, scholars in Japan and abroad sound an alarm for treating the Japanese system of criminal justice as a cultural anomaly, for it has started to follow other nations' examples of penal populism (Hamai & Ellis, 2006). They call for more rigorous examinations of the entire criminal justice system in Japan as well as its relationship to the members of society (Hamai & Ellis, 2006; Miyazawa, 1990).

While the field of scholarship on offenders' families in Japan is still in its infancy, there are several noteworthy studies. From the perspective of social work and welfare, Fukaya (2007, 2009) argues that the Japanese state has a tendency to treat the family as a social resource, automatically attributing to its members the role of caretaker for their mentally troubled kin who have committed offenses. Viewing the issue from a more practical standpoint, Abe (2015, p. 21) notes that one of the most serious repercussions of being related to an offender is marginalization. In his reportage, Suzuki (2010) documents a number of celebrated cases where family members of serious offenders in Japan met with severe harassment and disdain from the community, ranging from prank calls to hate mail, to vandalism and arson. Some of these family members and relatives have even been driven to commit suicide as a result. Similarly, Steinhoff's (2008) study of the Japanese New Left student activists demonstrates that such negative societal reactions to sensational crimes were not uncommon in Japanese society, even a half century ago. While these studies are all informative and insightful, they are limited in terms of both size and diversity of samples. Moreover, there are no published, comprehensive criminological studies about family members of offenders in Japan so far. This study attempts to close that gap as well as advance the literature of criminal justice in Japan by carefully examining the relationship between Japan's criminal justice authorities and the family members of offenders.

3 Gaps in the Literature

Although there have been a number of studies examining the lives of family members of prisoners in the West, they are not free from limitations. By and large, little has been written about the broader collateral consequences of violating the law and social norms (Comfort, 2007; Condry, 2007). In particular, there is a paucity of knowledge about the lives of family members of offenders *prior to* their kin's imprisonment. Several studies suggest that once individuals' behaviors come under the scrutiny of the police, the lives of their parents, partners, and other family members are significantly disrupted (Braman, 2007; Comfort, 2016).

Moreover, the majority of the previous literature in Japan and elsewhere has examined only *serious* cases of criminal offenses that resulted in imprisonment. Less is known about the family members of those who have committed a misdemeanor. It is, however, a well-known fact that the vast majority of criminal cases are routinely dismissed or dealt with through probation or other alternatives to confinement. Scholars indeed argue that examining routine and less serious cases such as drug offenses, bar fights, and prostitution is critical, for these cases are often relegated to minimal coverage in the shadow of more celebrated cases (Bach, 2010; Feeley, 1992). Thus, this study adds to the literature on the collateral consequences of crime that even a brief contact with law enforcement due to a non-serious offense can throw the lives of offenders' families into disarray.

In her study of the families of death row inmates, Sharp (2005, p. 17) notes that, "To truly understand the effects of the system of capital punishment on families, we must examine these families' experiences at all stages of the process." Using Sharp's contention as the point of departure, this study examines the experiences of the family members of less serious offenders by looking at each process in the criminal justice procedure. Pointing to the critique of "courthouse criminology," Condry (2007) also asserts that scholars must inquire into how the collateral consequences of crime affect offenders' families beyond courthouses and prisons. Hence, this study examines how the lives of offenders' families in Japan are affected by their kin's crime from the moment of police encounter and arrest through incarceration and reentry. To construct the most comprehensive image of the lives of offenders' kin, the present research pays particular attention to the interactions between the family members of offenders and major criminal justice personnel including police, prosecutors, defense attorneys, judges, correctional staff, and probation/parole officers.

4 Methods

To investigate the lives of offenders' families in Japan, I used qualitative methods, which are "particularly well suited for obtaining information about sensitive and emotional matters" (Sharp, 2005, p. 23). Because crime is commonly regarded as a sensitive topic that induces various emotional reactions, ethnography was an appropriate research method for this study. My field research lasted from January 2014 to August 2015, during which I observed 50 family members and interviewed 31 of them. Participants included thirty four mothers (68%), seven wives (14%), six fathers (12%), and three sisters (6%), which reflects the clear predominance of women in the field of prisoner and offender support activities (Comfort, 2008; Condry, 2007). All participants were of age 35 and up, of which the eldest was in her mid-70s. More than half of the women were working or had just started to work full time or part time during my field research. The rest were either housewives or receiving a pension. All men, except one, were working full time. Thirty-four family members (68%) experienced their kin's incarceration, including juvenile training schools (six parents), and all except for five family members (90%) experienced their kin's arrest. Table 3.1 shows the types of crime the offenders were charged with most recently. The offenders were predominantly male, with only five women (four daughters and one sister), including two drug offenders, two property offenders, and one violent offender.

During my preliminary fieldwork in the summers of 2012 and 2013, I located and gained entree to three organizations based in Tokyo, Kanagawa, Chiba, and Miyagi that specifically support the family members of substance users, juvenile delinquents, and offenders of other types of crime (i.e., violent crime, property crime, and sex crime). Because these organizations' meetings took place in either private or quasi-private settings, I sought and obtained formal permission to observe and interview meeting attendees prior to attending any family circle (Lofland, Snow, Anderson, & Lofland, 2005, p. 41). These organizations usually hold 90–120 minute-long family circles on a monthly basis, and I attended them regularly during the

Table 3.1 Kin's criminal charges by type

	Number	Percentage
Sex offense	14	28%
Drug offense	11	22%
Fraud	5	10%
Murder	4	8%
Theft	4	8%
Assault	3	6%
Others	2	4%
Unknown	2	4%
No arrest	5	10%
Total	50	100%

20 months of my field research from January 2014 to August 2015. Based on the information I gathered, I used purposive sampling to select those who had any interactions with various actors in the criminal justice system due to their kin's crime. Then I contacted the family members to ask if they would consent to be interviewed.

Family circles are a protected place that allows family members to share their detailed accounts of criminal events that have affected their lives. Because of my regular presence at circles, I was able to obtain a fair amount of information about each family, prior to the interviews. Hence, I was later able to avoid dwelling on the details of offenses committed, which could have been emotionally harmful to such at risk, vulnerable individuals (Beck & Britto, 2006). A typical family circle consisted of an average of 10–15 family members, who were predominantly female (75% or more), sitting in a circle in a meeting room at a local community center. To initiate the meeting, a facilitator or a director of the organization went over the ground rules. Attendees were reminded not to disclose any information outside the meeting and that they could skip their turn if they did not wish to speak. They were also highly discouraged to advise, criticize, and cross talk others, based on regulations borrowed from self-help organizations such as Alcoholic Anonymous and Narcotics Anonymous. This is often expressed in Japanese as "iippanashi kikippanashi" (talk, listen, and leave it at that), and attendees were encouraged to focus on merely speaking and listening. Note-taking was another matter that attendees were barred from, for the purpose of protecting the privacy of others. Thus, I always took extensive notes immediately after each family circle. In addition to listening to their thoughts, feelings, and insights, I let the family circle attendees know my background and intensions of coming to the meetings to openly conduct research (Lofland et al., 2005). In total, I sat in on these circles for more than 143 h during my 20 months of field research.

The interviews were semi-structured and took the form of intensive interviewing, which encourages participants to reflect on earlier events and share their significant experiences as experts (Charmaz, 2006, pp. 25–27). I asked broad, open-ended questions that covered a range of topics that related to their lives before and after their kin's crime. The interviewee and I exchanged phone calls and emails prior to the interview to carefully select a location where the family member would feel safe, comfortable, and familiar enough to tell his or her story. On many occasions, we sat in public spaces such as spacious restaurants and coffee shops where there was enough room between tables. At times, interviewees invited me to their homes when other family members were not present. On average, interviews lasted for two to two and a half hours. With the interviewees' permissions, I recorded every interview with a digital voice recorder, except for one occasion when an interviewee wished not to be recorded. All interviews were conducted in Japanese.

After transcribing all the interviews, I analyzed the transcriptions and field notes. During this process, the names of the study participants were replaced with pseudonyms to protect their identities. I used initial or open coding to identify emerging themes, which mainly consisted of family members' reactions to various stages of the criminal justice procedure. Although their responses varied greatly, in the stage of focused coding, I was able to synthesize them into several types of families' responses toward the criminal justice system as well as toward their own kin. Because the researchers' "stimulus involvement in data-gathering and analysis" is one of the core aspects of the grounded theory method (Charmaz, 2006, p. 504), I also reviewed and revised these analytical themes as well as interview protocols throughout the process of data collection and analysis. I had several occasions to share some of my findings with family members, as they invited me to speak at family circle meetings. Taking advantage of such opportunities, I asked the informants to see if they agreed that such categories matched their actual experiences.

5 Findings and Discussion

5.1 *Encounter with the Law*

Recent studies of family members of offenders in the USA reveal that their experiences of interacting with the criminal justice system start at a much earlier stage than the imprisonment of the offender (Braman, 2007; Fishman, 1990). When an individual's lawbreaking comes to the attention of law enforcement, family members are usually among the first ones to acknowledge the lawbreaking (Comfort, 2007). The consequences of coming into—often times unannounced—contact with law enforcement, however, are scantly documented in the literature (Koehler et al., 2003). In the present study, none of the family members reported any previous history or signs of crime in the family (although there were some reported cases of alcoholism and domestic violence). Moreover, all the participants were of the lower-middle to upper-middle class and had fairly respectable social standings. Thus, crime was something completely new and foreign to most of the family members until it became apparent that their kin had offended. Condry (2007) argues that after the discovery of their kin's crime, the relatives go through the "initial impact" stage, which is characterized by external events, intrapersonal processes, and interpersonal processes (p. 41). In this study, 12 family members reported that the arrest came as a shock. Some even wondered if it was a new type of scam when they received a call from the police.

Moreover, ten of them expressed developing fear or anxiety of picking up the phone, answering the doorbell, and seeing a police car, after having frequent and unpredicted contacts with the police. Noriko, whose son had a history of juvenile delinquency but was arrested for fraud as an adult, recalled:

> On top of phone calls, I also got scared of the sound of the doorbell, *in the morning!* They come in the morning, the police. Oh, how I was scared. It is around seven in the morning [that they ring the bell]. Nobody usually visits anyone that early in the morning, right? But that's when they come.

She added that she was also sensitive about phone calls and doorbells because she wanted to minimize contact between law enforcement officers and her daughter, who was a middle schooler at that time. Despite Noriko's efforts, her daughter wound up answering a phone call from the police once, experiencing house searches at least three times, and witnessing her brother's arrest at home twice. In his study of families of prisoners in the Washington, D.C. area, Braman (2002) similarly documented the case of a child witnessing her father's arrest at home. He noted that witnessing the police violently hunt down her father in front of her had a detrimental effect on her psychological well-being, which eventually led to the child's negative attitude toward schoolwork. Although there were no visible signs that Noriko's daughter was experiencing difficulties at school, Noriko felt a great need to shield her daughter from police investigations, which further added to Noriko's psychological distress.

During another interview, Machiko's cell phone rang. Getting slightly tense, she answered the call immediately. It turned out to be a wrong number but as she hung up the phone she remarked:

> My heart skipped a beat. I still get like this when I receive phone calls. In my head, I know that [my son] is in the rehab doing fine. But whenever I receive calls, I cannot help but think he might have done something again.

Constantly fearing criminal justice contact takes a toll on family members' psychological well-being. Kiyomi explained that she had to step in and completely take over her husband's role as the liaison between their son and the criminal justice authorities. She said, "I was afraid that he would have a nervous breakdown, going through such angst every day at the workplace where nobody knew about our son's crime." These accounts demonstrate that family members who reside with offenders at the time of the arrest also become the virtual target of "the same processes and regulations as the supervisee, inspiring feelings of being intruded upon, monitored, and controlled," despite their legal innocence (Comfort, 2007, p. 277).

Another instance where families experience intense interactions with the law enforcement is when they find themselves caught in pre-arrest investigations. Goffman's (2014) ethnography on African American youth in Philadelphia found that the police frequently turned to kin and intimates to obtain information about suspects who were on the run. Although much less violent than the American counterparts depicted in Goffman's work, the present study revealed that the Japanese police frequently exploited family ties to investigate and collect evidence, especially in organized crime cases. Kohei, whose son had been a member of *yakuza* and spent 3 years in prison for his involvement in fraud, explained how he helped the police after he was persuaded to do so for the benefit of his son and consequently for the family:

> MK: What were the police like?
>
> Kohei: Well, they more or less took advantage of my position [as a parent] and asked me to have my son's friends and associates come to my house to let them talk. Yeah, they asked me to cooperate on things like that. So, I invited them and had a chat. They brought over their girlfriends, too. As I was talking to them, detectives were in the room next to us, as well as outside, waiting. I go, "Well, I actually asked you all to come because I wanted to help my son as a parent. I was asked by the police to see if the detectives could speak to you." Then I say, "They will show up here once I give them a call." Their faces turned pale,

> of course. They go, "What?" But when I asked them again, they were like, "Ah… Ok." Then the detectives came in, and they all went to the police station. … I did think about [whether or not to cooperate] for a while, though, yeah. But fortunately, none of them [his friends] got arrested, yeah.

Noriko was also asked to inform on the whereabouts of her son for interrogation by the police. Once, she voluntarily went to his friend's house where she successfully located her son and let him know that the police were here. On another occasion, shortly after her son's urine test, she was asked by the police to call them once her son came home. Extremely distressed and unsure of what to do, she later caught her son sleeping in his room one night. She recalled, "It was rare to see him at night at home like that, sleeping so soundly. And once I saw his face, there was no way I could call the police." These instances demonstrate the pressure on families to turn into a "snitch," which causes internal anguish and distress among suspects' kin (Goffman, 2014). Steinhoff (2008) found that the Japanese police in the 1960s also used a similar tactic to obtain information about arrested student activists and their associates, a strategy carried over from the *Tokko* (Special Higher Police) in the prewar era. The present study indicates that such a strategy is still in use among police detectives in contemporary Japan. With little to no regard for emotional consequences on the family members, the law enforcement often successfully persuaded them to cooperate by taking advantage of their ignorance of the law, as well as their familial bond to the suspect.

Although arrest came as a shock to most family members in this study, nine family members stated that they were anticipating or even hoping for the arrest of their kin. In fact, in many drug-related cases, family members had started witnessing suspicious behaviors from their kin long before it came to the attention of the police. Some family members even suffered from physical abuse by their kin who were acting out under the influence of a substance. In desperate need for help, they took it upon themselves to dial 110 (the American equivalent of 911). Miyako, the mother of a 41-year-old drug addict who had been in and out of prison, spoke of her experience of calling the police twice on her son who was acting out. With teary eyes, she told me:

> I called … I mean we knew he was using it. He was crazy. And he didn't listen to anything we said, and it was too late when he had injured some … others. It was too late when something had happened, so I called the police. It was so, so hard. Really. [The police] asked, "Is he home now?" so I said, "Yes." Then they showed up in a group of about five or six people. I snuck out of the house and went to the other side of the field and hid. But I could hear my son yelling from his room on the second floor, "Mom! Mom!" So, I don't know, I just covered my ears like this [*covers her ears with both hands*]. But I couldn't leave either. I wanted to be near him. Yeah, it was very hard, just remembering it. I thought to myself, wow, I even have to go through things like this. Yeah, [calling the police] was the hardest thing for me.

Hideo, a father of a 25-year-old who was arrested for the possession of methamphetamine, recalled that he phoned the police twice because he thought his son's "life was in jeopardy." Haruko, whose teenage daughter has been abusing methamphetamine, reported that both her and her husband had taken their daughter to the police twice to have her arrested. These accounts of parents indicate a desperate need for social services in Japan that can provide appropriate care and advice *before* problematic behaviors come under the radar of the law enforcement. As much as the family members did not wish their kin to be apprehended, they were compelled to make it happen, to not only save the lives of their kin but also of their own.

Comfort (2008) argues that some of the wives and partners of prisoners in the USA are entangled in the mix of inadequate social services and a powerful penal system, which leaves carceral control as the only way to address men's criminality, abuse, substance use problems, and other social, financial, and health issues (pp. 163–182). This system failure is also faced by many families of death row inmates in the USA (Beck et al., 2009). Similarly, in Japan, the present study reveals that the system of control serves the function of providing relief and security for troubled families when social services are invisible or nonexistent. The inaccessibility to substance abuse treatment facilities, interpersonal violence programs, and family counseling contributes to making the police the only venue for family members to seek help and support.

5.2 Interactions with the Courtroom Workgroup

As mentioned above, prior to their kin's wrongdoing, all participants of this study were leading a life that was completely void of involvement with the law. Thus, when they suddenly faced the complex criminal justice process, they often felt at a loss (Christian & Kennedy, 2011). Eleven family members in this study expressed such concerns. At family circles, they often explained their situations in great detail and concluded by saying, "I don't know what to do." Moreover, I observed two occasions where family members bewilderingly asked other family circle attendees about the existence of parole/probation officers. On another occasion, a wife hesitantly admitted her past ignorance of public defenders at the time of her husband's arrest. This gross lack of basic knowledge about the criminal justice process places family members in an incredibly disadvantaged position within the power dynamics of the courtroom workgroup.

According to Eisenstein and Herbert (1991), the courtroom workgroup includes defense attorneys, prosecutors, judges, and to a lesser degree, defendants, who work together to "do justice." Amy Bach's (2010) compelling critique of the American judicial system reveals the customary practice among judges, prosecutors, and defense attorneys to promptly settle cases with plea bargains. According to Johnson (2002b), such teamwork is just as prevalent in Japan. The difference, however, is that Japan's prosecutors exert enormous power to firmly follow the established norms during criminal court proceedings by dominating police, judges, and defense attorneys. And the family members of the accused often get caught in their effort by providing testimonies that fit the workgroup's (or rather prosecutors') objectives, which are largely truth-finding, appropriate charging, remorse-invoking, and rehabilitation and reintegration (Johnson, 2002b). This pressure to cooperate is felt strongest by families when they are called in to testify as *jojo shonin*.

The role *of jojo shonin* is quite similar to that of a character witness in the USA. They attest to the defendant's moral character and "promise to 'supervise' (*kantoku suru*)" (D. T. Johnson, 2002a, p. 150) his or her behavior after release. If the defendant has already pled guilty, assessing character evidence becomes a crucial part of Japanese trials, for it can greatly influence the sentencing outcome (Ishimaru, Senba, Kawakami, & Hattori, 2005, p. 12). With no prior knowledge or experience of trials, family members often feel fearful of taking up this role. Four mothers reported such a feeling, and one of them noted that she even lost 5 kg during a lay-judge trial of her son's sexual assault case. Nonetheless, most family members were compelled to testify in front of the judge, recognizing intense pressure from defense attorneys as well as their accused kin.

When a family member appears at a trial as *jojo shonin*, the defense attorney asks if the defendant would be under proper supervision so he or she would not commit a crime again. Then prosecutors and judges cross-examine the family member if he or she would be capable of providing such supervision. Kohei, who appeared in court as *jojo shonin*, recounted his experience of being questioned by a prosecutor as follows:

> Kohei: … It was indeed painful when the prosecutor told me, "Well, your son was in the juvenile detention center once when he was sixteen." Yes, it was true. He was in it. Then the prosecutor went on and said, "Since then your son's behavior has just worsened. You really can't supervise him, *can you?*" That was … hard. I thought, maybe from the eyes of prosecutors it was right. As a parent, I thought, what the prosecutor told me was right. When he said that, the feeling that I had suppressed overcame me, and I couldn't say anything to defend myself. I couldn't say, "No, that's not true."
>
> MK: What kind of feeling overcame you?
>
> Kohei: Well, the feeling that it is the parents' responsibility, and that is how society will see it.

Similarly, in Noriko's case, not only did prosecutors criticize and comment on her and her husband's way of parenting but also defense attorneys, social workers, and police officers told them that they were at fault for their son's wrongdoing. Moreover, Miyako, Teruyo, and Yasuyo all reported that, at some point in the criminal justice procedure, they were blamed and told that it was their fault that their adult sons had committed crimes. This is understandable considering the fact that the prosecutors who dominate Japan's criminal court put rehabilitation and reintegration as one of their most important objectives. The way this is achieved, however, is only through moral instructions and lenient sanctions, which do little to actually rehabilitate offenders (Johnson, 2002a). As moral instructions most often come from parents, and leniency implies self-correction in communities, the families of offenders are by nature expected to cooperate with the courtroom workgroup who seek offender rehabilitation.

Most of the family members succumbed to this pressure, as they felt powerless with no knowledge of criminal law. More informed families, however, actively avoided to become a cog in the routinized criminal court procedure. Katsuko, Satomi, and Miyako all had sons who were drug addicts. Attending Nar-Anon and family support groups, the three women had been rigorously learning about addiction and the ways of recovery for their sons and themselves. The support groups for the drug addicts' kin are different from the support groups for other crimes, for the families are equipped with the language, knowledge, and conceptual tools to frame their kin's behavior, which were all borrowed from the drug rehabilitation community. Codependency is one such tool and is a prominent rhetoric to make sense of addiction. As Borovoy (2005) puts it, "The language of codependency allowed women to express tensions in family and public life that had previously been difficult to articulate" (p. 24). Thus, when they were asked to appear at trial and testify as character witness, they all refused to do so, as a part of "cutting off" (*tsukihanashi*) or "detaching with love" (*ai aru tsukihanashi*), a widely used strategy in the addiction community to end codependent relationships.

Satomi, who had been attending Nar-Anon meetings for a decade by the time she experienced her son's first arrest, explained that when she had initially said that she wouldn't testify in the court, the public defender referred to her as heartless (*tsumetai*). In Katsuko's case, although she originally refused to testify as a witness (because it was "complicated and frightening"), she still wound up appearing in court. Katsuko, who had kicked out her son as part of "*tsukihanashi*" long before the arrest, explained how she was caught between the defense lawyer's demand to act as a caring mother and her determination to cut off her drug-addicted son. She recounted:

> The defense lawyer tried to make me say [that I would take care of my son] in front of the judge again and again. But if I said so, that's the same as me saying he could come home. So, I got really torn listening as the attorney spoke. I still did not say it. Then in the end the attorney himself started saying things like, "You *will* look after him at home, won't you? That's what you mean, right?" But I did not say yes [*laughs*]. Of course, I couldn't say no but I didn't say yes, either.

For this defense attorney, the information that addiction cannot be cured by familial affection had no value to his proceeding needs. But as a mother who had been witnessing her son's struggle with addiction, Katsuko believed that it should be communicated to the judge that her support might exacerbate his addiction. In the end, she thought that the judge understood her claim and her son received a suspended sentence.

Satomi's and Katsuko's accounts reveal legal experts' ignorance of drug addiction as well as the institutional expectation for family members to cooperate in its concerted effort to follow the established judicial routines. Assumed to be the most suitable and convenient figures to provide supervision and moral guidance to offenders, family members are compelled to play the role of watchdogs—or de facto probation and parole officers with no specialized knowledge, skills, or experiences of offender rehabilitation. While prosecutors believe in the importance of corrections in Japan, they seek rehabilitation in a selective manner. First timers, for instance, are usually given suspended sentences and released without any practical rehabilitation measures (Johnson, 2002b). While it is a celebrating fact that Japanese prosecutors believe prison should be the last resort, this could be the beginning of a nightmare for the families, as offenders are not diverted or referred to the suitable rehabilitation programs. Families are left alone in society with the troubled kin until they commit more serious crimes and are dealt much harsher sentences such as incarceration, which could further exacerbate their addiction problem and delay their recovery.

5.3 Experiences at Correctional Facilities

When the participants of this study discussed prisons, jails, and juvenile training schools, their views represent complexity and ambivalence. As opposed to the generally negative perception of the prison system in the USA and the UK, such as racist (Wacquant, 2001), criminogenic (Alexander, 2012), and socially detrimental (Clear, Rose, & Ryder, 2001), in this study, some families actually appreciated incarceration. Out of 33 family members who experienced their kin's incarceration, the majority of the family members demonstrated a very mixed way of appreciating their kin's confinement. Corroborating the findings documented in Comfort's (2008) and Christian and Kennedy's (2011) works, family members in this study reported that they felt a sense of relief when their kin was imprisoned. Ryoko, whose son had been imprisoned for assault, demonstrated such sentiment by saying, "In the letters he says he wants to get straight when he comes out. He may think so now but when he gets out, I'm afraid he would make the same mistake again. To be honest, as a parent, I am relieved now [that he is in prison]." Haruko, whose teenage daughter had been abusing methamphetamine and suffering from eating disorders, explained her feelings during her daughter's incarceration as follows:

> I did feel sad when I saw her handcuffed behind her back at the court. But I couldn't stay alive if she was [living] with me. So the fact that she would be in the juvenile training school made me feel that I could live a little longer. … When I learned that there was a higher possibility of recidivism for meth users I got so depressed. I thought, if only she could stay in the juvenile training school for the rest of her life. But of course, it's impossible.

The fear of recidivism was one of the most frequently discussed topics by the family members. It was even more amplified for the family members of drug offenders and sex offenders. However, at the same time, family members made efforts to believe in the "possibility that after incarceration [the offender] would desist from criminal activity" (Christian & Kennedy, 2011, p. 391).

Eight parents demonstrated their belief that spending time in prisons and juvenile detention centers was indeed beneficial for their children and that it would teach them a good lesson. At a family circle, Kiyomi spoke of her 28-year-old son who was serving time for attempted murder as follows:

> On one hand, I feel bad for my son. But on the other hand, after the ten years of dealing with him and seeing him during the trial, of course I feel sorry for him but at the same time, I think this [prison] time was necessary for him. He has two sides almost like Dr. Jekyll and Mr. Hyde, and he has been swinging from one side to another. So I think this was really needed for him. God slammed on the brakes for him. I really think it was more of a necessary thing.

Such perspective was more common among the family members who had been witnessing their family members' long-term lawbreaking behavior prior to arrest than those who had not. Whether it was beneficial to the offender or not, the belief that the time spent behind bars is not completely useless was important for family members to maintain a positive mental state. However, this rather naïve perception of the prison as a place to foster penitence and desistence was shattered when an ex-inmate displayed a completely unexpected result. Kaori, whose substance-abusing son was imprisoned for an assault charge, said that during the tumultuous 16 years of her son's addiction, she felt the most shocked and enraged when she found out that her son had developed an addiction to prescription drugs inside prison. She recounted, "I personally experienced my son going to prison, thinking that he would get better but actually getting even worse. I was like, it's unforgivable!" Her account parallels what Sharp refers to as "a cycle of raised and diminished hopes" (2005, p. 54)—the phases of bargaining and frantic activities that the family members of death row inmates go through to save their kin, only to find they have grown disillusioned with the criminal justice system. Although to a lesser degree, the present study suggests that the family members of those who committed a less serious crime also experienced a cycle of hope and despair, possibly resulting in the diminished efficacy of offender rehabilitation.

As family members have been assigned the roles of scapegoats and watchdogs by the legal experts in court, they are likewise expected to play the role of caregivers for their confined kin. Because Japan's correctional system puts an enormous amount of restrictions on prisoners' conduct, from reading books and magazines, to wearing clean underwear and maintaining hygiene (Hayashi, Kitamura, & Natori, 2013), family members are often drawn into fulfilling various requests from their imprisoned kin. As was shown in Steinhoff's (1999) study of those who provided legal, material, and emotional support to political prisoners in Japan, the majority of family members with their loved ones behind bars discussed their current or previous routine of writing letters, visiting prisons, and sending in goods and money. Moreover, because convicts are sent to prisons depending on their classification such as the length of prison sentence, family members are required to cover the cost of travel every time they make a prison visit to a remote place where their kin is serving time. Noriko and Kazumi expressed frustration at not being able to see their sons as much as they would like, due to the financial constraint of buying plane tickets and renting a hotel room (see Christian (2005) for the costs of prison visitation on American families). Five family members including Noriko and Kazumi said visiting prison was something that they looked forward to, stating that being able to talk to the family members face-to-face was a benefit. It was evident, however, that they also made a conscious effort to make the prison visit as much a pleasurable experience as possible by including other fun activities, such as seeing friends or visiting tourist attractions, in the itinerary.

Others mentioned how physically and emotionally draining it was to make such visits. Mutsumi, whose brother had been serving time for murder, explained how she got exhausted every time she went to visit her brother, as follows:

> [The prison] is in [the suburb of Tokyo] but I get dead tired when I go visit. Even now, [after every prison visit] I go to karaoke with my husband and sing songs non-stop for a few

> hours. But in the beginning, our karaoke session used to last four to five hours because I was afraid I would go mad if it wasn't that long.

Moreover, a family's emotional strain is exacerbated by Japan's institutional regulations that limit visitation time and forbid contact visits altogether. Yoko, whose daughter was accused of aiding her boyfriend in a murder, expressed such pain as follows: "When I go visit my daughter, she tries to reach out to me, crying out 'Mom!' But I can't even hold her hand. … It is impossible to have a meaningful conversation in only ten minutes!" While the law states that the standard meeting time should be no more than 30 min, in case of unavoidable circumstance, it is considerably decreased to less than 5 min (Hayashi et al., 2013). Takeshi, a father of a sex offender, recounted that once they had visited a prison only to be denied meeting with his son because he was held incommunicado due to a minor prison regulation violation. Paralleling the experiences of prison visitors in the USA, the families in this study demonstrate how the pains of imprisonment extended to legally innocent prison visitors through vague, arbitrary, or un-communicated prison rules (Comfort, 2003).

Although some family members voluntarily and diligently work to fulfill their role as caregivers despite various difficulties, others take advantage of the physical distance between them and their incarcerated kin to reassert control in their familial relationship. As noted in Comfort (2008)'s work, for middle-class families with financial stability and higher levels of education, living in proximity to lawbreaking kin forces them to place the transgressor at the center of their lives. But once he or she is removed from home through imprisonment, the family members can leave behind a precarious life filled with unexpected encounters with law enforcement and regain a sense of control over their lives. Ayako and Tatsuyo, both a few years into their sons' imprisonment, stated in a family circle that they had decided to write letters to their sons less frequently, to move on and lead the normal life they used to have prior to their sons' arrests. Yoko expressed the same sentiment by saying, "I've decided to enjoy the time that my daughter is not around." Noriko, Ryoko, and Nobuo all spoke of how their sons were starting to occupy less and less amount of their thoughts in their everyday lives. Noriko told in a family circle, "I thought I should live a normal life.… Sorry to be like this, but I'm going to put my son aside for now." Indeed, Comfort (2008) notes that the penitentiary may be a powerful tool for wives and partners to exert control over the relationship with their abusive mates. Two other family members, however, expressed difficulty in getting their minds off of their confined kin, and even if they did, agony and sadness overcame them from time to time. Moreover, even those who had decided to become less devoted to supportive activities exhibited ambivalence, admitting feelings of guilt for caring less, as well as feelings of anxiety about their kin's future prospects.

Narratives provided by the family members with incarcerated kin reveal that prisons occasionally serve a positive function, especially for those who had experienced considerable disruptions in their lives due to their kin's offending. This is similar to another finding discussed previously, how some family members took advantage of law enforcement's power of arrest to deal with their kin's illicit drug use. Not only do these findings parallel what American criminologists have discovered about the wives and children of inmates in the USA (Hagan & Dinovitzer, 1999), but they also challenge previous understandings about the family members of offenders in Japan. While their function was previously understood as a mere social resource passively used by the state (Fukaya, 2007), these findings reveal that some family members of offenders in Japan also actively use the criminal justice system to their advantage. Some families can benefit from kin's apprehension as it restored peace and security in their life. Through imprisonment, they also appreciated an appropriate amount of mental and physical distance from inmates, as it helped establish healthy familial ties. What this suggests is a complex, almost codependent relationship between the criminal justice authorities and family members of offenders, in the absence of other effective social support. As a result of having to rely on the criminal justice system as the sole solution in dealing with their kin's deviant or delinquent behavior, family members suffer from conflicting feelings of solace and distress.

5.4 Release and Reentry

Criminologists have noted that the notion of self-correction seems to lay deeply in the foundation of Japan's criminal justice (Bayley, 1991, p. 183; Braithwaite, 1989, p. 65; Johnson, 1996). Extensive reliance on society's capacity for self-discipline leads to less government investment in prisoner reentry, thus, reintegrating ex-prisoners back into society ultimately becomes the burden for those who are closest to offenders. As the day of the prisoner's release approaches, the family members become increasingly anxious due to varying concerns for their kin's as well as their own future. Even with the existence of parole officers, the participants expressed a tremendous feeling of angst, specifically over their kin's potential recidivism and employment, as well as the changing dynamics within the family and the community. Asked about his emotional state at the time of his son's release, Kohei said he was "80 percent worried and 20 percent optimistic." According to Haruko, she felt as though she was holding "a ticking time bomb" when her daughter came out of the training school. Without proper guidance or assistance to treat an ex-inmate, family members grapple with conflicting feelings of hope and despair.

Takao, a father of a drug offender who was in prison for 18 months, repeatedly discussed his feelings of anxiety at three consecutive family circle meetings prior to his son's release on parole. On one occasion he spoke:

> I'm worried, yeah. … My daughter is worried, too if there would be any [negative] influence on her. She thinks maybe she should go some place else when her brother comes back. Well, the biggest thing I'm worried about is the neighbors who are a little strict, and I'm afraid it would cause trouble….It really concerns me, but I have no answer. Meanwhile, the time is fast approaching. I personally wanted his release to be [in another two months]. I almost told our parole officer to delay it [*laughs bitterly*].

Because prisoners' families are removed from the process of parole planning, they do not have any choice but to accept the release date, which solely is decided by the regional parole board. The parole board in Japan consists of professional probation/parole officers (PPOs) who work together with volunteer probation/parole officers

(VPOs) to rehabilitate those who have committed crime or delinquency. While PPOs mostly engage in administrative tasks as national governmental employees, VPOs are citizens who are commissioned by the state to help "recover" (*tachinaori*) people from deviance and delinquency on a voluntary basis (Angata, 2005). In the case of Takao, he maintained an exceptionally intimate relationship with his son's VPO. He described visiting the officer at least twice a month of his own will, which was quite rare in the sample of this study.

The majority of the families reported that they had limited interactions with VPOs or received insufficient support upon their kin's release. Yasuyo, whose son served time for robbery, said of the VPO, "in the end he seemed to not care at all." Haruko demonstrated her frustration that her daughter's probation officer did not understand the strategy of "cutting off," when she refused to let her daughter come home. She said that she wrote him a letter afterward, thanking him and detailing her daughter's addiction and the reasons behind her action. However, what in his reply, he called her "a heartless parent." In another case, however, the VPO actually helped a family member receive proper support and treatment for her drug-abusing son. In the case of Teruyo, she was recommended by her son's probation officer to attend a talk about addiction, which eventually led her getting connected to a drug rehabilitation center and its family circle. The narratives of the family members indicate that the quality of VPOs in Japan is vastly uneven. Some argue that there is a need for professionalization in order to improve the system of parole (Kitazawa, 2003, p. 108), although it is questionable that simple professionalization would solve many other fundamental issues of the VPO system, let alone a limited national budget for prisoner reentry services.

Two family members have also reported pressure from VPOs to become *migara hikiuke nin* to increase the possibility of parole. *Migara hikiuke nin* simply means a person to whom the prisoner is released; and for inmates, having one is a required condition of parole. The receiver does not have to be a family member but frequent visitation and exchange of letters with the prisoner are necessary criteria to become one (Kikuta, 2011, pp. 197–198). Because not all ex-prisoners are allowed admission to halfway houses,[1] family members acutely feel the pressure from VPOs and their imprisoned kin to provide shelter after release. When Tatsuyo showed reluctance to be on the receiving end of her son due to her age and health, the probation officer asked her daughter to become one instead. Feeling extremely torn, Tatsuyo asked at a family circle if she had done the right thing for her daughter, who was still having a tough time facing her younger brother's sex offenses. Eventually the daughter agreed but Tatsuyo later added that she had told her daughter to "treat [her brother] as if he is another troublesome child of hers and bear the burden as her fate." Her account demonstrates an enormous sense of duty felt by the family members of offenders to keep a close eye on their kin, even throughout their whole lifetime if necessary.

Expectations for family members to virtually aid the criminal justice agents are also seen in the system of parole in Japan. In a society where individuals are assumed

[1] Drug offenders, the elderly, and those who committed yakuza-related organized crimes are less likely to be admitted to halfway houses in Japan (Kikuta, 2002, p. 196).

to self-discipline themselves, prisoner reintegration is often left to the hands of those who are closest to ex-inmates. At this point, the pressure felt by the family members intensifies even more, for it could mean a lifelong responsibility to care and monitor their kin, a sense of burden also commonly felt by Japanese families of the mentally ill and the demented elderly (Arai & Washio, 1999; Hasui et al., 2002).

John Braithwaite (1989) writes of Japan as a culture that allows wrongdoers to be de-labeled and accepted in communities after reintegrative shaming. Indeed, the system of "community corrections" in Japan is much less authoritarian and punitive than that of the USA, with VPOs acting as the "moral influence," rather than the agents of crime control (Johnson & Johnson, 2000). However, with the lack of specialized knowledge and training (Angata, 2005), VPOs cannot provide bias-free, family-centered, and effective support for ex-prisoners, let alone their families. In contrast to the USA where parole violations account for one of the major causes for prison admission, the benefits of Japan's reliance on the less formal, less threatening method of supervision should be recognized. During the course of my fieldwork, I have come to know several VPOs who are passionate about learning the experiences of offenders' family members. Haruko was even invited by the rehabilitation bureau to talk regularly in front of VPOs and share her experiences as the mother of a drug addict. Initiatives like this can improve the current system of parole by catering to the needs of parolees and their families while maintaining the informal and non-punitive relationship. Being treated as a valuable asset rather than a mere convenient tool for crime control is a desire shared by many families of offenders in Japan.

6 Conclusion

Japan uses prison as a means to control crime and delinquency significantly less than other democratic nations (Johnson, 1996). Criminal justice in Japan is also known for its informality as well as its extensive reliance on the community to discipline itself; this is arguably the main reasons for Japan's lower crime rate (Bayley, 1991; Braithwaite, 1989). The experiences of the families of offenders in this study, however, reveal that Japan's criminal justice may be achieved at the significant cost of those who are closest to the offenders. In the absence of social services and programs that effectively assist those who are in trouble with the law, families are forced to rely on the system of control, which financially, emotionally, and socially debilitates them.

To change this reality, Japan's criminal justice system should seek ways to apprehend, prosecute, incarcerate, and rehabilitate individuals with less reliance on the offenders' kin. Collaborating with various governmental and non-governmental organizations such as the national welfare system, employment service centers, drug rehabilitation centers, halfway houses, homeless shelters, and hospitals is crucial. Moreover, all criminal justice authorities and health-care providers should equip themselves with accurate, bias-free understanding of drug addiction. Those with mental health and addiction problems must be promptly referred to hospitals and drug rehabilitation facilities not only for their benefit but also for the sake of their family members' mental and physical well-being.

Although a fundamental reform to allow for a criminal justice system that relies less on offenders' kin would be an ideal fix to the issues discussed in this chapter, a more practical approach may be to use the family as a constructive resource. The Prison Family Bill of Rights (Prisoner's Family Conference, 2013), which was adopted at the fifth International Prisoners' Family Conference in Dallas, reads, "The prison family has the right to be treated and integrated as a *positive* resource in the process of rehabilitation and reintegration preparation and parole planning of an incarcerated loved one [*emphasis added*]." Incorporating the voices of those who are closest to offenders in prisoner reentry, rehabilitation, and reintegration may enhance offenders' possibility of desistence, which in turn benefits their family, as well as society at large. It is important, however, to note that such an effort could face obstacles in communities like Japan, due to the considerable amount of shame and stigma attached to breaking social norms and regulations. Not all family members of offenders are willing to share their experiences with the wider public, as they gravely fear receiving negative publicity in their communities in the era of Internet and social media. This leads to another area that requires further research, that is, the social consequences of being related to an offender in contemporary Japan.

While the current study examined the criminal justice system's response to crime and its relationship to offenders' families, how society responds to offenders and their families is yet to be investigated. Close examination of the family members' lived experiences with neighbors, colleagues, friends, and acquaintances will create new knowledge about one of Japan's most marginalized populations and will aid in the recognition of their voices by criminal justice agents as well as members of society.

References

Abe, K. (2015). In H. Kusaba (Ed.), *Kagaisha Kazokun No Ronri To Jissen: Kazoku No Kaihuku To Kagaisha No Kousei Ni Mukete*. Tokyo: Gendai Jinbun Sha.

Alexander, M. (2012). *The new Jim Crow: Mass incarceration in the age of colorblindness*. New York: The New Press.

Angata, S. (2005). *Shakainai Shogu No Keisei To Tenkai*. Tokyo: Nihon Kosei Hogo Kyokai.

Arai, Y., & Washio, M. (1999). Burden felt by family caring for the elderly members needing care in southern Japan. *Aging & Mental Health, 3*(2), 158–164.

Bach, A. (2010). *Ordinary injustice: How America holds court*. New York: Holt Paperbacks.

Bayley, D. H. (1991). *Forces of order: Policing modern Japan* (2nd ed.). Berkeley: University of California Press.

Beck, E., & Britto, S. (2006). Using feminist methods and restorative justice to interview capital offenders' family members. *Affilia, 21*(1), 59–70.

Beck, E., Britto, S., & Andrews, A. B. (2009). *In the shadow of death: Restorative justice and death row families*. New York: Oxford University Press.

Borovoy, A. (2005). *The too-good wife: Alcohol, codependency, and the politics of nurturance in postwar Japan*. Berkeley: University of California Press.

Braithwaite, J. (1989). *Crime, shame and reintegration*. Cambridge, UK: Cambridge University Press.

Braman, D. (2002). Families and incarceration. In M. Mauer & M. Chesney-Lind (Eds.), *Invisible punishment: The collateral consequences of mass imprisonment* (pp. 117–135). New York: The New Press.

Braman, D. (2007). *Doing time on the outside: Incarceration and family life in urban America*. Ann Arbor, MI: University of Michigan Press.

Charmaz, K. (2006). *Constructing grounded theory: A practical guide through qualitative analysis*. Thousand Oaks, CA: SAGE Publications Ltd.

Christian, J. (2005). Riding the bus: Barriers to prison visitation and family management strategies. *Journal of Contemporary Criminal Justice, 21*(1), 31–48.

Christian, J., & Kennedy, L. W. (2011). Secondary narratives in the aftermath of crime: Defining family members' relationships with prisoners. *Punishment & Society, 13*(4), 379–402.

Christian, J., Mellow, J., & Thomas, S. (2006). Social and economic implications of family connections to prisoners. *Journal of Criminal Justice, 34*(4), 443–452.

Clear, T. R., Rose, D. R., & Ryder, J. A. (2001). Incarceration and the community: The problem of removing and returning offenders. *Crime & Delinquency, 47*(3), 335–351.

Comfort, M. (2003). In the tube at San Quentin the "secondary prisonization" of women visiting inmates. *Journal of Contemporary Ethnography, 32*(1), 77–107.

Comfort, M. (2007). Punishment beyond the legal offender. *Annual Review of Law and Social Science, 3*(1), 271–296.

Comfort, M. (2008). *Doing time together: Love and family in the shadow of the prison*. Chicago: University of Chicago Press.

Comfort, M. (2016). "A twenty-hour-a-day job": The impact of frequent low-level criminal justice involvement on family life. *The Annals of the American Academy, 665*, 63–79.

Condry, R. (2007). *Families shamed: The consequences of crime for relatives of serious offenders*. Cullompton: Willan.

Dressel, P. L., & Barnhill, S. K. (1994). Reframing gerontological thought and practice: The case of grandmothers with daughters in prison. *Gerontologist, 34*(5), 685–691.

Eisenstein, J., & Jacob, H. (1991). *Felony justice*. Lanham, MD: University Press of America.

Feeley, M. M. (1992). *The process is the punishment: Handling cases in a lower criminal court*. New York: Russell Sage Foundation.

Fishman, L. T. (1988). Stigmatization and prisoners' wives' feelings of shame. *Deviant Behavior, 9*(2), 169–192.

Fishman, L. T. (1990). *Women at the wall: A study of prisoners' wives doing time on the outside* (1st ed.). Albany, NY: State University of New York Press.

Fukaya, H. (2007). Shokuho Seishin Shogaisha Kazoku Eno Sekkin No Kokoromi: Seishin Shougaisha No Oya Ni Kaserareta Shakai Shigen Kinou Wo Megutte. *The Waseda Journal of Social Sciences, 10*, 342–356.

Fukaya, H. (2009). Shokuho Seishin Shogaisha Kazoku No Keiken Ni Tsuite Nani Wo Tou Bekika. *Japanese Journal of Forensic Social Sciences, 9*, 106–117.

Goffman, A. (2014). *On the run: Fugitive life in an American City*. Chicago: University Of Chicago Press.

Hagan, J., & Dinovitzer, R. (1999). Collateral consequences of imprisonment for children, communities, and prisoners. *Crime and Justice, 26*, 121–162.

Hamai, K., & Ellis, T. (2006). Crime and criminal justice in modern Japan: From re-integrative shaming to popular punitivism. *International Journal of Sociology of Law, 34*, 157–178.

Hamai, K., & Ellis, T. (2009). Nihon Ni Okeru Genbatsuka To Populism. In *Gurobaruka Suru Genbtasuka To Populism* (pp. 90–118). Tokyo: Gendai Jinbun Sha.

Hasui, C., Sakamoto, S., Sugiura, T., Miyata, R., Fujii, Y., Koshiishi, F., et al. (2002). Burden on family members of the mentally ill: A naturalistic study in Japan. *Comprehensive Psychiatry, 43*(3), 219–222.

Hayashi, M., Kitamura, A., & Natori, T. (2013). *Keiji Shuyo Shisetsu Ho* (2nd ed.). Tokyo: Yuhikaku.

Hirayama, M. (2012). Lay judge decisions in sex crime cases: The most controversial area of siban-in trials. *Yonsei Law Journal, 3*(1), 129–144.

Hirschi, A. E., Dietrich, S. M., Landau, R., Schneider, P. D., Ackelsberg, I., Bernstein-Baker, J., et al. (2002). *Every door closed: Barriers facing parents with criminal records*. Washington, DC: Center for Law and Social Policy.

Howarth, G., & Rock, P. (2000). Aftermath and the construction of victimisation: "The other victims of crime". *The Howard Journal, 39*(1), 58–78.

Ishimaru, T., Senba, A., Kawakami, T., & Hattori, S. (2005). *Keiji Sosho No Jitsumu* (Vol. 1, 2nd ed.). Tokyo: Shin Nihon Hoki.

Johnson, D. T. (2002a). Plea bargaining in Japan. In M. M. Feeley & S. Miyazawa (Eds.), *The Japanese adversary system in context: Controversies and context* (pp. 140–172). New York: Palgrave Macmillan.

Johnson, D. T. (2002b). *The Japanese way of justice*. New York: Oxford University Press.

Johnson, D. T. (2007). Crime and punishment in contemporary Japan. *Crime and Justice, 36*(1), 371–423.

Johnson, E. H. (1996). *Japanese corrections: Managing convicted offenders in an orderly society*. Carbondale, IL: Southern Illinois University Press.

Johnson, E. H., & Johnson, C. (2000). *Linking community and corrections in Japan* (1st ed.). Carbondale, IL: Southern Illinois University Press.

Kaeble, D., & Glaze, L. E. (2016). *Correctional populations in the United States, 2015*. Washington, DC: Bureau of Justice Statistics. Retrieved from https://www.bjs.gov/index.cfm?ty=pbdetail&iid=5870

Kikuta, K. (2002). *Nihon No Keimusho*. Tokyo: Iwanami Shoten.

Kikuta, K. (2011). *Keiji Shihou: Taiho, Saiban, Soshite Shakai Fukki*. Tokyo: Keiso Shobou.

Kitazawa, S. (2003). *Hanzaisha Shogu No Tenkai: Hogokansatsu Wo Shoten Toshite*. Tokyo: Seibundo.

Koehler, S. A., Weiss, H., Songer, T. J., Rozin, L., Shakir, A., Ladham, S., et al. (2003). Deaths among criminal suspects, law enforcement officers, civilians, and prison inmates: A coroner-based study. *The American Journal of Forensic Medicine and Pathology, 24*(4), 334–338.

Levin, M., & Tice, V. (2009). *Japan's new citizen judges: How secrecy imperils judicial reform*. Retrieved December 20, 2013, from http://www.japanfocus.org/-Virginia-Tice/3141

Lofland, J., Snow, D., Anderson, L., & Lofland, L. H. (2005). *Analyzing social settings: A guide to qualitative observation and analysis* (4th ed.). Belmont, CA: Wadsworth Publishing.

Ministry of Justice. (2016). *Number of people in correctional facilities (Keiji Shisetsu No Shuyo Jokyo)*. Retrieved February 13, 2017, from http://hakusyo1.moj.go.jp/jp/63/nfm/n63_2_2_4_1_1.html

Miyazawa, S. (1990). Learning lessons from Japanese experience in policing and crime: Challenge for Japanese criminologists. *Kobe University Departmental Bulletin, 24*, 29–61.

Petersilia, J. (2003). How we hinder: Legal and practical barriers to reintegration. In *When prisoners come home* (pp. 105–138). New York, NY: Oxford University Press.

Prisoner's Family Conference. (2013). *Prison family bill of rights*. Retrieved from http://prisonersfamilyconference.org/prisoner-family-bill-of-rights/

Rose, D. R., Clear, T. R., & Ryder, J. A. (2001). Addressing the unintended consequences of incarceration through community-oriented services at the neighborhood level. *Corrections Management Quarterly, 5*(3), 62–71.

Sampson, R. J. (2011). The incarceration ledger. *Criminology & Public Policy, 10*(3), 819–828.

Sharp, S. F. (2005). *Hidden victims: The effects of the death penalty on families of the accused*. New Brunswick, NJ: Rutgers University Press.

Steinhoff, P. G. (1999). Doing the defendant's laundry: Support groups as social movement organizations in contemporary Japan. *Japanstudien, Jahrbuch Des Deutschen Instituts Fur Japanstudien, 11*, 55–78.

Steinhoff, P. G. (2008). Mass arrests, sensational crimes and stranded children: Three crises for Japanese new left activists' families. In A. Hashimoto & J. W. Traphagan (Eds.), *Imagined families, lived families: Culture and kinship in contemporary Japan* (pp. 77–110). Albany, NY: SUNY Press.

Suzuki, N. (2010). *Kagaisha Kazoku*. Tokyo: Gentosha.

Wacquant, L. (2001). Deadly symbiosis: When ghetto and prison meet and mesh. In D. Garland (Ed.), *Mass imprisonment: Social causes and consequences* (pp. 82–120). London: Sage Publication Ltd..

Wakefield, S., & Wildeman, C. (2011). Mass imprisonment and racial disparities in childhood behavioral problems. *Criminology & Public Policy, 10*(3), 791–792.

Chapter 4
Incidents of Homicides or Murder–Suicides by Family Caregivers in Japan and Challenges for Prevention

Etsuko Yuhara

1 Introduction

Japan's demographic aging continues to progress each year. Whereas the proportion of elderly people aged 65 years and above was 7.1% of the total population in 1970, it sharply increased to 27.3% in 2016. The number of people requiring care due to aging has also increased. According to the Ministry of Health, Labour and Welfare and as disclosed in the monthly "Nursing Care Insurance Situation Report," as of January 2017, there were 6.29 million people (65 years old and above) in primary nursing care or recognized as needing support. The pressing need for examination of family care support is becoming one of society's most important issues. In addition, incidents of homicides and murder–suicides caused by fatigue due to care burdens continue to occur throughout the nation. However, in Japan, there have been few academic research studies regarding the features and trends of such incidents or measures toward their prevention.

This study clarifies the features and trends among incidents of homicides (including homicides by willful negligence), manslaughter, and murder–suicides committed by family members or resulting from care-related factors (homicides or murder–suicides by family caregivers). The study also examines the characteristics of perpetrators in precedent cases of murder by caregivers and how the often-cited motive of "pessimism about the future" was formed. In addition, the study analyzes why the perpetrators were unable to keep themselves from carrying out the crimes. The study's objective is to clarify the policies and support needed to prevent murder by caregivers.

E. Yuhara (✉)
Department of Social Welfare, Nihon Fukushi University, 〒4703295, Okuda, Mihama-cho, Aichi-pref, Chita-gun, Japan
e-mail: e-kato@n-fukushi.ac.jp

J. Liu, S. Miyazawa (eds.), *Crime and Justice in Contemporary Japan*, Springer Series on Asian Criminology and Criminal Justice Research,
https://doi.org/10.1007/978-3-319-69359-0_4

2 Current Situation of Murder by Caregivers

There are three good sources for understanding the current situation in which murders committed by caregivers occur in Japan: the "Incidents of Deaths Due to Abuse" investigation by the Ministry of Health, Labour and Welfare, crime statistics from the National Police Agency, and surveys conducted by social welfare researchers. Each source has been outlined below.

2.1 "Incidents of Death Due to Abuse" Survey by the Ministry of Health, Labour and Welfare

On the basis of a law that took effect in April 2006 to prevent the abuse of the elderly and laws related to supporting caregivers of the elderly (hereinafter referred to as the *Elderly Abuse Prevention Law*), the Ministry of Health, Labour and Welfare conducts an annual survey on abuse of the elderly in municipalities. The survey, titled "Incidents of Death Due to Abuse," indicates, nationwide, the number of cases acknowledged as "death due to abuse," number of victims, form of cases, gender of victims and perpetrators, and relationship between victim and perpetrator. As of October 2016, results spanning 7 years from 2006 to 2014 have been published, and they indicate 227 cases of "Incidents of Death Due to Abuse" and 230 victims.

2.2 Crime Statistics from the National Police Agency

The National Police Agency annually publishes domestic crime statistics, which are organized by motive. From 2007 onward, "fatigue from caregiving or nursing" was included as a direct motive or cause of a crime, which led to a greater understanding of the number of cases committed with this motive. As of October 2016, statistics have been published until 2015. These numbers show that there were 398 cases in which murderers were arrested who had the motive of "fatigue from caregiving or nursing" in the 6 years spanning 2007–2015, and there were 22 cases of manslaughter.

In addition, the 2008 edition of a white paper on crime by the National Police Agency contained a feature on crimes against the elderly, which revealed the reality of the situation and measures the agency has taken to address it. Regarding murderers, the following information was presented (National Police Agency, 2008, pp. 38–39).

The subjects examined by the Tokyo District Public Prosecutor's Office were 50 people, who were 65 years or older between January 1, 1998, and December 31, 2007, who were found guilty at their first hearing, and against whom material could be gathered. Twenty-eight of these people had killed their relatives, while 22 had killed unrelated persons. Concerning those who killed their relatives, the proportion was high of those who expressed "pessimism about the future" and "fatigue from caregiving or nursing" as motives for the crime. Moreover, fatigue from caregiving was observed in 28.6% of the murderers who killed their elderly relatives (19 males, 9 females), 71.4% expressed "pessimism about the future," and 25% had attempted a forced double suicide.

A comparison of the gender of the perpetrators shows that the motives of male perpetrators were "pessimism about the future" (68.4%), "crime of passion" (31.6%), and "forced double suicide" (26.3%), whereas for females, the motives were "pessimism about the future" (77.8%), "fatigue from caregiving" (55.6%), and either "miserable with life," "forced double suicide," "revenge," or "suffering" from a sense of victimization stemming from the feeling that one is being excluded from the mainstream society because of age or disabilities (22.2%). Gender-specific motives that constituted a high percentage were "crimes of passion" for males and "fatigue from caregiving" for women.

Of the nine victims of the cases in which the victim was killed by an elderly female family member, seven victims (77.8%) were found to have a disease. Moreover, in comparison to perpetrators in cases not involving murder of the elderly, there are more perpetrators who have attempted suicide before or after the incident in cases involving killing the elderly. It was observed that almost half of those involved in cases of killing elderly family members attempted suicide.

Moreover, in this white paper, one type of crime in which the elderly are murdered is illustrated through this statement "I was tired of nursing him and we were economically unstable, so I attempted to murder my husband." The details were the following: a "69-year-old female. No previous convictions or personal history. Retired from work just before this incident due to fatigue from caring for her 70-year-old husband who has dementia." There were also economic issues due to the couple's decrease in income. She attempted to kill her husband with an elastic cord but gave up halfway through the act. She received a two-and-a-half-year sentence with a 3-year suspended sentence.

The National Police Agency offered the following speculation about the results of the investigation (National Police Agency, 2008, pp. 43–44):

> Many of those who murder their relatives have no previous convictions or personal history, but spouses and children become first-time offenders because of 'fatigue from caregiving' or 'pessimism about the future.' In the investigation, there were nine female offenders. All had murdered their relatives. Moreover, majority of the female offenders in particular cited 'fatigue from caregiving' as the motive for the crime. One cause of the increase in the number of elderly people being killed could be the advancement of an 'aging society,' in which a family member gets tired of having to look after elderly family members." "It is not easy for the criminal justice system to intervene in the early stages to prevent the acts, such as aging and fatigue from caregiving, that lead to the so-called 'unexpected murder.' Since this is entirely in the domain of social welfare, it appears there is nothing else to do but wait for the social welfare system to be perfected.

From these remarks, one can confirm that the National Police Agency believes that cases of fatigue from caregiving that lead to murder are "in the domain of social welfare, and that it is necessary that the social welfare system play a major role in creating various countermeasures aimed at helping the elderly."

2.3 *Surveys Based on Newspaper Reports*

Surveys by social welfare researchers and others on murders by caregivers discuss actual conditions and issues on the basis of newspaper reports. Takako (2001), Kato (2005), and Hane (2006) have produced exemplary surveys.

Using a newspaper article database (Nikkei Telecom), incidents of homicides or murder–suicides by family caregivers who were also relatives were identified from among incidents of homicides occurring within the period from January 1, 1996, to December 31, 2015, where the age of victim is 60 years or older, as specified by the keywords "nursing care," "murder," "murder–suicide," "injury resulting in death," and "negligence as guardian" in 38 different newspapers across Japan. Features and trends of these incidents were then analyzed.

During the 20 years covered by the study, 754 incidents occurred, with background factors related to nursing care. Over half of the perpetrators were male (71.0%), while over half of the victims were female (74.1%) (Fig. 4.1). In terms of relationship, the highest proportion of incidents concerned husbands killing their wives (33.4%), followed by sons killing their parents (31.7%) (Table 4.1). Many victims were between the ages 80–85 (20.3%), while many perpetrators were in their 70s (22.8%). The proportion of older perpetrators was high; especially in 2010, perpetrators aged 60 or above accounted for over two-thirds of incidents (72.7%). Of the 754 incidents, 287 involved the caregiver's subsequent readiness to commit suicide (38.1%), while 237 involved disability or infirmities (depression), including illness on the part of the perpetrators (31.6%). Dementia on the part of the victim could be confirmed in 232 cases (30.8%).

Overall, notwithstanding the fact that women accounted for majority of the caregivers (approximately 70%), the perpetrator in approximately 70% of cases of homicides or murder–suicides by family caregivers was a male. Cases of husbands killing their wives are the most common. Since it is estimated that males are more likely than females to become impassive in caregiving roles, the improvement of support for male caregivers is called for to prevent the recurrence of similar incidents. In addition, cases of the perpetrator him- or herself being elderly (60 years of age and above) make up the average of 59.5% of the cases over the past 20 years. There was a particular increase in 2010, with the average being 72.7%. Furthermore, there were eight cases in 2009 of victims being 90 years old and older and nine such cases in 2011, suggesting that caregivers at home may become exhausted from providing prolonged care. In addition, since many perpetrators also suffered from infirmities immediately before the incidents, measures to ease depression in caregivers will also be effective in preventing similar incidents.

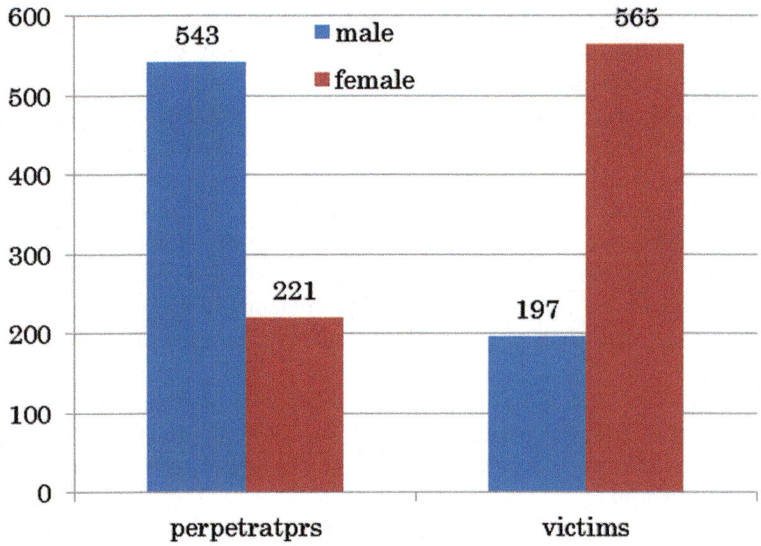

Fig. 4.1 Gender comparison of the perpetrators and the victims of homicides or murder–suicides by family caregivers

Table 4.1 Relationship between perpetrators and victims

	Perpetrator	Number of incidents (number of fatalities)	Percentage of incidents
Parent murders child	Father	1 (1)	0.1
	Mother	8 (8)	1.1
Child murders parent	Son	239 (242)	31.7
	Son's spouse	11 (11)	1.5
	Daughter	85 (87)	11.3
	Daughter's spouse	10 (11)	1.3
Murder between spouses	Husband	252 (252)	33.4
	Wife	100 (100)	13.3
Other	Sister	9 (9)	1.2
	Brother	15 (15)	2.0
	Grandchild	11 (11)	1.5
	Other	4 (6)	0.5
	Several murderers	9 (9)	1.2
Total		754 (762)	100

2.4 Overseas Research

In various countries, there are numerous studies being published on murder and suicide among relatives and loved ones. Using the database PubMed, Eliason (2009) performed a search with the keywords "murder–suicide," "homicide–suicide," and "families" and conducted reviews of the main literature, extracting information from this search from the United States and Western European countries from 1993 onward. The results showed that there were many cases of murder–suicide among the elderly in which men murdered their wives. If one looks at murder–suicide as a whole, the proportion of perpetrators judged to have depression is high, and they have often not received sufficient medical care. In a factual investigation, Salari (2007) examined 225 cases of homicide–suicide using newspaper reports, television news, police reports, and obituary notices from 1995 to 2005 to see whether victims and perpetrators were at least 60 years of age. The results showed that most perpetrators were male; 34% of the victims were judged to have health problems; 30% of the perpetrators were judged to have health problems; in 36% of the cases, both perpetrator and victim had health problems; and in 7.5% of the cases, the victim had dementia.

However, few studies have examined the context of cases and checked for difficulties related to caregiving or focused on cases in which family caregivers become perpetrators. Among the few studies in this area, Karch and Nunn's (2010) study is noteworthy.

Karch and Nunn (2010) used the National Violent Death Reporting System and conducted a situational analysis of 68 murder cases that occurred in the United States (between 2003 and 2007), wherein caregivers were the perpetrators. Their analysis focused on the characteristics of the victim and perpetrator, the role of the caregiver, and the time that the incident occurred. Their results indicate that approximately half of the victims (48.5%) were 80 years of age or above and slightly less than half of the incidents (44.1%) involved joint suicide. When examining cases wherein the victim's age was 50 or above, their relationship with the perpetrator was in descending order: husband (26.4%), son (20.8%), daughter (8.3%), and wife (6.9%). In addition, there was a tendency for either the victim or perpetrator to be suffering from some type of disease. With regard to incident prevention, the following three approaches can be determined from the study. First, it is necessary, particularly with regard to male caregivers, to introduce appropriate interventions and services, even when they have no history of abuse or instances of seeking support. Second, it is useful to understand the vulnerability of the victims, the characteristics of the suspects, and the various motives behind these crimes when establishing effective preventative measures. Finally, it is critical that medical professionals conduct thorough and effective risk assessments.

An article titled "Social workers 'failed' to monitor murdered elderly man" was published in the 2011 issue of Community Care Magazine (Dunning, 2011). The article focused on the murder of an English father by his caregiving son and determined several problems such as how the son had received no direct support from social workers, how he had not received a professional assessment (despite such an evaluation being stipulated in the Carers Act), and how there was no risk assessment conducted after the son had refused assistance. The article highlighted the importance of implementing caregiver or risk assessments as a means of prevention. It also indicated that with regard to benefit payments, local governments should not fail to determine whether such payments are being appropriately applied. However, it has been stated that the primary issue is currently how local governments should respond to the increasing number of benefit recipients.

2.5 Conclusion: The Current Status of and Issues Related to Murder by Caregivers

In Japan, in addition to enforcing the *Elderly Abuse Prevention Law*, the Ministry of Health, Labour and Welfare began conducting a yearly survey of "Incidents of Death as a Result of Abuse." Furthermore, since 2007, it has indicated the number of cases in which the direct cause of a crime was "fatigue from caregiving or nursing." It can be said that murder by caregivers has begun to be recognized as a problem that should be solved in Japanese society. However, several problems remain in terms of understanding the current situation regarding murder by caregivers and in aiming at preventing similar cases from occurring in the future. For example, there is ambiguity in the definition of a murder by a caregiver. To understand the actual context, it is essential to clarify the definition of this term, but as of 2017, there has been no agreed upon definition. One question is whether murder by a caregiver can be ranked as "abuse." In a majority of cases of double suicides, in which the motive was fatigue from caregiving, abuse has not occurred while the victim was alive. Conversely, cases of "contract murders" in which the victim requests that the perpetrator kill him or her by saying things such as "I want to die. Kill me." are not uncommon. There is another viewpoint that "no matter what reason is given, ending another's life is nothing other than abuse" (Nemoto, 2007, p. 40), but there are also cases in which up until right before the murder, the caregiver has been attentive to the point where he or she has been praised by others. It is essential to consider whether it is also acceptable to rank these types of cases as "death due to abuse."

The establishment of systems for examining cases that occurred in the past is also a crucial issue. In the case of the abuse and death of children, based on Article 4, Clause 5 of the *Child Welfare Law*, local public bodies are obligated to conduct investigations of such cases. In addition, based on the *Child Abuse Prevention Law*, the Ministry of Health, Labour and Welfare forms a committee of experts to look into the situation at the time of the incident and proposes countermeasures to prevent similar cases from occurring (Ministry of Health, Labour and Welfare, 2016). However, when it comes to murder by caregivers, investigation of cases has not been required by law, there is no examination of improvement nor are there surveys conducted by experts, and there have not been particularly many proposals for policies aimed at improving caregiving in general. I think it is necessary to take these steps regarding murder by caregivers and have local public bodies undertake investigations and offer preventive measures based on those investigations.

In addition, regarding the context of cases, it is essential to identify what drove the perpetrator to commit the crime and to analyze the situation from his or her viewpoint. A 2008 white paper on crimes presented the strategy of "removing the risk factors of crimes by conducting various countermeasures aimed at the elderly focused on welfare" (National Police Agency, 2008, p. 43), but it is unclear specifically what kind of countermeasures are needed and whether conducting these measures might curb such incidents. To answer this question, it is necessary to explore the process by which perpetrators come to experience "pessimism about the future" and to clarify what triggered the incident and why the caregivers could not take an action such as consulting those around them to prevent the incident from occurring. It is desirable to establish a system that examines these points in the course of judging a case of murder by a caregiver.

3 Traits of Caregivers Who Become Perpetrators in Murder by Caregiver Cases

Although a caregiver may have experienced stress building up from taking care of a person, he or she does not generally commit a crime at first even if they have thought about killing the person in their care. Rather, the caregiver probably seeks help from those around him or her, going to great effort to improve the situation by using welfare services and so forth. If one considers the number of caregivers in Japan as a whole, the occurrences of murder by caregivers are quite rare and are special cases. However, if that is true, then one needs to examine why those special circumstances are limited to particular cases and what caused them. What specific situation existed for the perpetrator and the victim, and what was unique about their surrounding environment? For example, in trials related to murders by caregivers, there is almost always prejudice against the perpetrator's way of thinking, and it is often pointed out that the perpetrator did not seek help from those around him or her. However, caregivers who murder of the person under their care are clearly different from regular caregivers. Perhaps they have an unusual way of thinking. Therefore, to draft effective preventive measures, it is necessary to clarify the caregiver's perspective.

Therefore, I will now analyze the particulars of murders and double suicides committed by relatives who are caregivers, specific cases of attempted murder, the thought process of perpetrators, and the circumstances that led to the crime and consider why the crime could not have been avoided. Simultaneously, I will examine accounts of the experiences of people who were "driven to thinking I would die and kill them, but gave up on the idea just before committing the crime," which were compiled for people with dementia and their families. I will clarify the reasons those people were able to avoid committing a crime.

3.1 Analysis of Precedent Cases Related to Crimes Committed by Relatives Who Were Caregivers

3.1.1 Aim of the Survey

The aim is to examine the reasons perpetrators were unable to avoid committing a crime through an investigation of murders by caregivers committed in the past. An additional goal is to clarify the defendants' ways of thinking as judged in court rulings and their reasons for not seeking help from those around them to avoid committing the crime.

3.1.2 Objects of Study in the Survey

First, I searched for cases that corresponded to any of the following keywords in the legal information database D1LAW COM, in which precedent cases are compiled: crimes committed by a relative, cases related to caregiving, cases in which the victim was at least 60 years of age, murder, attempted murder, manslaughter, and abandonment by a person responsible for protection that resulted in death.

Regarding cases that occurred between January 1, 1998, and September 1, 2014, I used the keywords "caregiving, murder," "caregiving, double suicide," caregiving, manslaughter," and "caregiving, abandonment by a person responsible for protection that resulted in death" and selected relevant cases, focusing my analysis on those cases in which caregiving somehow played a role.

3.1.3 Ethical Considerations

The precedent cases recorded in the database I used are already widely available to those in the legal profession and to researchers. In conducting my analysis, I omitted all information that could be used to identify individuals.

3.1.4 Analysis Method

On the basis of the descriptions of the precedent cases, I identified the reasons the crime could not be avoided, the defendants' way of thinking, and why the defendant did not seek help from those around him or her to avoid committing the crime.

3.1.5 Results

Through the search, I identified 140 cases related to "caregiving, murder," 39 cases related to "caregiving, double suicide," 15 cases related to "caregiving, manslaughter," and 6 cases related to "caregiving, abandonment by a person responsible for protection that resulted in death." Among these, caregiving had a direct influence on the occurrence of the crime in 17 cases. Moreover, while caregiving was not the main cause of an incident in two cases, the caregivers in other cases had attempted a double suicide with the person for whom they provide care. In another case, the person who would require care was not yet in need of assistance, but she feared that the need for her child to provide care in the future would cause trouble for the child, and therefore she attempted a double suicide. These 20 cases were the subject of analysis.

4 Reasons the Incident Could Not Be Avoided

I was able to identify the various primary reasons that drove the defendants to commit the crime: the person for whom they were caring was suffering from dementia and was bedridden or ill; the physical condition of the caregiver was worsening because of insomnia, lack of appetite, and so forth; and the household was experiencing economic distress and so on. If these factors are considered as single elements, they are all matters that can somehow be overcome, but when concentrated within a certain period of time, the combined difficulty of these issues accumulates, possibly resulting in enough emotional damage to cause the caregiver to decide to kill the person receiving care.

Among the 20 cases I analyzed, "depression" was suspected to be one of the main causes of the defendant committing a double suicide or of being unable to stop him- or herself from committing murder in seven cases (Table 4.2). Three patterns were observed: depression had been observed in the caregiver, in the person receiving care, or in both of them.

In the case of the caregiver having depression, he or she experienced insomnia, lack of appetite, a decrease in opportunities to leave the house, and suicidal thoughts during the time leading up to the incident. In Case 1, a woman was responsible for the care of both her mother, who had dementia, and her husband, who was bedridden after a stroke. The woman had insomnia and lost her appetite, losing nearly 10 kg in body weight over a short period of time. She had fewer chances to leave the house, she stopped answering phone calls from her children, and she hinted at suicide to those around her. At the time of the incident, the woman had been diagnosed with minor depression. In Case 2, a doctor had diagnosed a daughter-in-law with depression. Her depression worsened when her mother died, and she began taking her medication irregularly around 1 month before the incident. Other than caring for the victim, her mother-in-law, she often only lay in bed in her bedroom. The trigger for the incident was "not being able to control irritation at unexpectedly hearing the sound of a car somewhere." In the trial, she acknowledged that she "could not control herself and attacked the victim fitfully."

In contrast, in a number of cases, the person who was receiving care was judged to have a level of depression. Those who were under the care of another person and who were pessimistic about their own futures said things such as "I want to die" (Cases 3, 12), "I'm sorry to cause you so much trouble, if I could die right now, I would like to" (Case 4), and "There's no choice but to live" (Case 13). Sometimes the situation may have been one in which the person receiving care entreated his or her caregiver to "kill me." In these cases, the caregiver may have told the person "not to joke around," cheering him or her up by saying that one "must keep doing [one's] best to live" (Case 12), scolding the person and telling him or her "not to say such a thing" (Case 13), or somehow attempting to bring the situation to a close. However, when the situation began to take a toll on the caregiver's health and the task of caregiving started to become a hindrance in his or her daily life and the caregiver began to lose the will to encourage the care recipient, then, from that point

Table 4.2 Precedent cases of caregiving murder

Case number	Perpetrator	Victim	Background to the incident	Suspicion of depression
Case 1	Daughter	Mother	The defendant was sickly and in debt. Committing suicide would leave nobody behind to take care of her mother, who had dementia. She couldn't leave her mother alone, so she decided to kill herself and her mother	At the time of the incident, the defendant had minor depression
Case 2	Daughter-in-law	Mother-in-law	The defendant wanted to be liberated from caregiving, but she thought it was her duty to provide care and that she could not abandon her role. She was emotionally cornered, and decided to kill both herself and her mother-in-law	Nine years before the incident, the defendant was diagnosed with depression. At the time of the incident, she had relapsed
Case 3	Husband	Wife and mother-in-law	The defendant was in economic distress and unable to pay the mortgage. He was convinced that his wife's diabetes was no longer curable, so he was pessimistic about the future. He believed he was putting his wife out of her misery by killing her, as she thought was best. He accepted her request of "Kill me." He felt pity for his mother-in-law, who had severe dementia and would have nobody to take care of her, so he killed her too	The defendant was diagnosed with depression during the year of the incident. He complained that he wanted to die
Case 4	Son	Parents	The defendant was the oldest son and was a shut-in. His mother's condition continued to worsen, and he was unsure as to when his father would die. He was in despair over being in debt and not seeing a future, so he decided to kill his parents and himself	On the day of the incident, the victim told the defendant, "If I could die now, I would"

(continued)

Table 4.2 (continued)

Case number	Perpetrator	Victim	Background to the incident	Suspicion of depression
Case 5	Son	Parents	The defendant's younger sister and her partner worked. His wife also worked part time. If he and his father were hospitalized, there would be nobody to care for his mother. His father was old and didn't have long to live, so the defendant assumed the worst. He was pessimistic about the future for himself and his parents, and he was convinced that the three of them would be out of their misery if they all died. He decided to commit suicide after killing his parents	No record
Case 6	Son	Mother	The defendant was in serious debt. If his mother, who had dementia, died, his other relatives would be out of their misery and could return to their normal lives. He forced his mother into a double suicide with him	No record
Case 7	Husband	Wife	The defendant strongly wanted to release the pain of his wife to whom he had been married for many years. The wife also wished to die	In the year of the incident, the victim had retrogressive depression and had told the defendant, "It hurts. Kill me." Reactive depression had been observed in the defendant at the time of the incident
Case 8	Wife	Husband	The defendant was unable to rely on her family because she had eloped with her husband, practically abandoning her family and moving to a new prefecture. She had no friends or acquaintances with whom she could speak frankly about her worries. She suffered physical and mental fatigue while worrying alone and was pessimistic about the future. She decided to kill her husband and herself	No record

(continued)

Table 4.2 (continued)

Case number	Perpetrator	Victim	Background to the incident	Suspicion of depression
Case 9	Wife	Husband	The defendant's husband was being given the runaround by the hospital. She agonized over whether he would pass away. Phlegm was causing him to have shortness of breath, and she couldn't bear to see him in pain when he breathed. She wanted to put him out of his misery quickly and decided to kill him	No record
Case 10	Wife	Husband	Owing to bad relationships with her children and grandchildren, the defendant was brooding over whether to continue living with them. The defendant realized that if she moved away and left her home, there would be nobody to care for her husband. She preferred for both of them to die	No record
Case 11	Husband	Wife	The defendant awoke suddenly one night and saw his wife. His wife, who usually appeared to be in pain, was sleeping peacefully. While looking at her, he thought about how nice it would be for her to depart this world without pain and how happy she would be. He then committed the crime	No record
Case 12	Son	Parents	The defendant himself was handicapped and felt he could not care for his parents forever. He was exhausted from caring for them, and he felt that those around him would think he was pitiful if he were unable to care for them, so he killed his parents as they had wished for him to do and decided to commit suicide	Both parents were sad about their weakened state, and both said that they wanted to die. The day of the incident, the parents said they wanted to die and asked their son to kill them

(continued)

Table 4.2 (continued)

Case number	Perpetrator	Victim	Background to the incident	Suspicion of depression
Case 13	Son	Mother	The defendant's mother warned him about his drinking. Although he did his best to take care of her, he felt she did not understand him. He became sad and angry, which led to his thinking he had to end his life. He committed suicide after killing his mother	The mother told her son, "Even if I live, nothing can be done for me." A year before the incident, the two had agreed to die together
Case 14	Son	Mother	The defendant lived alone with his mother and showed tendencies of a shut-in. Around 2 months before the incident, the defendant's mother began repeating senseless words daily and 1 month prior began wetting and defecating herself, so he was pessimistic about the future. On the day of the incident, the mother suddenly began shouting in a loud voice, so the defendant despaired that things had gotten worse and drowned his mother in the bath	No record
Case 15	Son	Mother	The defendant was in economic distress and lied to his siblings that he was working. He was receiving ¥160,000 per month through his mother's pension, so at that point, he couldn't ask his siblings to lend him money because he had none. He was at his wit's end and completely tired of his living situation. He left his mother's home, and as a result, his mother died from weakness and starvation	No record
Case 16	Daughter	Mother	The defendant wanted her mother to listen to her, so she pushed her mother down by her shoulders onto the bed. Her mother died because of the resulting injury	No record

(continued)

Table 4.2 (continued)

Case number	Perpetrator	Victim	Background to the incident	Suspicion of depression
Case 17	Son	Father	The defendant was irritated that his father was not taking his medicine as he had told him to. He was exasperated and hit and punched his father. His father died as a result of the assault	No record
Case 18	Daughter	Mother	The defendant's husband had piled up a huge debt. She tormented herself with the thought that the only choice she now had was to die. Other than the nurses who visited the home thrice a week, the defendant was responsible for all her mother's care. Other relatives could not take on the responsibility. She knew there was nobody to whom to she can entrust her mother's care and decided to force her mother into a double suicide	No record
Case 19	Daughter	Mother	The defendant did not know when her husband would come to lend money, and she had no hope for the future. She began to think it better to die if this was her life. However, she realized that after she committed suicide, there would be nobody to take care of her mother, and she was convinced that placing her reluctant mother in an institution would be impossible. Finally, she decided to kill her mother and herself	No record
Case 20	Wife	Husband	The defendant had cared for her mother, who had dementia. She could not bring herself to burden her two daughters the same way in the future when she grew old. Considering the suitable assets she had left behind, she attempted a double suicide with her husband before it was too late, but only he died	No record

onward, when the caregiver began to experience anxiety about his or her own life and plot to commit double suicide with the care recipient (Case 12) and think that dying was the best way of escaping suffering (Cases 4, 7), the result was an incident.

In addition to depression, dementia in the person receiving care is another major cause that may drive the caregiver to commit a crime. In Case 8, behavioral and psychological symptoms of dementia (BPSD), such as delusions, acts of violence, and wandering, had been observed in the victim. The caregiver had to keep an eye on the person receiving care at all times. In Case 14, the victim's loud voice became a direct trigger for the incident. These types of symptoms can be controlled to some extent if the person receiving care takes medication, but if either the caregiver or the person receiving care dislikes going to the hospital, it can be difficult to get even a medical examination. Moreover, when no family member is available whom the caregiver or the patient can ask to drop them off and pick them up at the hospital, then it is difficult for the patient to receive regular medical examinations. Furthermore, children find it hard both mentally and emotionally to see a parent who has dementia. They recall the healthy, firm figure of their parent who was not suffering as he or she is now. These feelings on the part of the caregiver are linked to pessimism about the future and may become triggers for incidents (Case 6).

In addition, I was able to confirm factors not directly linked to caregiving but which appeared to contribute to the occurring incident. In cases where families experienced forced double suicides (Cases 18, 19), the caregivers had trouble with human relations, debts, and so on. They decided on suicide for reasons other than the pressures of caregiving and decided to also kill the person for whom they were caring with them. One reason for this was because there would be nobody to take care of that person after the caregiver was dead. There is also Case 20, in which an elderly couple, not yet in need of care, anticipated the troubles that would be involved in receiving care and plotted a double suicide, saying, "The future rests with our daughter." The defendant, the wife, had the experience of nursing her own mother, who had dementia. On the basis of this experience, the wife realized that she was aging from the changes in her own physical condition and feared living a life where she would not understand things and would be a terrible burden on her daughter. That fear was linked to her pessimism about the future and led her to decide on a double suicide with her husband.

4.1 Characteristics of Defendants' Mindsets

The mindset of the defendants at the time they decided to commit murder or a double suicide can be classified into ten categories: "knowing that even if the care recipient lived, nothing could be done for them," "having pity for the person for whom they are caring," "wanting to put the person for whom they are caring out of their misery," "thinking that the person for whom they are caring probably wants to die," "experiencing anger and sadness toward the person for whom they are caring," "wanting to be liberated from caregiving," "wanting to escape reality," "wanting to put themselves out of their misery," "wanting the person for whom they are caring to listen to them," and "not wanting to leave the burden of caregiving to somebody else."

The mindset of "knowing that even if the care recipient lived, nothing could be done for them" was identified in Cases 1, 3, and 8. In Case 1, a woman was in debt, and her life contained only herself and her mother for whom she was the caregiver. The woman loved her husband, who was hospitalized, but her own physical condition was worsening, and she needed an operation. She thought she might end up bedridden like her husband, who had no hope of recovery, and she was pessimistic about the future. In Case 3, a man was in financial trouble because he was unable to pay his mortgage. His mother-in-law, who lived with him, had dementia, and his wife, who was bedridden, often said that she wanted to die. The man figured that his wife's illness could no longer be cured and was pessimistic about the future. In Case 8, a woman was in great shock because her husband, upon whom she had relied solely up to that point, could not even speak. She thought he would only continue suffering in the same way if he lived on, and she decided to carry out a double suicide.

The mindset of "having pity for the person for whom they are caring" was identified in Cases 6, 9, 10, 11, and 12. In Case 6, a son thought of his mother as she had been in the past—healthy and vibrant—and watching her as her dementia progressed caused him grief. In Case 9, a wife suffered emotionally while her husband was given the runaround by the hospital. She was unable to stand the idea of him approaching death. In Case 10, a woman realized that if she moved away and left her home, there would be nobody to take care of her husband, so she felt pity for him. The wife of the man in Case 11 became weak and was hospitalized after moving home (without deciding on an appropriate address). She was in physical pain and had tubes attached to her while she was telling him that she wanted to go to the new house. Her husband thought that she was dying. The son in Case 12 was in poor health himself and suffering fatigue from caregiving. He thought his parents would be miserable if he became unable to care for them.

The mindset of "wanting to put the person for whom they are caring out of their misery" was identified in Cases 3, 7, and 9. In Case 3, the defendant said, "As my wife wished, I put her out of her misery, as she was better off dying." In Case 7, the defendant said he wanted to "free his wife from her pain and put her out of her misery." In Case 9, the wife said she "wanted to put him out of his misery quickly" after being unable to stand seeing her husband choking on phlegm and breathing as if he were in pain.

The mindset of "thinking that the person for whom they are caring probably wants to die" was identified in Case 11. A husband thought that his being next to his wife's peaceful sleeping form "felt good and it would be best [for her] to pass on to the next world with this feeling. After this there would be no pain, but happiness." He decided to commit murder.

"Experiencing anger and sadness toward the person for whom they are caring" was identified in Cases 13 and 14. Despite doing his best in his own way to think about his mother and take care of her, the son in Case 13 was warned about his drinking by his mother, and he felt that she did not understand him. He was angry and sad. In Case 14, as his mother's physical and mental state worsened, the son was provoked by her shouting, leading to the incident.

The idea of "wanting to be liberated from caregiving" was identified in Case 2. A daughter-in-law was caring for her mother-in-law against her will and in truth wanted to be liberated from caregiving, but she was convinced that caregiving was her duty as a daughter-in-law and that she could not abandon that duty.

The idea of "wanting to escape reality" was identified in Cases 4, 5, 15, 18, and 19. In Case 4, a son who was a shut-in saw the state of his declining mother and began to think it was necessary for him to overcome his social withdrawal and to work, but he felt as if he could not make progress toward this goal and continued to worry every day. In Case 5, a son's appetite declined, and he was losing sleep and was in bad health. He thought that if he died, he would be at peace. In Case 15, a son was at his wit's end regarding the lifestyle he was living in which he had no money. He left home and deserted his mother, who was bedridden and weak. In Cases 18 and 19, the defendants were worried about the large debts their husbands had piled up.

The mindset of "wanting to put the caregiver out of his or her misery" was identified in Case 6. Here, the son thought that his younger sister would be able to return to a normal life if he committed a double suicide with his mother, who needed care. The mindset of "wanting the person for whom they are caring to listen to them" was identified in Cases 16 and 17. In Case 16, a woman was irritated by her mother's retorts and resorted to hitting her mother to make her listen to her. In Case 17, a man's father had slow movements, and the man grew irritated because his father was not living by his rules.

In addition to these cases, there are cases of manslaughter in which the caregiver did not intend to kill the person for whom he or she was caring. However, on account of their dementia, the people being cared for continued to do actions that were against the caregiver's will. This irritated the caregiver and became a cause for violence.

4.2 Reasons Defendants Did Not Seek Help from Those Around Them to Avoid the Incident

In 13 of the 20 cases examined, there were records that explained why the defendants had not asked for help from those around them to avoid the incident. The six following reasons were "there was really nobody I could ask for help"; "there were relatives I should have asked, but I was unable to"; "consulting relatives did not improve the situation"; "consulting outsiders and institutions did not go well"; "I was convinced I could not ask for help from anyone"; and "I didn't want to cause trouble for my child."

The reason "there was really nobody I could ask for help" was identified in Case 8. Here, a wife had eloped with her husband, practically abandoning her family and moving to a different prefecture. She was therefore unable to rely on her relatives when her husband began to require care, and there were no friends or acquaintances with whom she could frankly speak about her worries. She suffered physical and mental fatigue while worrying alone.

The reason "there were relatives I should have asked, but I was unable to" was identified in Cases 1, 5, 10, 13, 14, 15, 18, and 19. In Case 1, the daughter and son of the (female) defendant did not live at home, and the defendant's relations with the daughter were bad. The son had his own family, so the defendant thought it would be useless to ask him for help. From the beginning, the defendant never thought she could rely on her children. In Case 5, the defendant's sister and brother-in-law worked, and his wife worked part time; therefore, the defendant decided that there would be nobody to care for his mother if he himself and his father were ever hospitalized. In Case 10, relations had fallen apart between the defendant and her children who lived with her. In Case 13, the siblings of the defendant refused to help with care for their mother, and the defendant was unable to rely on them. In Case 14, the defendant was a shut-in and unable to seek assistance from relatives. In Case 15, the defendant was in economic distress but lied to his siblings about working. Moreover, the defendant received about ¥160,000 a month from the mother's pension; therefore, he felt that he could not ask his siblings for financial support. In Case 18, the defendant's relatives were not in a situation to provide care. In Case 19, the defendant's siblings were in a situation where it would have been difficult for them to provide care for their mother. The defendant lived alone and did not work; therefore, the defendant was available to obtain care.

In Case 4, the reason for the incident was identified as "consulting relatives did not improve the situation." The defendant, who was a shut-in, did not know what to do. Nine months before the incident, the defendant visited an aunt and consulted her about the situation, but they were unable to come up with an effective solution.

In Cases 9 and 19, the reason was identified as "consulting outsiders and institutions did not go well." In Case 9, the defendant was unable to get advice at the city hall about caregiving. She was also constrained by the fact she had been told by the head nurse that her husband's leaving the hospital would be difficult, and therefore she was pessimistic about the future. In Case 19, a mother had been in temporary care for a month and hated it. The defendant had trouble with matters such as her mother's leaving untidy the bags she had packed the day before. For this reason, the defendant thought it was impossible to leave her reluctant mother in an institution.

In Case 2, the reason for the incident was "I was convinced I could not ask for help from anyone." A daughter-in-law who was providing care felt it was her duty and that she could not abandon it. She believed that even if she strongly appealed to her husband and those living with her for help, it would be impossible to exempt her from caregiving for economic reasons. Therefore, she was unable to ask for assistance.

In Case 20, the reason was identified as "I didn't want to cause trouble for my child." The defendant had cared for both her mother-in-law and her own mother, who had dementia; therefore, she wanted to avoid burdening her daughter in the future when she grew old.

4.3 Analysis of Stories of People Who Stopped Themselves Before They Committed a Crime

These concern people who were cornered to the point that they thought they would die or kill.

4.3.1 Purpose of the Survey

In 2009, the Alzheimer's Association of Japan and the Family Association collected the experiences of those who were driven to thinking they would commit a double suicide or would kill those whom they were taking care of and published these narratives in a single volume called *Don't Die! Don't Kill! Live!* On the basis of the experiences published in this book, I will investigate the reasons those people were somehow able to stop themselves even while experiencing the painful feeling of wanting to die.

4.3.2 Subject of the Study

Among the stories compiled in *Don't Die! Don't Kill! Live!*, those that contain concrete instances of people who thought about killing or committing a double suicide with the person for whom they were caring but somehow stopped themselves at the crucial moment have been chosen for discussion here.

4.3.3 Ethical Considerations

The narratives I analyzed are already available publicly as a book. I did not record information that might identify individuals by name.

4.3.4 Analysis Method

I organized the stories in relation to how the caregivers avoided committing murder or a double suicide while having such painful thoughts that they wished to die.

4.3.5 Results

A search result indicated that 22 of the 80 stories examined corresponded to the object of the investigation. From these 22 stories, I discovered six reasons people were able to avoid an incident: "I realized the person in my care had a purpose in living," "it crossed my mind that this person was precious to me," "I remembered the person before their illness," "I received support from somebody who was not a relative," "I did not want to cause trouble for people," and "I felt like I should cherish myself" (Table 4.3).

Table 4.3 Reasons caregivers were able to stop their actions

Case number	The trigger for stopping the murder or double suicide	Category
Case 1	The mother yelled "No!" at the crucial moment	Noticed that the person in care had the will to live
Case 2	Mother-in-law completely refused the invitation and told the daughter-in-law, "Hey, stop it! I won't die!"	Noticed that the person in care had the will to live
Case 3	Received a call from the care manager and went to the hospital. After an examination by the doctor, the doctor listened to the caregiver for 2 h	Support from somebody unrelated
Case 4	"I don't like it..."	Noticed that the person in care had the will to live
Case 5	Recalled that the mother had said suicide was for cowards and remembered the way the mother always did her best before the illness	Remembered the person in care before their illness
Case 6	Unusually, my mother-in-law looked my way with a kind smile. I wonder how much I was saved by that smiling face and calm gaze	Remembered the person in care before their illness
Case 7	That day my car was in for repairs, so I was using a loaner car. If I got into an accident, the staff at the garage would be troubled, as would my husband's insurance company (his place of employment)	Feeling that they shouldn't cause trouble for others
Case 8	My mother gave me a superb smile and said, "I want to live"	Noticed that the person in care had the will to live
Case 9	The faces of my children, grandchildren, and all those around me who were helping me came to mind	It crossed their mind that somebody was precious to them
Case 10	I was saved by the smiling faces of my daughter's children (I have two grandchildren, aged 5 and 2)	It crossed their mind that somebody was precious to them
Case 11	"I don't wanna die!"	Noticed that the person in care had the will to live
Case 12	My aged mother said to me while crying, "If you have come to kill me, go home. My grandchildren's lives will be pitiful if their mother is a murderer." When I saw her tears, I knew I couldn't kill her	It crossed their mind that somebody was precious to them

(continued)

Table 4.3 (continued)

Case number	The trigger for stopping the murder or double suicide	Category
Case 13	Thought of the family I would leave behind	It crossed their mind that somebody was precious to them
Case 14	"The life I get to live just once should not be interrupted by such a thing"	Feeling of cherishing oneself
Case 14	I couldn't make my own father sad	It crossed their mind that somebody was precious to them
Case 15	My husband said, "I won't die. You must not leave this house as someone who committed suicide or as a murderer." I began respecting him as the backbone of the family once again	Noticed that the person in care had the will to live and remembered the person in care before their illness
Case 16	I was saved by the words "You don't have to do your best, be defiant." They shocked me; it was like being struck by lightning	Support from somebody unrelated
Case 17	I put my hands around his neck, but his beard was rough and I didn't like the feel of it, so I let go	
Case 18	Images of the faces of my children and grandchildren rushed through my mind	It crossed their mind that somebody was precious to them
Case 19	Husband said, "Mom"	Noticed that the person in care had the will to live
Case 20	This is an illness. Only I can defend that person's dignity. I should not do such a thing simply for my own convenience…	
Case 21	I suddenly remembered walking through the city of Frankfurt with my wife in Germany	Remembered the person in care before their illness
Case 21	By chance it was a Sunday, and when I peeked in a church, I saw the figures of people praying. That's right; there are temples in Japan too. When I went to pray at the temple, the chief monk's sermon touched me	Support from somebody unrelated
Case 22	My husband whistled "Yuuyake Koyake." It was the first time I had heard him whistle. I sang while crying	Noticed that the person in care had the will to live

In Cases 1, 2, 4, 8, 11, 15, 19, and 22, the reason for avoiding an incident was identified as "I realized the person in my care had a purpose in living."

> When it came down to it, my mother said, 'No!' (Case 1).
>
> "My mother-in-law downright refused my invitation." She said, "Hey, stop it! Don't die" (Case 2).
>
> They said 'No way' to those words (Case 4).
>
> My mother gave me a superb smile and said, 'I want to live' (Case 8).
>
> I don't want to die! (Case 11).
>
> I ain't gonna die (Case 15).

> My husband called me honey (Case 19).

> My husband whistled 'Yuuyake Koyake.' It was the first time I had heard him whistle. I sang while crying (Case 22).

The reason "it crossed my mind that this person was precious to me" represents the caregiver's remembering that the person whom he or she thought should die was somebody precious and that the caregiver should not make that person sad. This reason was identified in Cases 9, 10, 12, 13, 14, and 18.

> The faces of my children, grandchildren, and all those around me who were helping me came to mind (Case 9).

> I was saved by the smiling faces of my daughter's children (I have two grandchildren, aged 5 and 2) (Case 10).

> At that time, my aged mother said to me while crying, 'If you have come to kill me, go home. My grandchildren's lives will be pitiful if their mother is a murderer.' When I saw her tears, I knew I couldn't kill her (Case 12).

> I thought of the family I would leave behind (Case 13).

> I couldn't make my own father sad (Case 14).

> Images of the faces of my children and grandchildren rushed through my mind (Case 18).

The reason identified in Cases 5, 6, 15, and 21 was "I remembered the person before their illness":

> I remembered my mother usually said that suicide was for cowards and how she was before, doing her best (Case 5).

> Unusually, my mother-in-law looked my way with a kind smile. I wonder how much I was saved by that smiling face and calm gaze (Case 6).

> My husband said, 'I won't die. You must not leave this house as someone who committed suicide or as a murderer.' I began respecting him as the backbone of the family once again (Case 15).

> I suddenly remembered walking through the city of Frankfurt with my wife in Germany (Case 21).

In Cases 3, 16, and 21 the reason identified was "I received support from somebody who was not a relative":

> I got a call from the care manager and went to the hospital. I was examined by the doctor, and the doctor listened to what I had to say for about 2 hours (Case 3).

> I was saved by the words 'you don't have to do your best, be defiant.' They shocked me; it was like being struck by lightning (Case 16).

> By chance it was a Sunday, and when I peeked in a church, I saw the figures of people praying. That's right, there are temples in Japan too. When I went to pray at the temple, the chief monk's sermon touched me (Case 21).

In Case 7, the reason identified was "I did not want to cause trouble for people":

> That day my car was in for repairs, so I was using a loaner car. If I got into an accident, the staff at the garage would be troubled, as would my husband's insurance company (his place of employment).

In Case 14, the reason identified was "I felt like I should cherish myself":

> The life I get to live just once should not be interrupted by such a thing.

Other than these explanations, the following reasons were discovered:

> This is an illness. Only I can defend that person's dignity. I should not do such a thing simply for my own convenience.

> I put my hands around his neck, but his beard was rough and I didn't like the feel of it, so I let go.

5 Discussion

5.1 Reasons Defendant Was Unable to Avoid an Incident

Cohen (2005) stated that, usually, the caregiver who commits a murder–suicide plans it months or even years ahead of time and that it is not an act of love or altruism; rather, it occurs as a result of despair or depression. At least half the perpetrators do not know they have depression, they have not been medically treated, or they suffer from other psychological problems. Loneliness or a sense of helplessness due to various stresses can be a trigger in the caregiver's decision to act. In this study, when I analyzed precedent cases of murder by caregivers, I was able to identify seven cases in which the effects of depression could be observed in the period leading up to the incident. There is a possibility that a care recipient or caregiver can improve his or her mental state through treatment for depression.

In the future, systems should be established locally in which health and medical professionals can provide services for a person who is receiving care or for a caregiver if it is suspected that either person has depression. Particularly in the case of depression in the caregiver, detection of early symptoms is important. One characteristic of depression is decrease in judgment and becoming unable to consider matters calmly. Even individuals capable of developing healthy methods of coping do not have a positive outlook when they are in a state of depression. They may then think of dying as the only way to escape their pain and end up not being able to come to their senses at the crucial moment. Therefore, prevention of murder by caregivers is linked to first detecting early symptoms of depression in caregivers and having appropriate medical institutions that can provide the necessary resources. It is important to watch over caregivers and care recipients and to support them as much as necessary. To this end, it is essential to establish a system that truly supports caregivers, such as enforcing assessment of caregivers and training those who can promptly support caregivers who may be at risk (Mitomi, 2010, p. 323).

Moreover, in the case of depression in a care recipient, it is extremely important to check whether that person has made statements to those around him or her, such as "I want to die" or "I want to be at peace." If caregivers have repeatedly been told by the person for whom they care that he or she wants to die, even if they do not take the remark seriously at the time, they may lose their willpower when they themselves are in bad health and may think that they would probably be happier if they died together with the person in their care. Double suicides and contract murders in care can be prevented by professionals focusing on cases in which a person receiving care often makes statements to his or her caregiver, such as "I want to die," checking how the caregiver reacts to those words, providing psychiatric services as necessary, and conducting meticulous observation. Support from the family as a whole also needs to be considered.

In the case of a patient with dementia, there is a high possibility that a caregiver might be unable to deal with and will worry about symptoms of BPSD such as shouting, delusions, acts of violence, and wandering. Therefore, it is important for support providers to advise caregivers about how to handle these symptoms. I would recommend checking whether the caregiver's willpower is weakening and whether he or she is having suicidal thoughts. Many caregivers are particularly worried by the patient's acts of wandering, but this behavior has a tendency to lessen with the weakening of the body and does not necessarily always happen. Caregivers may be unsure where their lives are going and may feel uneasy. If the professionals who provide support consider how caregivers are feeling and continue to provide careful advice about their lives, then the caregivers may gradually become able to prepare themselves for the future. While these professionals may have to guess the feelings of caregivers, they can offer perspectives and ideas, including taking future steps, thereby easing the anxiety of caregivers.

5.2 *Characteristics of Defendants' Mindsets*

"Even if they live, nothing can be done for them." In other words, the caregiver may not be able to find a way to escape his or her state of suffering and may think that things will never improve. This can be considered a manifestation of that person's despair about the future. In the case of cancer, dementia, and so forth, the condition progresses with time. Thus, the more the caregiver cherishes the person for whom he or she is caring, the more painful it is to see that person decline and greater the possibility that the caregiver may feel pessimistic about the future. In this situation, even if nothing changes, having somebody who will understand and explain the situation properly, and with whom the caregiver can consider the best options in times of trouble, can be a driving force in the caregiver's getting through the day.

People feel pity toward people in care, as well as anger and sadness. Particularly in cases where the caregiver had a good impression of or respected the person in his or her care, he or she may be unable to deal with how that person has completely changed and may suffer. Nursing and other care professionals probably do not experience much psychological repulsion even when they see adults excrete in diapers and exhibit symptoms of dementia. However, daughters and sons often cannot bear the sight of their own parent excreting in a diaper like an infant, not believing that their parent has declined to such an extent and feeling pity for him or her. They are conflicted in that they want to be able to endure the situation. In these circumstances, it is vital that caregivers have the support of somebody who can explain the reasons for these physical changes, who can listen to the caregivers talk about their surprise and sadness, and who can support them in coming to terms with and understanding the painful feelings they feel.

"I want to put the person in my care out of his/her misery" and "the person in my care probably also wants to die" are viewpoints that can be observed in cases in which the person receiving care is constantly suffering and the caregiver is considering suicide. In such cases, the caregiver may show signs indicating that he or she is at risk through actions such as attempted suicide. Particularly in cases of the caregiver's being repeatedly told by the person receiving care that he or she wants to die and when the caregiver has little motivation to live, the possibility of a double suicide occurring is high; therefore, it is important to focus on such signs.

The mindsets of "wanting to be liberated from caregiving" and "wanting to escape reality" can be found in many cases in which the person who is expected to play the role of caregiver is unable to respond adequately to the situation in the first place. The caregiver may have a mental disability or disorder or may hold ill will toward the person for whom he or she is caring. In such cases, even if there is an expected way for a caregiver to behave, it is impossible for the caregiver to fulfil that role. Attempting to make a shut-in into a caregiver fits this pattern. For a shut-in, going to the city hall to apply for primary nursing care requirement authorization, contacting the care manager, and using nursing insurance services can be awkward, and actually doing these activities may be impossible. Those professionals who support caregivers should ascertain the extent to which the caregiver can provide care and determine whether he or she has the ability and the will to do so. In cases in which the person's ability to provide care is insufficient, leaving the situation as it is can lead to a high possibility that the caregiver will abandon his or her role. In these instances, it is essential to conduct a positive intervention.

The thought "I want them to listen to me" can often be observed in those who care for dementia patients, in cases where the person in care does not follow the caregiver's instructions. The possibility of the caregiver's turning to violence to try to get the patient to listen is high if the person in care still does not listen after the caregiver says something. Because violence has the immediate effect of quieting a patient and making him or her listen and thus that person may then abide by the rules after being treated violently, the caregiver may end up continuing to use violence. In such cases, even if those who support the caregiver tell him or her, "You must not use violence," the caregiver will probably not cease using these methods; rather, the caregiver may be troubled by how difficult it is to get his or her intention across to the person in care. It is important for support providers to offer the caregiver several ways in which to express him- or herself before threatening violence, the means to reach an agreement with the person in care instead of using violence, and methods of putting these approaches into practice. If communication goes well between the caregiver and the person in care, then even when he or she does not rely on violence, one can expect the caregiver's use of violence to lessen.

Finally, cases in which a caregiver fears that he or she will also need care in the future, which can potentially lead to a double suicide, require one to consider the policies for caring for the elderly in Japan. The defendant in Case 20, for example, recalled her own painful experience of caregiving and did not want to burden her daughters by expecting them to take care of her in the future. Certainly, there are many elderly people who do not want to impose an excessive burden on their children. As long as the idea that "If I become ill, my family will also become victims" remains unchanged in Japan, incidents will probably continue to occur in which a caregiver feels pessimistic about the future, leading to murder by caregivers.

5.3 Reasons Defendants Did Not Seek Help from Those Around Them

In the case of an elderly person who requires care, but does not want to be a burden for his or her children, that person may not rely on his or her children unless it is an extreme circumstance. There are many people who have nobody to depend on in case of an emergency. It goes without saying that there are also cases in which people have no relatives and really have nobody on whom they can depend. A person might believe that there is "nobody to rely on" even, for example, when a family lives nearby whom they could ask for help. Caregivers may feel that only they can assume the burden of caregiving because other family members are busy with work or childcare, siblings will not cooperate in caregiving responsibilities, or the care recipient may have bad relations with his or her relatives. Therefore, caregivers may give up on consulting with relatives. Although caregivers can use nursing insurance-recognized care services according to the level of care required, it is not uncommon for individuals who need care not to want nurses in their home or to go into temporary care, no matter how much the caregiver urges them to do so. In these cases, the caregiver may think it is impossible to force the person in their care, who dislikes such services, to go into an institution and may give up on using care services although they are available.

The mindset that there is "nobody to rely on" is observed relatively more often in caregivers who are the eldest son or daughter or who are perfectionists. Particular attention needs to be paid to cases in which the eldest children feel they need to be responsible for caregiving although they do not want to do it. They should be evaluated for whether their assuming the responsibility of caregiving exceeds their subjective limit, and those that provide support services should conduct a positive intervention at times when the caregiver feels he or she can no longer provide care. Support providers tend to feel easy about perfectionistic caregivers who feel they must provide meticulous care and that they have no one on whom to rely. However, these providers should recognize that the caregiver probably cannot reach out for help to anyone. It is essential for support providers to conduct positive intervention if the state of the caregiver leads them to suspect that that person's perfectionistic actions are intensifying and creating torment for him or her.

5.4 Reasons Incidents Could Be Prevented at the Last Minute

Mr. Takami, the representative director of the Alzheimer's Association of Japan and the Family Association, pointed out that "More than thinking about the dignity of humans and the value of life, the reason caregivers stop themselves when they attempt to kill someone is that they realize how easy it would be to do it" (Alzheimer's Association of Japan and the Family Association, 2009, p. 6). In fact, in the stories published in *Do Not Die! Do Not Kill! Live!*, phrases such as "I returned to sanity" and "I came to my senses" crop up here and there. Therefore, in other words, if it is possible to create a situation in which the caregiver can begin to think reasonably again before committing a violent act, the incident can be avoided. In the stories I analyzed, what I observed most often was caregivers saying they "realized the person had a purpose in living." The typical pattern is that the caregiver broods over killing the person in his or her care or committing a double suicide and falls into a state of mind in which it is impossible think about anything else. However, when the care recipient shows a will to live by making statements such as "I want to live" or "I don't want to die," the caregiver is taken aback and becomes clear sighted again. This is also apparent in precedent cases: "The defendant came to her senses from her husband yelling that he was in pain" (Case 8). I also discovered cases in which the caregiver attempted murder and failed to kill the person under his or her care. The care recipient's somehow showing the caregiver that he or she wanted to live also brought the caregiver to terms with the situation. If caregivers can be jolted and brought to their senses, they may be able to stop what they are doing at a crucial moment. However, in cases in which the person in care desires to die and entrusts his or her caregiver with the task, in other words consensual murder, or if the caregiver is suffering from depression, it can be difficult for the caregiver to come to his or her senses or think rationally to avoid carrying out this action.

The next most common remark by a caregiver was that "it crossed my mind that this person is precious to me." In the field of criminology, there is a theory (social bond theory) that people turn to crime and that crime and delinquency occur not through the strengthening of people's will to commit those acts but rather through the weakening of the power of social regulations to stop crime. Hirschi (1969), a representative advocate of the theory, stated that the connections between the individual and society, or so-called bonds, are what differentiate those who turn to crime from those who do not. If one considers what those who stopped themselves from committing murder and a double suicide say—"it crossed my mind that this person is precious to me"—then this means that through the approach of "bonds," the caregiver was able to remember the connection he or she had with the other person leading up to just before that moment when the murder was to take place. If that is the case, then the key to prevent such incidents is helping the caregiver remember that he or she cherishes this person at the critical moment. However, surveys of caregivers show that the trend is for caregivers' time to be taken up by their responsibilities and for the human connections around them to diminish. There are fewer opportunities for the caregiver to leave the house because he or she cannot leave the care recipient unattended, chances of meeting with friends decrease, and the caregiver begins to feel socially isolated (Tsudome & Saito, 2007, p. 127). Therefore, before reaching this point, it is important for caregivers to deliberately create an environment in which they can maintain the same human relations they had with the care recipient before they took on the responsibility of caregiving.

From the statement "I remembered what they were like before they were ill," one might expect to find a deterrent effect in cases in which the caregiver and the care recipient once had a good relationship. It is difficult and painful for a caregiver who does not want to accept the current caregiving situation to remember what the person was like before he or she became ill. However, when a caregiver has good memories of the person under his or her care, this can be a trigger for the caregiver's remembering the feelings of affection he or she had for that person. Therefore, those who provide support to caregivers should listen to them as they recall their memories. Supporters should consider the caregiver's feelings and attentively offer support for the caregiver to be able to accept the care recipient's illness and to provide the very best care for that person.

In addition, I believe that reaching out to caregivers who feel that they are backed into a corner, listening to them, and promoting opportunities in which they can speak up would be effective in deterring such incidents in the future. Individuals who have also experienced caregiving in a similar manner and who said, "I am painfully aware of how the caregiver felt leading up to the incident" (Alzheimer's Association of Japan and the Family Association, 2009, p. 4) are not merely paying lip service. Meeting other caregivers at the Family Association can give caregivers considerable strength. They can begin to see that whatever care they can provide in the present situation is enough. It is acceptable even if they cannot offer the level of care that they wish they could, and they do not have to feel guilty because of this. In addition, those who feel lonely because they have come to have fewer relations with other people, and those who did not necessarily have good relationships with the person for whom they are caring before that person needed care, can make new personal connections at the Family Association. This might prevent caregivers from feeling lonely.

6 Conclusion

The trends and characteristics of the incidents in Japan were practically in complete accordance with the findings of a similar study conducted in the United States by Karch and Nunn (2010). To prevent such cases in the future, short-term improvements concerning the support offered to male caregivers are necessary as well as measures to tackle depression among caregivers. It is also important to establish a system in which professionals can discuss the details of the actions and the mental state of people with dementia and not allow caregivers to feel as if they are alone.

The number of elderly people requiring care will continue to increase in the future. Expectations for caregiving will be concentrated in particular families. Therefore, as long as the situation in which caregivers feel isolated from society does not improve, incidents of murder by caregivers will continue to occur. I would like to see a society in which even if a person becomes responsible for caregiving, he or she does not bear the burden any more than is necessary and is able to cherish his or her own life. The construction of a support system that allows people to value their own lives as citizens and not just as caregivers is desired.

Acknowledgment This work was supported by JSPS KAKENHI Grant-in-Aid for Scientific Research (C) Grant Number 24616019.

References

Alzheimer's Association and the Family Association. (2009). *Do not die! Do not kill! Live! A message to you in utmost pain because of caregiving*. Kyoto: Kamogawa Press.

Cohen, D. P. (2005). Caregiver stress increases risk of homicide–suicide. *Geriatric Times, 1*(4), 1–7.

Dunning, J. (2011, November 7). Social workers failed to monitor elderly man murdered by son. *Community Care*. http://www.communitycare.co.uk/2011/11/07/social-workers-failed-to-monitor-elderly-man-murdered-by-son. Accessed 20 June 2014.

Eliason, S. (2009). Murder–suicide: A review of the recent literature. *Journal of the American Academy of Psychiatry and the Law Online, 37*(3), 371–376.

Hane, A. (2006). Factors in murder of double suicide cases committed by male caregivers of the elderly – An analysis of newspaper articles. *Japanese Journal of Family Sociology, 18*(1), 27–39.

Hirschi, T. (1969). *Cause of delinquency*. Piscataway: Transaction Publishers. University of California Press.

Karch, D., & Nunn, K. C. (2010). Characteristics of elderly and other vulnerable adult victims of homicide by a caregiver: National violent death reporting system – 17 U.S. States, 2003–2007. *Journal of Interpersonal Violence, 26*(1), 137–157.

Kato, E. (2005). *'Kaigosatsujin -Shihofukushi no shitenkara.' (Homicides or murder–suicides by family caregivers – From the point of view of law and forensic social services)*. The Woodlands: Kress.

Ministry of Health, Labour and Welfare. (2016). Results of survey of incidents of death of children due to abuse (Summary of Tenth Report). http://www.mhlw.go.jp/file/06-Seisakujouhou-11900000-Koyoukintoujidoukateikyoku/0000137018.pdf. Accessed 20 September 2016.

Mitomi, K. (2010). *Long-term care and support of caregivers in Europe and America – Typology of family policy, social inclusion and the welfare state*. London: Minerva.

National Police Agency. (2008). *2008 White paper on crime – Reality and treatment of elderly offenders*. http://www.moj.go.jp/HOUSO/2008/hk1_2.pdf. Accessed 26 April 2017.

Nemoto, H. (2007). The necessity of cooperation between the medical treatment section, the welfare section and the administration of justice which was seen throughout the trial – From the point of view of the murder case relating to care. *The Japanese Journal of Law and Political Science, 43*(2), 39–51.

Salari, S. (2007). Patterns of intimate partner homicide suicide in later life: Strategies for prevention. *Clinical Interventions in Aging, 2*(3), 441.

Takako, I. (2001). The care problem which lies behind the double suicide event of the elderly: From the analysis of the newspaper articles about the double suicide in Nara Women's University. *Journal of Family Studies, 7*, 25–39.

Tsudome, M., & Saito, M. (Eds.). (2007). *White paper on male caregivers proposal to support family caregivers*. Kyoto: Kamogawa Press.

Chapter 5
The Effect of Disaster Damage on the Occurrence of Crime: A Survey of Residents of Four Prefectures Affected by the Great East Japan Earthquake

Hideo Okamoto, Takemi Mori, Tsuneyuki Abe, and Toyoji Saito

Japan is believed to be a country with fundamentally good public order, whereby almost no crime would occur even in areas affected by large-scale natural disasters. This is an assertion not limited to Japan; some even consider it normal anywhere in the world that outbreaks of crime will be controlled in areas affected by large-scale disasters (Solnit, 2009). Certainly, from the moment a natural disaster occurs and through the period immediately after, everyone would be fully committed to responding to the disaster, and even people with criminal tendencies are not in a position to commit crimes. However, as the situation calms with the passage of time, crimes start to be committed before long by those with criminal tendencies who are already in the affected area and by other malicious people coming into the area from elsewhere (Thornton & Voigt, 2010). In practice, we have all seen and heard of various types of crime being committed in affected areas in the wake of large-scale natural disasters. Looters plundered stores during the New York City Blackout of 1977 (Wohlenberg, 1982). There was also looting, for instance, when Hurricane Hugo hit the Virgin Islands in 1989 and following the San Francisco Earthquake of 1906 (Frailing & Harper, 2010). In Japan, there were reports of opportunistic crime such as swindling of evacuees, robbery from collapsed houses, and store burglaries amid the post-disaster chaos in areas affected by the Great Hanshin-Awaji Earthquake of 1995 (Saito, 1997). There were also reports of much

---

H. Okamoto (✉)
Division of Human Life and Environmental Sciences, Nara Women's University, Nara, Japan
e-mail: h.okamoto@cc.nara-wu.ac.jp

T. Mori
Faculty of Human Sciences, Konan Women's University, Kobe, Japan

T. Abe
Graduate School of Arts and Letters, Tohoku University, Sendai, Japan

T. Saito
Emeritus Professor of Konan University, Kobe, Japan

J. Liu, S. Miyazawa (eds.), *Crime and Justice in Contemporary Japan*,
Springer Series on Asian Criminology and Criminal Justice Research,
https://doi.org/10.1007/978-3-319-69359-0_5

opportunistic crime, such as breaking into houses left vacant by evacuated residents, theft of cash from ATMs, and car theft (Okamoto & Saito, 2011), as well as crimes committed by people hit by the disaster in order to obtain necessities for daily living (Abe, Wiwattanapantuwong, & Honda, 2014) in areas affected by the Great East Japan Earthquake of 2011. It would thus seem better to consider areas affected by large-scale disasters not as areas in which crime would be controlled, but rather as areas more prone to the occurrence of crime.

Why does crime become more likely to occur after large-scale natural disasters? There are theoretical frameworks to explain the occurrence of crime in areas affected by large-scale disasters, such as those which consider anonymity and the breakdown of society following the influx of poorer classes (Genevie et al., 1987; Wohlenberg, 1982) and those which use routine activity theory to look at the existence of factors that make crime likely to occur (Cromwell, Dunham, Akers, & Lanza-Kaduce, 1995). The relationship between crime and the scale of damage caused by a natural disaster can be explained particularly well through the routine activity theory approach, whereby crime is likely to occur when the following three factors are all in place: "likely offender(s)," "suitable target(s)," and "absence of capable guardian(s)" (Cohen & Felson, 1979). It would be natural to see crime as more likely to occur due to the greater likelihood of the following three factors as the scale of damage caused by a natural disaster increases: people lose property and experience excessive levels of stress following disasters (likely offenders); buildings are damaged and become easier to access from the outside (suitable targets); more homes and stores are vacant due to evacuations, criminal activity is easier to conduct at night due to blackouts, and security cameras are rendered useless (absence of capable guardians). Of course, these conditions facilitating the occurrence of crime become more severe as the degree of damage caused by the disaster increases. Yet even when there is great damage, surely once disaster recovery progresses, damaged buildings will be repaired, evacuees will return to their homes, blackouts will cease, and people affected by the disaster will become less stressed—namely, the three factors will disappear—and crime should be less likely to occur. Conversely, if recovery from disaster damage is delayed, the three factors that incite crime in routine theory will accordingly not disappear but will continue to exist, perpetuating the conditions that make crime likely to occur. In other words, we can consider that the greater the scale of damage caused by a disaster, the more likely crimes are to occur; and further, to the extent recovery from the disaster damage is delayed, crime accordingly is more likely to occur.

If we could obtain scientific confirmation of the relationship between the occurrence of crime, the scale of the damage caused by disasters, and/or any delay in recovery, then we could predict the levels of crime which would occur following a disaster and may also be able to obtain the knowledge required to think of effective methods of crime prevention. In particular, if it is clear that crime is more likely to occur with delays in recovery from damage caused by disasters, post-disaster recovery becomes an urgent necessity not only for the sake of rebuilding the lives of those affected but also for safety in daily life. There is thus a need for us to examine the relationship between disaster damage and crime empirically.

It is not suitable to use official data on reported numbers of criminal cases when examining the relationship between disasters and crime, because the reported numbers of criminal cases are for occurrences of crime of which the police are aware and do not account for crimes that have not been reported by victims. It has been pointed out previously that the occurrence of crime cannot be accurately understood from reported case numbers alone since reported case numbers do not include all crime (Maxfield & Babbie, 2015, pp. 137–165). Indeed, it is possible that they underreport crime more heavily than in normal situations in the chaotic conditions after a large-scale disaster, where it may be more common for victims of crime not to be able to notify the police as their highest priorities are ensuring their own physical safety and securing food supplies. This is clear in the following example from the Great Hanshin-Awaji Earthquake. The reported case numbers for the areas affected in the year in which the earthquake hit, 1995, show that while motorbike and vehicle theft increased, burglary decreased drastically. Between November 1999 and March 2000, 4–5 years after the Great Hanshin Earthquake, we conducted a questionnaire survey of all 891 local association leaders in the neighborhoods of Nishinomiya City and in Higashinada, Chūō, and Nagata Wards in Kobe City, Hyōgo Prefecture, which suffered considerable damage in the earthquake, and asked about issues such as the extent of damage and crime and about crime prevention (the results of the survey are reported in part in Okamoto (2011)). Accordingly, while there were certainly many reports of motorbike theft, reports of burglary were even greater in number. We also asked whether respondents notified the police of crimes and found that it was more common for the police not to be notified in areas more severely affected by the disaster. We may assume here that more crime occurred than the police were aware of, but residents were occupied with responding to the disaster and were rarely able to report any crime they suffered. Thus, when investigating the state of crime in areas affected by large-scale natural disasters, it is preferable to use personal statements by the residents subject to crime.

The results of the above questionnaire survey of local association leaders in areas affected by the Great Hanshin-Awaji Earthquake also revealed the following. Areas in which there were outbreaks of fire following the earthquake were more prone to theft from collapsed buildings, theft from intact buildings, bicycle and motorbike theft, and fights and altercations than those without fires. The same was confirmed for areas which saw higher numbers of fatalities following the quake. We also found that areas with longer periods of blackouts following the earthquake were more prone to theft from collapsed buildings, theft from intact buildings, and bicycle and motorbike theft. These findings from the Great Hanshin-Awaji Earthquake survey confirm that crime is more likely to occur the greater the scale of damage caused by a disaster and the greater the delay in disaster recovery.

In order to check whether our findings for the Great Hanshin-Awaji Earthquake can be confirmed for other disasters, we conducted an online survey in December 2012 of 1030 residents of Miyagi and Fukushima, two prefectures affected by the Great East Japan Earthquake, asking them how they were affected by the disaster and by crime. Accordingly, we found that gasoline theft was more common for people who experienced fatalities in their vicinity than those who did not, that bicycle and motorbike theft was more common for people who were near completely or partially destroyed buildings and/or were in areas with longer blackout

Table 5.1 Official details of damage following the Great East Japan Earthquake

	Deaths and missing persons		Completely and partially destroyed buildings	
	Number of people	Proportion per population of 1000 people	Number of buildings	Proportion per population of 1000 people
Iwate	6256	4.7	26,077	19.6
Miyagi	11,790	5.0	238,129	101.4
Fukushima	3955	1.9	95,846	47.2
Ibaraki	66	0.0	27,003	9.1
Total: 4 prefectures	22,067		387,055	
Total: Japan	22,118		401,928	

Note 1: Earthquake damage is dated March 8, 2017, and based on the FDMA' s *Report on the 2011 earthquake by the Pacific coast of the Tohoku region (Great East Japan Earthquake)* (No. 155)
Note 2: Population data is based on the national census dated October 1, 2010

periods, and that house robbery was more common for people who were evacuated after the quake and/or in areas with longer blackout periods (Okamoto et al., 2014). These surveys of residents of areas affected by the Great Hanshin-Awaji and Great East Japan Earthquakes showed that the scale of earthquake damage and any delay in disaster recovery influence the occurrence of crime.

The accuracy of responses regarding the occurrence of crime in the Great Hanshin-Awaji Earthquake survey is not entirely free of doubt, since the responses were given by local leaders regarding their area of jurisdiction, and in many cases these respondents themselves were not crime victims. Meanwhile, the Great East Japan Earthquake survey focused on general residents and asked about their own personal experiences of crime. Yet, despite the vast scale of the area affected by the earthquake, the survey only focused on residents from two prefectures and no population sampling was conducted, raising some questions of the validity of the results. For this study we therefore decided to broaden our survey area to include residents of four regions which suffered the most damage in the Great East Japan Earthquake—Iwate, Miyagi, Fukushima, and Ibaraki Prefectures—and to conduct a survey using sampling allocated proportionately to the population. The damage caused by the earthquake in these four regions is detailed in Table 5.1. The numbers of deaths, missing persons, and completely and partially destroyed buildings are highest for Miyagi Prefecture, both in actual figures and per 1000 people. This is followed by Iwate in deaths and missing persons and by Fukushima in completely and partially destroyed buildings. While Ibaraki has the smallest numbers of deaths and missing persons out of all four prefectures, it has greater numbers of completely and partially destroyed buildings than Iwate. The total damage suffered by these four regions accounted for most of the damage caused by the Great East Japan Earthquake across Japan (99.8% of all deaths and missing persons; 96.3% of all completely and partially destroyed buildings). We may assume therefore that we can attain sufficient validity by conducting a survey of the residents of these four regions, as they accounted for the majority of the damage caused by the Great East Japan Earthquake.

We conducted a survey in the four prefectures that accounted for most of the damage to clarify the relationship between disasters and crime. How did the scale of disaster damage and delays in recovery from damage effect on the crime occurrence?

1 Method

1.1 Survey Participants

We commissioned a survey company to conduct an online survey of the company's registered respondents. The survey participants were 3600 men and women aged between 20 and 80 who live in areas affected by the Great East Japan Earthquake—namely, Iwate, Miyagi, Fukushima, and Ibaraki prefectures. However, this study is based on data prorated according to the population distributions by gender and age range (within the four age ranges of the twenties, thirties, forties, and fifties) for each prefecture, which yielded data for 2800 men and women aged between 20 and 60. As will be described later, in order to investigate the relationship between crime and the degree of damage caused by the disaster in the region in which respondents were resident at the time of the earthquake and to investigate crime within 1 year after the quake, we removed respondents who had moved to other regions after the disaster and respondents whose areas of residence experienced blackouts lasting over 1 year and used the remaining 2335 people (1199 men; 1136 women; average age 41.5 years, SD 10.8) from this sample for the actual analysis.

1.2 Survey Details

Disaster Damage We used the same three factors as Okamoto et al. (2014) as indicators of the scale of disaster damage by asking respondents whether there were any fatalities near their area of residence (i.e., within 10-min walk from their residence; same for below) after the Great East Japan Earthquake hit on March 11, 2011 (hereinafter, "victims"), whether there were any buildings completely or partially destroyed near their area of residence following the Great East Japan Earthquake (hereinafter, "building damage"), and whether they were temporarily evacuated after the Great East Japan Earthquake (hereinafter, "evacuation").

We used the duration of blackouts (power outages) following the Great East Japan Earthquake in the vicinity of areas of residence, in number of days (hereinafter, "blackout days"), as indicator of the scale of delay in disaster recovery. We asked respondents for the date until which the blackout continued and estimated the number of days when processing the data. Cases in which blackouts lasted only for the day of the earthquake, even for short periods, were taken as 1 day; cases in which there were no blackouts whatsoever were taken as 0 days. We also excluded cases in which "blackout days" exceeded 1 year from analysis for the purposes of investigating the effect exerted on crime within 1 year after the earthquake.

Crime We asked respondents about any crime they had experienced since the Great East Japan Earthquake hit until the time of the survey. The types of crime were those predicted to occur comparatively frequently after large disasters: "bicycle and motorbike theft," "car theft," "gasoline theft," "house burglary," "violence and injuries," and "opportunistic swindling" (i.e., fraudulent activities which take advantage of damage caused by the disaster). Respondents were then asked for when (either 3 days, 2 months, within 1 year, or over 1 year since the earthquake or unsure) and where (e.g., within the vicinity of their own residence) they experienced each crime. If a respondent had experienced one type of crime two or more times, they were asked to provide answers on the time and place of the more severe incident only. If the respondent experienced the crime within 1 year after the day of the earthquake, they were considered as a subject of crime; if the respondent experienced the crime over 1 year after the quake or if they were unsure of the time of the crime, they were excluded from the analysis. The reason for using only those subject to crime within 1 year after the earthquake is that, once an extended period has passed since the quake, it may become difficult to discern whether or not the crime is a result of the earthquake. We also exclude from per-crime analysis cases in which the site of the crime was not in the vicinity of the respondent's residence. This is to make it possible to examine the relationship between crime and the degree of earthquake damage in a respondent's area of residence at the time of the disaster (because if a respondent experienced a crime somewhere distant from their area of residence, it is difficult to know whether or not it was influenced by the scale of disaster damage in their area of residence). Since this process of exclusion was undertaken separately for each type of crime, the number of cases excluded differs by type of crime. The number of excluded cases for each type is as follows: 75 for "bicycle and motorbike theft," 66 for "car theft," 73 for "gasoline theft," 71 for "house burglary," 69 for "violence and injuries," and 75 for "opportunistic swindling," each from a total of 2335 respondents. Note that no cases were excluded when detailing only disaster damage without addressing crime; in this case we show the results of the analysis of all 2335 respondents.

Survey Period September 2014.

2 Results

2.1 Confirming Variables

Disaster Damage Table 5.2 shows the results of responses regarding damage caused by the Great East Japan Earthquake. Out of 2335 responses, 132 (5.7%) had "victims," 609 (26.1%) had "building damage," and 330 (14.1%) had "evacuation." For "blackout days," 1797 (77.0%) had blackouts; taking no-blackout responses as 0 days, the average duration was 5.7 days (SD 14.4). The majority (75.8%) of responses with "victims" also had "building damage." This may be because the

Table 5.2 Earthquake damage based on questionnaire survey

	Victims (report rate)	Building damage (report rate)	Evacuation (report rate)	Average number of blackout days (standard deviation)
Yes	132 (5.7%)	609 (26.1%)	330 (14.1%)	
No	2203 (94.3%)	1726 (73.9%)	2005 (85.9%)	5.7 (14.4)
Total	2335 (100%)	2335 (100%)	2335 (100%)	

more victims an area has, the more building damage there will be. Meanwhile, no more than 17.0% of responses with "victims" also had "evacuation."

Crime Table 5.3 shows the results of responses regarding crime. As mentioned above, cases in which the respondent was subject to the crime elsewhere than in the vicinity of their residence have been excluded from the data for each type of crime. This was 18 (0.8%) of 2260 "bicycle and motorbike theft" responses, 6 (0.3%) of 2269 "car theft" responses, 18 (0.8%) of 2262 "gasoline theft" responses, 8 (0.4%) of 2264 "house burglary" responses, 4 (0.2%) of 2266 "violence and injuries" responses, and 8 (0.4%) of 2260 "opportunistic swindling" responses.

Figure 5.1 shows the time ranges within which crimes occurred. We can see that the peak period for most occurrences of crime was either within 3 days or 2 months after the Great East Japan Earthquake. Note that opportunistic swindling was at the same level for 2 months after the disaster, and later, this type of crime does not decrease with the passage of time.

2.2 *Investigation Per Prefecture*

Disaster Damage We totaled damage from the Great East Japan Earthquake by the questionnaire survey respondents' prefecture of residence (Table 5.4). Miyagi had the highest proportion of "victims" responses, the highest proportion of "building damage" responses, and the highest average value for "blackout days" out of the four prefectures. Miyagi also had almost the same level of "evacuation" as Fukushima; thus, we may consider Miyagi the prefecture with the greatest degree of damage. Fukushima was the prefecture with the second-highest proportions for "victims" and "building damage," yet it had the lowest "blackout days" of the four prefectures. According to the official damage data (Table 5.1), Miyagi had the highest numbers of deaths and missing persons and of completely and partially destroyed buildings; this matches the results of the questionnaire survey. However, some differences were observed between the official damage data and the questionnaire survey; for example, according to the official data, the prefecture with the second-highest number of deaths and missing persons was Iwate, but the prefecture with the second-highest number of victims in the survey was Fukushima. One possible cause of this difference may be the omission of people who moved residence after the earthquake from the data in this study.

Table 5.3 Crime experienced within 1 year of disaster

	Bicycle and motorbike theft (report rate)	Car theft (report rate)	Gasoline theft (report rate)	House burglary (report rate)	Violence and injuries (report rate)	Opportunistic swindling (report rate)
Yes	18 (0.8%)	6 (0.3%)	18 (0.8%)	8 (0.4%)	4 (0.2%)	8 (0.4%)
No	2242 (99.2%)	2263 (99.7%)	2244 (99.2%)	2256 (99.6%)	2262 (99.8%)	2252 (99.6%)
Total	2260 (100%)	2269 (100%)	2262 (100%)	2264 (100%)	2266 (100%)	2260 (100%)

Note: Cases whereby the crime was not experienced in the vicinity of the respondent's residence have been omitted from the data

Fig. 5.1 Time when crime occurred

Table 5.4 Earthquake damage report rate and average number of blackout days, per prefecture

	Victims	Building damage	Evacuation	Blackout days (SD)
Iwate	3. 9%	8. 9%	7. 0%	5.5 (11.1)
Miyagi	11.0%	41.0%	21.3%	9.6 (14.8)
Fukushima	5. 1%	34. 0%	21.7%	2.9 (10.6)
Ibaraki	3. 0%	17.8%	7. 3%	4.8 (16.8)

Crime We show crime by the numbers per 1000 questionnaire survey respondents per prefecture of residence (Table 5.5). From the questionnaire survey results, it appears that Miyagi was the prefecture with the most crime, as it had the highest figures for four of the six types of crime, namely, "bicycle and motorbike theft," "gasoline theft," "house burglary," and "violence and injuries." As noted in the preceding section, Miyagi was also the prefecture that suffered the greatest damage following the disaster.

Note that Table 5.5 also shows police-reported case numbers per 1000 people. Since there were no equivalents in police-reported case number data to the crimes which have been labelled "gasoline theft" and "opportunistic swindling" in the questionnaire survey, no data is shown for "gasoline theft" or "opportunistic swindling" reported case numbers. Also, while the questionnaire survey results are for crimes that occurred between March 11, 2011, and March 10, 2012, the reported case numbers are data for the year of 2011; though there may be a slight mismatch between the two periods covered, we may nonetheless compare the questionnaire survey results and the reported case numbers for reference. For the most part, the questionnaire survey results show higher figures than the reported case numbers.

Let us consider whether the crime report rates obtained from the questionnaire survey results are higher or lower than in general circumstances unrelated to the earthquake. Strict comparison is not possible, but we can make some degree of comparison by using the results of the Fourth Crime Victimization Survey (dark figure survey) conducted by the Research and Training Institute of the Ministry of Justice (Research and Training Institute of the Ministry of Justice of Japan, 2013) (hereinafter, "national survey"). This national survey was undertaken in January 2012 with survey participants sampled from across Japan and deals with crime in 2011, the year in which the Great East Japan Earthquake struck. The present study, which surveyed areas affected by the Great East Japan Earthquake, posed questions about the year spanning March 11, 2011, through March 10, 2012, and thus has a difference of a little over 2 months from the national survey; nonetheless, the two still cover roughly the same period.

The types of crime featured in this study and in the national survey are not entirely the same, but we may consider this study's "bicycle and motorbike theft" to match the national survey's "motorcycle theft" and "bicycle theft" and this study's "car theft" to match the national survey's "car theft." Note that these crimes in the national survey differ from in this survey in that the former poses questions about the respondent and any family with which they live, while the latter asks for responses about the respondent only. Looking at the crime rates in the national survey, "motorcycle theft" is 1.5%, "bicycle theft" is 5.9%, and "car theft" is 0.1%. While the results of this study show lower figures for "bicycle and motorbike theft" in any of the prefectures, "car theft" has higher figures than the national survey for Ibaraki, Miyagi, and Fukushima (0.4% for Ibaraki, 0.3% for Miyagi, 0.2% for Fukushima). At least three prefectures showed higher figures for "car theft" than the national survey crime rate.

2.3 *Investigation Using All Data*

Since the scale of earthquake damage differs even within the same prefecture, we cannot gain a clear understanding of the relationship between earthquake damage and crime by comparing and examining prefectures separately. We thus investigate the relationship between earthquake damage and crime for all data, not per-prefecture data. Our study also includes additional factors in earthquake damage (e.g., age and gender of respondents), since it is possible that they may also influence the occurrence of crime. We undertake logistic regression analysis, using earthquake damage indicators and respondent factors as independent variables and using as dependent variables whether or not the following crimes had been experienced (Yes/No): "bicycle and motorbike theft," "car theft," "gasoline theft," "house

Table 5.5 Crime report rate and number of reported cases (both per 1000 people)

	Bicycle and motorbike theft		Car theft		Gasoline theft	House burglary		Violence and injuries		Opportunistic swindling
	Questionnaire survey	Reported case numbers	Questionnaire survey	Reported case numbers	Questionnaire survey	Questionnaire survey	Reported case numbers	Questionnaire survey	Reported case numbers	Questionnaire survey
Iwate	5.70	1.16	0.00	0.02	11.43	2.86	0.15	0.00	0.20	5.71
Miyagi	15.54	2.31	3.44	0.07	13.84	10.33	0.39	6.88	0.33	3.46
Fukushima	1.95	1.48	1.93	0.11	11.63	0.00	0.61	0.00	0.30	3.88
Ibaraki	7.35	2.40	3.66	0.68	0.00	1.22	0.67	0.00	0.37	2.45

Note 1: Questionnaire survey figures cover the period of March 11, 2011, through March 10, 2012, but reported case number figures cover the whole of 2011
Note 2: No suitable figures for reported case numbers are available for gasoline theft or opportunistic swindling, hence their absence from this table
Note 3: Reported case numbers for bicycle and motorbike theft, and for violence and injuries, are the sums of bicycle theft and motorbike theft, and of violence and injuries
Note 4: Reported case numbers are based on National Police Agency data
Note 5: Population data is based on population estimates dated October 1, 2011

burglary," "violence and injuries," and "opportunistic swindling." Previously we treated "victims," "building damage," "evacuation," and "blackout days" as earthquake damage, but as explained in the *confirming variables* section, the positive responses for "victims" mostly overlap with "building damage," and thus it is inappropriate to use both "victims" and "building damage" simultaneously. We keep "victims," as this can indicate when the scale of earthquake damage is particularly great, and do not use "building damage" as an independent variable.

Our dependent variables have been turned into dummy variables, with experience of the crime ("Yes") as 1 and no experience of the crime ("No") as 0. For independent variables, we use the numerical values directly for "blackout days" and "age" and turn "victims" and "evacuation" into dummy variables with "Yes" as 1 and "No" as 0; "gender" is also turned into a dummy variable, with "male" as 1 and "female" as 0. We looked at the correlation between our independent variables to check whether or not there was multicollinearity, and while some of the correlation coefficients were statistically significant, none were of a high enough value to suggest that issues of multicollinearity may arise (Table 5.6); all independent variables were thus used in the model. Note that only the independent variables which were statistically significant in forward stepwise selection were used when performing logistic regression analysis.

The model with "bicycle and motorbike theft" as a dependent variable ultimately used "victims" (odds ratio 4.488; $p < 0.01$) and "blackout days" (odds ratio 1.014; $p < 0.05$) as independent variables (Table 5.7). The values for the Hosmer–Lemeshow test were $\chi^2 = 11.380$, df = 7, and $p = 0.123$, presenting no issues. The Nagelkerke R^2 value was 0.041.

The model with "car theft" as a dependent variable used none of the independent variables.

The model with "gasoline theft" as a dependent variable ultimately used "victims" (odds ratio 5.804; $p < 0.01$) and "evacuation" (odds ratio 3.350; $p < 0.05$) as independent variables (Table 5.8). The values for the Hosmer–Lemeshow test were $\chi^2 = 0.010$, df = 1, and $p = 0.919$, presenting no issues. The Nagelkerke R^2 value was 0.091.

The model with "house burglary" as a dependent variable ultimately used "victims" (odds ratio 27.104; $p < 0.001$) and "age" (odds ratio 0.930; $p < 0.05$) as independent variables (Table 5.9). The values for the Hosmer–Lemeshow test were $\chi^2 = 5.178$, df = 8, and $p = 0.738$, presenting no issues. The Nagelkerke R^2 value was 0.222.

The model with "violence and injuries" as a dependent variable ultimately used "victims" (odds ratio 16.672; $p < 0.01$) as an independent variable (Table 5.10). Since there was only one independent variable, we could not perform the Hosmer–Lemeshow test. The Nagelkerke R^2 value was 0.106.

The model with "opportunistic swindling" as a dependent variable ultimately used only "evacuation" (odds ratio 18.654; $p < 0.001$) as an independent variable (Table 5.11). Since there was only one independent variable, we could not perform the Hosmer–Lemeshow test. The Nagelkerke R^2 value was 0.146.

Table 5.6 Correlation between independent variables

	Victims	Evacuation	Blackout days	Gender	Age
Victims	–				
Evacuation	0.199**	–			
Blackout days	0.113**	0.093**	–		
Gender	−0.003	−0.048*	0.004	–	
Age	−0.026	−0.062**	−0.014	−0.001	–

$^{*}p < 0.05$, $^{**}P < 0.01$

Table 5.7 Logistic regression analysis using bicycle and motorbike theft as a dependent variable

Independent variable	*B*	Odds ratio	*P*
Victims	1.501	4.488	0.009
Number of blackout days	0.014	1.014	0.029

Nagelkerke $R^2 = 0.041$
Hosmer–Lemeshow test $\chi^2 = 11.380$, df = 7, $p = 0.123$

Table 5.8 Logistic regression analysis using gasoline theft as a dependent variable

Independent variable	*B*	Odds ratio	*P*
Victims	1.759	5.804	0.001
Evacuation	1.209	3.350	0.018

Nagelkerke $R^2 = 0.091$
Hosmer–Lemeshow test $\chi^2 = 0.010$, df = 1, $p = 0.919$

Table 5.9 Logistic regression analysis using house burglary as a dependent variable

Independent variable	*B*	Odds ratio	*P*
Age	−0.072	0.930	0.045
Victims	3.300	27.104	0.000

Nagelkerke $R^2 = 0.222$
Hosmer–Lemeshow test $\chi^2 = 5.178$, df = 8, $p = 0.738$

Table 5.10 Logistic regression analysis using violence and injuries as a dependent variable

Independent variable	*B*	Odds ratio	*P*
Victims	2.814	16.672	0.005

Nagelkerke $R^2 = 0.106$
Could not perform Hosmer–Lemeshow test with only one independent variable

Table 5.11 Logistic regression analysis using opportunistic swindling as a dependent variable

Independent variable	*B*	Odds ratio	*P*
Evacuation	2.926	18.654	0.000

Nagelkerke $R^2 = 0.146$
Could not perform Hosmer–Lemeshow test with only one independent variable

3 Discussion

The results of our study by prefecture show that Miyagi, the prefecture which suffered the most damage following the Great East Japan Earthquake, also had the highest occurrence of crime (Tables 5.4 and 5.5). This suggests that the amount of earthquake damage has an influence on the amount of crime. However, given that the amount of earthquake damage varied even within the same prefecture, there was a need for a method of investigation which was not on a per-prefecture basis. We combined data for the four prefectures and conducted logistic regression analysis; as a result, we were able to confirm significant independent variables for each model except "car theft," namely, the models with "bicycle and motorbike theft," "gasoline theft," "house burglary," "violence and injuries," and "opportunistic swindling" as independent variables, respectively.

"Bicycle and motorbike theft" was 4.488 times more likely to have occurred when there were "victims" than when there were not. This means that "bicycle and motorbike theft" is more likely to occur in areas where there had been deaths nearby. Additionally, as the number of "blackout days," which corresponds to the length of delay in recovery from the earthquake, increases by 1, "bicycle and motorbike theft" becomes 1.014 times more likely to occur.

"Gasoline theft" was 5.804 times more likely to have occurred when there were "victims" than when there were not. Further, "gasoline theft" was 3.350 times more likely to have occurred when there was "evacuation" than when there was not. This means that "gasoline theft" is more likely to occur when residents are evacuated from their houses, even if temporarily.

"House burglary" was 27.104 times more likely to have occurred when there were "victims" than when there were not. This is a risk factor considerably higher than that of other crimes such as "bicycle and motorbike theft" and "gasoline theft." We may also consider house burglary in particular to be more likely to occur if the scale of earthquake damage is such that people have died nearby. Additionally, as "age" increased by 1 year, "house burglary" decreased by a factor of 0.930 (conversely, as age decreased by 1 year, burglary increased by a factor of 1.075). We may consider this to be because people take more care when away from their house as they get older.

"Violence and injuries" were 16.672 times more likely to have occurred when there were "victims" than when there were not. This may be because, in the wake of great earthquake damage, interpersonal conflicts become more common amidst the varied confusion and chaos and violent crime becomes more likely to occur.

"Opportunistic swindling" was 18.654 times more likely to have occurred when there were "victims" than when there were not. Opportunistic swindling includes selling inferior daily necessities and fraudulently accepting fees for repairs of damaged houses. If a resident is evacuated, this occurs in a context where it has become dangerous to be inside the house where they had previously resided; namely, the house may have been damaged or destroyed. In such cases, house repairs become necessary, and opportunistic fraud (swindling) which exploits earthquake damage may be more likely to occur.

From the above, the crimes whose incidence was influenced by the presence of "victims" were "bicycle and motorbike theft," "gasoline theft," "house burglary," and "violence and injuries"; the crimes whose incidence was influenced by the occurrence of "evacuation" were "gasoline theft" and "opportunistic swindling"; and the crime whose incidence was influenced by the length of the period of "blackout days" was "bicycle and motorbike theft." Additionally, the crime whose incidence was influenced by "age" as a respondent factor was "house burglary." In summary, "bicycle and motorbike theft," "gasoline theft," "house burglary," "violence and injuries," and "opportunistic swindling" are more likely to occur the greater the scale of earthquake damage, and in particular the likelihood of "bicycle and motorbike theft" is affected by any delay in recovery from earthquake damage. Also, residents' young age influenced the likelihood of "house burglary."

The presence of "victims" indicates earthquake damage great enough for people to have died; it is clear that earthquake damage on such a scale influences the occurrence of more crimes. "Evacuation" indicates not only that people are more likely to experience theft because they are unable to adequately guard their possessions after leaving their houses but also that opportunistic swindling becomes more likely as, for instance, there is greater need for house repairs. "Blackout days" is an indicator of damage recovery, and the length of an area's blackout period indicates how delayed its disaster recovery was; however, the only crime this length influenced was "bicycle and motorbike theft." The odds ratio for this scenario appears small at 1.014, but as the number of days increases, so does the risk: 30 days is 1.518 times (1.014 to the power of 30), 60 days is 2.303 times (1.014 to the power of 60), and 90 days is 3.495 times (1.014 to the power of 90). Finally, the influence exerted by youth (i.e., lower values for "age") of respondents on "house burglary" suggests that it is not only factors such as the scale of damage and delay in disaster recovery but also the characteristics of residents which affects the occurrence of crimes. Youth is not a factor that can be easily changed, but clarifying related elements (e.g., lack of caution) may facilitate the implementation of effective crime prevention measures. This will be addressed in future research.

Furthermore, while our study took the influence of the Great East Japan Earthquake to be within 1 year of the quake, since the frequency of quake-related "opportunistic swindling" did not decrease with the passage of time (Fig. 5.1), it would appear that some types of crime continue to be strongly influenced by earthquakes for periods exceeding 1 year. Perhaps it is also necessary to investigate the details of how this long-term influence is manifested in the future. It is also said that the particulars of the crimes which occur after earthquake disasters change with the passage of time (Thornton & Voigt, 2010); in order to avoid complicating the results of this study, however, we did not conduct an analysis with that extent of detail. This is an issue we would like to investigate at another opportunity.

How should we best prevent the occurrence of crime when another large-scale natural disaster strikes in the future? Based on the conclusions of previous surveys and the present study, the greater the damage to an area, the more necessary it is to implement urgent measures to prevent crime. While state measures like dispatching more police to affected areas are indeed important for this, we may consider anti-crime efforts by residents to be rather more realistic. We will need to investigate the details of effective crime prevention efforts on a separate occasion in the future. We are unable to accurately predict when and where a large-scale disaster will occur, and we certainly cannot control the scale of any disaster. Reducing the magnitude of an earthquake is something far outside the realm of possibility. Large disasters occur suddenly, outside our expectations. However, we do know of one effective method for reducing crime following large-scale natural disasters: speeding up disaster recovery to any extent. This is not only a definite, effective measure for reducing crime but also a means of restoring the livelihoods of those affected by the disaster.

Acknowledgment This research was supported by JSPS KAKENHI Grant Number 25285025.

References

Abe, T., Wiwattanapantuwong, J., & Honda, A. (2014). Dark, cold and hungry, but full of mutual trust: Manners among the 2011 Great East Japan Earthquake victims. *Psychology in Russia: State of the Art, 7*(1), 4–13.

Cohen, L. E., & Felson, M. (1979). Social change and crime rate trends: A routine activity approach. *American Sociological Review, 44*, 588–608.

Cromwell, P., Dunham, R., Akers, R., & Lanza-Kaduce, L. (1995). Routine activities and social control in the aftermath of a natural catastrophe. *European Journal on Criminal Policy and Research, 3*(3), 56–69.

Frailing, K., & Harper, D. W. (2010). Crime and disaster in historical perspective. In D. W. Harper & K. Frailing (Eds.), *Crime and criminal justice in disaster* (pp. 7–25). Durham: Carolina Academic Press.

Genevie, L., Kaplan, S. R., Peck, H., Struening, E. L., Kallos, J. E., Muhlin, G. L., et al. (1987). Predictors of looting in selected neighborhoods of New York City during the blackout of 1977. *Sociology and Social Research, 71*(3), 228–231.

Maxfield, M. G., & Babbie, E. R. (2015). *Research methods for criminal justice and criminology* (7th ed.). Boston: Cengage Learning.

Okamoto, H. (2011, August). A study of relationship between the earthquake damage and crime. In T. Saito (Chair), *Disaster and crime (1): Major earthquake of 1995 and crime prevention in Kobe*. Symposium conducted at 16th World Congress of the International Society for Criminology, Kobe, Japan.

Okamoto, H., Mori, T., Abe, T., Saito, T., Yamamoto, M., Matsubara, H., et al. (2014). The effect of the Great East Japan Earthquake on the occurrence of crime in disaster-affected areas. *Japanese Journal of Sociological Criminology, 39*, 84–93. (in Japanese).

Okamoto, H., & Saito, T. (2011, October). The Great East Japan Earthquake and crime (2). In *The 38th annual meeting of Japanese Association of Sociological Criminology*, Kyoto, Japan.

Research and Training Institute of the Ministry of Justice of Japan. (2013). *The research department reports of Research and Training Institute of the Ministry of Justice:* Vol. 49. (in Japanese).

Saito, T. (1997). Earthquake and crime. In K. Shiomi (Ed.), *The great Hanshin-Awaji earthquake and law* (pp. 262–276). Kobe: Konan University. (in Japanese).

Solnit, R. (2009). *A paradise built in hell: The extraordinary communities: That arise in disaster*. New York: Penguin Books.
Thornton, W. E., & Voigt, L. (2010). Disaster phase analysis and crime facilitation patterns. In D. W. Harper & K. Frailing (Eds.), *Crime and criminal justice in disaster* (pp. 27–60). Durham: Carolina Academic Press.
Wohlenberg, E. H. (1982). The geography of civility' revisited: New York blackout looting, 1977. *Economic Geography, 58*(1), 29–44.

Chapter 6
Revisiting Japan's Postwar Homicide Trend: 1951–2014

Aki Roberts

When I was a graduate student studying criminology at the University of New Mexico in the 1990s, my advisor Dr. Gary LaFree gave a class assignment in which students were to plot the postwar homicide trend for a country of their choice and explain the trend using some major criminological theories. As I am originally from Japan, the Japanese homicide trend was naturally my choice for the assignment. Plotting the data made me realize that Japan's recent low rates of homicide, which had attracted the attention of many Western scholars like Adler (1983), Braithwaite (1989), and Bayley (1991), are in fact the result of a consistent decline through the whole postwar period. From a contemporary perspective, it was very surprising to see that Japan and other industrialized countries, including the United States, had much more similar homicide rates immediately after WWII than they do today (Fujimoto & Park, 1994). While Japan was experiencing its steadily decline in homicide rates, US rates went the other direction and increased during the 1970s and 1980s, creating the large gap in lethal violence rates that is now one of the features that most distinguishes Japan from the United States.

My dissertation topic then became the exploration of socio-structural explanations for postwar Japan's declining homicide rates via quantitative analyses. In 2004, I published the extension of my dissertation in the article "Explaining Japan's

---

Aki Roberts is Associate Professor of Sociology at the University of Wisconsin-Milwaukee. Her research interests include criminal justice outcomes, auto theft, homicide, and the National Incident-Based Reporting System (NIBRS). Her work has appeared in *Criminology*, *Journal of Quantitative Criminology*, *Journal of Research in Crime and Delinquency*, and *Homicide Studies*. She also recently published a Japanese-language book on American higher education, アメリカの大学の裏側 (朝日新書).

A. Roberts (✉)
Department of Sociology, University of Wisconsin-Milwaukee,
PO Box 413, Milwaukee, WI 53201, USA
e-mail: aki@uwm.edu

J. Liu, S. Miyazawa (eds.), *Crime and Justice in Contemporary Japan*,
Springer Series on Asian Criminology and Criminal Justice Research,
https://doi.org/10.1007/978-3-319-69359-0_6

Postwar Violent Crime Trends" in *Criminology* with Dr. LaFree (Roberts & LaFree, 2004).[1] Using national-level data from 1951 to 2000, our time-series analyses found that economic stress, in both absolute and relative measures, and young male population were negatively associated with homicide rates. These results suggested that, with other structural factors held constant, the strength of the postwar Japanese economy and the declining size of the "crime-prone" population are likely responsible for a good deal of the homicide drop. (Our work also included analyses of prefectural-level data over time.) With newly available data, the current analysis updates that earlier study by reexamining the impact of socio-structural variables on Japan's postwar homicide trends from 1951 to 2014.

1 Japanese Homicide Trends Between 1951 and 2014

Figure 6.1a shows Japanese homicide rates per 100,000 population between 1951 and 2014.[2] Homicide rates generally follow a declining trend throughout the postwar period. Rates became somewhat stable between 1990 and 2005 but started to decline again and reached a postwar low of 0.73 per 100,000 population in 2013. This is a remarkable 75% drop from 1951, when the rate was 3.39 per 100,000 population. It is astounding to think that a country of 127 million people now has only about 1,000 homicides per year.

Furthermore, the number of *completed* homicides in Japan is much lower still. Unlike US official crime statistics, in which attempted homicides are recorded as aggravated assaults, Japanese official statistics include attempted homicides in the homicide category (Finch, 2001). More than half of the Japanese incidents categorized as "homicide" were actually attempted homicides that were not completed. For example, in 2014, only 38% of reported homicides were completed acts.[3] That the recorded homicide incidents are mainly just attempts also argues against the possibility that the declining homicide trend simply stems from improving medical interventions that keep more potential victims alive.

It is true that Japanese homicide statistics exclude robberies that resulted in death, but those incidents are rare, with the number of completed robbery-murders averaging only about 35 per year during the 2000s. Figure 6.1b shows the trend of homicide rates calculated according to the US definition by excluding attempted murders and including completed robbery-murders, along with the official homicide rates for comparison. Regardless of which definition is used, homicide rates show a strong declining trend. Johnson (2008) suggested that homicide and suicide in Japan may represent the same "stream" of lethal violence, but expressed differently and directed

[1] We also conducted similar analyses of 1951–1997 data in Roberts and LaFree (2001).

[2] Data were obtained from the Historical Statistics of Japan and various years of the Japan Statistical Yearbook. http://www.stat.go.jp/english/data/.

[3] National Police Agency's Heisei 26nen no Hanzai http://www.npa.go.jp/toukei/soubunkan/h26/h26hanzaitoukei.htm.

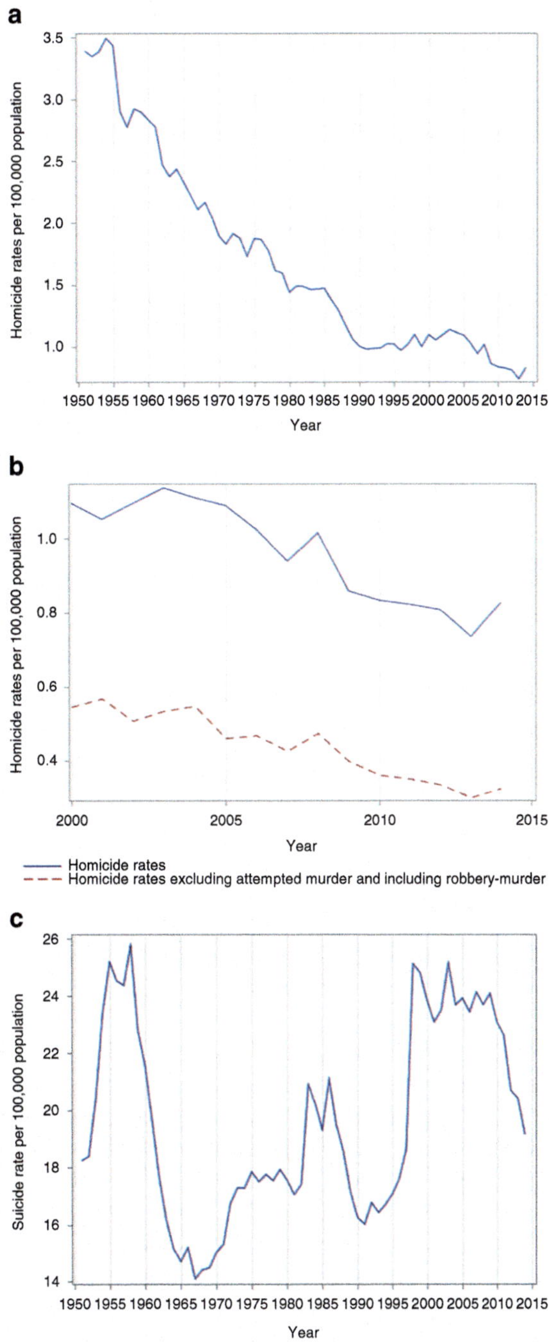

Fig. 6.1 (**a**) Homicide rates per 100,000 population, 1951–2014. (**b**) Homicide rates and homicide rates excluding attempted murder and including robbery-murder per 100,000 population, 1951–2014. (**c**) Suicide rates per 100,000 population, 1951–2014

at different targets (self or others). If this were the case, one might wonder if declining homicide rates had been compensated for by a trend of rising suicide rates. However, the long homicide decline has not been accompanied by steadily rising suicide, with the postwar era marked by several periods of higher and lower suicide rates and the most recent data showing several years of decline (see Fig. 6.1c).

In the world context, Japan's consistent decline in homicide rates throughout the postwar period is very unusual. LaFree and Drass' (2002) study of 34 developed and developing nations between 1956 and 1998 found that Japan was one of just a few countries with a declining homicide trend. However, more recently, other major industrialized nations have also experienced decreasing or stable homicide rates. For example, after more than two decades of growing violence, US homicide rates started to decline in the early 1990s. By 2014, the US homicide rate had declined to 4.5 per 100,000 population—a figure similar to the early postwar period before the rapid increase in the 1970s and 1980s (Federal Bureau of Investigation, 2014). Still, even with this recent improvement, the American homicide rate is still more than five times that of Japan.

2 Structural-Level Explanations of Homicide Decline in Postwar Japan

In this section, I briefly review four common structural-level explanations for declining Japanese homicide rates; these were also discussed in Roberts and LaFree (2004). In addition, I descriptively compare the homicide trend with trends in some major potential predictors that are derived from those four explanations.

2.1 Economic Stress in Postwar Japan

With an economy-crime link suggested by several otherwise competing theoretical frameworks, including social disorganization (Shaw & McKay, 1942), social strain (Merton, 1938), and conflict (Gordon, 1973), researchers have argued that Japan's strong postwar economy plays a crucial part in its low and declining crime rates (Park, 1992, 2006; Tsushima, 1996; Roberts & LaFree, 2004). Although other industrialized countries also experienced important periods of economic prosperity during the postwar period, the unique strength of Japan's postwar economy is indicated by low levels of economic stress in measures such as poverty, unemployment, and income inequality (Roberts & LaFree, 2004). However, after the collapse of the bubble economy in 1990, Japan has suffered from serious economic stagnation, with no or even negative growth. The 2011 Tōhoku earthquake and tsunami, the costliest natural disaster in history, further put a serious burden on the already deteriorating economy.

Postwar trends of poverty and unemployment (Fig. 6.2b) show the impact of these recent economic setbacks. Poverty, measured as the monthly average of

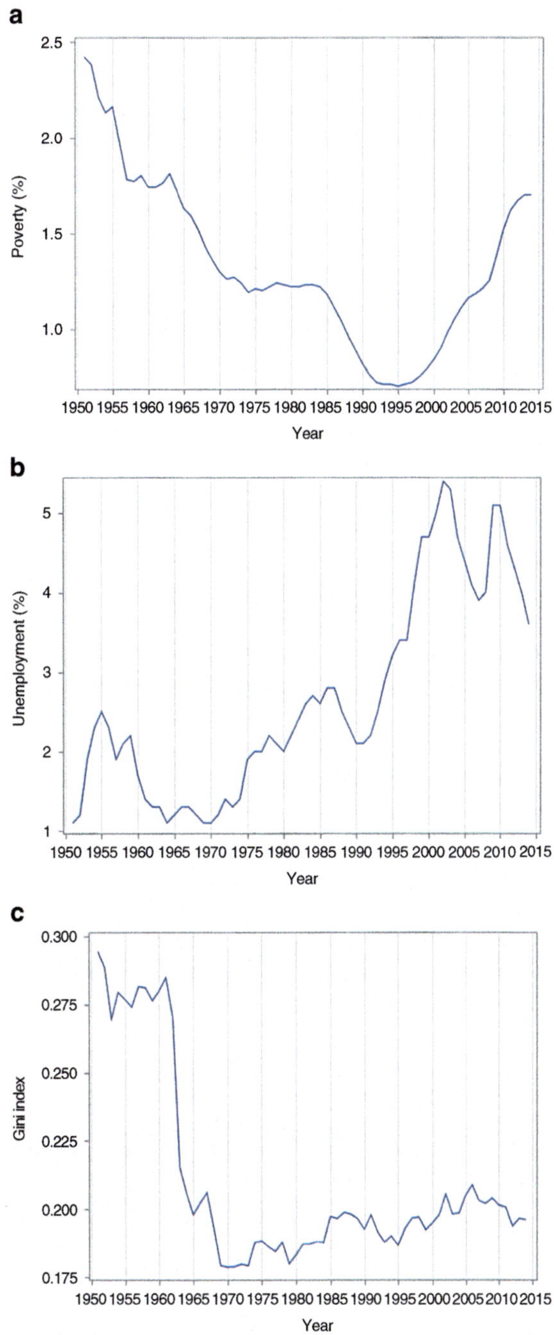

Fig. 6.2 (**a**) Poverty (percentage of public assistance recipients), 1951–2014. (**b**) Unemployment (percentage unemployed), 1951–2014. (**c**) Income inequality (Gini index), 1951–2014

persons receiving public assistance per 1000 population, reached its postwar low in 1995 but has steadily increased ever since. The economic stress argument would suggest a corresponding increase in homicide rates, but this did not happen. The unemployment trend also looks generally opposite that of homicide rates. After 1990, unemployment rapidly increased, to a postwar record high of 5.4% in 2002. Even with a later drop to 3.6% in 2014, unemployment still remains high compared to the earlier postwar period, when Japan's well-known guaranteed lifetime job security developed.

Poverty and unemployment are absolute measures of economic stress, as they are oriented to a fixed level of economic well-being. However, relative deprivation scholars argue that comparison of one's economic standing to others' is the key element of the economic stress-crime link (e.g., Messner, 1982). That is, people resort to crime and violence not just because they lack economic resources to meet basic needs but also due to their resentment and hostility toward wealthier groups in the society; this is more likely in societies with more unequal distributions of income (Roberts & Willits, 2015).

The level of income inequality—a relative measure of economic stress—is often captured by the Gini index.[4] The Gini index trend between 1951 and 2014 (in Fig. 6.2c) looks distinct from those of poverty and unemployment. After the declining in the 1960s, the level of income inequality has remained stable and low. This relative measure of economic stress did not seem to be influenced by the post-1990 economic stagnation nearly as much as the absolute measures poverty and unemployment were.

Why is Japan, one of the largest capitalist economies, so successful in suppressing income inequality? Higher taxes on the wealthy may make monopolization of wealth by a small group less likely in Japan than in other industrialized nations like the United States. The tax rate for inheritance recently increased to 55%, making it difficult to accumulate extreme wealth over generations; as measured income includes nonwage sources, limiting wealth accumulation will also contribute to lower income inequality. And even at a given level of income inequality, cultural norms against ostentatious displays of wealth may limit lower classes' feelings of relative deprivation (Koike, 2015).

---

[4] There are other measures of income inequality such as the inequality ratio, Theil index, and Atkinson index. However, Roberts and Willits' (2015) study found that those measures were highly correlated and produced similar results when examining the income inequality-homicide link in a multivariate context. The level of income inequality in society was calculated from data reporting the mean income in each quintile of the Japanese income distribution (restricted to households with two or more persons; see the Japan Statistical Yearbook). Following Brown's (1994) method, the Gini coefficient was calculated as:

$$G = 1 - \sum_{K-1}^{i=0} \left(X_{i+1} + X_i \right) P_{i+1}$$

with $i = 1$ to K indexing the five income groups (quintiles) from lowest to highest, X_i representing the proportion of total income earned by groups 1 to i (cumulative proportion), with $X_0 = 0$ by convention, and P_i representing the proportion of all households which fall in group i (equal to 1/5 for quintile data).

2.2 *Aging Population and Disappearance of "Crime-Prone" Population*

Because it is commonly understood that crime and violence, across different times and places, is disproportionately committed by young males (Daly & Wilson, 1988; Gottfredson & Hirschi, 1990), some researchers have suggested that an aging Japanese population is the major reason for the homicide decline (Hamai, 2013; Hiraiwa-Hasegawa, 2005). With declining fertility rates and growing life expectancies during the postwar era, Japan became a nation of the elderly. In 2015, the 65 or older group was nearly one third of the total population; this is expected to rise to about 40% by 2050.[5]

This rapidly aging population not only results in a smaller representation of typically violence-prone young people in Japanese society but also creates less resource competition among this group. As the reproduction rate dropped below two births per female,[6] children are much more valued than before, getting more emotional attention as well as financial support. Compared to earlier generations, young people now enjoy easier access to higher education as a path to successful socioeconomic outcomes (Hiraiwa-Hasegawa, 2005). Classic criminological theories such as social strain, criminal opportunity, and rational choice would therefore suggest that today's young Japanese are less motivated to commit crime than their counterparts in earlier generations.

As more resources become available to them, otherwise thrill-seeking young men are becoming more risk-averse, avoiding all types of risk-taking behavior associated with youth culture such as smoking, drinking, and driving fast cars (Johnson, 2006), activities that are associated with greater risk of taking another person's life. With a nearly perfect homicide clearance rate, the chance of getting caught is high, and the scarcity of guns means that perpetrators face a real risk of injury from close contact with their victims (Johnson, 2008).

Comparing data from 1970 to 2005, Hamai (2013) showed the tendency toward homicide avoidance by young Japanese today. In 1970, homicide offending rates (accounting for the size of different age groups) for young people aged 20–29 were noticeably higher than those for older age groups. However, by 2005, the homicide offending rate had dropped more for the 20–29-year-olds than for any other group, so that their rate was only slightly higher than those of other groups (see Fig. 7 in Hamai, 2013). The widely accepted "age-crime curve" thus became less apparent in Japan over time. This suggests that the declining young population may be making a typically crime-prone group much less so.

Figure 6.3 shows the postwar trend for percentage of males aged 20–29. The percentage has not consistently dropped during the postwar era, increasing somewhat between 1986 and 1996 as the children of early baby boomers reached young

[5] Based on the estimates in the 2017 Japan Statistical Yearbook.

[6] According to the Japan Statistical Yearbook, the postwar low for the reproduction rate was 1.26 births per female in 2005.

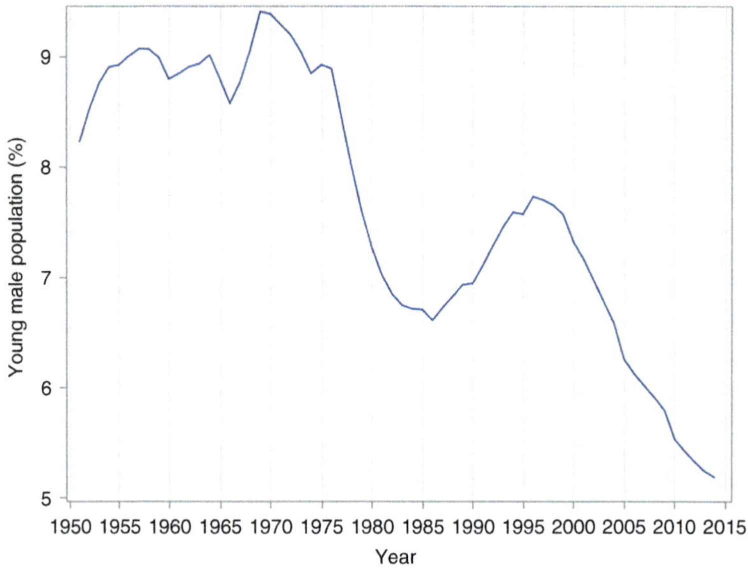

Fig. 6.3 Young male population (percentage of males ages 20–29), 1951–2014

adulthood. To an extent, this brief increase overlaps with the period in which homicide rates stabilized. The percentage of young males started to drop again after 1996 and, similar to homicide, reached a postwar low of 5.18% in 2014.

2.3 Informal Social Control, Social Change, and Modernization

Japanese society's unique valuing of group membership and the resulting strong informal social control mechanisms have long been popular explanations for Japan's low crime rates compared to other countries (e.g., Braithwaite, 1989; Bayley, 1991; Komiya, 1999). However, this explanation does not seem to explain Japan's *declining* homicide trend very well. Japan went through rapid social change and modernization during the postwar period. New values, roles, and lifestyles emerged that were not fully integrated or institutionalized and disrupted traditional support mechanisms (LaFree & Drass, 2002). These changes should also reduce informal social control's ability to limit crime, as in one way or another the major theories of crime link social change or modernization to increased crime rates.

Urbanization, female labor force participation, and divorce are common indicators of social change/modernization. High levels of those variables signal deviation from traditional society and effective informal social control, presumably resulting in increased crime rates. Figures 6.4a–c show postwar trends of urbanization, female

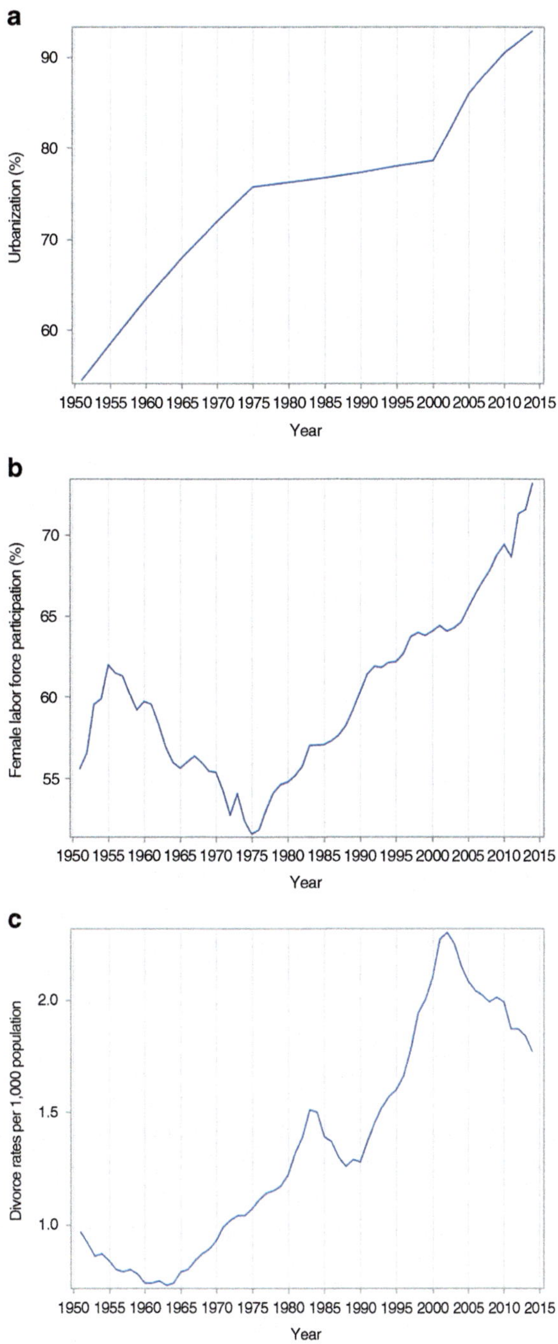

Fig. 6.4 (**a**) Urbanization (percentage living in urban areas), 1951–2014. (**b**) Female labor force participation (percentage of females in labor force), 1951–2014. (**c**) Divorce (per 1000 population), 1951–2014

labor force participation, and divorce. Urbanization, measured as the percentage living in urban areas, increased steadily during the postwar period. The acceleration of this increase since 2000 has concentrated the Japanese population in urban areas where traditional values and norms, and in turn the effectiveness of informal social control, are likely weaker than in rural areas.

The percentage of women participating in the labor force decreased somewhat from the mid-1950s to the mid-1970s but has risen steadily since then. The divorce rate also shows a generally upward, but less consistent, trend. Divorce rates declined during the 1950s and early 1960s and again in the 1980s. After reaching a high of 2.30 divorces per 1,000 population in 2002, divorce rates again decreased, though still remaining at a level higher than in the earlier postwar period. This recent decrease in divorce rate may not truly indicate recovery of traditional family values, because marriages also decreased during the same period. The divorce-to-marriage ratio (ranging from 0 to 1, with a higher value indicating more divorces per marriage) dropped below 0.1 in the earlier postwar period but steadily increased to nearly 0.4 in the 2000s.[7] As with divorce rates, the divorce-to-marriage ratio did decrease during the most recent period, but this decrease is very slight. In any case, divorce is still much more prevalent in contemporary Japan than it was in the earlier postwar period. Contrary to the expectation that crime increases as society goes through social change or modernization, the trends of those indicators are generally opposite the declining homicide rates.

2.4 *Certainty of Punishment*

Contemporary deterrence theorists argue that crime is effectively reduced by punishment, especially if certain (Marvell & Moody, 1994; Nagin, 2001). Certainty of punishment in a place is often indicated by the clearance rate—the proportion of cleared cases among cases reported to police.[8] In our 2004 paper, we used Japan's total clearance rate for all offenses to reflect the overall effectiveness of the country's criminal justice system. However, use of a clearance rate based on all offenses may be problematic. Deterrence theories assume that prospective offenders calculate and weigh costs and benefits. It is doubtful that potential homicide offenders would be influenced by the clearance likelihood for petty non-violent offenses, which naturally are the largest proportion of total crimes (Johnson, 2006). The media and general public will also be most concerned about the solvability of the most heinous offense, so that the specific homicide clearance rate is often used as an indicator of effectiveness of the criminal justice system (Roberts, 2014).

[7] Based on data in Historical Statistics of Japan and the Japan Statistical Yearbooks.

[8] In Japan, a crime incident is considered "cleared" if a suspect is in custody for investigation and/or sent for further prosecution.

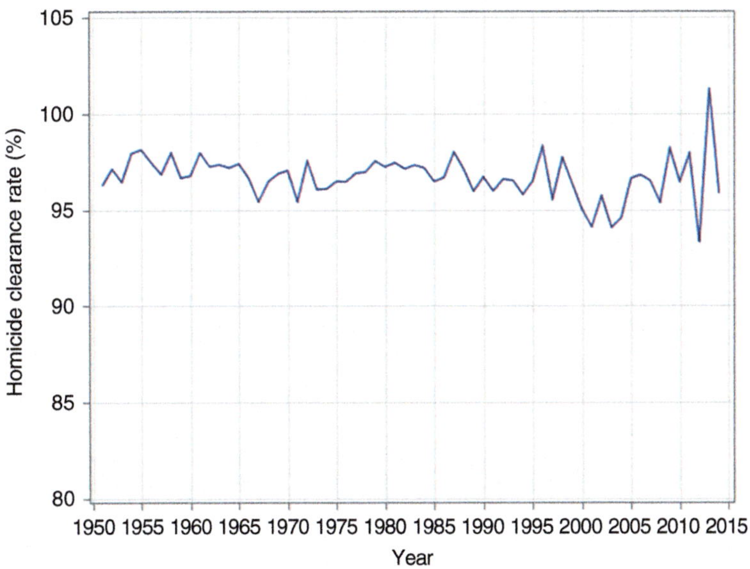

Fig. 6.5 Homicide clearance rate (percentage of cleared homicide incidents), 1951–2014

Furthermore, official crime statistics indicate a sudden increase in reported minor offenses in the late 1990s. Hamai and Ellis (2006) note that this could reflect an increase in reporting due to "moral panic"[9] and change in police policy and practice rather than an actual increase in the occurrence of those offenses. Because minor offenses represent the majority of total offenses, reported total offenses also increased. As the total number of reported offenses is the denominator of the total clearance rate, inflation of this figure would reduce the total clearance rate even if the true effectiveness of the criminal justice system were unchanged. Official statistics on homicide are less likely to be influenced by such external factors and will be more likely to reflect actual occurrence than is the case for less serious offenses. Therefore, in the current paper, I used homicide clearance rates (percentage of cleared homicide offenses among reported homicide incidents) to indicate the certainty of punishment.

Using homicide clearance rates to predict homicide rates could potentially raise simultaneity issues. However, with such low homicide rates, police investigators are far from overworked, at least not nearly to the extent they would be in the United States. Therefore, any relationship found between homicide clearance and homicide rates should reflect some aspect of deterrence rather than simultaneity. Figure 6.5

[9] Hamai and Ellis (2006) define moral panic as amplification of crime and deviance, often induced by the media. Moral panic is likely when existing social and economic institutions are weakened, and could lead to a punitive attitude among citizens, including reporting of incidents that previously were not considered crimes.

shows homicide clearance rates between 1951 and 2014. Postwar homicide clearance rates are consistently high and stable, varying from 93.31 to 101.28%.[10]

Homicide clearance rates are near-perfect for some other countries such as Germany (95.8% in 2013) (Research and Training Institute of the Ministry of Justice, 2015). The United States also cleared a very large proportion of its homicides in the 1960s, but these rates dropped throughout the postwar period, and currently the US homicide clearance rate stands at just 65% (Federal Bureau of Investigation, 2014). The recent gap between Japan and US homicide clearance rates could be due to differences in citizen-police cooperation and police workload. Also, Japanese homicides contain a higher proportion of "easy-to-investigate" cases, including those with non-firearm weapons, family member offenders, and child victims, than do American homicides (Roberts, 2008).

3 Multivariate Analysis of National Time-Series Data: 1951–2014

Informal comparison of trends is of course insufficient to understand the relationship between these independent variables and the homicide rate. The relationship between structural-level variables and homicide trends therefore should be examined in a multivariate analytic context. However, most previous multivariate time-series studies of Japanese postwar homicide have focused on limited sets of independent variables that did not permit full examination of potential structural influences on the Japanese homicide trend (e.g., Gartner & Parker, 1990; Merriman, 1991). Even studies with more comprehensive lists of independent variables often left out an appropriate measure for income inequality (Halicioglu, Andrés, & Yamamura, 2012; Ohtake & Kohara, 2010; Park, 1992, 2006; Tanaka, 2015).

As noted above, the idea of relative deprivation (associated with high levels of income inequality) has great theoretical importance. Like Japan's low homicide rates, its low level of income inequality is a major characteristic that distinguishes Japan from other industrialized nations. Furthermore, income inequality declined during the earlier postwar period and, especially importantly, did not rise when absolute measures of economic stress did in response to Japan's recent economic stagnation. Our 2004 analysis with Japanese data from a shorter time period found that income inequality, as well as absolute measures of economic stress, was significantly associated with homicide rates in the theoretically expected positive direction. Hiraiwa-Hasegawa's (2005) analysis of data between 1960 and 1996 also found that income inequality was positively associated with homicide committed by young males.

The current analysis included income inequality as well as absolute measures of economic stress, age structure, social change/modernization, and certainty of punishment in the multivariate analysis and explored how change in those relevant

[10] Note that homicide clearance rate could exceed 100% because the count of cleared incidents in a given year could include clearance of some incidents that had occurred in previous years.

structural variables is related to the postwar Japanese homicide trend. The current study also used data from a longer time period (1951–2014) than any of the previous multivariate time-series studies on Japanese crime that are known to me.

The dependent variable was homicide rate per 100,000 residents. Guided by the four structural explanations for Japanese crime trends discussed earlier, independent variables included measures of economic stress, young male population, social change/modernization, and certainty of punishment. Economic stress variables included both absolute and relative measures. Absolute measures of economic stress were poverty and unemployment, measured as the monthly average of public assistance recipients per 1000 population and the percentage of unemployed, respectively. The Gini index was the relative measure of economic stress.

The size of the young male population was measured as the percentage of men aged 20–29 in the population. Social change/modernization variables included urbanization, female labor force participation, and divorce. These were measured as percentage living in urban areas, the percentage of females aged 15–64 years old who are in the labor force, and the number of divorces per 1000 population, respectively. Certainty of punishment was indicated by the homicide clearance rate, specifically the percentage of cleared homicides among reported homicides. Data necessary to calculate independent and dependent variables were obtained from Historical Statistics of Japan and various years of the Japan Statistical Yearbooks. Appendix A gives descriptive statistics for those variables.

Table 6.1 shows the results of time-series analyses for homicide rates between 1951 and 2014. I conducted analyses using SAS software's implementation (in

Table 6.1 Regression results for Japanese postwar homicide rates per 100,000 population between 1951 and 2014 ($n = 64$)

	b
Economic hardship	
Poverty	0.064 (0.006)*
Unemployment	0.034 (0.037)
Income inequality	2.949 (1.025)*
Age structure	
Young male population	0.144 (0.028)*
Social change	
Urbanization	−0.014 (0.008)**
Female labor force participation	−0.024 (0.006)*
Divorce	−0.109 (0.127)
Certainty of punishment	
Homicide clearance rate	−0.008 (0.009)
First-order autoregressive error term (AR1)	−0.351 (0.127)*

Note: Standard errors are in parentheses
*$p < 0.01$, one-tailed
**$p < 0.05$, one-tailed

PROC AUTOREG) of the Yule-Walker method for regression with autoregressive error terms. Inspection of partial correlation plots of residuals and Durbin-Watson statistics indicated the presence of significant temporal autocorrelation, and in the regression, the estimated first-order autoregressive parameter significantly differed from zero. Reported regression estimates are therefore from a model with a first-order autoregressive error structure.

Among the three measures of economic stress, poverty and income inequality were statistically significantly associated with homicide rates in the expected positive direction. Unemployment was also positively associated with homicide rates, but this was not statistically significant. Supporting the argument that smaller size of young male population plays an important part in Japan's declining homicide trend, young male population was (net of other structural variables) positively and significantly associated with homicide rates.

Results for social change/modernization variables were less clear. Divorce rate was not significantly associated with homicide rates. While the associations between female labor force participation and urbanization and homicide rates were statistically significant, estimated coefficients were opposite in sign from the predictions of the social change/modernization perspective. The homicide clearance rate, measuring certainty of punishment, was not significantly associated with homicide. All of the statistically significant effects appeared meaningful in substantive terms, according to comparison of descriptive statistics with the size of the estimated coefficients.

4 Discussion and Conclusion

The current paper replicates and extends the national time-series analysis from Roberts and LaFree (2004) that examined the relationship between structural-level variables including economic stress, age structure, social change/modernization, and certainty of punishment and the 1951–2000 Japanese homicide trend. With newer years of data now available, the current study covered the time period between 1951 and 2014. Even though descriptive comparison of plotted rates showed poverty rising against falling homicide during the recent economic stagnation, poverty was actually significantly and positively associated with homicide rates when other structural-level variables were controlled and the entire time series was analyzed. The relationship between income inequality and homicide was also statistically significant and positive. These results indicate that even with the extended time series, economic stress variables remain important predictors of Japanese homicide trends.

Although income inequality has been relatively stable in recent years, the income gap between permanently contracted workers and those with less secure positions is now widening ("Inequality in Japan", 2015). Furthermore, Prime Minister Abe's current economic initiatives include reducing corporate taxes, and this may increase Japan's income inequality. Findings here suggest that these changes could result in a future rise in homicide rates. It is important to be clear, however, that the multivariate results reported here are based on statistically holding other factors constant, and economic changes that affect inequality will almost surely have other consequences too. Thus, it is dangerous to use these results to make a simple prediction of the possible impact of changes in one variable, with others not held constant, on homicide rates.

As in our 2004 paper, young male population was positively associated with homicide rates in the multivariate context, suggesting that a general decline in young male population is an important driver of Japan's postwar decline in homicides. As discussed above, the positive relationship between the size of the young male population and homicide could be due to less resource competition among young males leading to more risk-averse behavior by what is typically a thrill-seeking and violent population (Hiraiwa-Hasegawa, 2005; Johnson, 2008). Using the overall Gini index and college enrollment rate as resource competition measures, Hiraiwa-Hasegawa (2005) found that resource competition was significantly associated with young male homicide offending rates. Future research should further explore the resource competition-crime link, using age-specific resource competition measures that capture the generational gap.

Neither descriptive comparison of trends nor multivariate results supported the social change/modernization perspective's argument. Divorce did not have a statistically significant association with homicide. In an alternative analysis (not reported here), I replaced the divorce rate with the marriage rate, as a different measure of Japanese family stability, and again its effect was not statistically significant. The negative association between female labor force participation and homicide may indicate that social advancement of women has broadly beneficial impacts, signaling a more mature society that will more often eschew violence (Hamai, 2013). As we noted in the 2004 paper, measures of informal social control that rely on official statistics like these may not adequately capture the essence of this rich concept. Future researchers may want to consider designing surveys that can tap this idea more directly, though of course such data will never be available for the entire postwar period.

The homicide clearance rate had no significant association with Japan's homicide rate. Perhaps the near-perfect homicide clearance rate is not sufficiently salient to the public to exercise any effect, or citizens may misunderstand the frequency of homicide due to intense media coverage of serious offenses and therefore incorrectly perceive the declining overall clearance rate as if it applied to homicide (Hamai & Ellis, 2006). It is also possible that potential offenders are less likely to be deterred for an explosive, noneconomic offense like homicide. And it may be that with homicide clearance at such high levels throughout the entire postwar period, year-to-year variation is mostly just random rather than reflecting any systematic structural changes that would in turn influence homicide rates.

Roberts and LaFree (2004) examined robbery as well as homicide, but for the new analysis, I focused on homicide only. As discussed above, there is reason to suspect that recent official crime statistics for less serious offenses than homicide could be inflated compared to the earlier postwar era, due to increased reporting and change in police policy and practice regarding reported incidents (Hamai & Ellis,

2006). Inflation or deflation of crime statistics is not a problem for the multivariate analysis if it is consistent throughout the study period but becomes an issue if it occurs more at some times than at others, which is possible for robbery in Japan. Official statistics for homicide are less vulnerable to this concern, because official counts of homicide are less likely to be influenced by changes in public behavior or police policy and practice. However, in order to understand Japanese crime in its entirety, it will still be very important for researchers to conduct multivariate analyses that explore structural explanations for property offense rates. One approach to this dilemma may be for future studies to use data on particularly serious robbery cases, such as robbery involving serious injury, and analyze those specific rates instead of robbery rates in general.

Descriptive Statistics

	Mean	S.D.	Min.	Max.
Dependent variable				
Homicide rate	1.70	0.80	0.73	3.49
Independent variables				
Poverty	13.32	4.35	7.00	24.2
Unemployment	2.67	1.29	1.10	5.40
Income inequality	0.21	0.03	0.18	0.29
Young male population	7.67	1.23	5.18	9.41
Urbanization	74.94	9.59	54.4	92.9
Female labor force participation	60.04	5.24	51.55	73.18
Divorce	1.35	0.49	0.73	2.30
Homicide clearance rate	96.69	1.17	93.31	101.28

References

Adler, F. (1983). *Nation not obsessed with crime*. Littleton, CO: Fred B. Rothman & Co..

Bayley, D. H. (1991). *Forces of order: Policing modern Japan*. Berkeley: University of California Press.

Braithwaite, J. (1989). *Crime, shame, and reintegration*. Cambridge: Cambridge University Press.

Brown, M. C. (1994). Using Gini-style indices to evaluate the spatial patterns of health practitioners: Theoretical considerations and an application based on Alberta data. *Social Science and Medicine, 38*, 1243–1256.

Daly, M., & Wilson, M. (1988). *Homicide*. Hawthorne, NY: Aldine de Gruyter.

Federal Bureau of Investigation. (2014). *2014 Crime in the United States*. Retrieved from https://ucr.fbi.gov/crime-in-the-u.s/2014/crime-in-the-u.s.-2014

Finch, A. (2001). Homicide in contemporary Japan. *British Journal of Criminology, 41*, 219–235.

Fujimoto, T., & Park, W. (1994). Is Japan exceptional? Reconsidering Japanese crime rates. *Social Justice: A Journal of Crime, Conflict and World Order, 21*, 110–135.

Gartner, R., & Parker, R. N. (1990). Cross-national evidence on homicide and the age structure of the population. *Social Forces, 69*, 351–371.

Gordon, D. M. (1973). Capitalism, class, and crime in America. *Crime & Delinquency, 19*, 163–186.

Gottfredson, M. R., & Hirschi, T. (1990). *A general theory of crime*. Palo Alto, CA: Stanford University Press.

Halicioglu, F., Andrés, A. R., & Yamamura, E. (2012). Modeling crime in Japan. *Economic Modeling, 29*, 1640–1645.

Hamai, K. (2013). Why has the number of crimes reported to the police declined for 10 years in Japan? Is it a real reduction in crime or police artifact? *Japanese Journal of Sociological Criminology, 38*, 53–77.

Hamai, K., & Ellis, T. (2006). Crime and criminal justice in modern Japan: From re-integrative shaming to popular punitivism. *International Journal of the Sociology of Law, 34*, 157–178.

Hiraiwa-Hasegawa, M. (2005). Homicide by men in Japan, and its relationship to age, resources, and risk taking. *Evolution and Human Behavior, 26*, 332–343.

Inequality in Japan: The secure v the poor. (2015, February 12). *The Economist*. Retrieved from https://www.economist.com/news/finance-and-economics/21643202-problem-not-super-rich-secure-v-poor

Johnson, D. T. (2006). The vanishing killer: Japan's Postwar homicide decline. *Social Science Journal Japan, 9*, 73–90.

Johnson, D. T. (2008). The homicide drop in postwar Japan. *Homicide Studies, 12*, 146–160.

Koike, Y. (2015, March 2). Why inequality is different in Japan. *World Economic Forum*. Retrieved from https://www.weforum.org

Komiya, N. (1999). A cultural study of the low crime rate in Japan. *British Journal of Criminology, 39*, 369–390.

LaFree, G., & Drass, K. A. (2002). Counting crime booms among nations: Evidence for homicide victimization rates, 1956 to 1998. *Criminology, 40*, 769–800.

Marvell, T. B., & Moody, C. E. (1994). Prison population and crime reduction. *Journal of Quantitative Criminology, 10*, 109–139.

Merriman, D. (1991). An economic analysis of the post world war II decline in the Japanese crime rate. *Journal of Quantitative Criminology, 7*, 19–39.

Merton, R. K. (1938). *Social theory and social structure*. New York: Free Press.

Messner, S. F. (1982). Poverty, inequality, and the urban homicide rate. *Criminology, 20*, 103–114.

Nagin, D. S. (2001). Integrating celerity, impulsivity, and extralegal sanction threats into a model of general deterrence: Theory and evidence. *Criminology, 39*, 865–891.

Ohtake, F., & Kohara, M. (2010). The relationship between unemployment and crime: Evidence from time-series data and prefectural panel data. *Japanese Journal of Sociological Criminology, 35*, 54–71.

Park, W. K. (1992). *Trends in crime rates in postwar Japan: A structural perspective* (Doctoral dissertation). Florida State University, Tallahassee, FL.

Park, W. K. (2006). *Trends in crime rates in postwar Japan: A structural perspective*. Tokyo: Shinzansha Publishing Co..

Research and Training Institute of the Ministry of Justice. (2015). *White paper on crime*. Tokyo: Ministry of Justice.

Roberts, A. (2008). Explaining differences in homicide clearance rates between Japan and the United States. *Homicide Studies, 12*, 136–145.

Roberts, A. (2014). Adjusting rates of homicide clearance by arrest for investigation difficulty: Modeling incident- and jurisdictional-level obstacles. *Homicide Studies, 19*, 273–300.

Roberts, A., & LaFree, G. (2001). The role of declining economic stress in explaining Japan's remarkable postwar crime decreases, 1951 to 1997. *Japanese Journal of Sociological Criminology, 26*, 11–34.

Roberts, A., & LaFree, G. (2004). Explaining Japan's postwar violent crime trends. *Criminology, 42*, 179–209.

Roberts, A., & Willits, D. (2015). Income inequality and homicide in the United States: Consistency across different income inequality measures and disaggregated homicide types. *Homicide Studies, 19*, 28–57.

Shaw, C. R., & McKay, H. D. (1942). *Juvenile delinquency and urban areas: A study of rates of delinquency in relation to differential characteristics of local communities in American cities.* Chicago: University of Chicago Press.

Tanaka, D. (2015). *Exploring factors affecting crime rates in Japan (1955–2012)* (Master's thesis). Southern Illinois University Carbondale, Carbondale, IL.

Tsushima, M. (1996). Economic structure and crime: The case of Japan. *Journal of Socio-Economics, 25*, 497–515.

Part II
Testing and Developing Theories of Crime and Delinquency

Chapter 7
Potential Risk Factors for Serious Delinquency: Findings from Osaka Male Youths

Laura Bui, David P. Farrington, and Mitsuaki Ueda

1 Introduction

The perception that Japanese youths are one of the main reasons for the "law and order collapse" has been a prominent concern in the Japanese mass media, with newspapers focused on "the rising tide of youth violence," and dubbing these youths as *shinjinrui* (a "new human species"), who dress outside of the norm, steal from their parents, shoplift, and are involved in street gangs (Hamai & Ellis, 2008; Laser, Luster, & Oshio, 2007; Maeda, 2003). The sensationalizing of youth offending[1] is attributed to a string of extremely violent youth-on-youth murders (Nawa, 2006). The 2012 White Paper on Crime reveals that, in 2011, theft (62.6%) and embezzlement (17.3%) were the most common offenses within total juvenile non-traffic penal code offenses. Since 2004, the number of juveniles cleared (e.g., processed by the police or any other investigative authority) for penal code offenses has declined each year, and in 2011, 116,089 juveniles were cleared for penal code offenses,

[1] Japanese juvenile delinquency as specified in the Juvenile Law comprises the following: (1) criminal acts by juveniles aged 14 (the minimum age for criminal liability) or over but less than age 20, (2) illegal acts by juveniles under 14 years of age, and (3) predelinquency (deviant acts such as smoking and loitering) by juveniles under 20 years of age (Research and Training Institute of the Ministry of Justice 2000).

L. Bui (✉)
Department of Social Science, Liverpool Hope University, Liverpool, UK
e-mail: buil@hope.ac.uk

D.P. Farrington
Institute of Criminology, University of Cambridge, Cambridge, UK
e-mail: dpf1@cam.ac.uk

M. Ueda
Institute of Advanced Research and Education, Doshisha University, Kamigyo-ku, Kyoto, Japan
e-mail: miueda@mail.doshisha.ac.jp

J. Liu, S. Miyazawa (eds.), *Crime and Justice in Contemporary Japan*, Springer Series on Asian Criminology and Criminal Justice Research, https://doi.org/10.1007/978-3-319-69359-0_7

8.7% fewer than 2010. Based on the official youth offending rates, the media hype is not fully supported (Foljanty-Jost & Metzler, 2003).

Although scholars point to increases in Japanese youth offending, the official numbers are still relatively lower than in other industrialized countries (Finch, 2000; Miller & Kanazawa, 2000; Nakanishi, 2003). Interestingly, while criminological knowledge has established that youth offending is not specific to any particular social or educational background, this "generalization" of youth offending appears to be a comparatively new concept in Japan: the majority of juvenile offenders are raised in two-parent households with no financial difficulties (Erbe, 2003; Nawa, 2006; Yonekawa, 2003), although there are conflicting findings. Okabe (2014), for example, conducted a longitudinal analysis of police statistics and concluded that a disproportionate amount of delinquency was found among youths from low social and educational backgrounds.

According to commentators and critics, reasons for the perceived increase in youth offending are the following: urbanization and lower levels of social cohesion, the breakdown of family and effective parenting, an intense focus on exams and entering prestigious schools, an increase in materialism and commercialism, and harmful forms of popular culture and opportunities for illicit sexual activity (Ambaras, 2006). The majority of arrested youths have reported that the thrill of risk-taking is the motivator for their delinquency and that peers are important influences in their lives (Toyama-Bialke, 2003; White, 1994). These are plausible risk factors for Japanese youth offending.

1.1 Prior Studies of Risk Factors for Japanese Youth Offending

A few English language studies of self-reported Japanese youth offending and deviance exist (see Bui, 2014; Fukushima, Sharp, & Kobayashi, 2009; Kobayashi, Sharp, & Grasmick, 2008; Kobayashi, Vazsonyi, Chen, & Sharp, 2010; Kobayashi, Akers, & Sharp, 2011; Osamu, 1998; Tanioka & Glaser, 1991; Tanioka, 1989; Tsutomi, 1991). Although Bui (2014) used the same data as the present study, her study examined the mediating effects of high risk-taking between poor parenting and serious delinquency and whether established knowledge about poor parenting applied to Japan. The present study is different because it investigates factors for self-reported youth offending using the risk factor prevention paradigm (Farrington, 2000). Studying dichotomous risk factors has several advantages in that they make it easy to interpret interaction effects, to identify individuals with multiple risk factors, and to communicate results to a broader audience (Farrington & Loeber, 2000).

Only three English language self-reported studies of risk factors for Japanese youth offending are known: Laser et al. (2007) collected data from 555 postsecondary youths in the Sapporo area. Known Western risk factors for deviance were measured in this sample such as low parental monitoring, living in an unsafe neighborhood, moving home frequently, poor moral development, poor maternal relationship, and watching sex and violence on television. The strength of Laser et al.'s (2007) study was the consideration of prospective risk and promotive[2] factors specific to Japan. Factors such as "mother's involvement in *telekura*" (telephone sex) and "father visiting *fūzoku*" (brothels) were included. Risk factors for males were the absence of a positive maternal relationship, low parental monitoring, frequency of moving, and father visiting brothels; for females, a history of sexual abuse potentially increased risk for deviant behavior.

A comparison of risk factors for violence between Japanese and American male youths yielded unexpected results (Bui, Farrington, Ueda, & Hill, 2014). Compared to American males from Seattle, Washington, Japanese males from Osaka self-reported a significantly higher prevalence of violence: 47.7% versus 35.2%. Having more friends involved with the police and a higher level of risk-taking explained why Japanese male youths reported a higher prevalence of violence relative to American male youths. What was regarded as a strength was also considered a limitation: in attempting to ensure cultural relevance, the violence measure was altered from "hitting someone with the idea of seriously hurting them" to "hurting someone in the context of a fight" for the Japanese context. It is unclear whether the higher prevalence of violence was because the measure tapped into "hidden violence" or assessed a more innocuous level of violence compared to the original American measure. Only replication using both violence measures will clarify this issue.

Potential risk and promotive factors for Japanese females were explored by Bui, Farrington, and Ueda (2016). Results from a sample of 219 Osaka female youths, aged 15–18 years, showed that high risk-taking and having troubled peers are the strongest risk factors, whereas having a nonworking mother was a promotive factor. These factors differ from Laser et al. (2007), but more so because history of sexual abuse had not been examined.

Because of the paucity of research on risk factors for Japanese youth offending, the aims of the present research are to (1) investigate which risk factors are significantly related to delinquency and deviance in the Japanese context, (2) investigate which risk factors are independently related to delinquency and deviance, (3) identify any interaction effects, and (4) explore how the prevalence of delinquency and deviance increases with cumulative risk.

2 Methods

Data were collected in May 2011, and a total of 878 secondary students located in the Osaka prefecture area participated in the survey. For the present study, however, only the male sample ($N = 637$) is examined. The male respondents ranged from 15 to 18 years old; their mean age was 16.13 (SD = 0.92). More results based on this data may be found in previous studies (Bui, 2014; Bui et al., 2014).

Although the students were from two high schools, the classes in each school were randomly chosen to participate in the survey. Therefore, the sample should be

[2] Promotive factors predict a low probability of offending (Farrington, Loeber, & Ttofi, 2012).

representative of these schools. The survey comprises questions on living arrangements, attitudes about shame and embarrassment, youths' relationships with their parents, schools, communities, and delinquent involvement. The survey was originally designed in English, and a back translation (Matsumoto & Juang, 2004) was conducted where the survey was translated from English to Japanese and then translated again into English without reference to the original text.

2.1 *Measures*

2.1.1 Outcome: Delinquency (and Deviance)

Respondents were asked how many times (none, one to two times, three or more times) in the past year they had committed the following acts: (1) smoking cigarettes; (2) drawing graffiti on buildings or other property (without the owner's permission); (3) breaking into a house, store, school, or other building without the owner's permission; (4) taking a bicycle/scooter/motorbike for a ride without the owner's permission; (5) shoplifting; (6) picking a fight with someone; (7) hurting someone in a fight; (8) running away from home; (9) pachinko (gambling slots); (10) staying overnight without parents' permission; and (11) taking parents' money without permission.

The study drew upon the seriousness scale of Wolfgang, Figlio, Tracy, and Singer (1985) and the average seriousness scores of LeBlanc and Frechette (1989).[3] The method consists of multiplying these scores[4] by the response of each delinquency item, where each new score from each item was successively added together, resulting in a cumulative "offending gravity score." The purpose of using these scores is to ensure that more serious offenses are given more weight than less serious ones while accounting for both frequency and seriousness (Kazemian, Farrington, & Le Blanc, 2009). The scores of the 11 items were subsequently added together to form the final delinquency score. Next, the measure was dichotomized to represent the 25% most delinquent and deviant versus the remaining 75% of males; these top 25% will be referred to as serious delinquents. Table 7.1 presents the items of the outcome measure in more detail.

[3] The seriousness scale is rated as follows: personal attack, 13.21 (picking a fight with someone, hurting someone in a fight); motor vehicle theft, 6.70 (taking a bicycle/scooter/motorbike for a ride without the owner's permission); burglary, 6.43 (breaking into a house, store, school, or other building without the owner's permission); common theft, 5.07 (taking parents' money without permission); shoplifting, 2.20 (shoplifting); vandalism, 1.80 (drawing graffiti on buildings or other property); public mischief, 0.70 (smoking cigarettes, running away from home, pachinko, staying out somewhere other than home).

[4] The categories were scored as none = 1, one to two times = 1, three or more times = 2.

Table 7.1 Prevalence of delinquent and deviant acts among Japanese male youths ($N = 637$)

Delinquency	Prevalence *N* (%)	Seriousness score
Drawn graffiti on buildings or other property	55 (8.63)	1.80
Broke into someone's house, store, school, or other building	86 (13.50)	6.43
Taking someone's scooter, bike, or motorcycle for a ride	90 (14.13)	6.70
Shoplifted	69 (10.83)	2.20
Picked a fight with someone	70 (10.99)	13.21
Hit someone in a fight	131 (20.57)	13.21
Took parents' money without permission	50 (7.85)	5.07
Deviance		
Smoked cigarettes	122 (19.15)	0.70
Ran away from home	34 (5.34)	0.70
Pachinko	68 (10.68)	0.70
Staying out somewhere other than home	79 (12.40)	0.70
Offending gravity score, *M* (SD), range	*M* (SD) 22.28 (26.85)	Range 0–102.84

2.2 *Explanatory Variables*

2.2.1 Prospective Risk Factors Related to Delinquency

The survey contained a total of 63 explanatory variables that were divided into the following categories: individual, family, peers, and school. Each variable was dichotomized so that a score of one meant at risk, whereas a score of zero meant not at risk. For variables that were on a four-point Likert scale, they were dichotomized in half to represent low (i.e., 0) versus high (i.e., 1) scores.

Unadjusted relationships were examined through logistic regression to identify which factors were significantly related to serious delinquency (the 25% top quartile of the outcome measure). A total of 21 individual significant risk factors were identified, and they were the subject of further investigation. Table 7.2 shows the 21 significant risk factors that are analyzed in the study (26 risk factors if combined items were included).

Some of the items were conceptually similar and exhibited multicollinearity (identified through tetrachoric correlations) with each other, so they were subsequently combined. These items were the following: (1) for high risk-taking, items combined were "often shock people for the fun of it," "often do what feels good regardless of the consequences," "often do something dangerous because someone dares me," "often do risky things even if a little frightening," and "often do crazy things just to see the effect on others"; (2) for parental monitoring, paternal and maternal monitoring were combined; (3) for low school bonding, "getting good grades is unimportant," "don't finish homework on time," and "don't care what

Table 7.2 Prevalence of risk factors and effect size of significant unadjusted relationships with serious delinquency

	Prevalence of delinquency/risk factor *N* (%)			
	Yes/yes (a)	Yes/no (c)	OR	95% CI
Individual				
High risk-taking ($N = 5$; $\alpha = 0.82$)	47.67 (82/172)	16.85 (76/451)	4.50***	3.05–6.62
1. Often shock people for the fun of it	30.35 (112/369)	17.74 (47/265)	2.02***	1.37–2.97
2. Often do what feels good regardless of the consequences	29.15 (100/343)	20.21 (58/287)	1.62*	1.12–2.35
3. Often do something dangerous because someone dares me	49.18 (60/122)	19.49 (99/508)	4.00***	2.63–6.07
4. Often do risky things even if a little frightening	46.91 (91/194)	15.53 (68/438)	4.81***	3.28–7.05
5. Often do crazy things just to see the effect on others	40.26 (93/231)	16.21 (65/401)	3.48***	2.40–5.06
Beliefs				
Wouldn't get caught if illegally gambled	39.08 (34/87)	22.95 (126/549)	2.15**	1.34–3.46
Attitudes				
Not courteous to people who are disagreeable	29.64 (75/253)	21.90 (83/379)	1.50*	1.04–2.16
Not willing to admit a mistake	32.00 (48/150)	22.93 (111/484)	1.58*	1.06–2.37
Try to get even rather than forgive and forget	30.32 (94/310)	20.12 (65/323)	1.73**	1.20–2.49
Parents				
Parental monitoring ($N = 2$; KR-20 = 0.66)	42.65 (58/136)	19.72 (70/355)	3.03***	1.97–4.65
Father				
Low monitoring ($N = 2$; $\alpha = 0.81$)	37.29 (44/118)	22.34 (88/394)	2.07**	1.33–3.22
1. Seldom or never knows where I am	36.00 (81/225)	17.71 (51/288)	2.61***	1.74–3.93
2. Seldom or never knows who I am with	29.75 (97/326)	18.72 (35/187)	1.84**	1.19–2.85
Mother				
Low monitoring ($N = 2$; $\alpha = 0.83$)	42.25 (60/142)	20.26 (95/469)	2.88***	1.93–4.31
1. Seldom or never knows where I am	39.24 (62/158)	20.44 (93/455)	2.51***	1.70–3.72
2. Seldom or never knows who I am with	34.65 (79/228)	19.84 (76/383)	2.14***	1.48–3.10
Low attachment—seldom or never understands my thoughts or feelings	31.18 (53/170)	23.08 (102/442)	1.51*	1.02–2.24
Discipline—locks me out of the house	40.43 (19/47)	23.75 (133/560)	2.18*	1.18–4.03

(continued)

Table 7.2 (continued)

	Prevalence of delinquency/risk factor *N* (%)			
	Yes/yes (a)	Yes/no (c)	OR	95% CI
Peers				
One or more close friends picked up by police	34.25 (149/435)	5.10 (10/196)	9.69***	4.98–18.87
School				
Low school bonding ($N = 3$; $\alpha = 0.63$)	35.88 (47/131)	22.47 (113/503)	1.93**	1.28–2.92
1. Getting good grades is unimportant	33.33 (49/147)	22.75 (111/488)	1.70*	1.13–2.54
2. Don't finish homework on time	35.07 (94/268)	17.98 (66/367)	2.46***	1.71–3.55
3. Don't care what teacher thinks of me	28.41 (100/352)	21.13 (60/284)	1.48*	1.03–2.14
Compared to others, academic ability is below average or worst	31.51 (75/238)	20.34 (72/354)	1.80**	1.24–2.63
No plans to attend 4-year university	31.68 (51/161)	22.89 (106/463)	1.56*	1.05–2.32

***$p < 0.001$
**$p < 0.01$
*$p < 0.05$

teacher thinks of me" were combined. A total of 11 risk factors were analyzed.[5] These 11 factors (shown in italics in Table 7.2) were the following: high risk-taking, wouldn't get caught if illegally gambled, not courteous to people who are disagreeable, not willing to admit a mistake, try to get even rather than forgive and forget, low monitoring, mother locks child out of house as punishment, one or more close friends picked up by police, low school bonding, low academic ability, and no plans to attend 4-year university.

2.3 *Plan of Analysis*

Logistic regression was used to obtain odds ratios (ORs) of unadjusted and adjusted relationships between significant risk factors and delinquency. Interactions between significant individual and environmental factors among the most delinquent were analyzed. The totals and percentages of each risk factor and outcome measure in a 2 × 2 table were also included as these give an idea of the extent to which each item was prevalent. In addition, cumulative risk was investigated, as it is established criminological knowledge that many risk factors in combination with few protective factors predict future criminal outcomes (Herrenkohl et al., 2000).

[5] Maternal attachment was dropped from the analyses because, conceptually, it did not fit with parental monitoring, yet it was highly correlated with parental monitoring.

To further examine cumulative risk, the area under the receiver operating characteristic (ROC) curve (AUC) was used. Similar to the OR, the ROC is independent of the base rate of the outcome measure in the sample, and it is unaffected by changes in the sample size and in the row and column totals (Farrington, Loeber, Stouthamer-Loeber, Van Kammen, & Schmidt, 1996; Farrington, Jolliffe, & Johnstone, 2008). The ROC curve plots the probability of a true positive (i.e., the percentage of offenders identified at any selection criterion) versus the probability of a false positive (i.e., the percentage of non-offenders identified at this selection criterion; Farrington et al., 1996). The AUC is derived from the ROC. If predictive accuracy was no better than chance, then the area would be 0.5; with perfect discrimination, the AUC value would be 1.0. The AUC, therefore, measures predictive accuracy.

The AROC was calculated using the formula 2*(AUC-0.5). The measure of cumulative risk is derived from a 4 × 2 table (Farrington et al., 1996). In other words, the cumulative risk measure has four categories (i.e., low, medium, high, and very high), and the outcome has two categories (high and low risk for serious delinquency). The AROC is a better measure of efficiency in a 4 × 2 table than the chi-square because it measures the linearity of the relationship (Piquero, Farrington, & Blumstein, 2007). Essentially, the AROC converts the AUC to a 0–1 scale (0 = chance to 1 = perfect discrimination).

3 Results

3.1 Risk Factors for Delinquency

As previously stated, Table 7.2 presents the original 21 risk factors that were significantly related to delinquency. Each of these relationships is based on a 2 × 2 table: a = respondents who had both the risk factor and the outcome (i.e., true positive); b = respondents who had the risk factor but not the outcome (i.e., false positive); c = respondents who had the outcome but not the risk factor (i.e., false negative); and d = respondents who neither had the outcome nor the risk factor (i.e., true negative). For instance, the overall high risk-taking measure shows that 47.67% of those who had the risk factor were serious delinquents (true positives), whereas 16.85% of those who did not have the risk factor were serious delinquents (false negatives) (OR = 4.50, $p < 0.001$).

The strongest risk factor for serious delinquency was having one or more close friends who were picked up by the police (34.25% delinquents of those with the risk factor vs. 5.10% of those without it; OR = 9.69, $p < 0.001$). The weakest risk factor was apathy toward what the teacher thought of the respondent (28.41% delinquents at risk vs. 21.13% delinquents not at risk; OR = 1.48, $p < 0.05$). But when this risk factor was combined with the two other school bonding items ("getting good grades is unimportant" and "don't finish homework on time"), the combined strength was OR = 1.93 ($p < 0.01$). Further, low parental monitoring followed peers and high

Table 7.3 Strength of adjusted relationships between significant risk factors and delinquency based on logistic regression analysis ($N = 431$)

	OR	95% CI
Individual		
High risk-taking	3.10***	1.83–5.23
Wouldn't get caught if illegally gambled	1.11	0.57–2.14
Not courteous to people who are disagreeable	1.39	0.82–2.36
Not willing to admit a mistake	1.23	0.69–2.20
Try to get even rather than forgive and forget	1.40	0.84–2.34
Parents		
Low monitoring	2.36*	1.22–4.58
Mother locks child out of house as punishment	1.61	0.69–3.72
Peers		
One or more close friends picked up by police	5.73***	2.70–12.13
School		
Low school bonding	1.25	0.69–2.27
Compared to others, academic ability is below average or worst	1.69*	1.00–2.85
No plans to attend 4-year university	1.06	0.61–1.85

***$p < 0.001$
**$p < 0.01$
*$p < 0.05$

risk-taking in strength: 42.65% of poorly monitored males were serious delinquents (OR = 3.03, $p < 0.001$).

As previously mentioned, because some risk factors exhibited multicollinearity, some of them were combined. Table 7.3 shows the strength of the adjusted relationships when the combined and single risk factors ($N = 11$) were inserted into the same logistic model. High risk-taking (OR = 3.10, $p < 0.001$), low parental monitoring (OR = 2.36, $p < 0.05$), having one or more close friends picked up by the police (OR = 5.73, $p < 0.001$), and low academic ability (OR = 1.69, $p < 0.05$) were the only significant risk factors.

3.2 *Interaction Effects*

The percentage of serious delinquents within each interaction category between individual and environmental risk was examined. The overall pattern of interaction effects reveals that, when two risk factors interact with each other, there is an increased risk as demonstrated by the disproportionately higher prevalence of serious delinquents in the high individual-high environmental risk category. For example, the interaction between the belief that one would not get caught if one illegally gambled and low school bonding was the only significant interaction term (OR = 4.01, $p < 0.05$). Compared to the other groups in this interaction analysis

(22.35% low individual-low environmental risk, 24% high individual-low environmental risk, and 26.32% low individual-high environmental risk), 61.11% of those who had both risk factors were serious delinquents. Therefore, an amplifying effect (Farrington, 1997) occurred, which increased the risk for serious delinquency more so than the simple addition of the two risk factors.

3.3 Cumulative Risk

The 11 significant risk factors were added together to form an overall risk scale. Scores ranged from 0 to 11 with the average Japanese male youth having 3.83 risk factors. The scale was subsequently divided into four categories according to quartiles: low (0–1), medium (2–3), high (4–5), and serious (6+) risks. The delinquency and deviance items were dichotomized to signify having committed either none (0) or one or more (1) of each act. Table 7.4 shows how the prevalence of delinquency and deviance varies with the risk score.

Table 7.4 Prevalence of delinquency and deviance versus risk score ($N = 431$)

Delinquency	Low (0–1)	Medium (2–3)	High (4–5)	Serious (6+)	AROC[a]	95% CI
25% highest combined delinquency score	3 (2.70)	18 (16.22)	37 (33.33)	53 (47.75)	0.52	0.42–0.61
Drawn graffiti on buildings or other property	2 (4.55)	6 (13.64)	10 (22.73)	26 (59.09)	0.49	0.33–0.64
Broke into someone's house, store, school, or other building	2 (3.33)	13 (21.67)	20 (33.33)	25 (41.67)	0.36	0.23–0.49
Taking someone's scooter, bike, or motorcycle for a ride	4 (6.35)	9 (14.29)	17 (26.98)	33 (52.38)	0.45	0.31–0.58
Shoplifted	1 (2.17)	6 (13.04)	10 (21.74)	29 (63.04)	0.54	0.41–0.68
Picked a fight with someone	1 (1.96)	6 (11.76)	16 (31.37)	28 (54.90)	0.52	0.39–0.64
Hit someone in a fight	5 (5.49)	21 (23.08)	25 (27.47)	41 (43.96)	0.39	0.25–0.49
Took parents' money without permission	0 (0.00)	9 (23.68)	11 (28.95)	18 (47.37)	0.40	0.25–0.55
Deviance						
Smoked cigarettes	1 (1.25)	12 (15.00)	29 (36.25)	38 (47.50)	0.50	0.40–0.60
Ran away from home	0 (0.00)	3 (12.50)	6 (25.00)	15 (62.50)	0.54	0.38–0.70
Pachinko	2 (4.88)	9 (21.95)	16 (39.02)	14 (34.15)	0.28	0.13–0.44
Staying out somewhere other than home	1 (2.00)	8 (16.00)	15 (30.00)	26 (52.00)	0.47	0.34–0.60

[a]AROC = 2*(AUC-0.5)

For each delinquent and deviant outcome, those who had six or more risk factors had the highest prevalence compared to the other risk categories. For example, 2.17% of those who were rated as low risk committed shoplifting in the past year compared to 63.04% who were rated as serious risk. The prevalence of the delinquent or deviant act increased as one went from low to high risk, and the relationships between each outcome and the risk score was significant. But the only exception for this observation was having engaged in pachinko (gambling slots).

The AROC was calculated to examine the extent to which the cumulative risk scale can accurately predict a particular delinquent or deviant outcome better than chance (= 0). The cumulative risk scale was useful in predicting overall serious delinquents (AROC = 0.52, 95% CI = 0.42–0.61), shoplifting (AROC = 0.54, 95% CI = 0.41–0.68), picking fights with people (AROC = 0.52, 95% CI = 0.39–0.64), and running away from home (AROC = 0.54, 95% CI = 0.38–0.70). The lowest AROC values were for pachinko involvement (AROC = 0.28) and hitting someone in a fight (AROC = 0.39), and their confidence interval range was below 0.50 (pachinko, 0.13–0.44; hitting someone, 0.25–0.49) meaning their performance to accurately predict pachinko involvement and hitting someone in a fight was not very good.

4 Discussion

The main purpose of the present study was to identify important risk factors for delinquency and deviance in Japanese male youths and explore whether issues in risk were applicable to Japan. One may argue that delinquency and deviance are not important to study because of the mistaken belief that youth crimes are not as pervasively damaging as white-collar crimes or homicide. Studying youth offending, however, is important because failure in targeting the specific factors of youth crime results in major financial losses at the societal level. For example, in the UK, youth crime costs the government £1.2 billion in 2009 (Prince's Trust, 2010). The economic costs of serious antisocial behavior in youth are substantial, and its implications for society can be enormous, including costs related to accessing health, mental health, child welfare, and special education (De Ruiter & Augimeri, 2012).

Japanese society believes that increases in problems within the youth population indicate problems for posterity (White, 1994). What aggravates the issue of youth offending in Japan is that the country has the highest proportion of people aged 65 and over in the world as well as a declining fertility rate (Muramatsu & Akiyama, 2011). The growing trend among young men and women is to postpone marriage and delay having children, and a higher fraction of women have chosen to remain single for the long term because of educational advancement and participation in the workforce (White, 2002). In addition, the mass media's sensational reporting of the violent youth-on-youth crime and rises in police arrests for juvenile crime only increases the public's fear of youth behavior (Tokuoka, 2003; Yoder, 2011). Taken together, youth offending is an important issue within Japan.

Four risk factors were significantly related to delinquency and deviance for Japanese male youths when accounting for other factors: low parental monitoring, high risk-taking, having one or more close friends picked up by the police, and low academic ability. These risk factors were similar to risk factors established in Western criminological studies (Farrington, 2005).

In Japanese society, being monitored by others is a common occurrence. According to Sugimoto (2014), this phenomenon is called *seken*, and it is an imagined but real entity, "encompassing a web of people who provide the moral yardsticks that favor the status quo and traditional practices" (p. 301). It is embedded in the Japanese mind and has the ability to approve and disapprove individual behavior (Holloway, 2010). The *seken* exists because Japan's societal structure emphasizes groups, and failure to behave appropriately and adhere to the expectations of these groups will result in gossip, criticism, and ridicule (Westermann & Burfeind, 1991). The idea of the *seken* relates to *relational centrality* of Messner (2014), which is the extent to which interpersonal relationships with accompanying obligations are central to people's everyday lives. Relational centrality explains why self-control is high in collectivist cultures like Japan; the basis of this theory is from previous cultural psychology research conducted by Kitayama and Uchida (2005). Because parents are primarily responsible for the socialization of their children, low parental monitoring should be particularly saliently linked to youth offending. The combination of two important facets in Japanese society, parenting and monitoring the behavior of others, makes low parental monitoring an important risk factor.

In a previous paper, using the same dataset, Bui et al. (2014) compared common risk factors for violence between Japanese and American male youths. The two most significant risk factors that explained violence for Japanese male youths were high risk-taking and having peers who were picked up by the police. The present study also finds that these two risk factors are highly salient for delinquency and deviance in Japanese male youths. These findings are different from the previous findings using the same data because the present analyses examined all available risk factors for delinquency, accounting for the severity and frequency of offenses and deviant acts. Having delinquent peers could reflect the same underlying construct as the male's own delinquency, because of co-offending. If one offends, one must have delinquent peers because one co-offends, but there is no evidence that delinquent peers have a causal effect (Farrington, Loeber, Yin, & Anderson, 2002). Similar to Bui et al. (2014), high risk-taking and having troubled friends produced the strongest relationships to crime. What these two risk factors may represent are defiance against Japanese norms and conventional rules.

Security and safety are highly valued in uncertainty avoidance cultures such as Japan; to promote these options, rules for correct behavior must be followed in order to prevent conflict and dissent (Kobayashi et al., 2008). High risk-taking and having delinquent friends are indicative of a lifestyle that encourages marginalization from these values. It is assumed that having low academic ability (though the strength of the relationship between it and serious delinquency was weak, nevertheless, it should be considered) would only encourage such a lifestyle. It may be argued that these two risk factors may be measuring the same underlying concept as delinquency. These risk factors, however, contain nothing that refers explicitly to delinquent or deviant acts.

Only one interaction effect was significant for Japanese male youths. This interaction, however, revealed that a disproportionately increased risk of serious delinquency occurred when two risk factors coincided. Having both the belief that one would not get caught illegally gambling and having low school bonding increased the risk for serious delinquent involvement disproportionately (not additively but multiplicatively) compared to other combinations of the risk categories. Perhaps confidence in one's ability to elude authorities and the attitude that school is not worthwhile makes deviant prospects attractive.

Having no close friends who were picked up by the police was the strongest risk factor, and it was also the strongest promotive factor, when the opposite direction is considered. Protective factors have been studied less than the risk factors. The benefit of studying protective factors is that it is a more positive approach and is more attractive to communities than studying only risk factors, which emphasizes deficits and problems (Pollard, Hawkins, & Arthur, 1999). Loeber, Farrington, Stouthamer-Loeber, and White (2008) suggested that protective factors should be defined as factors that predict a low probability of offending among persons in a risk category, and promotive factors should be defined as factors that predict a low probability of offending in general, as in main effects (Farrington, Loeber, & Ttofi, 2012). A future study will investigate protective factors for delinquency in Japan. In addition, cumulative risk was also an applicable concept in the Japanese context. The findings show that the more risk factors an individual is exposed to, the higher the likelihood that they will be involved in a greater and more serious level of delinquency and deviance.

4.1 Policy Implications

It is an apparent solution to target the risk and protective factors identified through intervention programs for parental monitoring, peer groups, and risk-taking. The idea is simple: decrease the risk factors and increase the protective factors (Farrington, 2000). Not only should these risk and protective factors be targeted, but placing these factors in the wider context of the current issues faced by Japanese youths will make relevant programs more effective.

The overall findings are indicative of the wider context that Japanese youths confront: the very rigorous schooling system, societal pressure to conform, and declining employment opportunities (Ackerman, 2004; Mathews, 2004; Sugimoto, 2014). Offending is linked to other youth social issues in Japan such as suicide, school refusal, and family violence, and it should be viewed as a symptom of an "adolescent crisis" (Murai, 1988). Promoting opportunities where Japanese youth feel that they have different prosocial career and lifestyle options other than the status quo may also improve interventions targeting risk factors such as youth mentoring schemes or life coaching, which may help at-risk youth discover new possibilities for themselves.

It is also possible to use the four risk factors (high risk-taking, having close friends picked up by the police, low parental monitoring, and low academic ability) to identify at-risk youth and implement cognitive behavioral therapy (CBT) to reduce risk-taking, parent training to reduce poor parental monitoring, and tutoring to reduce low academic ability.

5 Conclusions

The findings show that established criminological risk factors are applicable in Japan as they are in the West, for example, delinquent peers, high risk-taking, poor parental monitoring, and low academic ability. These four risk factors are similar to results from longitudinal studies in the USA and the UK, and they are important in Japan. Thus, theories of delinquency may also be applicable.

Acknowledgments The authors wish to thank 社会安全研究財団 (Research Foundation for Safe Society) and the Great Britain Sasakawa Foundation for their generous support.

References

Ackerman, P. (2004). How Japanese teenagers cope: Social pressures and personal response. In G. Mathews & B. White (Eds.), *Japan's changing generations: Are young people creating a new society?* (pp. 67–82). New York: Routledge.

Ambaras, D. R. (2006). *Bad youth: Juvenile delinquency and the politics of everyday life in modern Japan*. Berkeley, CA: University of California Press.

Bui, L. (2014). Examining the relationship between parenting, risk-taking, and delinquency in Japan: Context and empirical applicability. *Asian Journal of Criminology, 9*(3), 171–187.

Bui, L., Farrington, D. P., & Ueda, M. (2016). Potential risk and promotive factors for serious delinquency in Japanese female youths. *International Journal of Comparative and Applied Criminal Justice, 40(3)*, 209–224.

Bui, L., Farrington, D. P., Ueda, M., & Hill, K. G. (2014). Prevalence and risk factors for self-reported violence of Osaka and Seattle male youths. *International Journal of Offender Therapy and Comparative Criminology, 58*(12), 1540–1557.

De Ruiter, C., & Augimeri, L. K. (2012). Making delinquency prevention work with children and adolescents: From risk assessment to effective interventions. In C. Logan & L. Johnstone (Eds.), *Managing clinical risk* (pp. 199–223). London: Routledge.

Erbe, A. (2003). Youth in crisis: Public perceptions and discourse on deviance and juvenile problem behavior in Japan. In G. Foljanty-Jost (Ed.), *Juvenile Delinquency in Japan: Reconsidering the "Crisis"* (pp. 51–74). Leiden: Brill.

Farrington, D. P. (1997). The relationship between low resting heart rate and violence. In A. Raine, P. A. Brennan, & D. P. Farrington (Eds.), *Biosocial bases of violence* (pp. 89–105). New York: Plenum.

Farrington, D. P. (2000). Explaining and preventing crime: The globalisation of knowledge—The American Society of Criminology 1999 Presidential Address. *Criminology, 38*(1), 1–24.

Farrington, D. P. (2005). Childhood origins of antisocial behavior. *Clinical Psychology & Psychotherapy, 12*(3), 177–190.

Farrington, D. P., Jolliffe, D., & Johnstone, L. (2008). *Assessing violence risk: A framework for practice*. Edinburgh: Risk Management Authority.

Farrington, D. P., & Loeber, R. (2000). Some benefits of dichotomization in psychiatric and criminological research. *Criminal Behavior and Mental Health, 10*(2), 100–122.

Farrington, D. P., Loeber, R., Stouthamer-Loeber, M., Van Kammen, W., & Schmidt, L. (1996). Self-reported delinquency and a combined delinquency seriousness scale based on boys, mothers, and teachers: Concurrent and predictive validity for African-Americans and Caucasians. *Criminology, 34*(4), 493–517.

Farrington, D. P., Loeber, R., & Ttofi, M. M. (2012). Risk and protective factors for offending. In B. Welsh & D. P. Farrington (Eds.), *The Oxford handbook in criminology and criminal justice* (pp. 46–69). New York: Oxford University Press.

Farrington, D. P., Loeber, R., Yin, Y., & Anderson, S. J. (2002). Are within-individual causes of delinquency the same as between-individual causes? *Criminal Behaviour and Mental Health, 12*(1), 53–68.

Finch, A. (2000). Criminal statistics in Japan: The white paper on crime, hanzai hakusho and hanzai tokeisho. *Social Science Japan Journal, 3*(2), 237–249.

Foljanty-Jost, G., & Metzler, M. (2003). Juvenile delinquency in Japan: Reconsidering the crisis. In G. Foljanty-Jost (Ed.), *Juvenile delinquency in Japan: Reconsidering the "Crisis"* (pp. 1–17). Leiden: Brill.

Fukushima, M., Sharp, S. F., & Kobayashi, E. (2009). Bond to society, collectivism, and conformity: A comparative study of Japanese and American College Students. *Deviant Behavior, 30*(5), 434–466.

Hamai, K., & Ellis, T. (2008). Japanese criminal justice: Was reintegrative shaming a chimera? *Punishment & Society, 10*(1), 25–46.

Herrenkohl, T. I., Maguin, E., Hill, K. G., Hawkins, J. D., Abbott, R., & Catalano, R. F. (2000). Developmental risk factors for youth violence. *Journal of Adolescent Health, 26*(3), 176–186.

Holloway, S. (2010). *Women and family in contemporary Japan*. Cambridge: Cambridge University Press.

Kazemian, L., Farrington, D. P., & Le Blanc, M. (2009). Can we make accurate long-term predictions about patterns of de-escalation in offending behavior? *Journal of Youth and Adolescence, 38*(3), 384–400.

Kitayama, S., & Uchida, Y. (2005). Interdependent agency: An alternative system for action. In R. M. Sorrentino, C. Dov, J. M. Olson, & M. P. Zanna (Eds.), *Culture and social behavior: The Ontario Symposium* (10th ed., pp. 137–164). Mahwah, NJ: Erlbaum.

Kobayashi, E., Akers, R. L., & Sharp, S. F. (2011). Attitude transference and deviant behavior: A comparative study in Japan and the United States. *Deviant Behavior, 32*(5), 405–440.

Kobayashi, E., Sharp, S. F., & Grasmick, H. G. (2008). Gender and deviance: A comparison of college students in Japan and the United States. *Deviant Behavior, 29*(5), 413–439.

Kobayashi, E., Vazsonyi, A. T., Chen, P., & Sharp, S. F. (2010). A culturally nuanced test of Gottfredson and Hirschi's general theory: Dimensionality and generalizability in Japan and the United States. *International Criminal Justice Review, 20*(2), 112–131.

Laser, J., Luster, T., & Oshio, T. (2007). Promotive and risk factors related to deviant behavior in Japanese youth. *Criminal Justice and Behavior, 34*(11), 1463–1480.

LeBlanc, M., & Frechette, M. (1989). *Male criminal activity from childhood through youth: Multilevel and developmental perspectives*. New York: Springer-Verlag.

Loeber, R., Farrington, D. P., Stouthamer-Loeber, M., & White, H. R. (2008). *Violence and serious theft: Development and prediction from childhood to adulthood.* New York: Routledge.

Maeda, M. (2003). *Nihon no chian wa saisei dekiru ka [Can Japan resurrect social order?]*. Tokyo: Chikuma Shinsho.

Mathews, G. (2004). Seeking a career, finding a job: How young people enter and resist the Japanese world of work. In G. Mathews & B. White (Eds.), *Japan's changing generations: Are young people creating a new society?* (pp. 121–136). New York: Routledge.

Matsumoto, D., & Juang, L. (2004). *Culture and psychology*. Belmont, CA: Wadsworth/Thompson Learning.

Messner, S. F. (2014). Social institutions, theory development, and the promise of comparative criminological research. *Asian Journal of Criminology, 9*(1), 49–63.

Miller, A., & Kanazawa, S. (2000). *Order by accident: The origins and consequences of conformity in contemporary Japan*. Boulder, CO: Westview Press.

Murai, T. (1988). Current problems of juvenile delinquency in Japan Hitotsubashi. *Journal of Law and Politics, 16*, 1–10.

Muramatsu, N., & Akiyama, H. (2011). Japan: Super-aging society preparing for the future. *The Gerontologist, 51*(4), 425–432.

Nakanishi, Y. (2003). Making sense of Japanese juvenile crime statistics: Beyond an economic approach and policy implications. *Radical Statistics, 81*(81), 34–50.

Nawa, S. (2006). Postwar fourth wave of juvenile delinquency and tasks of juvenile police. *Journal of Police Science, 1*(58), 1–19.

Okabe, T. (2014). *Gendai nihon no shonen hikou (Juvenile delinquency in today's Japan)*. Tokyo: Gendaijinbunsha.

Osamu, M. (1998). Youth under siege in a world of drugs. *Japan Quarterly, 54*(4), 76–83.

Piquero, A. R., Farrington, D. P., & Blumstein, A. (2007). *Key issues in criminal career research*. New York: Cambridge University Press.

Pollard, J., Hawkins, J. D., & Arthur, M. W. (1999). Risk and protection: Are both necessary to understand diverse behavioral outcomes in adolescence? *Social Work Research, 23*(3), 145–158.

Prince's Trust. (2010). *The cost of exclusion: Counting the cost of youth disadvantage in the UK*. London: Prince's Trust.

Research and Training Institute of the Ministry of Justice. (2000). *White paper on crime*. Tokyo: Ministry of Justice.

Sugimoto, Y. (2014). *An introduction to Japanese society* (4th ed.). Cambridge: Cambridge University Press.

Tanioka, I. (1989). *The informal social control of high school student behavior in Osaka, Japan: A test of "the web of informal control" theory of delinquency causation*. Los Angeles, CA: University of Southern California.

Tanioka, I., & Glaser, D. (1991). School uniforms, routine activities, and the social control of delinquency in Japan. *Youth & Society, 23*(1), 50–75.

Tokuoka, H. (2003). Repression of deviancy as a reason for new deviancy. In G. Foljanty-Jost (Ed.), *Juvenile delinquency in Japan: Reconsidering the "crisis"* (pp. 103–114). Leiden: Brill.

Toyama-Bialke, C. (2003). The "Japanese triangle" for preventing adolescent delinquency—Strengths and weaknesses of the family-school adolescent relationship from a comparative perspective. In G. Foljanty-Jost (Ed.), *Juvenile delinquency in Japan: Reconsidering the "crisis"* (pp. 19–50). Leiden: Brill.

Tsutomi, H. (1991). Do delinquent children obey their parents in Japan?: Examination of effects of parental controls for Japanese institutionalized delinquents. *Japanese Journal of Criminal Psychology, 29*(2), 13–30.

Westermann, T., & Burfeind, J. (1991). *Crime and justice in two societies*. Pacific Grove, CA: Brooks/Cole.

White, M. (1994). *The material child: Coming of age in Japan and America*. Berkeley, CA: University of California Press.

White, M. (2002). *Perfectly Japanese: Making families in an era of upheaval*. Berkeley, CA: University of California Press.

Wolfgang, M. E., Figlio, R. M., Tracy, P., & Singer, S. I. (1985). *The national survey of crime severity*. Washington, DC: U.S. Bureau of Justice Statistics.

Yoder, R. S. (2011). *Deviance and inequality in Japan: Japanese youth and foreign migrants*. Bristol: The Policy Press.

Yonekawa, S. (2003). Inequality in family background as a reason for juvenile Delinquency. In G. Foljanty-Jost (Ed.), *Juvenile delinquency in Japan: Reconsidering the "crisis"* (pp. 115–128). Leiden: Brill.

Chapter 8
Laying the Groundwork for Testing Routine Activity Theory at the Microlevel Using Japanese Satellite Positioning Technology

Yutaka Harada

1 Introduction

In their original paper that proposed the routine activity theory of crime victimization, Cohen and Felson argued that "structural changes in routine activity patterns can influence crime rates by affecting *the convergence in space and time* of the three minimal elements of direct-contact predatory violations: (1) motivated offenders, (2) suitable targets, and (3) the absence of capable guardians against a violation" (Cohen & Felson, 1979, p. 589, emphasis added). Although their theoretical framework focused on the microlevel concept of "the convergence in space and time" of the three elements of crime victimization, the supportive evidence they provided was macro-level observations on the relationship between crime rates and various lifestyle indicators or "demographic proxies."

Developments in satellite positioning technology in recent years provide opportunities for directly tracking and recording the routine activities of individuals in public spaces. One of the most attractive aspects of these satellite positioning devices is that they can determine *location* at each *time* of measurement, which opens the door for operationally defining and measuring "the convergence in space and time" of two or more individuals—the key concept in Cohen and Felson's original theoretical framework.

This chapter illustrates our efforts to lay the groundwork for testing routine activity theory at the microlevel, which we undertook in the course of our research project to devise a way to prevent predatory victimizations of elementary school students in public spaces (Harada, 2012). The chapter first reviews the theoretical aspects of the issue, with a special reference to the similarities and differences between the two

Y. Harada (✉)
Crime Prevention Section, Department of Criminology and Behavioral Sciences, National Research Institute of Police Science, Kashiwa, Japan
e-mail: harada@nrips.go.jp

J. Liu, S. Miyazawa (eds.), *Crime and Justice in Contemporary Japan*, Springer Series on Asian Criminology and Criminal Justice Research, https://doi.org/10.1007/978-3-319-69359-0_8

theoretical conceptions: "the three elements" of crime victimization in routine activity theory and "the crime triangle" in the problem-solving literature. It then refers to recent works by Felson and his collaborators that shed new light on Cohen and Felson's original routine activity theory. In accordance with these theoretical considerations, the latter part of the chapter presents and discusses our own studies, which attempt to measure some of the key components of routine activity theory at the microlevel with the aid of satellite positioning and related technologies.

2 Reconsidering Routine Activity Theory and the "Crime Triangle"

As cited above, Cohen and Felson (1979) stated that (1) motivated offenders, (2) suitable targets, and (3) the absence of capable guardians are the three minimal elements of victimization. Their formulation was adopted and developed by the advocates of "problem-oriented policing" (Center for Problem-Oriented Policing, 2003; Clarke & Eck, 2003) into what is called the "crime triangle" (Fig. 8.1).

Although they claim that "the crime triangle (also known as the problem analysis triangle) comes straight out of … routine activity theory" (Center for Problem-Oriented Policing, 2003), there is an important difference between the two: "absence of capable guardians" in Cohen and Felson's original formulation was substituted by "place" in the crime triangle, as shown in Fig. 8.1.

It appears that such a reformulation was first introduced by Eck (1994), who criticized Felson's theory for not emphasizing place as a key explanatory variable. He argued:

> In fact, until Felson (1987), place and time serve as logical necessities and not as variables to be explained. Recent micro-level research has focused attention on place aspects of this theory … and demonstrated that place is becoming a variable in need of explanation. (Eck, 1994, p. 26)

Thus, he restated the crime event equation as:

> Crime occurs when there is the convergence in time of a desirable target without an effective guardian, a motivated offender without an effective handler, at a facilitating place without an attentive manager. (Eck, 1994, p. 27)

Eck's reformulation appears to have contributed to the reconciliation of routine activity theory with microlevel, practically oriented crime control concepts such as situational crime prevention and crime prevention through environmental design. However, this reformulation resulted in the breakup of "time and place," which used to be treated together as they provided the "opportunity for crime" in Cohen and Felson's original routine activity theory. In fact, the current explanation of the "crime triangle" by the Center for Problem-Oriented Policing (Center for Problem-Oriented Policing, 2003) uses the word "place" 21 times, whereas there are practically no occurrences of the word "time" (the sole hit of my word search was "some*time*s"). As such, the "crime triangle" has lost the dynamic character of Cohen

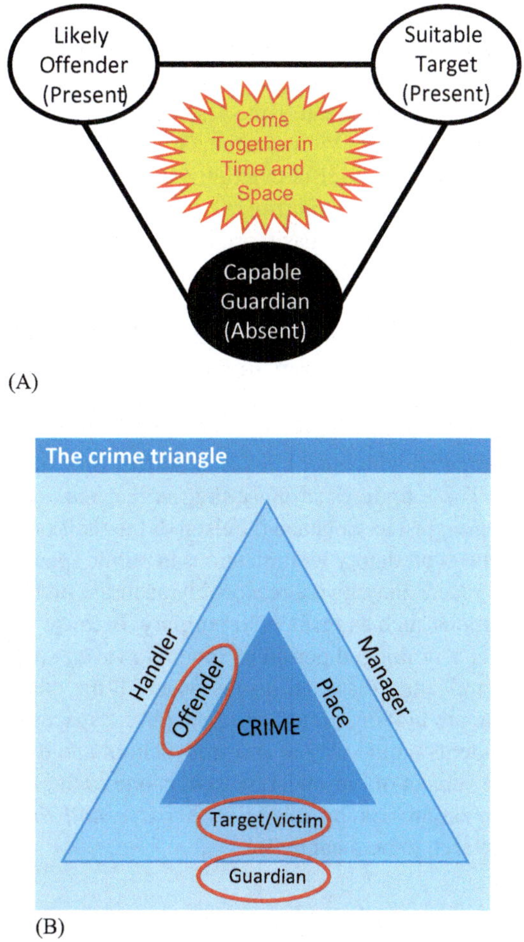

Fig. 8.1 Routine activity theory vs. "the crime triangle." (**a**) The "three elements" of crime victimization in the routine activity theory. (**b**) "The crime triangle"

and Felson's original notion of the *convergence in space and time* of the three elements of crime victimization. The "crime triangle" has become nothing but a static *place theory of crime*.

Recent works by Felson and his collaborators (e.g., Lemieux & Felson, 2012) shed new light on Cohen and Felson's original formulation of routine activity theory. Based on their view that "exposure to risk of violent crime is best understood after considering *where* people are, *what* they do, and for *how long* they do it" (Lemieux & Felson, 2012, p. 635, emphases added), they state that place-based victimization research "has been plagued by a limited ability to quantify respondent exposures to risk … and instead has been forced to rely on summary measures of risk" (Lemieux & Felson, 2012, p. 636) and that the complexity of quantifying "exposure to risk" has served as "the practical rationale for using general time use measures such as demographic proxy variables and frequency counts" (Lemieux & Felson, 2012, p. 637).

As an alternative approach, they employ "person-hour" as the denominator in calculating what they call "time-adjusted rates" of criminal victimization, as Cohen and Felson did in their original paper (see Cohen & Felson, 1979; Table 1, Panel D). Using the American Time Use Survey (ATUS) data as the denominator and the National Crime Victimization Survey (NCVS) data as the numerator, they calculated the time-adjusted victimization rates of violent offenses, defined as "the number of *violent victimizations per 10 million person-hours*" (Lemieux & Felson, 2012, p. 639, emphasis original) during the times respondents were engaging in nine broad activity categories.

As shown in Table 3 (Lemieux & Felson, 2012, p. 644) and in Figure 1 (Lemieux & Felson, 2012, p. 645), the time-adjusted rates indicated that the risks of violent victimization were very different from those calculated with conventional denominators. Particularly astonishing was the finding that the victimization risks tended to be much higher during the class of activities that they refer to as "in transit," when compared with other classes of activities.

These findings strongly suggest that *space and time* should be treated *in combination*, just as Cohen and Felson did in their original works, especially when direct-contact predatory victimizations in public spaces are an issue. Analyses solely based on places may give a reasonably accurate picture with regard to household victimizations such as residential burglary, because houses are always in a fixed location over a prolonged period of time. However, such place-based analyses may lead to significantly distorted results when all the "three elements" of criminal victimization are moving around in open, public spaces. Victimization of elementary school students on the way to and from school and during leisure time activities, which is the subject of our own research, is one such example. Measures that depict the victimization risk by taking *both space and time* into account are crucial for our research to be meaningful.[1]

3 Efforts Toward Empirical Examinations at the Microlevel

The developments in satellite positioning technology in recent years may bring about a breakthrough in the measurement issue that has long prevented routine activity theory from being tested at the microlevel by providing a way to locate the positions of moving objects in terms of *space and time*. As such, this technology may open the door for operationally defining and measuring "the convergence in space and time" of the three elements of criminal victimization, which is the key concept of Cohen and Felson's original theoretical framework.

Figure 8.2 shows a diagram that represents Cohen and Felson's formulation of victimization risks in the context of criminal victimization of elementary school students in public spaces. The "likely offender" in Fig. 8.2 is grayed out because (1)

[1] From the same point of view, Amemiya (2013) examines the victimization risk of on-street purse snatching using Japan's Person Trip Survey data as the denominator.

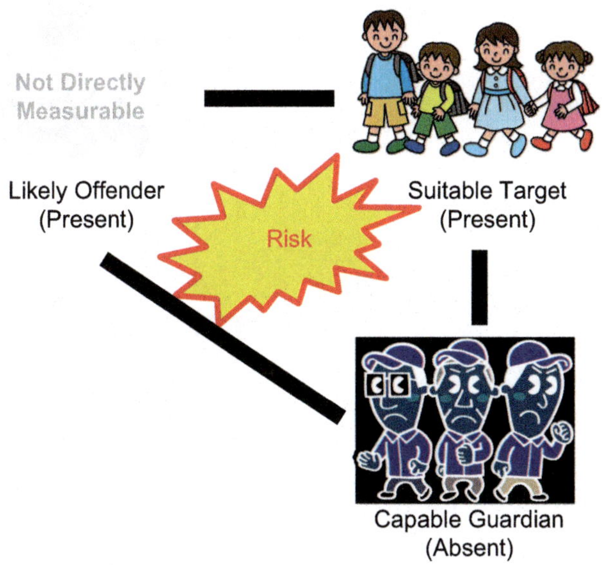

Fig. 8.2 A diagram of victimization risks experienced by elementary school children

her/his existence is "taken for granted" in the routine activity theory, and (2) her/his activities are not directly observable. By contrast, the "suitable target" (in this case, elementary school children) and the "capable guardian" (e.g., crime prevention volunteers) are displayed as clear images because they can be observed and/or tracked, if consent is obtained from the subjects. The "capable guardian" is shown as a negative image because the existence of the capable guardian is expected to be related negatively to the risk of victimization. The risks of victimization can be estimated by examining the time when and locations where the children are present and the guardians are absent.

Drawing on the above conceptual framework, we have developed what we call two *measuring rods* for assessing the victimization risks faced by elementary school students in their routine activities. One approach is a self-report victimization survey. The other is a "probe person" survey that makes use of lightweight "GPS loggers" (Fig. 8.3).

Self-reported victimizations can be seen as "observed" outcomes of victimization risks. Minor victimizations can also be seen as potential precursors of more serious kinds of victimization. In the study of industrial accidents, for example, there are said to be 29 minor accidents for each serious accident, and 300 potentially dangerous incidents per minor accident. In heuristics it is known as "Heinrich's law." Therefore, we would like to examine the occurrence of various kinds of child victimizations, including minor ones, by means of self-report victimization surveys.

Figure 8.4 shows a prototypical version of our instrument for measuring child victimization, as of the year 2014.

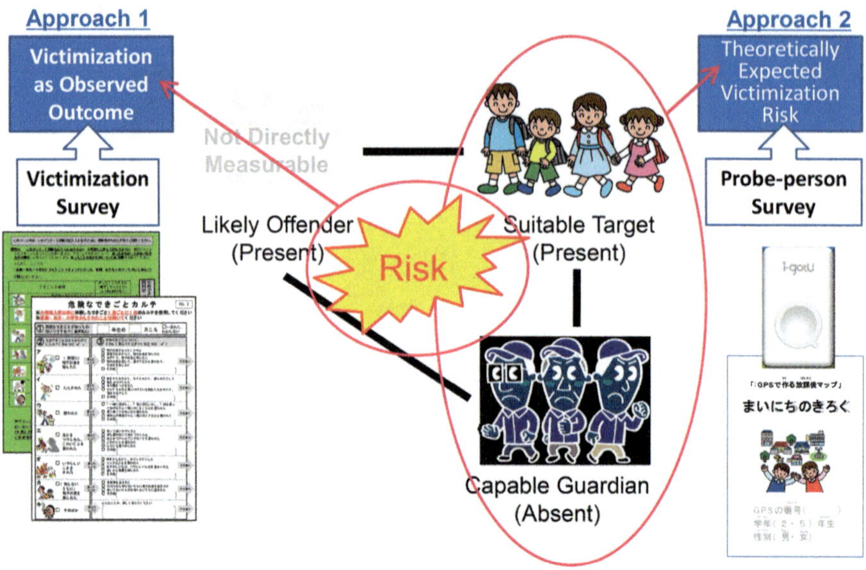

Fig. 8.3 Two "measuring rods" for assessing victimization risks e xperienced by elementary school students

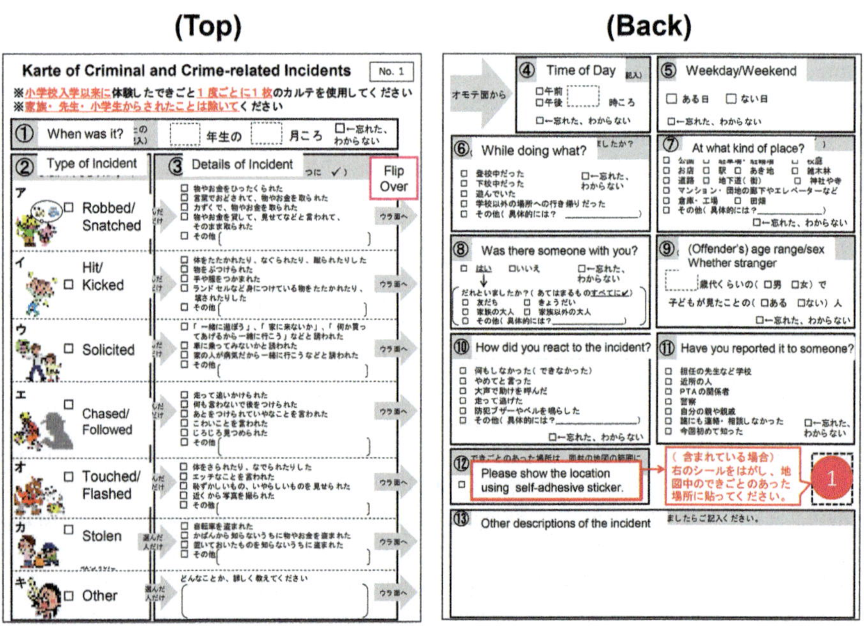

Fig. 8.4 "Karte" of criminal and crime-related incidents

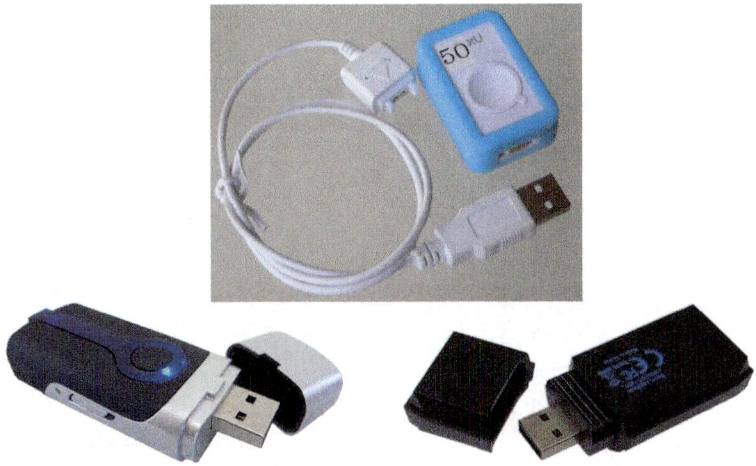

Fig. 8.5 Examples of lightweight GPS loggers

At the top are screening questions that ask respondents about their experiences in incidents belonging to seven broad categories, while the back lists detailed questions to be answered only by those respondents who have indicated that they experienced an incident during the reference period. Each sheet is designed to correspond to a single incident of victimization, and therefore we call it a "Karte" of criminal and crime-related incidents, because it looks like a medical sheet (which Japanese doctors refer to using the German word "Karte").

A "probe person" survey is a method of studying the everyday activities of persons and/or vehicles with the combined use of GPS devices and web-based diaries. In order to implement it in an elementary school-based study of students' after-school activities, we made use of lightweight GPS loggers (Fig. 8.5) and paper-based diaries (Fig. 8.6) that collected quantitative and qualitative data on the students' activities.

In addition to these two "measuring rods," we developed several software tools so that crime prevention volunteers can record their own activities and share them with others, with minimal effort and cost. One such example is what we call the "Kiki-Gaki Map" (Harada et al., 2011; Harada, Saito, Yamane, Hosoda, & Amemiya, 2013; Harada, 2014), which literally translates to "Listen-Write Map." Although this software tool was designed primarily to help crime prevention volunteers find potentially problematic situations in their neighborhoods and seek solutions for themselves, it may also be used as a tool to record the routine activities of crime prevention volunteers such as *guardians who are moving around* in their own neighborhoods.

Using these measurement tools, we carried out several studies that may lay the groundwork for testing routine activity theory in its original form. These include:

1. A survey of criminal and crime-related incidents against elementary school students, which was carried out in five elementary schools using a combination of questionnaires and maps.

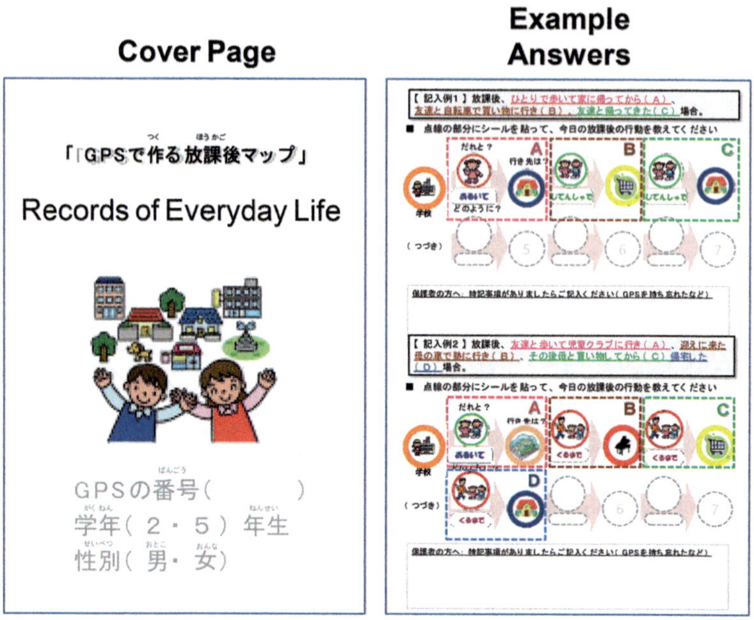

Fig. 8.6 "Records of everyday life"

2. A survey of the routine activities of 80 elementary school students, which recorded and analyzed the after-school activities of second-grade and fifth-grade students for 2 weeks, using GPS loggers as tracking devices.
3. Studies of town-watch activities by voluntary crime prevention groups that used a software tool that integrates GPS track-logs, digital photos, and descriptive texts (derived from voice recordings) into spatial-temporal datasets.

Below are brief descriptions of each of these studies and discussions on their findings and on their theoretical and practical implications.

3.1 *A Survey of Criminal and Crime-Related Incidents Against Elementary School Students*

We conducted a victimization survey at five elementary schools in a local city in December 2009 (Harada, 2012). The questionnaires (including the Kartes) were delivered in the classrooms to all the students in the five elementary schools. The students were asked to fill out the questionnaires at home, with the assistance of their parents, and to submit the filled-out questionnaires by enclosing them in the envelopes provided. Valid responses were obtained from 2258 students and the valid response rate was 78.9%.

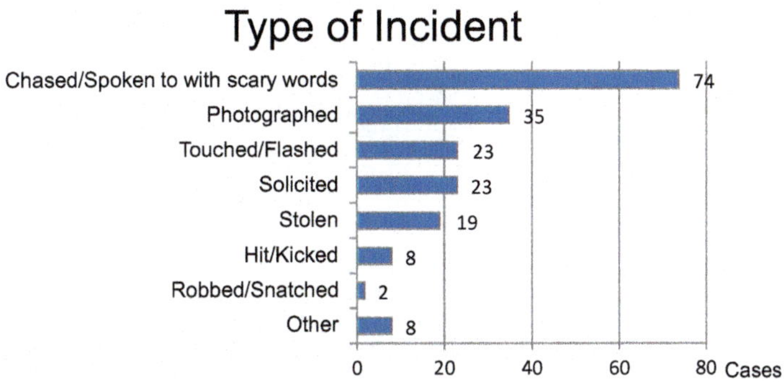

- Overall victimization rate: Approx. 6.4%
- Most frequent = Minor incidents:
  e.g., "Chased" "Spoken to with scary words"
- A few potentially more serious incidents:
  e.g., "Touched/Flashed" "Hit"

Fig. 8.7 Victimization rates

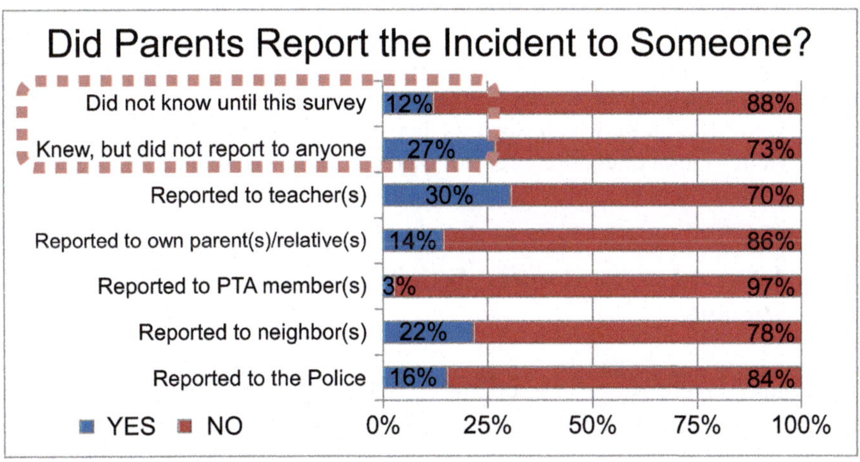

- Approx. 40% of all incidents were either not known to parents or not reported to anyone else.

Fig. 8.8 Parents' knowledge about victimization

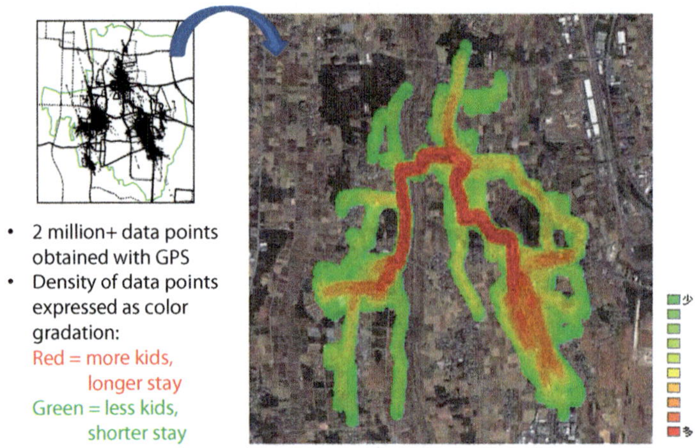

Fig. 8.9 A kernel density map of the routine activities of elementary school children

Figures 8.7 and 8.8 show the basic findings of the survey. The overall victimization rate among the respondents since entering the elementary schools was 6.4% (Fig. 8.7), which was considerably lower than the rate measured in a large city in our previous study (approximately 15%). With regard to the types of victimization, relatively minor ones such as "being chased" or "being spoken to with scary words" were reported most frequently, whereas a few potentially more serious incidents such as "being touched/flashed" or "being hit" were also reported (Fig. 8.7). The survey also revealed that approximately 40% of the parents either "did not know of the victimization until this survey" or "knew of the victimization but did not report it to anyone" (Fig. 8.8), which suggests that a considerable amount of information on the victimization of children was not shared in the local community.

3.2 A Survey of the Routine Activities of Elementary School Students

A simplified "probe person" survey was carried out in one elementary school in the same city, in which the after-school activities of 80 students were tracked with lightweight GPS loggers for 2 weeks (except for weekends) in May 2009. During the 2-week period of the study, the location of each student was tracked at 5 s intervals from the time they left school until they finally arrived home. The more than two million data points obtained from the GPS loggers were imported into the GIS software and visualized using kernel density estimation. The results are shown in Figs. 8.9 and 8.10.

These figures indicate that the everyday activities of elementary school students can be recorded and analyzed (e.g., by time zones) by way of our simplified "probe person" survey and that the visualized results of the survey may provide valuable

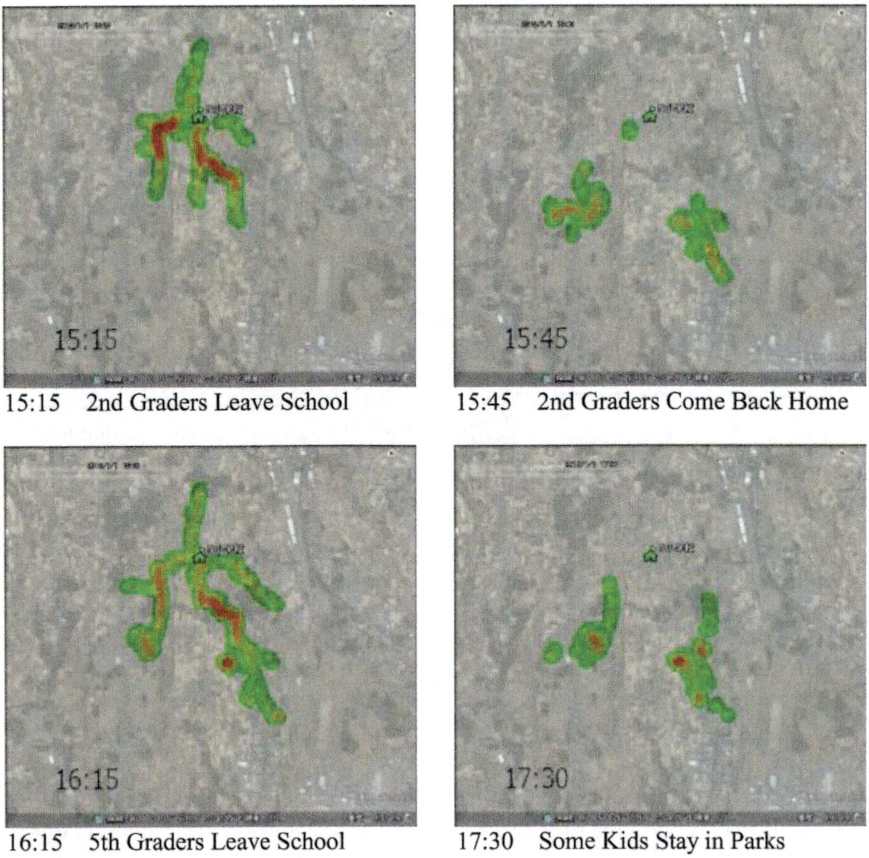

Fig. 8.10 Kernel density maps of the routine activities of elementary school children (changes by time zones)

pieces of information about the students' everyday activities that are both easy to understand and scientifically well founded (Kikuchi, Amemiya, & Shimada, 2012).

3.3 Studies of Town-Watch Activities by Voluntary Crime Prevention Groups Using a GPS-Assisted Software Tool

The "Kiki-Gaki Map" is an easy-to-use software tool for recording the process and findings of field observations in a systematic and objective manner (Harada et al., 2011; Harada et al., 2013; Harada, 2014). It is called the "Kiki-Gaki Map" because it makes use of a voice recording device instead of a paper-based field notebook.

Figure 8.11 illustrates how the "Kiki-Gaki Map" works. A GPS logger is used to record the route of field observation. Pictures taken along the way are placed on the

Fig. 8.11 "Kiki-Gaki Map" (Listen-Write Map)

map at the locations where they were taken by searching through the GPS log records using the shooting time of each picture as a search key. The shooting time is also used to "cue" the voice recording, so that one can instantly jump to the verbal comments that correspond to the picture from the continuous sound data. This way, one can easily "listen" to these comments and "write" them down in the "Memo" field in the software.

The "Kiki-Gaki Map" has so far been field tested in six neighborhoods. In all these field tests, the software tool worked as intended and obtained mostly positive feedback from the users.

Although the "Kiki-Gaki Map" can handle only one track-log (i.e., the data that represents the route along which the holder of a GPS logger proceeds) at a time, one can export each of the track-logs recorded by a number of different persons and/or groups during their town-watch activities and import these track-logs into a general-purpose GIS (Geographic Information System) software, so that all of these track-logs are shown on a digital map and accumulated as more and more data is collected, as shown in Fig. 8.12.

When these pieces of information are collected and accumulated for all town-watch and/or preventive patrol groups in a neighborhood, they may be considered as microlevel indicators of guardianship in that neighborhood, recorded in a form that takes *both space and time* into account.

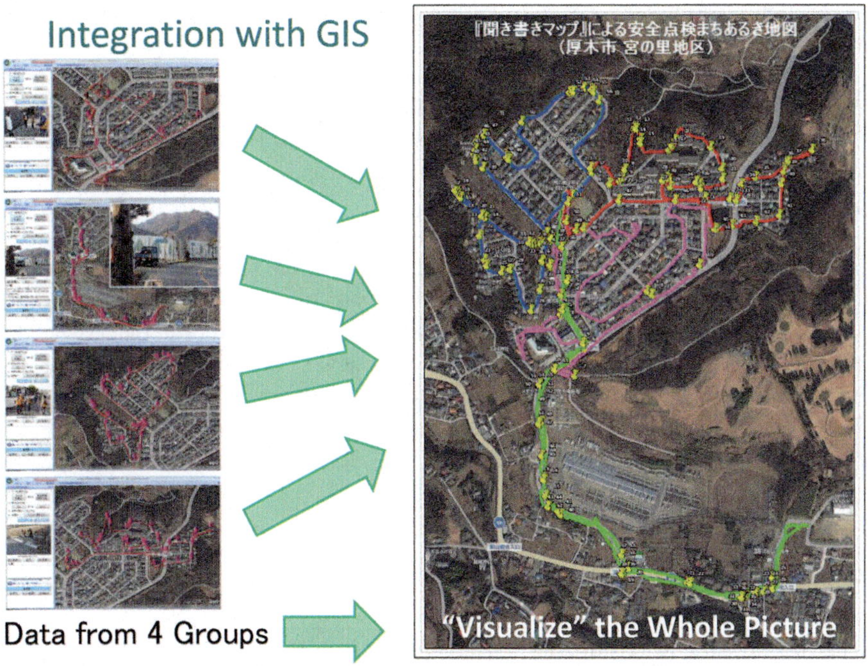

Fig. 8.12 Integrating and visualizing neighborhood-watch activities by crime prevention volunteers using the "Kiki-Gaki Map" and general-purpose GIS

It should be noted, however, that the GPS, a satellite positioning system developed by the United States, has a well-known weakness in that the positioning accuracy goes down significantly in large urban settings due to reflected waves from high-rise buildings. This is a particularly serious weakness for crime prevention research and practice because crime problems are often associated with densely populated urban areas. Fundamental solutions to overcome this weakness are urgently needed.

4 Discussion

The results of these pilot studies strongly suggest that (a) the routine activities of potential targets of crime (e.g., elementary school students) and guardians (e.g., crime prevention volunteers) can be tracked and recorded with reasonable accuracy using low-cost, easy-to-use satellite positioning devices such as GPS loggers; (b) the survey of criminal victimization and potentially dangerous incidents may be a preferable candidate for the dependent variable in testing routine activity theory, since a considerable number of these incidents are not reported to official institutions; and (c) although the GPS works reasonably well in suburban and rural settings, the level of positioning accuracy tends to be far less than satisfactory in highly urbanized settings, which is where crime problems tend to be most overwhelming.

With the hope of overcoming the problem of poor GPS positioning accuracy in urban settings, we aim to make our toolkits compatible with the Quasi-Zenith Satellite System (QZSS), the latest Japanese satellite positioning infrastructure that is scheduled to go into full-scale operation in the year 2018 (National Space Policy Secretariat, Cabinet Office, 2015).

It is expected that QZSS will provide much better positioning accuracy in urban settings, as well as in mountainous areas, than the current GPS. Further, its benefits will not be limited to Japan but also spread in many other countries in Asia and the Pacific region because of the satellites' special figure-8-shaped orbit that covers the region. We are eagerly looking forward to this new system and are making every effort to promote its application in the area of crime prevention and community safety promotion, which has had little connection with space technology until very recently.

5 Conclusion

The use of satellite positioning technology, in combination with routine activity theory, may have great practical implications in the area of community-based crime prevention. By recording the routine activities of potential targets and capable guardians, one may make inferences about the places where, and the times when, potential crime targets are present and capable guardians are absent in a given community. Such pieces of information can then be used for space-time-focused efforts for the prevention of victimization in high-vulnerability situations. In this way, routine activity theory may prove to be a guiding theoretical framework for the everyday practice of community-based crime prevention.

Acknowledgments This work was supported by JSPS KAKENHI (Grant-in-Aid for Challenging Exploratory Research), Grant Number 25560395.

The preceding study, in which the first version of the "Kiki-Gaki Map" was developed, was supported by the Research Institute of Science and Technology for Society (RISTEX).

References

Amemiya, M. (2013). Estimating on-street crime victimization risk using person trip survey data [in Japanese]. *Papers and Proceedings of the Geographic Information Systems Association of Japan*, CD-ROM, 22.

Center for Problem-Oriented Policing. (2003). *A theory of crime problems*. Retrieved from http://www.popcenter.org/learning/pam/help/theory.cfm

Clarke, R. V., & Eck, J. (2003). *Become a problem-solving crime analyst*. London: Jill Dando Institute of Crime Science.

Cohen, L. E., & Felson, M. (1979). Social change and crime rate trends: A routine activity approach. *American Sociological Review, 44*, 588–608.

Eck, J. E. (1994). *Drug markets and drug places: A case-control study of the spatial structure of illicit drug dealing.* (Unpublished Ph.D. dissertation). University of Maryland, College Park.

Harada, Y., Kikuchi, G., Arai, T., Amemiya, M., Imai, O., Inoue, Y., & Hirohara, T. (2011). Developing a field note taking support software using continuous sound recording [in Japanese]. *Papers and Proceedings of the Geographic Information Systems Association of Japan*, CD-ROM, 20.

Harada, Y., Saito, T., Yamane, Y., Hosoda, K., & Amemiya, M. (2013). Enhancing the functions of a field note taking support software through test installations [in Japanese]. *Papers and Proceedings of the Geographic Information Systems Association of Japan*, CD-ROM, 22.

Harada, Y. (2012). *The measurement of childhood victimization and the establishment of empirical bases for crime prevention activities* (Final Report [in Japanese]). Tokyo: Research Institute of Science and Technology for Society (RISTEX).

Harada, Y. (2014). Citizen-led safety promotion using the 'Kiki-Gaki (Listen-Write) Map'. [in Japanese] *Japanese. Journal of School Health, 55*, 499–506.

Kikuchi, G., Amemiya, M., & Shimada, T. (2012). An analysis of crime hot spots using GPS tracking data of children and agent-based simulation modeling. *Annals of GIS, 18*, 207–223.

Lemieux, A. M., & Felson, M. (2012). Risk of violent crime victimization during major daily activities. *Violence and Victims, 27*(5), 635–655.

National Space Policy Secretariat, Cabinet Office. (2015). *Overview of the quasi-zenith satellite system (QZSS).* Retrieved from http://qzss.go.jp/en/overview/services/sv01_what.html

Chapter 9
Analysis of Current Criminals in Japan Based on Typology of Relationships with Others

Kyoko Fujino

1 Introduction

Psychologists who treat juvenile delinquents and adult criminals tend to interpret the causes of their deviant behavior as due to individual psychological factors, such as personality and distortions of cognition based on medical models. However, psychological treatment is not sufficient for the prevention of delinquency and crime. The environmental context of individuals also influences the promotion or inhibition of deviant behavior. Recently, the importance of the biological-psychological-sociological (biopsychosocial) model has been recognized in the field of psychology. Thought and behavior may change depending on the social context of the person, such as reactions from society and family relationships. The broader cultural context can have various influences, including influence on criminal behavior.

Markus and Kitayama (1991) contend that Asian people have an interdependent view of the self, while European people have an independent view of the self. If their contention is correct, then Asian people will be more influenced by others than European people. In this context, I will discuss how people promote or deter actions of crime in relationships with others.

First of all, I classify four patterns of relationships of a person with intimates and mainstream society and examine Japanese crime phenomena as related to each pattern. Next, I discuss relationships with others among criminals and delinquents from the viewpoint of developmental psychology, including attachment theory. In this context, I also discuss not only self-control presented by Gottfredson and Hirschi (1990) but also bonds such as attachments to others, as presented by Hirschi (1969), which work to deter deviant activities. In addition, I discuss how relationships develop among law-abiding people and among antisocial people.

K. Fujino (✉)
Department of Letters, Arts and Sciences, Waseda University, Tokyo, Japan
e-mail: fujino@waseda.jp

J. Liu, S. Miyazawa (eds.), *Crime and Justice in Contemporary Japan*,
Springer Series on Asian Criminology and Criminal Justice Research,
https://doi.org/10.1007/978-3-319-69359-0_9

Furthermore, I mention whether or not shame, the feeling brought about by the relationship with others, contributes to deterring or promoting further crimes. In this context, I refer to reintegration involving shaming, as presented by Braithwaite (1989). Then, I introduce some recent attempts for social reintegration of criminals and delinquents in Japan.

2 Degree of Influence by Others

Markus and Kitayama (1991) provide the results of experiments that indicate Asian people are more influenced by others than European people. Then, they propose a model indicating that Asian people have an interdependent view of the self, namely, that specific others are included within the boundaries of the self. In contrast, European people have an independent view of the self, where even intimate people are located outside of the self.

According to Markus and Kitayama, people in different cultures have strikingly different constructions of the self, of others, and of the interdependence of the two. The independent self, as found in European people, is separate from the social context, while the dependent self, as found in Asian people, connects with the social context. In other words, the structure of the former is bounded, unitary, and stable, while the latter is flexible and variable.

In Japanese, the word *jibun* means self. Writing in Japanese using Chinese characters, *jibun* includes not only the meaning of "self" but also the meaning of "share": thus *jibun* refers to "one's share of the shared life space." The Japanese culture has a distinctive conception of individuality that insists on the fundamental relatedness of individuals to each other.

The Japanese language has many words for "I" which are used depending on the audience and context. For instance, when a female talks to her child, she uses the word *okasan* or *mama* to refer to herself. She uses the word *watashi* in the presence of her friends, while she may use the word *watakushi*, which gives a more formal impression, in her ceremonial speech. Nisbett (2003) refers to research showing that Japanese tend to describe themselves in particular contexts, while Americans tend to describe themselves without specifying context. Thus for the Japanese, selfness is not a constant like the ego, but denotes a fluid concept which changes with time and situation according to interpersonal relationships. On the other hand, American and Western European languages use neither, nor do they assume such overt valuing of connectedness among individuals.

Hall (1976) introduced the notion of "low-context" versus "high-context" societies to capture differences in self-understanding. The differences may come from their views of humanity. Westerners believe that humans can freely manipulate their environment for their own purposes, while Japanese reject that belief and instead believe that humans adjust themselves to their environment. The Japanese proverb *deru kui wa utareru* means the peg that stands out is pounded down. This suggests that maintaining harmonious social relations is more important than showing off individual excellence.

In this context, we may understand behavior including crime in relationship with the situation, particularly in Asia.

Yamagishi (2010) presents the concept of "action depending on frequency," which means that the larger the number of people who select an action grows, the more others will also select that action. His research asks students whether they would join in to stop bullying in situations where different numbers of classmates try to stop bullying. His findings show that the greater the number of people who attempt to stop bullying becomes, the greater the number of people who join in to stop bullying will increase.

The phenomenon of action depending on frequency may be applied to the phenomenon of crime, which would imply that crime may increase rapidly once many people engage in crime. Fortunately, the crime rate is low in Japan, but there is a risk that this could change in the future.

From the viewpoint of interpersonal development, the stage of maintaining friendships and accepting the differences of others is more mature than those who are not conscious of individual differences. The latter may try to behave similarly to others in order to be accepted by others. Thus, a society which forces conformity with others might be composed of people at a more immature stage of interpersonal relationships. In this context, Western people might be considered to be more mature in interpersonal relationships than Asian people. However, there may be different in interpersonal development between Asian people and Western people. Markus and Kitayama (1991) indicate that conformity in Asian people may be explained by cultural differences of self-construction.

Yamagishi (2010), from a different viewpoint, asserts that people in Asian societies cooperate with others because they know that this cooperation benefits their own welfare. Since the Japanese social structure brings people together to take advantage of cooperation with others, Japanese people may cooperate with others according to their calculation of loss and gain. However, this social structure is beginning to be destroyed in the trend of Westernization within Japan.

If Yamagishi's insight is correct, then the degree of influence by others may decrease in the near future in Japan. It is necessary to pay attention to this trend. However, at least for the present in Japan, focusing on relationships with others is effective as a countermeasure for the prevention of crime.

3 Various Contexts where Crime Occurs

Crime is an act of breaking a law. How the individual views the mainstream society, which consists of the government which makes the laws and governs based on them and the people who support the government, influences the individual's decisions about committing crimes.

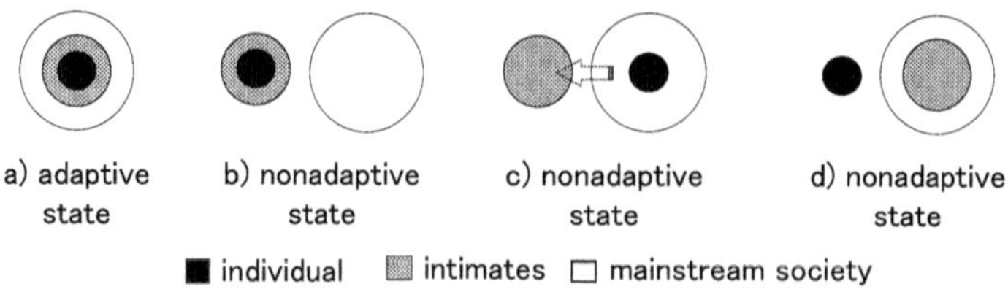

Fig. 9.1 Relationship of individual to intimates and mainstream society

In addition, people do not receive equal amounts of influence from everyone. People are influenced more strongly by intimates than by non-intimates. Fujino and Naganuma (2013), using a bullying situation in the classroom, demonstrate this. It is a truism that bullying should not be permitted in our society irrespective of the relationship to the victims of bullying. However, research indicates that people feel that bullying conducted by intimates is more acceptable than bullying conducted by non-intimates. In addition, bullying of non-intimates is considered more permissible than bullying of intimates. Thus, the intimacy level of the persons influences peoples' judgment and behavior.

Figure 9.1 presents conceptual diagrams which show the relationships of the individual to intimates and mainstream society. I use the four patterns shown in Fig. 9.1 to discuss crime phenomena and criminological theory. I particularly contend that the criminal's relationship to others is important for understanding crime in Japan.

Figure 9.1a shows the situation where both the individual and his or her intimates belong to mainstream society. This is an adaptive state. The person typed in Fig. 9.1a is a socially integrated individual. On the other hand, Fig. 9.1b–d shows several types of nonadaptive states.

Figure 9.1b shows that both the individual and his or her intimates do not belong to mainstream society. The person typed in Fig. 9.1b is the individual in a deviant subculture. Members of *boryokudan*, antisocial groups indigenous to Japan which are similar to criminal gangs, are a typical example of Fig. 9.1b because they spend their daily life mainly with other members of the *boryokudan*.

The social structure approach in criminology focuses on the crime phenomena corresponding to Fig. 9.1b. Cohen's theory of delinquent subculture is an example. According to Cohen (1955), people in the lower class felt that the social system and social order are established as reflections of the values of people in the middle class, and consequently they believe that the mainstream society does not benefit them. In this context, they form their own unique culture and cope with their actual circumstances by themselves, disregarding the social order of the mainstream society.

It is understandable that people would ignore the social order of mainstream society if they feel that the mainstream society does not care about them and their intimates. In this context, how people regard the mainstream society influences their motivation for following the rules within that mainstream society.

Figure 9.1c shows the situation where the individuals stay in the mainstream society, while their intimates do not belong to the mainstream society. The person typed in Fig. 9.1c is a conflicted individual. His or her intimates may have recently moved from the mainstream society to an antisocial group. Individuals may have good friendships with those in antisocial groups while not noticing their deviancy.

The situation induces individuals to be deviant since people are influenced more strongly by intimates than by non-intimates, as shown in Fujino and Naganuma (2013). Therefore, their level of resistance to deviant behavior will be lowered by observing their intimates' deviant behavior, even if the intimates do not actively tempt them to join their antisocial group.

Figure 9.1d shows the situation where the individual is isolated from not only mainstream society but also from intimates. In Fig. 9.1d, the borderline between the mainstream society and intimates is not shown, and the color shown for the intimates is a lighter gray than the color in Fig. 9.1a–c. This description indicates that the individual may not have intimates. The person typed in Fig. 9.1d is an asocial individual.

A representative case illustrating Fig. 9.1d would be to commit a crime alone in order to attract others' attention. One example is the so-called Akihabara indiscriminate bloodshed case where seven people were killed and ten people were wounded by a male aged 25 in Akihabara, Tokyo, on June 8, 2008. After he drove his truck into a pedestrian area and hit pedestrians, he stepped out of the truck and, brandishing a knife, stabbed one bystander after another.

After the incident, the perpetrator testified that he decided to commit the crime to get people to notice his existence, because he was solitary not only in the real world but also in the world of the Internet at the time. The aim of crimes like this is not restricted to obtaining something directly. In this case, he might get both stimulation in his boring life and others' attention. He might seek to escape and/or avoid the situation where he had difficulty adjusting by means of being arrested for the crime.

While I classify the above four patterns, there are no external criteria for making the judgment about belonging to the mainstream society. Each person subjectively judges the position of the self and intimates within the society. However, whether or not people identify themselves and their intimates as members of the mainstream society is important because their consciousness of this membership influences their law-abiding behavior in the mainstream society, as social identity theory posits. How one deals with the individual subjectivities is the key to deterring crimes.

4 Trends of Isolated Delinquents and Criminals in Japan

The types of people who become delinquents and criminals change according to the circumstances of that particular society. Recent trends in Japanese crime and delinquency show that the pattern of asocial individuals classified in Fig. 9.1d seems to be increasing, while the pattern of individuals in deviant subculture classified in Fig. 9.1b seems to be decreasing.

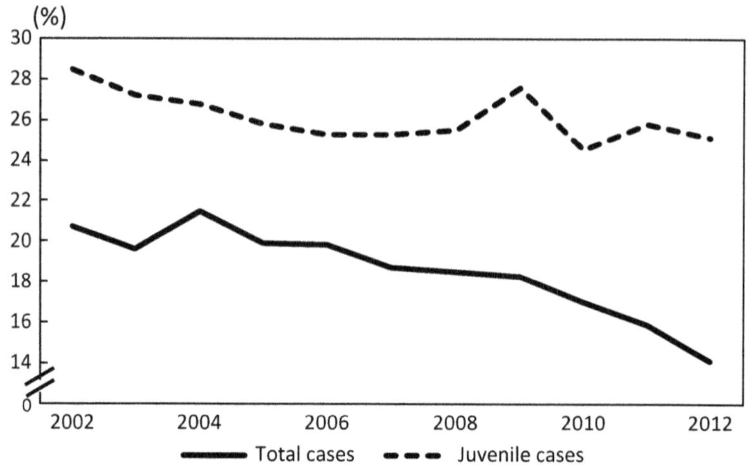

Fig. 9.2 The complicity rate for people who have been cleared of charges for non-traffic penal code offenses. Note: The data are from white paper on crime 2012

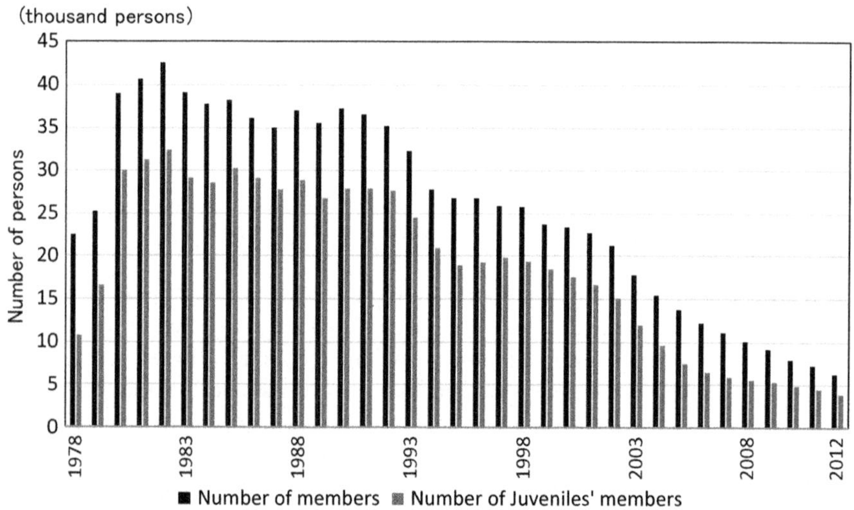

Fig. 9.3 The number of members of *bosozoku*. Note: The data are from white paper on crime 2012

For instance, the complicity rate (i.e., when two or more people conspire to commit a crime) for people who have been cleared of charges for non-traffic penal code offenses has been decreasing in recent years, as shown in Fig. 9.2. The behavior patterns seen in criminal activity may be reflected in their patterns of daily behavior. In this context, recently criminals and delinquents seem to act alone.

Recently, the number of members of *bosozoku*, motorcycle gangs composed mainly of juvenile delinquents, has decreased remarkably, as shown in Fig. 9.3. Generally speaking, juvenile delinquents in Japan have not teamed up into groups.

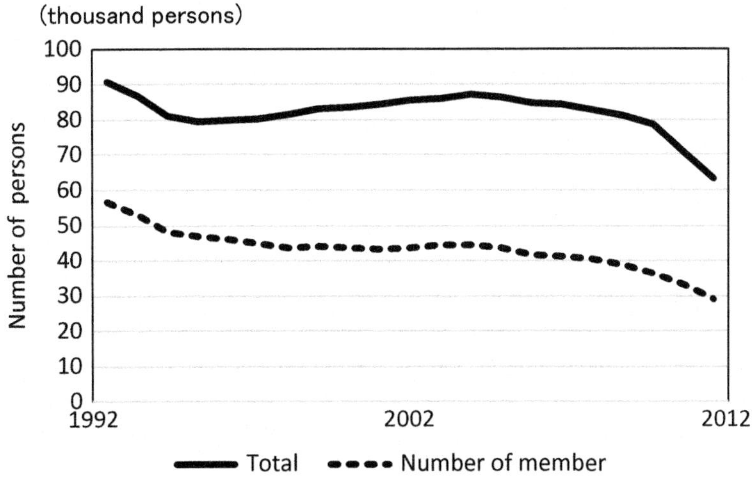

Fig. 9.4 The number of members of *boryokudan*. Note: The data are from white paper on crime 2012. The total numbers indicate the number of members and associate members

This phenomenon is not limited to juvenile delinquency, such as *bosozoku*. The number of members of *boryokudan*, adult gangs, is also decreasing. While the number of members and associate members of *boryokudan*, respectively, was 56,600 and 34,000 in 1992, in 2012 they were 28,800 and 34,400 (white paper on crime 2012) (Fig. 9.4).

In the 1980s, some members of motorcycle gangs said that it was fun to race with police, and other members said that they demonstrated their existence through their motorcycle gang's activity, including reckless driving. Although their behavior is not legal, their explanation of their motivation indicates that they take notice of mainstream society and seek to connect to it. On the other hand, recently juveniles have become extremely self-focused. As long as they feel that their desires are not directly interfered with, they tend to be indifferent toward mainstream society.

In summary, a recent trend in Japan is that asocial people who lack sociability, rather than antisocial people who try to oppose the existing mainstream society, tend to commit crimes. In this context, rather than fighting against their rejection of mainstream society, encouragement to help them adjust to the mainstream society may be an effective measure for reducing crime.

5 Attachment to Others

To examine interpersonal relationships, I use the concept of attachment presented by Hirschi (1969). According to his bonding theory, one element which deters crime is attachment to others. His work is influenced by Bowlby, who posits that having a secure attachment in early childhood is developmentally important.

Starting off at a disadvantage does not necessarily mean having to finish up at a disadvantage: early disadvantages do not inevitably set off a chain reaction of more and more disadvantages (Schaffer, 2004). However, since the child's first relationship tends to be a prototype of relationships in general, failure to develop an attachment of any kind is likely to affect adversely subsequent relationships. If people cannot develop attachment to their parents, it will be difficult for them to attach to other people such as teachers and classmates.

From the viewpoint of deterrence of delinquency and crime, those who do not develop an attachment to parents in a poor parenting environment may have difficulty imagining their parents' upset expression when they are motivated to commit crimes. In the same way, for people who have no attachment to law-abiding peers, the existence of law-abiding peers does not work as a deterrent from delinquency and crime.

In addition, the experience of maintaining relationships with others contributes to developing psychological functions. For instance, in order to maintain a relationship, people consider other parties' viewpoints and take responsibility for their own behavior. In this process, they cannot be selfish.

Even if people have secure attachment in early childhood, they may become criminals through various pathways based on experiences in later life. However, since those who do not have a secure attachment to others are at high risk of becoming maladjusted to society in general from the early period of their lives, the onset of their criminal behavior tends to start early. Delinquents and criminals who do not have secure attachments tend to be classified as the asocial individuals shown in Fig. 9.1d because the situation shown in Fig. 9.1d refers to people who are not attached to anyone. For these people, accumulation of experiences of healthy relationships with others is necessary. Thus, interventions that help them develop secure attachments may be important.

Whether the relationships among delinquents are weaker than the relationships among nondelinquents remains a contentious issue; both possibilities will be considered. Delinquents and criminals who did not develop secure attachments in early childhood tend to have a weak relationship with others, including other delinquents and criminals. On the other hand, delinquents and criminals who did develop secure attachments may become attached to deviant peers and criminal peers, which may facilitate deviant behavior.

Since Hirschi proposed another theory, self-control theory, with Gottfredson (Gottfredson and Hirschi, 1990), I will discuss the relationship between the bonding theory and the self-control theory, which many criminologists also have discussed. My research focuses on how concepts used in the above two theories influence delinquent activities. In my research (Fujino, 2006), the concepts related to the theories are interpreted broadly in psychological research, not restricted to the definitions of the theory, since the purpose of the research is not verification of these two theories in a strict sense.

According to Gottfredson and Hirschi (1990), low self-control is a synonym for criminality, that is, individual criminal tendencies which are formed in their life experiences in communication with surrounding people. In other words, low

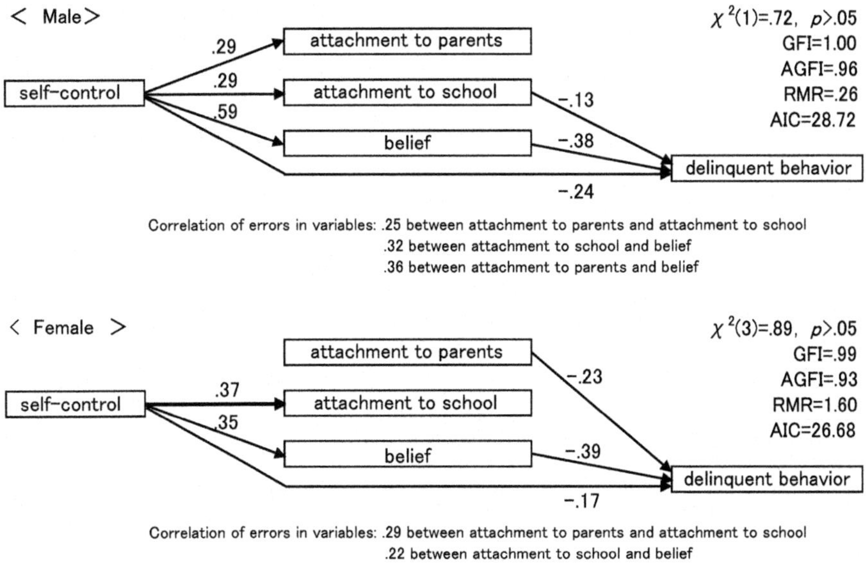

Fig. 9.5 Relationship of self-control and bonds to delinquent behavior. Note: Result of covariance structure analysis for research of Fujino (2006). The numbers indicate estimates of standardized regression weight

self-control is a latent factor of crime related to traits. According to them, once this tendency is formed in the infancy stage, it is assumed that it does not change in later life.

On the other hand, the bonding theory of Hirschi (1969) focuses on the individual situations related to deterring crimes. While Hirschi did not refer to the stability of the bond, it looks changeable based on the experiences of the individual's life.

Based on these considerations, I assumed that self-control might influence bonding since self-control is formed in infancy. Figure 9.5 shows the results of my research on high school students in Japan (Fujino, 2006). In this research, self-control is measured by a Japanese version of self-control scale by Grasmick, Tittle, Bursik, and Arneklev (1993), and bonds are measured by the scales of Nishimura, Suzuki, and Takahashi (1984) who examined bonding theory in Japan.

The results show that attachment to school, as well as belief, is influenced by self-control. Perhaps persons who cannot exercise self-control do not easily become attached to school because the school does not accept behavior which lacks self-control, and sometimes these individuals are criticized or avoid having close relationships. In addition, these persons might not believe in the moral validity of social rules since they cannot obey the rules because of their low self-control.

The results also show that not only bonding but also self-control influences delinquent behavior directly, while the influence of self-control on delinquent behavior is indirect through bonding according to my assumption. The concepts presented in WikstrÖm's situational action theory (WikstrÖm, 2010), propensity and situation, can be applied to these results. The influence of self-control is not restricted within the propensity. The direct influence of self-control on delinquent behavior indicates that those with low self-control tend to have difficulty controlling themselves during exposure to criminogenic settings.

As shown above, self-control is also an important factor in deterring crime. However, bonding directly influences delinquent behavior, and the degree of the influence of bonding is larger than that of self-control in my research. Depending on the correspondence of the surroundings, the strength of bonding might change more easily than the strength of self-control. In this context, to focus on bonds such as relationship to others is effective.

6 Viewpoint of Reciprocal Relationship

While I clarified that having relationships with others is one of the keys to deter crime, how do people select others to maintain relationships? In this context, the viewpoint of reciprocal relationships is useful.

When one person acts toward another, the other reacts. And then the first person reacts to the other's response. In this process, both sides influence each other. Thus, human relationships are reciprocally constructed. In addition, the process is often repeated so that the experience of being on both sides accumulates. Depending on the consequences, some relationships weaken and other relationships are strengthened because people naturally seek pleasure and avoid displeasure.

Here I discuss the process whereby criminals and delinquents come together with those who have similar deviant tendencies, as shown for individuals in deviant subculture in Fig. 9.1b. In some social structures, some persons might have few contacts with law-abiding people. However, in the recent Japanese situation, the crime rate is low and cultural conflict is not severe. Even many members of *boryokudan* want their children to become law-abiding persons, although they regard their own deviant behavior as unavoidably necessary to survive. In other words, all people in Japan have a position as a member of mainstream society as a starting point.

First, I describe how criminals' and delinquents' bonds with law-abiding persons gradually weaken. For instance, A misbehaves, and B, noticing A's misbehavior, scolds A. Then, A reacts with aggressive behavior toward B. B attempts to avoid A's aggressive behavior. Meanwhile, A cuts off the relationship with B by him/herself because A would not like to be excluded or alienated from B.

Next, I describe how the relationship with law-breaking people could be strengthened. Following A's misbehavior, B imitates A's behavior. Then, A's misbehavior is escalated to get into A's stride. Since B praises A's behavior, A feels comfortable. In this process, the relationship deepens.

While the asocial people corresponding to Fig. 9.1d experience only the former, people in deviant subculture corresponding to Fig. 9.1b experience both the above phenomena. To the extent that people corresponding to Fig. 9.1b can maintain interpersonal relationships with someone, they may form secure attachments to others who are not desirable from the viewpoint of mainstream society.

In the field of science, attention tends to be paid to specify causes of a result. However, the abovementioned phenomenon shows that the relation of causes and results is not one-way but more interactive. This perspective is very important.

In criminological theory, Thornberry's interactional theory pays attention to the interactive relationship. For instance, an empirical study showed that less attachment to parents induced delinquent behavior, and the delinquent behavior further induced weaker attachments to parents (Thornberry, Lizotte, Krohn, Farnworth, and Jang, 1991).

Effective intervention would involve breaking this interactive vicious circle. If one person behaves differently as a result of developing communication skills and modifying cognitions, then people in his/her surrounding environment will react differently to this person. At the same time, if these surrounding people act differently, then he/she will change. In other words, change of the sociological factors influences change of the psychological factors, based on the biopsychosocial model.

Of course, people do not change automatically even though their environment changes. Even when parents change their children's living environment in order to cut off friendships with deviant peers, their children may still make new friendships with other deviant peers.

Human nature tends to seek a psychologically comfortable place and settle down there. If people cannot make friends with law-abiding persons or feel happy to be with law-abiding persons, they will seek new friendships with deviant peers in the new place. The key is whether the person feels comfortable in a law-abiding environment.

7 Deterrence of Criminal Behavior by Shame and Guilt

In this section, I discuss two kinds of feelings, shame and guilt, which often occur after people engage in deviant acts. Benedict (1946) described Japan as having a culture of shame, where shame is a feeling brought about within relationships with others.

According to Nisbett (2003), Asians are trained to anticipate the reactions of other people, where they need to coordinate their behavior and blend harmoniously within a network of supportive social relationships. In contrast, Americans tend to overestimate their distinctiveness.

Japanese people use the word *seken*, meaning a community composed of the whole people's group including those who share an interest not only in the past but also in the future. *Seken* is not restricted to specific others, such as intimates. Japanese people tend to feel shame when they do not and/or cannot behave as others in *seken* expect them.

According to Braithwaite (1989), mutual monitoring contributes to the low rate of crime in Japan. Japanese people tend to behave according to others' expectations, as well as expect others to behave consistent with their expectations. Their monitoring of others' behavior, and their feeling of being monitored by others, deters them from engaging in deviant acts such as crimes.

However, once people have engaged in acts which do not seem to be forgiven by the society, how do they then behave? They will fear they are viewed negatively because of their acts and excluded by the society. They may avoid intimate interpersonal relationships in the mainstream society in order to conceal their acts, rather than feel guilt. Thus, they may put themselves in the isolated situation shown in Fig. 9.1d, or they may seek a community composed of deviant people who engage in similar behavior, as shown in Fig. 9.1b. Thus, while the feeling of shame may function as a deterrent for deviant acts at one time, it may function to worsen the situation at a later time.

Braithwaite (1989) presents the idea of shaming for deterring crime. On the other hand, the feeling often referred to after having committed a crime is guilt. How are these feelings different?

According to Benedict (1946), shame has been assumed to be a sign of guilt that is undeveloped, a pre-guilty feeling. From this perspective, shame disappears with the appearance of the guilt. If this assumption is correct, it means that the Japanese people are not psychologically well-developed.

However, this opinion came to be doubted in the 1970s to the 1980s. After the 1990s, research suggested a difference between guilt and shame. For instance, according to Lewis (1971), we feel shame if we focus on the negative act as being influenced by temporary factors such as the situation, while we feel guilty if we attribute the cause to ourselves. Harris (1989) found that the above two feelings can be identified by children as young as age 8.

Braithwaite (1989) insists that society should reintegrate criminals, if they have the mind-set of an apology after society shames the criminals. He suggests that society should not attribute the cause of the crime to criminals themselves.

But what conditions are necessary for an apology? First, the recognition of a causal relation between the event and the act of the person concerned is necessary. Second, the person needs to recognize that what he/she did is harmful to others. People do not apologize if they recognize that their behavior is harmless. Third, the person acknowledges his/her own responsibility to the victim. If people do not recognize their responsibility, then what they say is just an excuse. When the above three conditions are satisfied, we arrive at the act of apology (Tanaka, 2013).

Even if people apologize, others may not accept their apology. Several empirical research studies have shown that an apology without guilt feelings tends not to be accepted. For instance, an apology which is proffered to achieve some purpose, such as creating an impression of evading and/or reducing punishment, typically would not be accepted. An apology not based on guilt feelings but on pity for the victim tends not to be accepted. In addition, an apology which is not voluntary but comes from urging by others is unlikely to be accepted. When the other party feels that the person concerned sincerely wants to apologize, then the personal conflict may move toward a solution. Thus, even if people apologize superficially forced by surrounding people, the victims of the case as well as *seken* may not forgive him/her.

Some criminals and delinquents in Japan do not have strong feelings of guilt. One of the reasons is that they interpret their deviant acts as not very serious and believe they should be overlooked. Another is that their defense mechanism works against the feeling of guilt. For instance, it may be difficult to confront some situations such as fatal incidents because they are irreparable. In this context, it is not difficult to imagine that individuals would rely upon their defense mechanisms, avoid thinking about the incidents, or attribute the causes to others, rather than try to undertake responsibility without the wishful view of being forgiven even if they do their best.

To those who interpret their deviant acts as not so serious, people should show them that most people follow the rules and orders of the society because they are member of the society. Fortunately, Japanese people tend to be sensitive to the influence of others. For those who do not feel guilty because of their defense mechanism, people may contribute to work for their ego strength, because the purpose of defense mechanisms is to protect the ego. People in the community may encourage them through the affirmative evaluation of their efforts in confronting reality, as well as working to develop their ego strength.

8 Recent Attempts to Socially Reintegrate Criminals and Delinquents in Japan

Repeat offenders in Japan often say *seken ga tsumetai*, which means that people in their community treat them indifferently. Of course, some repeat offenders are not motivated to be law-abiding persons from the start. However, others give up on trying to become law-abiding persons along the way. Specifically, they give up because they feel they are excluded when their family refuses to live with them, or they are discriminated against when they are confronted with the difficult reality of becoming employed in the mainstream society.

The public fears crime and tries to keep criminals away as much as possible. This is a natural phenomenon. However, if those who committed crimes once cannot feel that they will ever be treated as members of the mainstream society, then they will ignore the rules and orders of the society. They may re-offend, which becomes a vicious cycle.

A comprehensive strategy for reducing re-offense was constituted by the Japanese government at the Ministerial Meeting Concerning Measures against Crime on July 20, 2012. The strategies include "building and preparing a place where one belongs" and providing "opportunities in the community" and "constructing a supported rehabilitation system, including public understanding." The Ministry of Justice has recruited "cooperating employers" who willingly offer employment to offenders despite their past records and treat them with understanding of their feelings, in the same manner as other workers. At present, about 10,000 such employers are registered throughout Japan (Ministry of Justice website).

In addition, subsidies for work support for criminals have been implemented in collaboration with the Ministry of Health, Labour and Welfare. A subsidy is for promoting trial employment, which is provided to enterprises that employ those released from prison.

Some local public entities have also begun to employ probationers and/or parolees as part-time staff. There are also private initiatives. In 2009, *Keidanren*, the Japan Business Federation, proposed the establishment of a Specified Nonprofit Cooperation National Organization for Employment of Offenders. This organization provides support to employ criminals and education about the importance of employment for deterring further crimes.

These show that understanding and cooperation concerning criminals' employment support has expanded. People are beginning to recognize that deterring further crime by involving only government agencies taking charge of the treatment of criminals is limited. The state will not change for the better as long as criminals are excluded from mainstream society. Therefore, various attempts to reintegrate criminals in society are being devised by different types of social groups.

The number of criminals applying to these support programs is not large, since many want to conceal their past crimes from employers and the community. However, being employed and continuing to work means not only getting money to live but also being accepted as a member of society. Through supportive social experiences, criminals may gain motivation to readjust to mainstream society.

Restorative justice aims to enable criminals to take responsibility for their crimes by engaging in activities of compensation, going beyond simple verbal apologies. Since the apology is embodied in the activity, restorative justice approaches may offer constructive ways for some resolution of the effects of crime.

However, many criminals and delinquents in Japan want to conclude their case at the time of the punishment, such as incarceration and fines. While a lot of criminals and delinquents consider their future without anticipating similar offenses, there are not very many criminals and delinquents who reflect on their own attempts at compensation for their past criminal behavior with feelings of guilt. Many of them desire to forget their past offenses, if possible.

Ideally, after compensation for the crime is completed, people should be reintegrated into mainstream society. However, as discussed in the previous section, many criminals and delinquents do not develop enough ego strength to confront their own serious reality, such as their past failures. Because of this, in Japan, measures for deterring re-offense place emphasis on readjustment to mainstream society rather than on compensation for past crimes.

9 Conclusion

Since Japanese people live in a high-context society, the influence of the social environment is large. Using this context, this paper has focused on relationships with others for deterring crimes and delinquency.

I have identified four patterns of relationships of individuals to intimates and mainstream society, as shown in Fig. 9.1. I have discussed measures for deterring crimes for each pattern.

Using statistical data, such as the complicity rate and the number of members of *bosozoku* and *boryokudan*, this paper indicates the phenomenon represented in Fig. 9.1d has increased recently in Japan. Compared with the phenomenon represented in Fig. 9.1b, these criminals' ability to develop and maintain interpersonal relationships, such as attachments, tends to be a problem because they stay alone. In this context, to prevent recidivism, psychological treatment for developing healthy interpersonal relationships, such as facilitating secure attachments to others and training in interpersonal skills, may be necessary. In addition, it is important that they believe they can come back as members of mainstream society, and the people in the mainstream society expect them to. Recent provisions to offer employment for criminals and delinquents may encourage them to become reintegrated into mainstream society. How to support them so that they do not give up trying to become law-abiding people is an important task for society.

To help prevent criminals of the type shown in Fig. 9.1c from returning to an antisocial subculture, it is important that they develop many interpersonal relationships in the mainstream society. Even if some intimates begin to belong to an antisocial group and tempt them to participate in an antisocial subculture, they may stay in the mainstream society because they want to maintain friendships with others in that society. In addition, their friends in mainstream society may persuade them not to associate with others in an antisocial subculture.

Individuals who persist in relationships with intimates in an antisocial subculture often do not have other relationships. Since they are afraid of being alone, they may seek to maintain those relationships. In addition, many of those vaguely feel that they do not fit in the mainstream society. Therefore, they may accept invitations from antisocial people because they share similar feelings toward mainstream society. Removing or reducing these feelings can be effective.

For those criminals of the type shown in Fig. 9.1b, the focus is how their attitudes toward the mainstream society, as well as that of their intimates, can change in a positive way. Mainstream society should examine the content of their dissatisfaction. If their dissatisfaction partly corresponds to realities in the mainstream society, then society should take some countermeasures.

For the treatment of criminals and delinquents, the risk-need-responsivity model presented by Andrews and Bonta (2010) has attracted positive attention. This model proffers that the treatment of criminals should focus on matters related to crime. On the other hand, the Good Lives Model proposed by Ward (2012) has recently gained influence. This model stresses that clarification of the values of the person concerned is important. Treatment should be provided leading to the realization of their values because human nature is "people do not change their behavior until they feel they can select their behavior and they take responsibility for their behavior."

Even if society forces people to obey rules and laws, people may not follow them. Japanese society has a low rate of crime since most people in Japan feel that they do not benefit by committing crimes or by dropping out of mainstream society.

The mission of society to reduce crime is to establish an attractive society where (potential) criminals and delinquents can cooperate with others and realize their desires more easily in mainstream society than outside of that society.

References

Andrews, D. A., & Bonta, J. (2010). Rehabilitating criminal justice policy and practice. *Psychology, Public Policy, and Law, 16*, 39–55.

Benedict, R. (1946). *The chrysanthemum and the sword.* Boston, MA: Houghton Mifflin.

Braithwaite, J. (1989). *Crime, shame, and reintegration*. Cambridge: Cambridge University Press.

Cohen, A. (1955). *Delinquent boys*. New York: Free Press.

Fujino, K. (2006). The relationship between social bond and self-control: Outcomes of the survey for high school students. In *The Japanese Journal of Sociological Criminology, 33th Annual Conference*, 55–56. (In Japanese).

Fujino, K., & Naganuma, Y. (2013). Contributions of situational and personal factors to third party's reactions to bullying. *Japanese Journal of Criminal Psychology, 50*(1), 1–13. (In Japanese).

Gottfredson, M. R., & Hirschi, T. (1990). *A general theory of crime*. Stanford, CA: Stanford University Press.

Grasmick, H. G., Tittle, C. R., Bursik, R. J., & Arneklev, B. J. (1993). Testing the core empirical implications of Gottfredson and Hirschi's general theory of crime. *Journal of Research in Crime and Delinquency, 30*(1), 5–29.

Harris, P. (1989). *Children and emotion: The development of psychological understanding*. New York: Basil Blackwell.

Hall, E. T. (1976). *Beyond culture*. New York: Anchor Books.

Hirschi, T. (1969). *Causes of delinquency*. Berkeley and Los Angeles, CA: University of California Press.

Lewis, M. (1971). *Shame and guilt in neurosis*. New York: International Universities Press.

Markus, H. R., & Kitayama, S. (1991). Culture and the self: Implications for cognition, emotion, and motivation. *Psychological Review, 98*, 224–253.

Nisbett, R. E. (2003). *The geography of thought*. New York: Free Press.

Nishimura, H., Suzuki, S., & Takahashi, Y. (1984). Comparison Study of inhabitation of delinquency and promotion of delinquency: Examination of control theory. *Reports of the National Research Institute of Police Science, 25*(2), 107–117. (In Japanese).

Schaffer, H. R. (2004). *Introducing child psychology*. Oxford: Blackwell Publishing.

Tanaka, A. (2013). *Cognitive developmental psychology of apologies and feelings of guilt*. Tokyo: Nakanishiya Press. (In Japanese).

Thornberry, T. P., Lizotte, A. J., Krohn, M. D., Farnworth, M., & Jang, S. J. (1991). Testing interactional theory: An examination of reciprocal causal relationships among family, school, and delinquency. *The Journal of Criminal Law and Criminology, 82*(1), 3–35.

Ward, T. (2012). The rehabilitation of offenders: Risk management and seeking good lives. *Japanese Journal of Offenders Rehabilitation, 1*, 57–76.

Wikström, P.-O. H. (2010). Explaining crime as moral actions. In S. Hitlin & S. Vaisey (Eds.), *Handbook of the sociology of morality* (pp. 211–239). New York: Springer Science.

Yamagishi, T. (2010). *Mind-heavy Japanese: Illusion of groupism culture*. Tokyo: Chikuma-shobo. (In Japanese).

Resources

Ministry of Justice (http://www.moj.go.jp/ENGLISH/RB/rb-01.html). Rehabilitation bureau: What is the rehabilitation of offenders?

Research and Training Institute of the Ministry of Justice. (2012). *White paper on crime 2012*.

Part III
Challenges and Trends in Criminal Justice Reform

Chapter 10
Considering Japanese Criminal Justice from an Original Position

Mark A. Levin

> The African American community is also knowledgeable that there is a history of racial disparities in the application of our criminal laws -- everything from the death penalty to enforcement of our drug laws. (Obama 2013)
>
> Prosecutor: What? You are being tricky, aren't you? Why don't you look me in the eye when you say such things? You haven't looked me in the eye much for quite a while.
>
> Sugaya: I'm sorry. I'm very sorry. Sorry, please stop this. Please, please stop doing this to me. Please stop doing this to me... I'm sorry.[1]

1 Learning from Differences

For over 20 years, I have had the good fortune to teach Japanese law at the William S. Richardson Law School at the University of Hawai'i. Every year, we cover a range of topics including history, constitutional law, legal education and legal careers, business transactions, and of course criminal justice. My lesson plan for the course includes the 2007 film by Director Masayuki Suo titled "I Just Didn't Do It," which tells a story of a young man accused of groping on a crowded Tokyo commuter train who maintains his innocence through an investigation, trial, and conviction. It dramatically portrays Japan's system as a failure that is woefully indifferent

Mark A. Levin, Professor of Law and Director, Pacific-Asian Legal Studies Program, of the William S. Richardson School of Law, the University of Hawai'i at Mānoa, Honolulu, Hawai'i, United States. Thanks to Professors David Johnson and Lawrence Repeta for thoughtful comments on an earlier draft of this article. Of course, any errors or omissions are mine. This article is dedicated to the memory of Justice Shigemitsu Dando, a courageous campaigner for criminal justice in Japan. I treasure my autographed copy of his *Shikei Haishi Ron*.

[1] Transcript of a tape recording of murder suspect Toshikazu Sugaya recorded during interrogations on December 7 and 8, 1992. Despite repeatedly recanting a confession he had given under duress in the interrogations, Sugaya was convicted and incarcerated for 17 years before being fully exonerated by modern DNA testing.

M.A. Levin (✉)
William S. Richardson School of Law, University of Hawai'i at Mānoa, Honolulu, HI, USA
e-mail: levin@hawaii.edu

J. Liu, S. Miyazawa (eds.), *Crime and Justice in Contemporary Japan*, Springer Series on Asian Criminology and Criminal Justice Research,
https://doi.org/10.1007/978-3-319-69359-0_10

to the rights of an accused. As the story is told, viewers seem likely to conclude that criminal justice reform is urgently necessary in Japan.

My students are always surprised by the story. After we watch the film together, my students, even those who have previously lived or worked in Japan, often express disbelief that circumstances could be as the film portrays. Recently, one student described herself as "incensed," concluding that "the film not only illustrates the difference between the American and Japanese criminal systems but also highlights the lack of fairness in the Japanese system."

Some years ago, we had a former Japanese judge sit in the class and attend the film showing. His comments, based upon over 5 years of experience with criminal matters, were also shocking to my students. Though they expected him to deny the essence of the film, he instead confirmed it. He thought the film correctly showed criminal justice as he had witnessed it. He deeply feared that the system may be failing to protect the public from wrongful convictions.[2]

With this, I wonder what causes these diametrically opposing perceptions. And I wonder what Japanese people who are not legal professionals or otherwise associated with the criminal justice system think of the film's story. Would most Japanese people leave the film "shocked?" Would most be "incensed?" I hope so, yet these are certainly interesting questions that I don't know the answers to.

I agree with my student that the film illustrates a difference between the American and Japanese criminal justice systems. However, I think the main point is not whether either system achieves perfect fairness. Neither does. Both nations deserve criticism, though for different major flaws, and arguably, circumstances in the United States are far worse, particularly for suspects and convicted persons of color.[3]

For me, however, there are also key differences with regard to *public perceptions* and *social engagement*. Who in the two populations will be sufficiently *informed* and actively *engaged* in order to ensure grassroots pressure for positive change, especially with regard to protecting the interests of suspects and convicted persons?

As I observe criminal justice reform efforts in the two nations, my clear impression is that Japan's reform process is driven almost entirely by legal and governmental elites; there is little participation by the broader public.[4] In contrast, US legal elites have historically engaged with powerful community interests with regard to debates over criminal justice policy. Though debates in the United States may be polarized,

[2] I do not have permission to share this judge's name. However, his views match those recently published by Hiroshi Segi. Concerning the same film, Segi writes: "frankly, this movie was neither particularly shocking nor interesting for me. The reason is that any right-minded legal professional knows that the situation portrayed in the movie can happen anytime in Japan's criminal justice system" (Segi, 2014, p. 146).

[3] Professor Michelle Alexander's profound work, *The New Jim Crow: Mass Incarceration in the Age of Colorblindness*, a compelling and distressing account of the horrific social failure of the US system, may be the best place to begin learning more (Alexander, 2012; see also Davis, 2007).

[4] Exceptions are vocal interests supporting stronger victims' rights protections, described below. Another crucial exception is the important work done by the Buraku Liberation League in partnership with the International Movement Against All Forms of Discrimination and Racism—Japan Committee (IMADR-JC).

justice reform efforts in the United States ordinarily include voices from communities that identify with and aim to protect suspects and convicted persons, particularly minority communities of color.

This difference may have much to tell us. I believe that differing perceptions concerning criminal justice substantially arise from differences in perceptions of social homogeneity, including perceptions of racial or ethnic homogeneity, in the two nations. And I hope that this insight can help guide the people of Japan toward a more just society in better compliance with the nation's fundamental international human rights obligations.[5]

2 Hoping and Waiting for Improvement in Japan

It would be challenging to catalog and explain all of my concerns with regard to Japan's criminal justice system in the limited space here. I briefly mention three concerns, leaving the door open for more careful explanations by other authors and omitting many important topics.[6]

First is Japan's extraordinary reliance upon interrogations of suspects in oppressive circumstances during sustained police custody opportunities, which may continue for days or weeks in isolated police holding cells, with minimal opportunity for meaningful oversight by an attorney on behalf of the suspect.

The problems in this area pertain to many elements of criminal investigations in Japan, including the duty to submit to questioning, the continuing use of "substitute prisons" (*daiyō kangoku*), questionable use of voluntary accompaniment, and arrest for separate incidents, all of which have been criticized by lawyers and scholars in Japan as well as international human rights organizations.[7] And all of which have come to light especially with regard to horrifying stories of convictions and sentences to lengthy imprisonments or death later discovered to have been erroneous, leading to dramatic stories in the news recently.[8]

These issues all relate to a powerful desire to procure confessions from suspects. This is so much that my colleague David Johnson has described confessions as "the

[5] My choice here to write "obligations" as compared to "norms" is because these are not merely matters of ethics and morality, but are directly tied to *legal commitments* by Japan pursuant to international human rights law, particularly its obligations under the Universal Declaration of Human Rights and the International Covenant on Civil and Political Rights.

[6] For example, problems concerning the adequacy of court interpretation at criminal trials for non-native speakers of Japanese.

[7] For example, the United Nations Human Rights Committee's action of April 15, 2013, adopting a Working Group Report with harsh criticisms of Japan on all of these issues.

[8] The 2014 release of Mr. Iwao Hakamada after 46 years on death row became famous in the news, just as Mr. Sugaya's exoneration after 17 years of imprisonment in 2009. It was deeply regrettable that prosecutors decided to appeal against his release, though without success to date (see Johnson, 2015; McNeill, 2016).

heart" of Japanese criminal justice (Johnson, 2002, p. 243).[9] Sadly, however, this intransigent force in the Japanese system underlies the limited quality of recent reforms. Until May 2016, perhaps the only recent countermeasure was to begin partial video recording of interrogations, which may in some ways be a step backward, while all of the other structures remained firmly in place.[10]

Contrast then Justice Arthur Goldberg's astute writing in the famous 1964 US Supreme Court decision of *Escobedo* vs. *Illinois*:

> We have learned the lesson of history, ancient and modern, that a system of criminal law enforcement which comes to depend on the "confession" will, in the long run, be less reliable and more subject to abuses than a system which depends on extrinsic evidence independently secured through skillful investigation.... (Escobedo, 1964, pp. 488–489)

The Escobedo decision may be less famous in Japan than its successor, Miranda v. Arizona (1996),[11] but *Escobedo* (more so even than *Miranda*) suggests a vast difference between practices in Japan and the US. *Escobedo* precisely rejects Japan's so-called duty to submit to questioning and the national government's systematic refusal to allow legal counsel to be present with suspects who wish to have a lawyer with them during interrogation. Moreover, *Escobedo's* rationale highlights where reform is still vitally necessary for Japan. Neither the introduction of Japan's lay judge system in 2009 nor the use of partial video recording of interrogations sufficiently improves the troubling circumstances here.

The second problem that I wish to focus on is Japan's death penalty. For purposes of my discussion, I set aside the fundamental human rights question of whether or not the death penalty should exist at all.[12] However, if one allows that a nation ought to be able to impose and carry out the death penalty in its criminal justice system, then it becomes all the more important that the nation adheres to the highest responsibilities in terms of fairness and procedural justice in doing so. Unfortunately, Japan is far from the goal.[13]

In this, once again, Professor Johnson provides an insightful report. Unfortunately, we learn from him how Japan's system fails in numerous respects:

> Japan has capital punishment, but it does not have capital trials.... In Japan this means that there are no special guarantees for ensuring adequate representation by defense counsel even when the defendant's life is at stake, there is no special sentencing hearing separate from the adjudication of guilt (where a variety of factors could be carefully considered), and there are no special rights to appeal or request clemency. There is not even a requirement for judges and lay judges to agree that a death sentence is deserved—a mere "mixed major-

[9] See also Foote (1991).

[10] As to legislative actions in May 2016 and since, see below.

[11] *Miranda* restated the rule from *Escobedo* and then obligated police authorities to meaningfully advise suspects of their rights.

[12] I oppose the death penalty, but I repeat that my writing here pertains to how the death penalty is imposed and carried out in Japan, rather than whether it should continue.

[13] The United States also misses. As a starting point, see, for example, McCleskey v. Kemp (1987) (dissenting opinions by Justices Brennan, Blackmun, and Stevens); see also The Innocence List, Death Penalty Information Center, www.deathpenaltyinfo.org (listing 159 cases between 1973 and June 1, 2017, in which innocent people were freed from death row in the United States).

> ity" is enough. By this rule, four of the nine persons sitting in judgment can conclude that the defendant should not be sentenced to death and a death sentence may still be imposed. (Johnson, 2009)

The simple point is that while "death is different in kind from any other punishment,… [i]n Japan, death is not different" (Johnson, 2009). Justice, fairness, and the responsibility of the nation to those who face the awesome power of the state to lawfully kill demand that this be done better.

Finally, my third major area of concern is the tremendous expansion of legal structures within the Japanese criminal justice system that pursue victims' rights as a superior value, subordinating due process protections for criminal defendants as a result (Matsui, 2011).

From an American observer's perspective, the changes made to the Japanese Code of Criminal Procedure in 2000 and the subsequent enactment of Japan's Fundamental Act of Protection of Victims of Crime in 2004, amended in 2007, have put into place surprisingly strong protections for victims. Many changes were overdue, bringing Japan up to speed with approaches common elsewhere. But others, such as letting victims or their representatives sit alongside the prosecutor in criminal proceedings, question the defendant, recommend a sentence, and question the prosecutor about the handling of the case, have brought forward criticism that the extraordinarily enhanced degree of victim protection might increase erroneous convictions, lengthen sentences, and otherwise be unfair to defendants (Matsui, 2011).

The sociopolitical aspects of these changes are especially interesting. In recent papers, Professor Setsuo Miyazawa has described the dynamics as "penal populism," which has arisen "in spite of the low and stable crime rate," to achieve a nearly hegemonic dominance in public policy development (Miyazawa, 2008). Thus, Japan's National Association of Crime Victims and Surviving Families (NAVS) founded in January 2000 "has acquired the position to represent public opinion in the policymaking process." Moreover, "only those scholars, lawyers, and practitioners who support or accommodate the NAVS' demands have access to the policy-making process, so there seems to be no political opportunity for opponents right now" (Miyazawa, 2008).

Accordingly, as an outside observer, I cannot help but ask who speaks for suspects and convicted persons in policy discussions so as to ensure a proper balance among competing interests in the criminal justice process for Japan. When victim organizations are permitted to "represent public opinion," who in the society has the empathetic vision to recognize that they, their son or daughter, or another loved one might become a suspect, so as to hold on to hopes for fairness?

3 Race as a Policy Impetus for Progressive Criminal Justice Reform Efforts in the United States

Here then, one can begin to see a major difference between the United States and Japan. In the United States, our horrible history of race relations, beginning from the seizure of the lands of native peoples and the enslavement of Black Africans, carrying through to various means of discrimination and subordination of minorities still present in today's American society, has caused a sensitivity among minority communities that they or their loved ones could easily be wrongfully accused of criminal behavior. As President Obama noted after the tragic shooting of an African-American teen returning from a neighborhood convenience store: "You know, when Trayvon Martin was first shot I said that this could have been my son.... Trayvon Martin could have been me 35 years ago" (Obama, 2013).

Consequently, community organizations representing racial minorities and their allies have historically been vigilant and engaged in criminal justice reform debates in the United States. The clearest example of this was death penalty reform litigation beginning from the mid-1960s when the National Association for the Advancement of Colored People Legal Defense and Educational Fund (NAACP LDF) launched the first major constitutional challenge to the death penalty in the United States.[14] As told by Jack Greenberg, its former Director-Counsel, NAACP LDF litigation challenging the death penalty began as an attack on the southern states' awful record of executing black men accused of raping white women.[15] But "very soon, we got into the capital punishment business generally, in murder as well as rape cases, representing whites as well as blacks, dealing with non-racial issues as well as racial ones" (Greenberg, 1994, p. 443).

These dynamics remain, though perhaps not as centrally as they appeared with death penalty reform litigation decades ago. Voices, such as Professor Alexander's, argue that civil rights organizations have been insufficiently engaged in criminal justice issues in recent years.[16] Nevertheless, discussion of criminal justice reform in the United States, whether in the media or legislatures, still brings forward expressions of deep concerns from communities of color and their allies.[17]

My suggestions that race underlies progressive criminal justice reform efforts in the United States does not mean that those efforts have brought successful *results*. Race remains at the foundation of terribly deep flaws in the American system including aggressive policing, the war on drugs, and multigenerational implications of mass incarceration that have created what Professor Alexander deplores as a new

[14] "The features of the 1960s, however, made capital punishment an obvious target for an organization like the NAACP LDF, which focused on racial justice" (Blume & Steiker, 2009, p. 95, 98).

[15] "Almost 90% of the 455 defendants executed for rape since 1930 were blacks convicted of raping white women" (Greenberg, 1994, p. 440).

[16] Professor Alexander forcefully criticizes US mainstream civil rights organizations for abandoning criminal justice issues in recent years. "Challenging mass incarceration requires something civil rights advocates have long been reluctant to do: advocacy on behalf of criminals" (Alexander, 2012, p. 226). At the same time, her involvement and those standing with her precisely demonstrate my point that racial justice issues remain a vital entry point for criminal justice policy debates in the United States.

[17] Another marker of difference is evident in a recent study finding support for the death penalty to be significantly lower among Hispanics (50% opposing, 40% supporting) and African Americans (55% opposing, 36% supporting) in contrast to 55% support overall (Pew Research Center, 2014).

racial undercaste in the United States.[18] Though space limitations here prevent me from adding further detail, Professor Michael Tonry, a leading criminologist succinctly states the point: "malign neglect of the interests of black Americans continues to drive American crime policies" (Tonry, 2008).

My point in this essay is narrower, which is simply to identify that communities of color and their allies in the United States, either through the voices of individuals or organizations, routinely come forward to push for the interests of criminal suspects and convicted persons. For the most part, Japan appears different in this regard.[19]

4 Looking from an Original Position

Although the proportion of minority persons is lower in Japan than in the United States, it must be stated clearly: Japan is *not* a homogeneous mono-ethnic society. I am among many authors who have tried to make more visible the important minority communities in Japan who painfully experience realities of discrimination and subordination on a daily basis (Levin, 2008). However, I believe that many, perhaps even most, privileged members of the mainstream Japanese society (those who I have suggested should be referenced as *Wajin* (id. at 82)), carelessly still believe Japan to be ethnically homogeneous or nearly so.[20]

While setting aside the question of the factual accuracy of their belief, the perception alone has tremendous power to shape the society. Thus, I believe that this perception makes it more difficult to move Japan toward criminal justice system that sufficiently contemplates the rights and circumstances of suspects and convicted persons. In the United States, at a minimum, even if majority whites are oblivious to criminal justice matters, minority communities who have suffered unfair circumstances in criminal justice know that they must watch the law with care. However, while Japan's *Wajin* may be oblivious to the minority experience, minority voices often seem to be too quiet, distracted by other concerns, or simply silenced to impact

---

[18] These wrongs are also imposed on Native Hawaiians in my home state (see Office of Hawaiian Affairs, 2010; Hawai'i Advisory Committee to the US Commission on Civil Rights, 2011).

[19] Again, the most important exception is the Buraku Liberation League's partnership with IAMDR-JC. Their engagement with international human rights bodies such as the United Nations Human Rights Committee represents a vital voice of civil society in these issues. More recently, there are 17 Muslim plaintiffs who sued to stop the Tokyo Metropolitan Police's massive surveillance of over 70,000 individuals, all profiled as "suspects," discussed in more detail below (Blakkarly, 2016; Spying on Muslims in Tokyo and New York-"Necessary and Unavoidable?", 2016).

[20] "I believe Japan's Wajin-dominated racial discourse represents the epitome of majority race transparency" (Levin, 2008, p. 87). However, it is important to note that Japan also incorporates growing populations of *visible* minorities, and Debito Arudou's work on this subject offers a vital contribution (e.g., Arudō, 2015). Arudou, a Japanese national, writes forcefully against racist institutional biases in Japan, including ones accomplished via civil and criminal justice processes, in both his comprehensive monograph and via a regular column in the Japan Times.

debates about criminal justice.[21] Too few Japanese people imagine they or their loved ones could be wrongfully accused or otherwise involved with the criminal justice system.[22]

At the broadest level, Japan could benefit from greater public empathy for suspects and convicted persons among *Wajin* and minorities alike.[23] If this can be accomplished, better solutions for problems in the system may become apparent and more politically feasible. Importantly as well, the debate will not be controlled by those who see the world only through the eyes of victims or innocent bystanders.

To do this, one may not want to look at Japan from the inside or the outside but from an "original position" behind a "veil of ignorance" as suggested in the work of Professor John Rawls in his famous 1971 text titled *A Theory of Justice* (Rawls, 1999). Rawls invites his readers to imagine that they are invited to participate in social debates over justice only if they cannot know what their place in society will be.[24] Simplifying his work greatly, this leads to an appreciation of principles of fairness and the protection of liberty.

I suggest that we approach criminal justice policy in the same manner. Let's go behind Rawls' veil of ignorance. From there, we can appreciate that one might be a victim, a bystander, an innocent accused, or a guilty accused. What system of justice should we aspire to then? In the United States, we substitute the veil of ignorance with a burden of historical knowledge—minority communities who know they may be unfairly treated. However, without that history and those communities in Japan, the work can instead be done by anyone and should be done by everyone.

Imagine, for example, that you are a young man named Teppei, standing in a crowded commuter train, in a hurry to an important meeting, jostled by the movement of the train and fumbling with your suit jacket caught in the door. You've done nothing wrong. But when the train doors open and you walk off, a young woman grabs your wrist and loudly accuses you of having sexually groped her.[25]

Or imagine one night the police come to your door at 9:30 p.m. and ask you about your whereabouts on a particular evening a few weeks before. When you can't immediately account for that evening's events, they ask you to come down to

---

[21] Again, one appreciates the exceptions mentioned above of IAMDR-JC, the Muslim plaintiffs in the police surveillance litigation and Dr. Arudou's scholarship. Perhaps these give hope for positive changes to come.

[22] It seems difficult to imagine Prime Minister Abe expressing that he could have experienced Iwao Hakamada's life history in the way that President Obama spoke about what happened to Trayvon Martin.

[23] This is admittedly idealistic; increasing social empathy seems to be a likely route toward better circumstances, but benefits are not guaranteed (see Bloom 2013).

[24] "They do not know how the various alternatives will affect their own particular case and they are obliged to evaluate principles solely on the basis of general considerations" (Rawls, 1999, pp. 136–137).

[25] This is the opening plot of "I Just Didn't Do It" (Suo, 2006).

the station to answer some more questions… (about a multiple murder, but you do not yet know that).[26]

Your journey begins from one of those two places into a criminal justice system that has the lawful power to incarcerate or even to kill you. Now, what kind of justice system do you want your country to provide?

5 Afterward: June 2017s Vantage Point[27]

This chapter is revised from the English draft of an article that appeared in Japanese language translation in SEKAI in June 2014 (Levin, 2014, Iwakawa transl.). Despite the clarity of calls for criminal justice reform in both the United States and Japan in the intervening years, it seems that little progress has been made in either nation.

5.1 *Looking at the United States: "More Dangerous than Trump"*

While the focus of this chapter is on Japan, it seems essential to take note of dynamics in the United States since 2014. In the United States, communities of color have not only maintained engagement with issues concerning criminal justice, but they have grown in the reach and level of that engagement. Most notable is the Black Lives Matter movement, launched in 2012 after the death of Trayvon Martin, which has taken root and grown into a powerful change mechanism and is now well established in the American political arena.[28] Together with this popular movement, both the public and intellectual communities have become better versed in issues surrounding racial justice and criminal justice system, as writings such as *The New Jim Crow* (Alexander, 2012; Joseph, 2016),[29] and research focused on impacts of implicit bias are now much more widely understood (e.g., Levinson & Smith, 2012).

---

[26] This began Mr. Sakae Menda's true-life encounters with the police on January 13, 1948, leading to his wrongful conviction and 33 years of incarceration on death row until being completely exonerated on July 29, 1983, the first of Japan's four famous death penalty retrial cases of the 1980s (Foote, 1992).

[27] In writing this section, I benefited greatly from conversations with my colleague Kenneth Lawson, Co-Director of the Hawai'i Innocence Project at the Richardson Law School and Professor Makoto Ibusuki of Seijo University Law School in Tokyo, Japan. Of course, the responsibility for any errors or omissions in this report is entirely mine.

[28] Perhaps one measure of the movement's reach is its 239,000 followers on Twitter.

[29] Taking quick counts, the book has been cited in 1141 law review and journal articles, 17 judicial opinions, and drawn nearly one million views on YouTube to Professor Alexander's talks and online documentaries considering her work.

If I were writing this chapter in the Spring of 2016 with anticipation of a Democratic majority in the Congress putting forward legislation to the presidential administration of Hillary Clinton or Bernie Sanders, I would see circumstances offering some degree of optimism for progressive reform. One year ago, one could see some of these movements gaining traction not only in public discourse but even in policy initiatives (e.g., Drabold, 2016; Glanton, 2016). Granted, the power of the movement reflected worsening conditions in the society, and some, including Professor Alexander, did not trust the prospect of a Hillary Clinton administration (Alexander, 2016), but nevertheless, the late 2015 and into 2016 presented any number of news items pointing toward positive change (e.g., Dyson, 2015; Hulse, 2016; Joseph, 2016; Zapotosky & Harlan, 2016).

Regrettably, the story is not nearly as sanguine in June 2017. Even before Donald Trump's nomination as the Republican candidate for the US presidency and his subsequent election, racial dynamics in the American criminal justice system remained deeply problematic. The incarceration of millions described in *The New Jim Crow* had barely changed, and violent deaths at the hands of police and in similar acts continued to tally up. Following Donald Trump's ascendency to the Republican Party nomination, a progressive bipartisan crime bill loosening devastating constraints such as mandatory minimums in federal sentencing lost momentum and died in the Senate (Hulse, 2016).

Whatever optimism may have been emerging in 2015 and 2016 under an Obama administration has been absolutely obliterated by the Trump administration and the leadership of Jeff Sessions at the Department of Justice (e.g., Ruiz, 2017). Even in his first weeks in office, the Attorney General directed the Bureau of Prisons to "return to its previous approach" and use private prisons to house federal inmates without restriction (Zapotosky, 2017).

More recently, Professor David Cole of Georgetown University Law School and the National Legal Director for the American Civil Liberties Union, describing Attorney General Sessions as "more dangerous than Trump," issued this harsh criticism:

> Reversing course from the Obama Justice Department on virtually every front, … *Sessions has been especially focused, and particularly retrograde, on criminal justice….* He has rescinded Eric Holder's directive to federal prosecutors to reserve the harshest criminal charges for the worst offenders…. At the same time, Sessions has promised to reduce the Justice Departments critical oversight of policing." (Cole, 2017, emphasis added)

As of this writing, the latest news is of the police officer who killed Philando Castile at a traffic stop in a Minneapolis suburban community being acquitted of any criminal charges (Meyerson, 2017; Smith, 2017). After the verdict brought hundreds out into the streets, marchers shut down the interstate highway in the city leading to 18 arrests (Chao, 2017).

In short, things in the United States were not good when I wrote in 2014. They are worse today. After some improvements to criminal justice policy at the federal level under the leadership of President Barack Obama and Attorneys General Eric

Holder and Loretta Lynch, we are now seeing a rapid retrenchment to failed and distressing criminal justice policy choices at the behest of President Donald Trump and his first Attorney General Jeff Sessions. As before, many remain engaged with these issues. But there is enormous work to be done for lawyers and activists both to overcome the devastating impacts of new policies being brought forward by the Trump administration and complete Republican majorities in the US Congress and 32 state legislatures (e.g., Butler, 2017).

5.2 *Looking at Japan:* Plus Ça Change, Plus C'est la Même Chose

Next we turn to Japan, where circumstances may not be as bleak as in the United States in 2017, but again it seems that progress has been limited and many problems remain. Again we can see indications of policy reform, while the overall direction has been retrograde. And, as before, a vast majority of Japanese citizens remain disengaged with criminal justice policy issues, leaving whatever comes to the legal professionals and scholars, bureaucrats, and politicians.

At the time of my earlier writing, Japan was in the middle of a criminal reform process, born out of a high-profile case which publicly revealed significant prosecutorial misconduct, including altered evidence and forced confessions, aiming to convict Atsuko Muraki, a senior bureaucrat, on forgery charges. The scandal led to operations of a high-level bureaucratic study and major reforms passed by the Japanese parliament in May 2016 (Osaki, 2016; Problematic criminal justice reforms, 2016).

The new legislation was centered around three core revisions to investigative procedures in Japan: an obligation to videotape certain criminal investigations, the establishment of a limited plea-bargaining system, and broadening the statutory license allowed for investigators to wiretap telecommunications. These ostensible reforms achieved little for progressives concerned about criminal justice in Japan and much for police and prosecutorial authorities (*id.*; see also Kyodo news, 2016).

First of all, the core enabling structures that have been at the root of failures in Japanese criminal justice, discussed above, were essentially unchanged. Aside from the fact that video recordings are being used in many investigations (Kyodo news, 2017b), nothing has improved for issues relating to inadequate access to counsel, sustained detentions in isolated police holding cells, and the like (More chances of false charges? 2015). Thus even in recent months, Japanese authorities kept one of the leaders of Okinawa's movement against US military base expansion detained without trial from October 2016 until March 2017, calling forth disapproving reports in international media, criticism from human rights organizations such as Amnesty International, and ultimately proceedings inside the United Nations Human Rights Council in Geneva (Fifield, 2017; Shimabukuro, 2017; Repeta, 2017).

Secondly, despite the impetus of the 2016 reforms being investigative excesses, the enacted legislation not only left open enormous loopholes in the rules regarding video recordings of interrogations, but investigative authorities obtained vastly *more* power in other respects (Problematic criminal justice reforms, 2016). Thus, both the plea-bargaining system and the expansion of wiretapping *only* benefit government authorities. Many have expressed concerns that the new capabilities will lead to more false charges and abusive prosecutions. Even a safeguard injected into the plea-bargaining system, that legal counsel be present, has been questioned owing to the loyalty of counsel to the bargaining suspect who may be offering up false testimony against others (*id.*, Kyodo news, 2016).

Meanwhile, in Japan where it is said that the Supreme Court "has never found a single case in which the actions of the police violated the free-speech rights of anyone" (Repeta, 2014), the likelihood of courts significantly improving criminal justice circumstances in Japan seems low. This may be best demonstrated by the Japanese Supreme Court's May 2016 dismissal of an appeal by 17 Muslim plaintiffs objecting to police surveillance of over 70,000 residents in Japan, including 1600 children,[30] owing to the intelligence gathering being "necessary and inevitable," particularly if one puts that case in contrast with judicial rulings in US federal courts facing nearly identical circumstances (Blakkarly, 2016; Spying on Muslims in Tokyo and New York-"Necessary and Unavoidable?" 2016).

Granted, one may find an inkling of hope in the Japanese Supreme Court's March 2017 unanimous ruling that warrantless collection of GPS data by police authorities was illegal and that existing statutory warrant mechanisms did not allow for such. But one can assume conservative members of Japan's parliament will move quickly to facilitate broad GPS surveillance powers and that the Court will not object to this on any constitutional grounds (Kyodo news, 2017a; Set rules on GPS data collection, 2017).

Lastly, it seems things in Japan have just gone from bad to worse. With the legislative process described as "railroaded," on June 15, 2017, Japan's parliament passed a controversial law targeting conspiracies to commit terrorism and other serious crimes, with provisions described as "what may prove to be this century's most dramatic expansion of state coercive powers" (Conspiracy crime bill railroaded through the Diet, 2017; Jones, 2017; McCurry, 2017).

Risks pertain most significantly to dangers that the legislation will enable police and prosecutorial overreach, far beyond its purported intent to prevent terrorist acts. The Japan Federation of Bar Associations noted how the law might be used to investigate and prosecute individuals for benign activities such as citizens protesting construction of buildings or to suppress dissent by community activists in civil society. United Nations human rights observers have also criticized this enactment owing to the risks of restrictions on rights to privacy and freedom of expression (*id.*).

[30] In the leaked documentation from the Tokyo Metropolitan Police, all 70,000 profiled individuals were listed as "suspects." In other words, TMP criminalized an entire minority community on the basis of their religious affiliation (*Id.*).

While there is much to criticize in this new enactment, assessment in the context of this chapter considers the likely chilling effects of the law on free expression in Japan. Even more than is already the case, the law's threatening sword will surely constrain public social engagement on controversial or unpopular issues such as protecting the interests of criminal suspects and convicted persons.

5.3 Closing Thoughts: Two Steps Forward and Five Steps Backward

In both the United States and Japan, the recent years have revealed similar, sad patterns. Differences in public engagements, described above, appear to remain constant. Communities of color in the United States are still (or perhaps even more) deeply engaged with these issues. The vast majority of Japanese citizens are still disconnected and unlikely to see the threats as being ones against them as individuals (McNeill, 2016). However, looking at recent dynamics in the two countries, another difference becomes evident. Regressive policies in the United States being brought forward by the Trump administration and complete Republican majorities in the US Congress and 32 state legislatures have been, for the most part, blatant and undisguised. But Japan's leaders seem to prefer camouflage and diversion by making pretenses of progress even while driving national policies backward toward authoritarian possibilities.

For example, in Japan's 2016 criminal justice reforms, national leaders issued grand pronouncements celebrating the mandatory recording of suspect interrogations in respect to human rights and dignity, but in fact the rule applies to only 3% of cases; prosecutions can declare exceptions, and there are countless ways authorities are able to work around the rule. Wiretaps were added to just nine new crimes from the previous four, except that theft is in the list, and theft accounts for about 70% of all crimes recognized by the police. And of course the conspiracy law is justified in order to bring Japan into international treaty compliance, but this is as if the national leadership cared when there are inconvenient international obligations in human rights or other treaty commitments.

I find myself wondering which approach is more distressing—being openly regressive, as one sees in Jeff Sessions' rollback of Obama administration policies, or covert actions, such as with Japan national leadership's feignt of care about human rights in criminal justice mechanisms.

If Rawls's veil of ignorance is designed to generate empathy, Japan's cloak of obscurity is designed to generate apathy. And Japan's approach, particularly in light of the new conspiracy law, makes it vastly harder for public citizens to organize and fight back even when they would choose to do.

On the other hand, perhaps the difference is inconsequential. Horrid is horrid regardless of whether it is naked or clothed.

References

Alexander, M. (2012). *The New Jim Crow: Mass incarceration in the age of colorblindness*. New York: The New Press.

Alexander, M. (2016, February 10). Why Hillary Clinton doesn't deserve the black vote. *The Nation*. Retrieved from https://www.thenation.com/article/hillary-clinton-does-not-deserve-black-peoples-votes/

Arudō, D. (2015). *Embedded racism: Japan's visible minorities and racial discrimination*. Lanham, MD: Lexington Books.

Asia-Pacific Journal Report (2016). Spying on muslims in Tokyo and New York-"Necessary and unavoidable"? *Asia-Pacific Journal: Japan Focus, 14*(18), 2. Retrieved from http://apjjf.org/--Asia-Pacific-Journal-Report/4956/article.pdf

Blakkarly, J. (2016, July 13). Shadow of surveillance looms over Japan's Muslims. *The Japan Times*.

Bloom, P. (2013, May 20). The baby in the well. *The New Yorker*. Retrieved from http://www.newyorker.com/magazine/2013/05/20/the-baby-in-the-well

Blume, J., & Steiker, J. (2009). *Death penalty stories*. St. Paul: West Academic.

Butler, P. (2017, June 20). Opinion | lawyers can't save America from Trump. *The New York Times*. Retrieved from https://www.nytimes.com/2017/06/20/opinion/trump-obstruction-of-justice.html

Chao, X. (2017, June 17). Hours after officer Yanez is found not guilty in fatal shooting of Philando Castile, marchers close I-94. *Star Tribune*. Retrieved from http://www.startribune.com/fifth-day-of-jury-deliberationsunderway-in-yanez-trial/428862473/

Cole, D. (2017, May 24). More dangerous than Trump. *The New York Review of Books*. Retrieved from http://www.nybooks.com/daily/2017/05/23/more-dangerous-than-trump-jeff-sessions/

Conspiracy crime bill railroaded through the Diet. (2017, June 15). *The Japan Times*.

Davis, A. J. (2007). *Arbitrary justice: The power of the American prosecutor*. Oxford; New York: Oxford University Press.

Drabold, W. (2016, July 26). DNC: Meet the mothers of the movement. *Time*. Retrieved from http://time.com/4423920/dnc-mothers-movement-speakers/

Dyson, M. E. (2015, August 1). Opinion|President Obama's racial renaissance. *The New York Times*. Retrieved from https://www.nytimes.com/2015/08/02/opinion/sunday/president-obamas-racial-renaissance.html

Escobedo v. Illinois, 378 U.S. 478, 488–89 (1964).

Fifield, A. (2017, March 19). Okinawan anti-base activist released after five months in detention. *The Washington Post*. Retrieved from https://www.washingtonpost.com/world/asia_pacific/okinawan-anti-base-activist-released-after-five-months-in-detention/2017/03/19/68be4502-0c9c-11e7-b2bb-417e331877d9_story.html

Foote, D. H. (1991). Confessions and the right to silence in Japan. *Georgia Journal of International and Comparative Law, 21*, 415–488.

Foote, D. H. (1992). From Japan's death row to freedom. *Pacific Rim Law & Policy Journal, 1*, 11–104.

Glanton, D. (2016, July 27). Hillary Clinton isn't afraid to say black lives matter. *Chigago Tribune*. Retrieved from http://www.chicagotribune.com/news/columnists/ct-clinton-black-lives-matter-glanton-20160727-column.html

Greenberg, J. (1994). *Crusaders in the courts: How a dedicated band of lawyers fought for the civil rights revolution*. New York: Basic Books.

Hawai'i Advisory Committee to the U.S. Commission on Civil Rights (2011). *Is there an Uneven Administration of Justice for Native Hawaiians in Hawai'i?* Retrieved from http://www.usccr.gov/pubs/HawaiiAdministrationJusticeNativeHawaiiansReport.pdf

Hulse, C. (2016, September 16). Why the senate couldn't pass a crime bill both parties backed. *The New York Times*. Retrieved from https://www.nytimes.com/2016/09/17/us/politics/senate-dysfunction-blocks-bipartisancriminal-justice-overhaul.html

Johnson, D. (2009). Capital punishment without capital trials in Japan's lay judge system. Asia-Pacific Journal: Japan Focus, 14(0). Retrieved from http://apjjf.org/-David-T.-Johnson/3461/article.html

Johnson, D. T. (2002). *The Japanese way of justice: Prosecuting crime in Japan*. New York: Oxford University Press.

Johnson, D. T. (2015). An innocent man: Hakamada Iwao and the problem of wrongful convictions in Japan. *The Asia-Pacific Journal, 13*(6). Retrieved from http://apjjf.org/-David-T--Johnson/4272/article.pdf

Jones, C. P. A. (2017, June 14). Conspiracy theory becomes frightening reality for Japan. *The Japan Times*.

Joseph, P. E. (2016, April 27). Obama is chipping away at the "New Jim Crow". But more needs to be done. *The Guardian*. Retrieved from https://www.theguardian.com/commentisfree/2016/apr/27/barack-obama-new-jim-crowprogress-mass-incarceration

Levinson, J. D., & Smith, R. J. (2012). *Implicit racial bias across the law*. New York: Cambridge University Press.

Kyodo News. (2016, May 29). Critics hit Japan's new plea-bargaining system, say it opens door to false testimony. *The Japan Times*.

Kyodo News. (2017a, May 24). GPS data collection illegal without warrants, top court rules. *The Japan Times*.

Kyodo News. (2017b, May 25). Police getting better about providing fully recorded interrogations for serious crimes. *The Japan Times*.

Levin, M. (2008). The Wajin's Whiteness: Law and race privilege in Japan (批判的人種理論と日本法—和人の人種的特権について). Hōritsu Jihō, (法律時報), 80(2), 80–91. Available in English at: https://ssrn.com/abstract=1551462

Levin, M. (2014). 無知のヴェールから日本の刑事司法を考える. *SEKAI, 857*, 112–121.

Matsui, S. (2011). Justice for the accused or justice for victims: The protection of victims' rights in Japan. *Asian-Pacific Law and Policy Journal, 13*, 54–95.

McCleskey v. Kemp, 481 U.S. 279, 320–67 (1987)

McCurry, J. (2017, June 15). Japan passes "brutal" counter-terror law despite fears over civil liberties. *The Guardian*. Retrieved from https://www.theguardian.com/world/2017/jun/15/japan-passes-brutal-new-terror-law-which-opponents-fear-will-quash-freedoms

McNeill, D. (2016, January 16). Travesty of justice: Legal reform unlikely despite erroneous convictions. *The Japan Times*.

Meyerson, C. (2017, June 16). The police officer who killed Philando Castile is found not guilty. *The Nation*. Retrieved from https://www.thenation.com/article/police-officer-who-killed-philando-castile-is-found-not-guilty/

Miranda v. Arizona, 384 U.S. 436 (1966).

Miyazawa, S. (2008). Globalized penal populism and its countermeasures: Will penal populism decline in Japan? *Japanese Journal of Sociological Criminology, 33*.

More chances of false charges? (2015, March 18). *The Japan Times*.

Obama, B. (2013, July 19). Remarks by the President on Trayvon Martin. *The Washington Post*. Retrieved from https://www.washingtonpost.com/politics/president-obamas-remarks-on-trayvon-martin-fulltranscript/2013/07/19/5e33ebea-f09a-11e2-a1f9-ea873b7e0424_story.html

Office of Hawaiian Affairs (2010). *The disparate treatment of native Hawaiians in the criminal justice system*. Retrieved from http://www.oha.org/sites/default/files/ir_final_web_rev.pdf

Osaki, T. (2016, May 24). Diet passes legislation to revamp Japan's criminal justice system. *The Japan Times*.

Pew Research Center (2014, February 12). *Support for death penalty drops among Americans*. Retrieved from http://www.pewresearch.org/fact-tank/2014/02/12/support-for-death-penalty-drops-among-americans/

Problematic criminal justice reforms. (2016, June 1). *The Japan Times*.

Rawls, J. (1999). *A theory of justice* (Revised Edn). Cambridge, MA: Belknap Press of Harvard University Press.

Repeta, L. (2014). Limiting fundamental rights protection in Japan: The role of the Supreme Court. In J. Kingston (Ed.), *Critical issues in contemporary Japan* (pp. 36–51). London; New York: Routledge, Taylor & Francis Group.

Repeta, L. (2017, January 4). The silencing of an anti-US base protester in Okinawa. *The Japan Times*.

Ruiz, R. R. (2017, May 12). Attorney general orders tougher sentences, rolling Back Obama policy. *The New York Times*. Retrieved from https://www.nytimes.com/2017/05/12/us/politics/attorney-general-jeff-sessions-drugoffenses-penalties.html

Segi, H. (2014). *Zetsubō no Saibansho*. Tokyo, Japan: Kodansha Gendai Shinsho.

Set rules on GPS data collection. (2017, March 25). *The Japan Times*.

Shimabukuro, R. (2017). *In UN speech Hiroji Yamashiro calls out Japanese government human rights violations in Okinawa*.

Smith, M. (2017, June 20). Video of police killing of Philando Castile is publicly released. *The New York Times*. Retrieved from https://www.nytimes.com/2017/06/20/us/police-shooting-castile-trial-video.html

Spying on Muslims in Tokyo and New York-"Necessary and Unavoidable"? (2016). *Asia-Pacific journal: Japan focus*, 14(18, No. 2). Retrieved from http://apjjf.org/--Asia-Pacific-Journal-Report/4956/article.pdf

Suo, M. (2006). *I just didn't do it*. Japan: Altamira Pictures.

Tonry, M. (2008). Why are American penal policies so harsh? *Journal of Sociological Criminology, 33*.

Zapotosky, M. (2017, February 23). Justice department will again use private prisons. *The Washington Post*. Retrieved from https://www.washingtonpost.com/world/national-security/justice-department-will-again-useprivate-prisons/2017/02/23/da395d02-fa0e-11e6-be05-1a3817ac21a5_story.html

Zapotosky, M., & Harlan, C. (2016, August 8). Justice Department says it will end use of private prisons. *The Washington Post*. Retrieved from https://www.washingtonpost.com/news/post-nation/wp/2016/08/18/justicedepartment-says-it-will-end-use-of-private-prisons/

Chapter 11
Sentencing and Punishment in Japan and England: A Comparative Discussion

Julius Weitzdörfer, Yuji Shiroshita, and Nicola Padfield

This is a discussion on two traditional, yet increasingly punitive jurisdictions that strongly adhere to the rule of law, yet face criticism for the way in which they exercise penal powers: England, over whole-life sentences, and Japan, over the death penalty. Following a comparative introduction and an overview of sentencing laws, institutions, and discourses in both criminal justice systems (Sects. 1 and 2), our analysis is structured along important aspects under consideration at sentencing: prevention (Sect. 3), consistency (Sect. 4), efficiency (Sect. 5), lay participation (Sect. 6), the protection of offender's human rights (Sect. 7), and public demands for retribution (Sect. 8). Finally, we will draw a number of comparative conclusions by highlighting recent, parallel trends in the penal policies of both jurisdictions (Sect. 9).

1 Introduction: Criminal Justice in England and Japan

At first sight, the criminal justice systems of Japan and England and Wales differ vastly. Both jurisdictions have been shaped by distinct developments over centuries. England's criminal law, although based on common law, adversarial trials and

J. Weitzdörfer (✉)
Faculty of Law, University of Cambridge, Cambridge, UK
e-mail: jfww2@cam.ac.uk

Y. Shiroshita
Faculty of Law, Hokkaido University, Sapporo, Japan
e-mail: sirosita@juris.hokudai.ac.jp

N. Padfield
Institute of Criminology, University of Cambridge, Cambridge, UK
e-mail: nmp21@cam.ac.uk

J. Liu, S. Miyazawa (eds.), *Crime and Justice in Contemporary Japan*, Springer Series on Asian Criminology and Criminal Justice Research,
https://doi.org/10.1007/978-3-319-69359-0_11

judicially developed, today is largely statutory and under scrutiny of the European Convention of Human Rights. In Japan's mixed jurisdiction, semi-inquisitorial trials are held under procedural and substantive criminal law that was largely modelled after the French and German civil law systems. Despite the rise of American influence on criminal procedure following Japan's occupation, in substantive criminal law, comparative inspiration drawn from Germany and France continues to be strong (subsequent to the major Japanese codifications and the academic reception of legal theories in the late nineteenth and the early twentieth century, European influence continued, albeit less so with regard to criminal law). In these ways, the criminal justice systems of the British and of the Japanese islands demonstrate common, normative continental European influences.

Such foreign influences include criticism: while England and Wales is one of only two EU jurisdictions in which the law still explicitly provides for indefinite imprisonment without a chance of parole (section 239 English Criminal Justice Act 2003; sections 28, 30 (1) Crime (Sentences) Act 1997), Japan is one of only two jurisdictions in the G7 that retain the death penalty (article 11 I Penal Code (*Keihô*), Law No. 45/1907, as amended by Law No. 54/2016; for an English translation (see Ministry of Justice, 2009; for a partial commentary, see Dando, 1997). After the abolition of capital punishment and transportation, it is the whole-life sentence that is now facing controversy with regard to England and Wales, where both the incarceration rate in general and the number of indeterminate sentence prisoners are the highest in Western Europe (to compare, more than twice as many people are serving indeterminate sentences than in France, Germany, and Italy combined; Ashworth, 2015). At the same time, Japan's death penalty is under discussion for the circumstances of extended prior incarceration and sudden execution of convicts.

On closer examination, however, we will explore how recent penal policies in both jurisdictions converge. A common, particularly hotly debated issue is that of doing justice to the most serious offenders, including sexual offenders and murderers, for which, as we will conclude, human rights discourses provide pressure for reform in similar directions. Examining death sentences and life sentences together, we connect the two discourses on severe punishment in both countries, adopting a new comparative perspective on sentencing.

These parallel and to a significant extent internationally driven debates are why we compare sentencing in England and Japan and why we focus on their severest forms of punishment, respectively. In addition, we are addressing an astonishing lack of English language scholarship comparing the Japanese criminal justice system with England and Wales and generally on sentencing in Japan. These gaps are due to two trends in the scholarship.

With regard to Anglo-Japanese comparisons, on the one hand, criminal justice research from the UK either focusses on domestic issues or rather draws comparisons to European, American, and Commonwealth jurisdictions (see also National Audit Office, 2012; a laudable exception are Lewis, Brooks, Ellis, and Hamai, 2009). On the other hand, works on Japan in English mainly use the USA, Germany, France, China, or Australia as reference points or remain non-comparative 'one-way' descriptions. The most comprehensive of these monodirectional studies was conducted by an American sociologist (Johnson, 2002, with references to sentencing at 62–63, 66–71, 158–159, 174, 183, and 196–198; see also Herber, 2009). He also contrasted incarceration rates, death sentences, and penal populism with other Asian countries (Johnson, 2008, comparatively on death sentences at 54–57). Some remarks from an English perspective (Oda, 2011) and a very brief overview on Asian and the Anglo-American criminal justice systems are also available (Thaman, 2012). Non-comparative, separate sections on both criminal jurisdictions are included in a number of recent edited volumes (Dammer and Albanese, 2014; Jennings, 2015; Sieber, Jarvers, and Silverman, 2013), but other international studies of sentencing exclude Japan (Sieber, 2004).

With regard to sentencing law in particular, a brief taxonomy of Japanese sentencing law is available in English (Jones, 2016), but the only legal commentary available is from half a century ago (Dando, 1965) and does not refer to sentencing in the parts on adjudication. As a result, merely two legal articles in the English language focus on sentencing in Japan (Sher, 2011; Shiroshita, 2010).

In publishing the subsequent discussion on sentencing and punishment, we follow the Japanese academic approach of 'learning through dialogues' (*taiwa de manabu*), where actual discussions between leading scholars are published for educational purposes, particularly in philosophy and law. For example, Japan's leading educational law journal, *Hôgaku kyôshitsu* [Law Classroom], runs a series of instructive discussions entitled *Hanrei kôza: Taiwa de manabu keiso-hô hanrei* [A Course on Case law: Learning Criminal Procedure Precedents Through Dialogues], and discussions of leading Japanese legal academics were published on other areas of law (Uga, Takahashi, & Ôhashi, 2003). To this end, we assembled a former judge, barrister, and criminologist from England, a professor of criminal law from Japan, and a comparatist working in both jurisdictions.

What follows is a revised transcript of this discussion, held as a public outreach event at the University of Cambridge on 20 October 2015. While bilingual references to relevant statutes, cases, policy documents, and the most recent scholarship have been added for the reader in footnotes, the discussion itself is kept in its accessible and engaging original form.

***

JW: Good evening, welcome to Darwin College and this event of the Cambridge Festival of Ideas on criminal justice and sentencing in England and Japan.

To my right is *Nicky Padfield* (NP), reader in Criminal and Penal Justice at the Faculty of Law and at the Institute of Criminology, Master of Fitzwilliam College, and recently elected Honorary Fellow of Darwin College, Cambridge. As a former Crown Court judge and barrister, she has very broad interests in 'all things criminal', particularly sentencing and the release from prison. In addition to writing a number of books on the topic, she has also spent, I understand, considerable time in prison, of course purely for academic purposes!

To my left is *Yuji Shiroshita* (YS), Professor of criminal law at Hokkaido University, from which he also received his doctorate. He first came to the Faculty of Law nearly 20 years ago and currently is a Visiting Fellow at Wolfson College and a Visiting Scholar at the Centre for Law, Medicine and Life Sciences. Adopting a comparative perspective, he has published widely on criminal responsibility, sentencing theory, and medical law in Japan and beyond.

My name is *Julius Weitzdörfer* (JW). I am a Fellow and Director of Studies in Law and an Affiliated Lecturer at the Law Faculty, and as a Japanologist and lawyer by training, I am delighted to host this discussion. Now, Nicky, let us first leave the floor to you, to briefly introduce the relevant legislation and the key institutions of the English criminal justice system with regard to sentencing.

2 Institutions: Sentencing Laws, Guidelines, and Precedents

NP: Thank you very much, thank you for your welcome, and thank you to Darwin College, the Master, for welcoming us here this evening.

This is the Festival of Ideas, and we are discussing criminal justice and sentencing. We could spend hours on 'criminal'; how we define what is criminal and what is not criminal is not at all self-evident; we could of course discuss justice forever, what we mean by justice and how you have justice within a rather unjust society, in many ways—huge, huge issues. When we come to sentencing, we could talk about sentencing theory, a subject which we are both interested to discuss, to explore why we do it, and what the justifications are for not only who we punish and how much we punish people.[1]

The first point I would make about sentencing is that we have far, far too much law in this country.[2] Let me show you my much fumbled with Criminal Justice Act 2003. We have Criminal Justice Acts every year and sometimes more than one. And here is the Powers of the Criminal Courts (Sentencing) Act 2000, just on sentencing. Actually this Act of Parliament only stood the test of time for 3 weeks before it was amended. Politicians make law, because in one sense that is all they can do and we have far, far too much. The law is far too complicated in this area. And if the sentencing judges find it difficult to apply, as you can see from the many appeals going to the Court of Appeal and the Supreme Court, think of poor old prisoners who do not have a clue how to calculate the realities of their sentence.

The other point which has to be made by way of introduction is that we have quite complicated sentencing guidelines nowadays, guidelines for both Magistrates and Crown Court judges.[3] I thought I would bring along some of them for you to have a look at, if you are interested in what they actually look like.

---

[1] On these questions, cf. already Walker and Padfield (1999), and the edited volume by Tonry (2010); for Japan, cf. e.g. the special journal issue by Akaike (2012).

[2] Relevant legislation is listed in Ashworth (2015, at 20–22); for a recent critique, cf. Roberts and Ashworth (2016).

[3] On the guidelines, see Roberts (2013); for a multitude of perspectives, including comparative approaches, see the edited volume by Ashworth and Roberts (2013); including Padfield (2013); explanations to the Sentencing Council's Guidelines to the Criminal Justice Act 2003 in Japanese

YS: Thank you very much for your kind introductions. With regard to the Japanese criminal justice system, as introduced, there are four very interesting recent developments we will discuss today, among which the most unexpected and controversial change was the introduction of the Lay Judges Act in 2004.[4] We will return to this, so let me also introduce the legal institutions of sentencing in Japan.

Our Penal Code does not comprise provisions directly relating to sentencing guidelines, and statutory offences each carry a very wide range of punishment (*keibatsu*).[5] Imprisonment with work (*chôeki*) can be imposed for up to 20 years, while multiple offences can lead to longer tariffs. In homicide cases, for instance, judges and lay judges can impose the death penalty (*shikei*), life imprisonment with work (*muki chôeki*), or imprisonment with work between 5 and 20 years.[6] Court precedents have given rise to several so-called de facto guidelines, which are said to exist in judges' minds, informed by a newly introduced database system, and not open to the public. So in order to prevent sentencing in a black box, we will have to create actual guidelines, which has not been successful so far.

Traditionally, the determination of sentences had lain almost entirely with judicial discretion. However, prosecutors' demands in closing arguments, although without binding force, also strongly influence the sentence. In general, prison terms pronounced by judges tend to represent around 70–80% of the prosecutors' demands.

3 Prevention: Sentencing Levels, Deterrence, and Crime Rates

JW: Japan famously prides itself on one of the lowest crime rates, one of the lowest incarceration rates, and one of the lowest rates of recidivism in the world, which give us a good starting point for our comparative inquiry.[7] The first intriguing question with regard to both jurisdictions seems to be whether the increased severity of judgements handed down and of the sanctions imposed by substantive law today has led to successes in bringing down the crime rates. Higher sentences do not break the vicious cycle of 'revolving door' prisons, as Nicky often puts it. So what kind of punitiveness is based on criminological evidence, and what does merely reflect (alleged) public pressure?

are provided by Ido (2007). All offence-specific and the generic guidelines are available from the websites of the Sentencing Council (2016).

[4] Act Concerning Participation of Lay Judges in Criminal Trials (*Saiban-in no sanka suru keiji saiban ni kansuru hôritsu*), Law No. 63/2004, as amended by Law No. 44/2009; English translation by Anderson and Saint (2005).

[5] For a Japanese commentary on the general provisions on the six types of punishments (see Itô and Matsumiya, 2013).

[6] Art 199 of the Penal Code; individual sentences will depend on circumstances relating to the person of the defendant and the criminal act itself, see recently Shiroshita (2015).

[7] For a comparison of Japanese crime rates, which have declined by almost 50% after 2002, with the UK, see Miyazawa (2013); for the most recent figures, see inter alia Table 1-1-1-2, Hômu-sho Hômu sôgô kenkyû-jo (2015); for context on these statistics, particularly on the dark figures, see Finch (2000).

NP: You talked about longer sentences: that is of course an issue. One of my main interests is looking at sentencing not just as something that the judge or magistrate does at the point of sentencing but to look at it as an ongoing process. People are serving much longer, not least, because the sentences are becoming longer, but we can also look at decisions to grant early release and so on.[8] So defining what we mean by sentencing I think is really interesting.[9]

However, measuring the amount of crime in society is a nightmare, whether we measure it by crime recorded by the police[10] or by what victims report to the Crime Survey for England and Wales.[11] The government at the moment wants you to know that the amount of crime out there is reducing, but actually it depends very much which crime you look at. We could explore the increase at the moment of sexual offending, or is it simply that people are reporting a crime that has been severely under-reported in the past? So there are lots of big issues about data (Table 11.1).

YS: In Japan, crime rates are reported to have declined slightly, but this can hardly be attributed to…

JW: … the recent amendments to the Penal Code.[12]

YS: Indeed, in 2004, we raised the maximum statutory sentences.[13] And in 2007, we tightened the provisions on traffic offences in the Penal Code.[14]

JW: For some offences, the maximum tariff was raised from 20 to 30 years—quite substantially (*kyôaku-ka*). Yet this has not led to measurable positive effects.

NP: Yes, with regard to the length of the sentence, not with regard to the probability of apprehension by the police. And, for example, if you are a Cambridge burglar, if you put plastic bags over your shoes and if you put gloves on, and you're lucky in the first 24 hours, they are very unlikely to catch you; so if they are not going to catch you, you are not going to worry about the threat.

That's not recommending we all become burglars, of course! But we can explore this in relation to the death penalty. Of course there are very interesting issues why people in countries which have the death penalty still commit crimes. They are not deterred; in many cases they are more frightened of their criminal minders than of the systems there to execute them.[15]

---

[8] On the increase of the use and length of custodial sentences, cf., e.g. Ashworth (2015, at 5 and 10); on the questions surrounding the topic of 'back-door sentencing', see the contributions in Padfield (2012).

[9] Cf. also Padfield (2014, 2016c).

[10] For police recorded crime data, see Office for National Statistics (2016).

[11] For the crime survey, see TNS RMBB and Office for National Statistics (2016).

[12] On this trend in Japan, cf. Shiroshita (2009); Shiroshita (2005); on other punitive amendments, cf. Miyazawa (2008).

[13] Act partially amending the Penal Code (*Keihô no ichibu o kaisei suru hôritsu*), Law No. 156/2004; for an overview of the old and new statutory sentences, see Shiroshita (2010, at 244).

[14] Act partially amending the Penal Code (*Keihô no ichibu o kaisei suru hôritsu*), Law No. 57/2007.

[15] On the question of deterrence by capital punishment, see comparatively Hood and Hoyle (2015, pp. 317–349), on the contestations of capital punishment in Asia at 84–102, particularly on Japan at 94–95, 148, 173, and 260.

Table 11.1 Severe crime and serious punishment in Japan and England and Wales

	Japan	England and Wales
Homicides		(Murder, manslaughter, corporate manslaughter, infanticide)
- Per year	1054 (2015)	681 (year ending June 2016)
- Per 100,000 of national population	0.8 (2014)	1.2 (year ending June 2016)
Rapes - Per year	1250 rapes; 44 with robbery (2014)	36,483 (year ending June 2016)
- Per 100,000 of national population	1.0 (2014)	21.1 (year ending June 2016)
Death sentences and executions (first instance/final instance/ executed)	2/7/3 (2014) 5/8/8 (2013) 3/10/7 (2012) 10/22/0 (2011)	–
Indeterminate sentences (first instance/final instance)	30/28 (2014) 39/38 (2013) 24/38 (2012) 23/46 (2011) (Life imprisonment with work)	Indeterminate sentence offenders (imprisonment for life, detention during Her Majesty's pleasure, custody for life, automatic life sentence, imprisonment and detention for public protection, whole-life orders) account for 19% of the prison population (see below, December 2016)
Correction facilities	188 (2014)	123 (2016)
Official capacity of prison system	90,536 (31 December 2014)	76,578 (29 July 2016)
Incarceration rate (per 100,000 of national population)	47 (mid-2015)	147 (end of October 2016)
Prison population (including pre-trial detainees and remand prisoners)	59,620 (mid-2015)	85,998 (28 October 2016; including immigration removal centres, not including secure training centres and local authority secure children's homes)
- Pre-trial and remand prisoners	11.0% (mid-2015)	10.9% (30 June 2016)
- Female prisoners	8.4% (mid-2015)	4.5% (28 October 2016)
- Juvenile prisoners	0.04% (31 December 2014; under the age of 20; not including classification homes and training schools)	0.7% (30 June 2016; under the age of 18; not including secure training centres and local authority secure children's homes)
- Foreign prisoners	5.8% (mid-2015)	11.9% (30 June 2016)

Based on World Prison Brief & Birkbeck Institute for Criminal Policy Research (2016), TNS RMBB and Office for National Statistics (2016, at 2, 22, 25, 29, and 30), and Keisatsu-Chô (2016, Tables 1-1-1-2, 2-3-1-1, 2-3-2-2, and 6-2-1-1). For a comparison of incarceration rates (Ashworth, 2015, at 299–302); for the definition of indeterminate sentences in England and Wales (HM Prison Service, 2012). Though Japanese and English crime data are among the world's most comprehensive, methodological limitations of direct comparisons remain (e.g. Pakes, 2012).

4 Consistency: Sentencing Guidelines and Databases

NP: There are many issues we can raise in relation to who is getting the sentences nowadays, and one of the big issues in this country, of which I have no idea if it is also an issue in Japan, is the very real problem of historic sex abuse cases. What are the right sentences for people who are being convicted today, of crimes they committed in the 1970s or 1980s, who are undoubtedly getting much, much longer sentences today than they would have done, had they been convicted at the time?[16]

YS: In Japan, it will depend on the severity of the sexual offences. We can observe that the variety of tariffs handed down for comparable cases has become broader after the introduction of jury trials. While it depends on the type of offence whether juries are now stricter than judges were before, sentences have certainly become less predictable.[17] One related idea is to raise the minimum tariff from 3 to 5 years—a proposal which I think will be realized.

JW: Some in our audience will have heard that cases of sexual harassment quite frequently occur in Japan (*chikan mondai*), both in professional settings in offices and also while commuting on trains and subways. While there are still significant difficulties in getting such cases reported and offenders convicted, it is safe to say that the awareness of such crime has risen both among the Japanese public and within the judiciary.[18]

However, what Nicky raises is the problem of coherence in the severity of sentences for such crimes, not only over time but also across gender, social stratification, and race.[19] In the UK, bias against black defendants and other ethnic minorities, manifested in unexplained overrepresentation in prisons, is a hotly debated topic. And in Japan, the question is asked whether sentences handed down in lay judge trials are stricter than before 2009.[20] One means of addressing such inconsistencies of course is sentencing guidelines. We know that a similar system was introduced in Japan; can you tell us how this plays out?

---

[16] Padfield (2005, 2010).

[17] For an empirical comparison of the sentences handed down by juries today versus those of professional judges before, see Saikô saiban-sho jimu sôkyoku [General Secretariat, Supreme Court] (2012).

[18] For a holistic, critical examination of judicial decision-making in such cases, see Burns (2005); for a recent overview of the sentences handed down between 2009 and February 2016, cf. Suzuki (2016).

[19] For overviews on equality and difference in punishment, see Easton and Piper (2016, p. 386) and Ashworth (2015, pp. 250–271).

[20] In contrast to other recent developments in Japan's criminal justice system, the body of literature on Japanese lay judge trials in Western languages has grown rapidly. For a collection of references, cf. Levin and Mackie (2013). For the latest in-depth monographs in English, see, firstly, Vanoverbeke (2015), focussing on sociolegal and historical backgrounds, where the point is made that more than a trend towards more severe sentencing by lay judges, the concern by Japanese professional judges is that the norm established in the past has to be respected, which prevents departures from it (see 141, 173, and 189) and, secondly, Wilson, Fukurai, and Maruta (2015) arguing for an expansion into the civil law realm.

YS: As I mentioned in the beginning, we have no 'visible' sentencing guidelines. Precedents, generally called sentencing standards, gradually gave rise to a number of so-called factual guidelines. The Japanese Supreme Court (*Saikô saiban-sho*) initiated a database in 2008 to provide both lay judges and professional judges with a set of standards to determine approximate sentences (*Ryôkei kensaku shisutemu*). This database, not open to the public, originally contained over 3000 past cases and is expanding continually. The Supreme Court's officials emphasized that the material from past sentences is merely for reference and does not constitute binding precedent.[21]

So the lay judges and the judges use a database system, which does not have binding force and should merely be used as material for consideration. They can search comparable cases using keywords relating to information such as the motive of the offender, the type of weapon, the seriousness of the crime, and the number of victims, etc.

NP: The problem with a database of actual cases, I suspect, is whether you can record enough for it to be meaningful. We can find out that the typical sentence for a person who goes and looks (unsuccessfully!) for a hitman to kill their wife is 5 years, but this is actually a gross simplification of all the factors that go into the equation, such as the harm caused, assessing the level of culpability, etc., and in this country we had huge problems collecting that data. Yes, it is in the public domain rather than private, and you can go and look at the late David Thomas' 'Sentencing Encyclopaedia'[22] or Robert Banks' book,[23] a slightly smaller summary of cases. The summaries are very brief.

Increasingly, judges' sentencing remarks are put on the internet in serious cases, but nobody has done any serious analysis of what individual judges are doing. We have got this body called the Sentencing Council nowadays which conducted a Crown Court sentencing survey, where all judges over a period of 2 years were asked to tick 'Mickey Mouse' boxes, but much better than nothing, on the factors which they took into account on sentencing. Sadly, this has recently been stopped as an economy measure, and we desperately need more data. In fact, we do not really know what judges do in practice.

In the Crown Court, where I sat as a judge for 12 years, you rarely have a defendant in front of you on one charge only. If he is a burglar, he is likely to have 3 or 4 burglaries and maybe even 20 others 'taken into consideration'. So how much more do you get for the subsequent burglaries? Because oddly we think, or maybe not oddly, if you are a many-time burglar, you are not as 'bad' as a rapist. So the fact that you are a burglar with 10 burglaries, with each one getting you, say, 3 years, we would never give you 30 years for burglary, so there is a sort of 'discount' for bulk offending. Now there are academics who want to understand this 'discount' and

[21] Cf. also Shiroshita (2010, pp. 243 and 246).

[22] Thomas (1982–2016).

[23] Banks (2016).

how it works in practice, but we really do not have any data to help us understand it, and we desperately, I think, need it.[24]

Audience: Speaking of sentencing guidelines, the American system, in federal jurisdiction, has very lengthy, binding sentencing guidelines and has had them for 24 years I think, which is much longer than in England. And of course case law stacks up upon it as well, e.g. as to what qualifies as 'substantial', etc. Now, instead of merely an advisory, data-driven approach of 'here's what's actually happening in practice and let's see if we can get uniformity in light of these data', do you think an American-style system, i.e. binding guidelines, is better, or does it perhaps exacerbate the problem of too much law that then confuses?

NP: I am nervous of talking about America any more than I would be happy telling you about the Japanese legal system. I have chosen not to look at the American criminal justice system in the last 40 years, because, in brief, I do not like what I see. I have focused on comparative research in Europe. Now, America got its guidelines because of the problems of inconsistency before that. Their guidelines are more mandatory than ours.

I do not know of any evidence that tells us that guidelines have done anything but to talk up sentencing levels. So I am nervous about our sentencing guidelines, in that it is much easier to identify aggravating factors than mitigating factors.[25] We see our increasing prison population: the guidelines are not causing the prison population to go down. So I am nervous that if you have a rigid system of guidelines, you can constrain judicial discretion—but in my eyes, in the wrong direction.

YS: I was also quite frightened to see the US federal sentencing guidelines. They seem to be as heavy as the Yellow Pages! My impression, however, is that the system under the US guidelines is more functional and closer to the ideal of fairness. All depends on the concept of fairness you want to adopt: in the guidelines of England and Wales, the goal seems to be logical consistency rather than strict uniformity of sentences. Perhaps in the USA, the importance lies more on the uniformity of outcomes.

JW: A general comparative observation is that the more specific the substantive law of a jurisdiction is, the less one will have to rely on sentencing guidelines. For instance, various degrees of rape are stipulated in the Japanese Penal Code, all carrying different, cascaded penal sanctions.[26] As another example, this code, like its German counterpart, sets forth even more differentiated elements of the crime of arson, which come with a whole system of aggravating circumstances and factors that must be considered, in turn imposing differentiated custodial penalties.[27]

---

[24] Padfield (2003, 2011).

[25] Cf., e.g. Roberts (2011) and Jacobson and Hough (2011).

[26] See the various degrees and combinations of elements of the crime of rape (*gôkan-zai*) in Arts. 177; 178; 178–182; 179; 181 I, II, III; 241; and 243 of the Penal Code.

[27] See the various degrees and combinations of elements of the crime of arson (*hôka-zai*) in Arts. 108; 109 I and II; 110 I and II; 111 I and II; 112; 113; 114; 116; 117; and 117–122 of the Penal Code.

YS: So the UK guidelines concern past cases and there is no connection between them? The Halliday Report, a public research report from 2001, which is said to have inspired the Criminal Justice Act 2003, said that the sentencing guidelines should have a common starting point.[28] This starting point is consistency to preventing disparity, rather than uniformity of outcomes, correct?

NP: Absolutely! For example, what I pick up here is the Drugs Offences Guideline, and let's start sentencing somebody for importing heroin.[29] We can see the starting point would be whether you had a leading role, a significant role, the amount of heroin you had, etc., etc., but it does not help us work out, for example, whether somebody has a leading role or a significant role or a lesser role. This is really, really difficult.[30]

Most people in our system plead guilty, and that is something you can tell us about Japan in a minute. Even if you have a trial, getting at the truth of the facts is really difficult. I once tried a case in which somebody was pleading not guilty to being involved in a major drug deal case, and he was sitting in the back of a car when the car was stopped by the police with a large amount of heroin in front of the front passenger. So in order for the jury to be convinced of the guilt of the person in the back seat, there was lots of evidence by mobile phone calls and linkages to people, but that did not help the sentencer work out whether the person in the back seat had a lesser role, a significant role, or a leading role. All the people involved in this drug conspiracy were not there to tell honest answers and help the judge sentence!

I think, perhaps, my greatest naivety when I first became a judge was a belief that the lawyers in the court were there to help me. The lawyers in the court were not there to help me, the judge. The lawyers there had their own agendas. Actually, the system is now trying to push the lawyers to help judges a bit more. The prosecution will now bring guidelines to the attention of the judge to make sure they are on the right page and thinking about it. And we are moving into a world of what is called 'active case management', which challenges the traditional role of the lawyers in the case.[31]

5 Efficiency: Plea Bargaining and Conviction Rates

JW: Let us take out and compare two aspects illustrated in your vivid examples. First, the role of plea bargaining you have just referred to: The introduction of a system of plea bargaining was under survey in Japan, yet the adoption of the concept seems to have been abandoned?

---

[28] Halliday (2001).

[29] Sentencing Council (2012).

[30] For definitions of the three roles, a defendant can be held to have had in drug cases, and on the four categories relating to the quantity of illegal substances determining the harm done, cf., e.g. Padfield (2013, at 35–37).

[31] *Cain* [2006] EWCA Crim. 3233, [2007] Crim. L.R. 310; *James* [2007] EWCA Crim. 1906.

NP: Does that mean nobody can plead guilty?

YS: You can. Indeed, the Legislation Council of the Ministry of Justice of Japan published its final report on the reform of the criminal justice system in 2014. In the beginning of the discussions, they considered the possibility of introducing a plea bargaining system, and a first draft was published in April 2014. It proposed that the punishment of a person who had committed a crime and stated the crime by the facts that are important for the probe of his or her crime and unknown to the investigative agencies may be reduced.[32]

The proposal was explained to be based on the necessity of cost reduction and the collection of evidence in cases that are hard to be investigated. But the proposal was exposed to reservation. Some members of the council pointed out the risk of concessions by the investigative agency. They feared that this system would prevent revelation of the true facts and appropriate punishment of the offender. They also mentioned that there had already been a provision for optional reduction of the sentence due to surrender (*jishu*) in Japan's substantive criminal law.[33] So the additional prescription was deemed unnecessary for now.[34]

NP: In our system, there is such a 'bribery' on you to plead guilty, because your lawyer will tell you that if you plead guilty, you will get a third off your sentence. You are nuts not to plead guilty if you are guilty, because of the discount in your sentence. If you are a judge sentencing on the basis of a guilty plea, which is, therefore, most cases, you have the agreed version of the facts.

Actually, a lot of people I think get under-sentenced because the defendant pleads guilty on the basis of facts, which the prosecution does not bother to challenge because they're delighted to have a guilty plea to save money. The judge can say 'I do not believe this version of facts, we will have a trial anyhow', but that is such a waste of money you do not tend to have those trials within trials[35].

JW: It would be quite striking to hear that Japanese courts seemingly have the efficiency and the resources at their disposal, so that Japan is not tempted to adopt a plea bargaining system, which also, for example, in my home jurisdiction, Germany, is something courts rely on heavily. In fact, all other things equal, they would hardly be able to handle the cases if they did not, so it is intriguing that Japan has so far withstood the temptations of such a system.[36]

---

[32] The proposals are to be found in Hômu-sho hôsei shingi-kai tokubetsu bukai (2014)

[33] Art 42 I of the Penal Code.

[34] However, plea bargaining was eventually introduced for a limited range of offences. Under the framework of a significant readjustment of the penal process in Japan in May 2016, a plea bargaining system was introduced by the law partially amending the Code of Criminal Procedure, etc. (*Keiji soshô-hô-tô no ichibu o kaisei suru hôritsu*), Law No. 54/2016. Inter alia, it allows to offer defendants lighter sentences or dropped charges in cases of drug trafficking and certain white-collar crimes, e.g. bribery and tax evasion, in exchange for information not on the defendant but on others, such as accomplices and ringleaders. While critics already argue that such a reform will open doors to false accusations, a first overview in English is provided by Osaki (2016).

[35] *Newton* [1982] 4 Cr. App. R.(S) 388; *Underwood* [2005] 1 Cr. App. R. 13.

[36] On similar, unofficial practices in Japan, however, cf. Johnson (2002, pp. 246–248).

Having said that, not all cases by far solved by the police are brought to court. Those cases that seem comparatively clear and easy to win, secured on the back of a confession or with sufficient evidence to satisfy the principle of the presumption of innocence (*muzai suitei no gensoku*; *utagawashiki wa bassezu*) beyond reasonable doubt (*gôri-teki na utagai*), will have a higher chance of being taken to court. This preselection by suspension of prosecution (*kiso yûyo*), due to the limited time prosecutors have for each case, helps demystify Japan's 99% conviction rate.[37]

YS: Yes, that is true. The conviction rate is very, very high.[38] According to the figures covering the time from the introduction of the lay judge system in 2009 to the end of February 2015, a total of 7414 defendants were held guilty at first instance, 23 of which were sentenced to death, while the acquittal rate was only 0.5%. Many scholars indeed see the root of this in the wide discretionary powers of prosecutors. The flipside of the high conviction rate is that nearly 60% of suspects are not prosecuted at all![39]

NP: We find it very difficult to understand how you can have such a high conviction rate in Japan, and therefore if you are a Japanese, you will find it quite bewildering that we prosecute, say, sexual offences, where there is a 50% acquittal rate.[40]

Audience: Given the 99% conviction rate in Japan, and that 60% of solved cases do not get to the stage of trial, it seems as though perhaps the stage where the public prosecutor decides whether or not to try is more important than the trial itself. Could you tell us more about this process and what the public knows about it?

YS: You are making a very good point. The root of this is a combination of judges' attitudes and prosecutors' discretion.[41] In Japan, judges tend to use records of statements, so the Japanese justice system was sometimes referred to as 'record justice', as written statements were the principal method of conversation between those involved in a trial. In principle, these should be written in a style of questions and answers. Japanese investigators, however, tend to write records as a 'story', and fact-finding is very important to the judges.

NP: So when they get to court, judges rely on the 'story' as written by the prosecution, but who verifies that the prosecutor's version is accurate?

YS: The judges do this, but maybe they rely on the prosecutors too much...

---

[37] Cf. Article 248 of the Code of Criminal Procedure, which draws on the principle of expediency with regard to the discretionary powers of the prosecution under German law of criminal procedure. With a comparison of Japan Rasmusen, Raghav, and Ramseyer (2009).

[38] Calculated as 99.79% for ordinary trials in 2014, based on the absolute figures in Table 2-3-2-1 in Hômu-sho Hômu sôgô kenkyû-jo (2015, p. 47). On the methodological problems of calculating and comparing such rates, see Johnson (2002, p. 215); on possible explanations, see Ramseyer and Rasmusen (2001).

[39] The 2014 prosecution rate is 34% (Hômu-sho Hômu sôgô kenkyû-jo, 2015, p 45, Table 2-2-3-1).

[40] Depending on how you read the recent figures, compare Crown Prosecution Service (2016), with Dodd and Bengtsson (2016).

[41] As Johnson (2002), summarizes at 63, prosecutors have more power over life, liberty, and reputation of suspects than anyone else in the Japanese justice system; on the prosecutors' discretion at *id.* 104–118.

JW: Some contend that the reason why the Japanese Bar was largely in favour of the adoption of a lay judge system is that it seemed to offer better possibilities of defence in some cases, in order to reduce convictions.

It is interesting though that in Europe, at least in continental Europe, we regard it as one of the main legal achievements of the Enlightenment, historically speaking, that trials are held in oral proceedings nowadays and that they are not administered as inquisitorial trials based on records and evidence prepared in advance like was common practice in the Middle Ages.[42]

6 Participation: Juries, Lay Magistrates, and Lay Judges

NP: You have also mentioned the role of laymen, and of course in England and Wales, the jury has no role in sentencing, but the lay element, which is really important in sentencing, is the Lay Magistracy.[43] And even in a world where many cases, minor cases, are diverted from prosecution, still Lay Magistrates decide about 96%of those cases that actually go to court. If Magistrates convict, they may commit the most serious cases for sentence in the Crown Court, but the great majority of cases begin and end in the Magistrates' Court.[44]

However, I am not convinced by our system of trial by jury, for two main reasons. One is that the jury gives no reasons, so it is impossible to challenge a jury's verdict.[45] Presumably this is different in Japan due to the professional judges involved, so you can appeal it?

YS: Yes. Lay judge trials were introduced by the Lay Judges Act we have already mentioned, which came into force in May 2009. Under this system, so-called lay judges (*saiban-in*) are randomly selected for each case from among the voters through a procedure similar to that in common law jurisdictions. Cases are tried by a mixed panel of three professional judges and six lay judges, collaborating both on fact-finding and on sentencing. So as in Germany, lay judges both decide on the question of guilt and, if held guilty, on the tariff to be imposed. While lay judges and professional judges have equal voting powers, procedural issues and legal interpretation are left to the professional judges.

---

[42] Cf. again, e.g. Thaman (2012, p. 242).

[43] In England and Wales, the jury decides the facts and the judge decides the law. In summary, juries are used in criminal cases in the Crown Court (where defendants plead 'not guilty'), in civil cases in the High Court and County Court (in cases involving defamation, false imprisonment, malicious prosecution, and fraud), and in Coroners' Courts (to inquire into deaths occurring in prison, police custody, industrial accidents, and other cases with implications for public health and safety); the basic qualifications are laid out by the Juries Act 1974.

[44] For an overview of the court and sentencing system in England and Wales, see, e.g. Ashworth (2015, at 1–7); on Japan, see, e.g. Oda (2011, pp. 57–65); and for the references on both jurisdictions, see note 6.

[45] Padfield (2016a, 2016c).

Only 3% of all trials are lay judge trials, as they are only held for very serious offences: those punishable by death or by imprisonment for life and for any intentional behaviour resulting in another person's death, for which, a minimum term of 1 year is stipulated.[46] These offences include serious drug offences but are mainly set forth in the Penal Code, such as murder (*satsujin-zai*),[47] robbery resulting in death or injury (*gôtô chi-shishô-zai*),[48] rape resulting in death or injury (*gôkan chi-shishô-zai*),[49] and arson of inhabited buildings (*genjû kenzô-butsu hôka-zai*).[50] Lay judge trials are mandatory in these cases,[51] so defendants may not waive them and request bench trials.[52]

The purpose of this system, inter alia, was to reflect ordinary citizens' common sense in proceedings formerly monopolized by the legal professions. It was also hoped that the participation of lay people in criminal trials would contribute to the promotion of the people's understanding of the judicial system, thereby also raising confidence in it.

NP: The second reason why I am not convinced by our system is that I have heard enough stories about sleepy jurors, or jurors wanting to go home, or dreadful things occasionally happening in jury rooms. I am desperately keen that we should do more research into what happens in our jury rooms, but most people say 'don't look because you won't like what you find'.[53] Well, that is no reason for doing what we do, because even if we do not like what we find, we ought to look.

My proposed solution for this country, as an experiment, would be: Why do we not let the judge retire with the 12 jurors and be the conductor of the orchestra, the chair of the debate, which, many people say to me, 'no, the judge would dominate'. I think it's very unlikely in modern Britain; if I was chairing a jury of 12 lay people, I do not think they would all think they have to agree with me, and I would just be chairing the discussion. So are those issues under public debate in Japan?

YS: Your point relates to the attitude of the lay people. The problem is that the reality of the circumstances of the discussions of the civil judges is not public and no records of them are kept. But we are looking forward to lay judges speaking out after they have fulfilled their duties.

NP: You said that one of the reasons for introducing the lay judges was to increase people's confidence in criminal justice. What serious study, academic or other, is

[46] Art 2 I of Lay Judges Act; cf. Shiroshita (2009, pp. 273–287); and the references in *supra* notes 8; 13.

[47] Art 199 of the Penal Code. For translations of Japanese terms of criminal law, including substance control legislation, see the contributions to the edited volume by Okuda, Anderson, and Baum (2013). For an overview of the murder cases tried between 2010 and 2015, see Shiroshita (2015, pp. 128–129); and Ellis and Hamai (2017).

[48] Art 240 of the Penal Code.

[49] Art 181 II and III of the Penal Code.

[50] Art 108 of the Penal Code.

[51] Art 9 of Lay Judges Act.

[52] The preceding paragraphs partly draw on Shiroshita (2010, p. 246).

[53] Smith (1998).

being done about this introduction? I would be intrigued to know when you send three professional judges and six lay judges into their room together, do the lay judges open their mouth or do they just do what the professional judges tell them to do?

YS: In Japan, lay judges are prohibited to speak anything after their verdict, so they may not tell us about their reasons. However, recently, some have attempted to comment on the deliberations after the judgement, and scholars have just begun to survey this.[54]

Some former lay judges have spoken out about the stress they are faced with dealing with serious cases involving the death penalty. In response, members of the Ministry of Justice committee tasked with reviewing the system of criminal justice (*Saiban-in seido no un'yô-tô ni kansuru yûshiki-sha kondan-kai*) pointed out that the emotional burden on lay judges is severe, so they called for the exclusion of cases that could involve a death sentence, but the committee eventually decided to maintain the current setup, holding that citizens' opinions are needed for due process in very serious crimes.

7 Human Rights: Death Penalty and Life Sentence

JW: You are leading over to the last aspects of our comparison: the death penalty in Japan and whole-life imprisonment in England and Wales and the respective roles of the public.

YS: As we all know, unlike in the member states of the European Union and the Council of Europe, the death penalty is not abolished in Japan.[55] Inter alia, it is stipulated for 12 types of crime in the Penal Code, among which I have already mentioned the examples of homicide and robbery resulting in death, and is carried out by hanging (*keishû-kei*) at a penal institution, pursuant to provisions in the Penal Code and the Penal Detention Facilities Act.[56] However, there is no mandatory death sentence, and in court practice, it is only resorted to in very serious murder cases nowadays.[57] In fact, it was only declared in two cases at the first instance in 2014, and since then we had exactly three executions each year.

JW: All crimes that carry capital punishment in Japan are tried under the lay judge system. In a number of these decisions, death penalties were handed down, but none of the 23 convicts on death row as a result of this have been executed so far. Leaving aside the fundamental questions about the death penalty as such, this

[54] For a recent sociological study on this in a Western language, see Vanoverbeke (2016).

[55] Cf. Art 2 II of Charter of Fundamental Rights of the European Union 2000, bindingly in force since 2009; Art 2 I 2 of Convention for the Protection of Human Rights and Fundamental Freedoms, in force since 1953.

[56] Art 11 I of the Penal Code; Art 71 of the Act Concerning Penal Detention of Detainees (*Keiji shûyô shisetsu oyobi hi-shûyô-sha-tô no shogû ni kansuru hôritsu*), Law No. 50/2005, as amended by Law No. 69/2014.

[57] For the leading judgement on the standards for selecting capital punishment from 1983, see Supreme Court, KEISHÛ 37, 609.

situation leads to the widely raised question of whether the agonizing time of up to a decade between conviction and execution of the prisoners can be deemed humane.[58] Can you tell us about the reasons for this time lag?

YS: According to the Code of Criminal Procedure,[59] the death penalty must be executed within 6 months after the failure of the prisoner's final appeal upon order of the Minister of Justice.[60] However, the period for requesting retrial or pardon is exempt from this provision, and so the typical period on death row is between 5 and 7 years. Yet, a quarter of the prisoners (*jukei-sha*) have been incarcerated on death row for over 10 years. For several, detention has even exceeded 13 years!

This, at least in part, has to do with the attitude of the respective Minister of Justice who is in office. It is at their discretion when to order carrying out the sentences. While some of them are very eager to increase the record of executions, others are more reluctant.

JW: Another explanation for this is that the authorities want to ensure that the judgement was not handed down on the basis of an assessment of facts that is later called into question by new evidence. In this way, the timespan could be seen as a means to further decrease the probability of executing innocents. If I am not mistaken, so far there is no known case in Japan in which that happened. So in one way this could be seen as an effective way of avoiding miscarriages of justice, which on the other hand entails arguably inhumane treatment by keeping convicts in their cells on death row in constant fear (or expectation) of sudden execution.

In England, questions comparable to Japan have been raised with regard to the humanity of whole-life tariffs in cases where no chance of review, early release, parole, or pardon is granted at all.[61] Can you tell us about the discussion on the human rights of those who do not have any hope of ever getting out?

NP: Yes, there is controversy about whole-life tariffs in murder cases in this country, and indeed this is going back to the European Court of Human Rights at this moment. There are really interesting relations, arguments, between our domestic courts[62] and the judges of the European Court of Human Rights.[63]

[58] Art 11 II of the Penal Code does not set forth a maximum term of imprisonment before execution. In 2014, for example, prisoner Iwao Hakamada was released after a retrial and having spent 46 years on death row. For human rights relevant in this context in Japan, cf. Articles 13, 14, 31, 36, 37, and 38 of the Japanese Constitution (*Nihon-koku kenpô*), 1946; the overview by Oda (2011, pp. 105–107) and Iwasawa (1998).

[59] Code of Criminal Procedure (*Keiji soshô-hô*), Law No. 131/1948, as amended by Law No. 54/2016; English definitions of its key terms are available in Okuda, Anderson, and Baum (2013).

[60] Art 475 II Code of Criminal Procedure.

[61] For human rights relevant in this context in England and Wales, cf. Articles 3, 5, 6, and 7 of European Convention of Human Rights 1950, as amended by Protocol Nos. 11 and 13, supplemented by Protocol Nos. 1, 4, 6, 7, 12, and 13; the Human Rights Act 1998; the in-depth commentary by Emmerson, Ashworth, and Macdonald (2012); and recently van Zyl Smit, Weatherby, and Creighton (2014)

[62] *R v Oaks* [2012] EWCA Crim. 2435; Attorney General's Reference No. 69 of 2013 [2014] EWCA Crim. 188.

[63] Cf., e.g. *Vinter v UK* (Grand Chamber, July 2013) and van Zyl Smit, Weatherby, and Creighton (2014); *McLoughlin and Newell* [2014] EWCA Crim. 188, [2014] Crim. L.R. 471; and most recently *Hutchinson v UK*, 17 January 2017.

Currently there are only 53 people in England and Wales being told they are never to come out.[64] Of course a lot more will die in prison, either by their own hands or somebody else's hands or natural causes. Regarding the prisoners who will never come out, most people who work in the prison system would like there to be a review after, let's say, 25 years, because people are much more difficult to manage if they have got no hope. Whether there should be a right to hope I think is a really interesting issue. I suspect that most of the 53 individuals with a whole-life tariff in this country would never come out, even if we introduced parole board reviews. That in my opinion does not constitute a reason not to give them parole board reviews.

JW: From a comparative viewpoint, Japanese convicts on death row also do not have a right of their own to ever petition for clemency. Even if a probation officer was to request a pardon for the prisoner, firstly, this would not suspend an execution, and, secondly, no such commutations have been issued since 1975. So in practice there is no 'right to hope' for everyone in Japan either, and this raises questions under international human rights law that are, in this way, similar to those regarding England![65]

YS: Only convicts sentenced to imprisonment, who then demonstrate substantial reformation, may be paroled at the discretion of an agency (*Chihô kôsei hogo i'in-kai*) after having served either one third of the term or, in case of a life sentence, 10 years (*kari shakuhô*).[66]

NP: There are many, in my view, even bigger issues with our life sentence,[67] for example the length of the minimum term that those who aid and abet other people committing murders get. Particularly, there is the problem area of 'joint enterprise', that if you are, say, two 19-year-olds on a night bus in Croydon,[68] and you get out your knife out and stab someone dead, and I am asked whether I knew that you had a knife on you, I say 'Of course I knew; we all have knives on us'. I do not have to have much of an idea that you ended up killing someone to also be convicted of murder, in that I aided and abetted you because I was on the bus with you and knew you had a knife with you and it was reasonably foreseeable that you might use it, etc., etc. But these young men receive extraordinarily long tariffs.[69] And another little rule of thumb, I would like to say, is that you could not have a minimum term that is longer than the number of years you have already been alive. Because to give

[64] As of December 2016, this number has grown to 60, while Japan's death row population was at 129.

[65] On clemency in Japan, see Art 13 of Pardon Act (*Onsha-hô*), Law No. 20/1947 as amended by Law No. 49/2013 and Arts 1, 1-2, 8, 10, and 11 of Pardon Act Enforcement Ordinance (*Onsha-hô shikkô kisoku*) No. 78/1947 as amended by Ordinance No. 59/2006; for English translation of both laws, as of 2009, see Ministry of Justice, Japanese Law Translation Database (2009). On the question of a human rights violation, see Death Penalty Project (2013).

[66] On paroles in Japan, see Arts. 28–30 of the Penal Code.

[67] Padfield (2016b) and Mitchell (2013).

[68] Croydon is a borough of London.

[69] Crewe, Liebling, Padfield, and Virgo (2015).

a 19-year-old a 20-year minimum term is an awful, long minimum term. People do not come out when they have achieved their minimum term anyhow, because you then have to satisfy the parole board and say that they have to release you. So there are lots of difficult issues about the mandatory life sentence for murder.

JW: Your example of joint enterprise might remind some of us of the famous Derek Bentley case from 1952, which later inspired the film *Let Him Have It*. We see a mentally challenged young man sentenced to death and hanged for committing nothing more than burglary and for being at the scene when his accomplice shoots a policeman. Ironically, the accomplice is spared from death as he is a minor.

NP: Yes. Everybody should see it; it should be compulsory viewing! The title of the film plays with the ambiguity of language (which was disputed at trial): imagine we are on a factory roof, where we are burgling, and the police arrive. If I say to you 'let him have it!', does that mean 'shoot the policeman!' or does it mean 'give your gun to the policeman!'? See the film![70]

8 Retribution: Public Demands for Punishment

JW: Sentencing and criminal justice are high-profile issues, not only in films. Be it in British tabloids or in Japanese private television, we know that the media tend to focus on gruesome crimes, on the perpetrators, and on erratic sentencing. Strikingly, while decreasing crime rates particularly in Japan are rarely reported on in the media, calls for more severe punishment for serious crime make headline news and stir continuing debates. However, higher sentences alone do not cut the crime rate, and sensationalized or inaccurate reporting of complex cases does not make it easier to understand this issue.[71]

YS: According to a public opinion poll of the Cabinet in 2015, 80% of the Japanese nation still supports the death penalty. On the other hand, there is criticism that the way of questioning for the public opinion poll is sometimes inductive. While there is no sign that the death penalty will be abolished in Japan, perhaps challenges could be made to if and how lay judges decide over them.[72]

---

[70] And read the case in which his conviction was quashed by the Court of Appeal more than 45 years after his execution: *Bentley* [2001] 1 Cr. App. R. 21, [1999] Crim. L.R. 330.

[71] On the role of the media in the UK, cf. Easton and Piper (2016, p. xv, 15–19); on Japan, cf. Ohba (2011); Ohba (2013).

[72] Arguments against the death penalty in Japan include that it has no proven effect in relation to reducing heinous crimes; it is contradictory for a law prohibiting homicide to stipulate a punishment that deprives people of life; it constitutes cruel punishment prohibited under Article 36 of the Japanese Constitution; and it cannot be reversed in the event of a misjudgement. Supporters argue that abolition may result in an increase of heinous crimes; based on the principle of proportionality, it is the only suitable punishment for certain heinous crimes; Article 31 of the Constitution is premised on the existence of such punishment, which hence cannot be prohibited under Article 36; and other punishments, such as time spent in prison, also cannot be undone. For reform proposals, cf. already Sher (2011).

JW: Public opinion, expressed through electoral choice, polls, focus groups, victims' statements, or laymen's verdicts of course, is a key variable in how crime is responded to. Many would argue that it has been the main influence on penal policy and levels of punishment. Public pressure on the one hand is a legitimate element of democracy. On the other hand, it can lead to lawmaking that is not based on sound empirical evidence and, worse, to 'tough on crime' rhetoric, retributivism, and populist punitiveness.[73] One example for a politically successful punitive movement is the Japanese 'National Association of Crime Victims and Surviving Families' (*Zenkoku hanzai higai-sha no kai*), which supports victim's procedural rights but also the death penalty and the introduction of new offences.[74]

NP: You rightly mention the role of public opinion, a hugely difficult area because what we understand about public opinion, in sentencing in particular, is that the public are not nearly as punitive as politicians would think they are, if they are well informed. So the more people know, either about individual cases or about the criminal justice system, the less punitive they are. In fact, what they are often much more interested in is stopping offenders from reoffending, rather than punishing them.[75]

YS: Indeed, there is criticism that the Japanese nation is not given the necessary information about the correctional institutions and the executions for answering the opinion polls. The media were admitted to access and to photograph an execution chamber for the first time in 2010, under the abolitionist female Minister of Justice Keiko Chiba, yet no ropes were displayed.

Audience: You have said a lot about consistency and the prevention of crime with regard to sentencing. Yet there is more, such as responding to the feelings of the victims' families or re-establishing the ideal of justice. What are the roles of other justifications for punishment?

NP: A wonderful question! With regard to sentencing, of course you can be consistently wrong or consistently right. So to know what is the right sentence is inherently difficult. We have to justify and try and understand what is the right sentence. There obviously is a huge area of the philosophy of punishment which explores this.

English law takes a pathetically compromised position on this. We say that, well, we must have proportionate sentences; the sentence must be commensurate with the harm caused, but this does not help you tack it on the graph at all. First, we are balancing harm and culpability, and these are very difficult to balance. You then work out whether you are punishing people for instrumental reasons, such as that you are protecting or trying to reform them or rehabilitate them. To all this we have what Andrew Ashworth called a 'cafeteria approach'—the judge can really choose whichever aim of punishment makes sense in the particular case at hand.[76]

---

[73] Easton and Piper (2016).

[74] On victims' procedural rights in Japan, see Matsui (2011) and Herber (2016).

[75] Cf. Wood (2009), Gray (2009), Roberts and Hough (2011), and *supra* note 78.

[76] Cf. the five purposes of punishment listed in Criminal Justice Act 2003, s 142. On the 'cafeteria approach', see Ashworth (1995, p. 331); this is not mentioned anymore in the current edition Ashworth (2015), but cf. the critical remarks at 42–53.

YS: Our situation is quite similar. The theories on the justifications of punishment by a Cambridge legal scholar, Andrew von Hirsch, are very famous in Japan, and many scholars are inspired by his system.[77]

NP: As a practitioner, I am intrigued to read philosophy of punishment, because I would have thought that philosophers, who have been arguing about this at least since Plato, would have got the answer by now. But the truth is the philosophers are still arguing, and since they have not really worked out why we punish people, it is not surprising that we lawyers have not worked it out either!

JW: Although we could only provide an overview of the trends in sentencing and punishment in Japan and England, at least our discussion must now come to a conclusion. Certainly, governments in both countries have become increasingly eager to raise public confidence in the criminal justice systems. If research suggests that while the public are often ill-informed about sentencing, the level of punitiveness in their attitude declines, and leniency increases when given further information.[78] I hope we had good reason to have this legal discussion in public and with the public. Thank you all very much!

9 Conclusions: Converging Trends in Sentencing and Penal Policy

This discussion provided a first systematic, legal introduction to the laws and practices, institutions and policies, and trends and discourses of sentencing in Japan. It introduced four recent reforms around Japan's sentencing regime, which, except for the lay judge system, have not received scholarly attention in English: the raise of maximum tariffs in 2004 and 2007, the sentencing database introduced in 2008, the lay judge trials that commenced in 2009, and the introduction of plea bargaining in 2016.

At the same time, this discussion highlighted converging trends in the penal policies in England and Japan.

Firstly, custodial sentences have become longer in both jurisdictions, through amendments of the law and through sentencing practice. On the one hand, our comparison shows that the absolute and relative figures of life sentences are several magnitudes higher in England every year. On the other hand, penal populism and punitiveness have risen (*kei no genbatsu-ka*) despite low and stable crime rates in Japan, leading to the question how or if at all penal moderation will take place after the recent decreases in recorded crime (see also Miyazawa, 2008, p. 124). Here, we discussed the doubts as to whether the inflations in sentencing provide deterrence and to what extent an informed public would be less supportive of such punishment.

[77] von Hirsch (1976, pp. 45–55); cf. also Hirsch and Ashworth (2005).

[78] On England and Wales, see Easton and Piper (2016, pp. 17–19) and the references in *supra* note 81; on Japan, see Miyazawa (2007); for a recent study on Japanese punitive attitudes and public information, see Sato (2014).

Secondly, having examined death sentences and life sentences together, we have identified parallel issues with regard to the most severe forms of punishment. Specifically, this concerns the 'right to hope' for convicts. Japanese prisoners on death row do not have a right to ever petition for clemency, just as English law provides for whole-life orders without a chance of parole, which de facto renders sentences irreducible. As a result, human rights, including equality, dignity, liberty, and fair trial, even for the most serious offenders, in both countries, provide pressure, including from abroad, for reform in a number of directions.

Thirdly, along with the increase in punitiveness, the role of the public at large, and that of lay people in particular, is taken increasingly serious in both judicial processes, albeit in different procedural ways. Against the background of the long tradition of juries in England, in Japan, pressure to further involve the public in the judicial system has led to the introduction of the lay judge system, inter alia in order to promote public understanding of the judicial process.

In publishing this discussion, we hope to start and stimulate more comparative research on the criminal justice systems of Japan and England.

Acknowledgements We are grateful to Darwin College, the Judicial Association of Japan (*Ippan Shadan Hôjin Shihô Kyôkai*), the Templeton World Charity Foundation for research grants, and the Volkswagen Foundation's 'Key Issues for Research and Society' initiative funding on the project 'Protecting the Weak: Entangled Processes of Framing, Mobilization and Institutionalization in East Asia' at the Interdisciplinary Centre for East Asian Studies, Frankfurt (AZ 87382). We thank Moritz Bälz and Fumihiko Sakamoto for comments on an early draft.

References

Akaike, K. (Ed.). (2012). *Hanzai shakai-gaku kenkyû. Kadai kenkyû keibatsu toshite no kôkin no imi o toikaesu* [Japanese Journal of Sociological Criminology. Special Issue: Why Prison? Reconsidering the Imprisonment as a Punishment].

Anderson, K., & Saint, E. (2005). Japan's quasi-jury (saiban-in) law: An annotated translation of the Act concerning participation of lay assessors in criminal trials. *Asian-Pacific Law and Policy Journal, 6*, 233–283.

Ashworth, A. (1995). *Sentencing and criminal justice*. Cambridge: Cambridge University Press.

Ashworth, A. (2005). *Proportionate sentencing: Exploring the principles*. Oxford: Oxford University Press.

Ashworth, A. (2015). *Sentencing and criminal justice*. Cambridge: Cambridge University Press.

Ashworth, A., & Roberts, J. V. (2013). *Sentencing guidelines: Exploring the English model*. Oxford: Oxford University Press.

Banks, R. (2016). *Banks on sentence* (Vols. 1–2, 11th ed.). Etchingham: Robert Banks.

Burns, C. (2005). *Sexual violence and the law in Japan*. London/New York: RoutledgeCurzon.

Crewe, B., Liebling, A., Padfield, N., & Virgo, G. (2015). Joint enterprise: The implications of an unfair and unclear law. *Criminal Law Review, 4*, 252–269.

Crown Prosecution Service. (2016). *Violence against women and girls (VAWG) crime report 2015–2016*. Retrieved from Crown Prosecution Service website: http://www.cps.gov.uk/publications/docs/cps_vawg_report_2016.pdf

Dammer, H. R., & Albanese, J. S. (2014). *Comparative criminal justice systems*. Belmont, CA: Wadsworth Cengage Learning.

Dando, S. (1965). *Japanese criminal procedure*. South Hackensack, NJ: Fred B. Rothman.

Dando, S. (1997). *The criminal law of Japan: The general part*. Littleton, CO: Fred B. Rothman.

Death Penalty Project. (2013). *The death penalty in Japan: A report on Japan's legal obligations under the international covenant on civil and political rights and an assessment of public attitudes to capital punishment*. Retrieved from: http://www.deathpenaltyproject.org/wp-content/uploads/2013/03/DPP-Japan-report.pdf

Dodd, V., & Bengtsson, H. (2016, October 13). Reported rapes in England and Wales double in four years. *The Guardian*. Retrieved from: https://www.theguardian.com/society/2016/oct/13/reported-rapes-in-england-and-wales-double-in-five-years

Easton, S., & Piper, C. (2016). *Sentencing and punishment: The quest for justice*. Oxford: Oxford University Press.

Ellis, T., & Hamai, K. (2017). Homicide in Japan. In F. Brookman, E. R. Maguire, & M. Maguire (Eds.), *The handbook of homicide* (pp. 388–411). Chichester: Wiley Blackwell.

Emmerson, B., Ashworth, A., & Macdonald, A. (2012). *Human rights and criminal justice* (3rd ed.). London: Sweet & Maxwell.

Finch, A. (2000). Criminal statistics in Japan: The White Paper on Crime, Hanzai Hakusho and Hanzai Tôkeisho. *Social Science Japan Journal, 3*, 237–249.

Gray, J. M. (2009). What shapes public opinion on the criminal justice system? In J. Wood & T. A. Gannon (Eds.), *Public opinion and criminal justice* (pp. 49–71). Cullompton: Willan.

Halliday, J. (2001). *Making punishments work: Report of a review of the sentencing framework for England and wales*. Retrieved from: http://webarchive.nationalarchives.gov.uk/+/http:/www.homeoffice.gov.uk/documents/halliday-report-sppu/chap-1-2-halliday2835.pdf?view=Binary

Herber, E. (2009). Japanese sentencing practices: Creating an opportunity for "formal" paternalism. *International Journal of Criminology and Sociological Theory, 2*(2), 303–313.

Herber, E. (2016). Victim participation in Japan: When therapeutic jurisprudence meets prosecutor justice. *Asian Journal of Law and Society, 3(1)*, 135–157.

HM Prison Service. (2012). *Life sentenced prisoners*. Retrieved from: http://www.justice.gov.uk/offenders/types-of-offender/life

Hômu-sho Hômu Sôgô Kenkyû-jo [Legal Research Institute, Ministry of Justice]. (2015). *Hanzai hakusho heisei 27-nen-ban* (White Paper on Crime 2015).

Hômu-sho Hôsei Shingi-Kai Tokubetsu Bukai [Special Committee, Legislation Council, Ministry of Justice]. (2014). *Arata na keiji shihô seido no kôchiku ni tsuite no chôsa shingi no kekka (an) – kaitei-ban [Revised edition – (Draft) Results of the Study and Deliberation about the Construction of a new Criminal Justice System]*. Retrieved from http://www.moj.go.jp/content/000125864.pdf

Hood, R., & Hoyle, C. (2015). *The death penalty: A worldwide perspective*. Oxford: Oxford University Press.

Ido, S. (2007). Igirisu no ryôkei gaidorain ni tsuite [About the English Sentencing Guidelines]. *Hanrei Taimuzu, 1238*, 67–92.

Itô, K., & Matsumiya, T. (Eds.). (2013). *Shin konmentâru keihô [New Commentary on the Japanese Penal Code]*. Tokyo: Nihon hyôron-sha.

Iwasawa, Y. (1998). *International law, human rights, and Japanese law: The impact of international law on Japanese law*. Oxford: Oxford University Press.

Jacobson, J., & Hough, M. (2011). Personal mitigation: An empirical analysis in England and Wales. In J. V. Roberts (Ed.), *Mitigation and aggravation at sentencing* (pp. 146–167). Cambridge: Cambridge University Press.

Jennings, W. G. (Ed.). (2015). *The encyclopedia of crime and punishment*. New York: Wiley-Blackwell.

Johnson, D. T. (2002). *The Japanese way of justice: Prosecuting crime in Japan*. Oxford: Oxford University Press.

Johnson, D. T. (2008). Japanese punishment in comparative perspective. *Hanzai shakai-gaku kenkyû [Japanese Journal of Sociological Criminology], 33*, 46–61.

Jones, C. P. A. (2016, February 8). Words about sentences: The Japanese vocab of crime and punishment. *The Japan Times*. Retrieved from http://www.japantimes.co.jp/life/2016/02/08/language/words-sentences-japanese-vocab-crime-punishment/

Keisatsu-Chô [National Police Agency]. (2016). *Heisei 27-nenban hanzai hakusho* (White Paper on Crime 2015). Retrieved from http://hakusyo1.moj.go.jp/jp/62/nfm/mokuji.html

Levin, M., & Mackie, A. (2013). Truth or consequences of the justice system reform council: An English language bibliography from Japan's millennial legal reforms. *Journal of Japanese Law, 35*, 299–311.

Lewis, C., Brooks, G., Ellis, T., & Hamai, K. (2009). Comparing Japanese and English juvenile justice: Reflections on change in the twenty-first century. *Crime Prevention and Community Safety, 11*(2), 75–89.

Matsui, S. (2011). Justice for the accused or justice for victims? The protection of victims' rights in Japan. *Asian-Pacific Law and Policy Journal, 13(1)*, 54–95.

Ministry of Justice. (2009). Japanese law translation database. *Penal Code*. Retrieved from http://www.japaneselawtranslation.go.jp

Mitchell, B. (2013). Sentencing guidelines for murder: From political schedule to principled guidelines. In A. Ashworth & J. V. Roberts (Eds.), *Sentencing guidelines: Exploring the English model* (pp. 52–70). Oxford: Oxford University Press.

Miyazawa, S. (2007). The politics of increasing punitiveness and the rising populism in Japanese criminal justice policy. *Punishment and Society, 10(1)*, 47–77.

Miyazawa, S. (2008). Will penal populism in Japan decline? A discussion. *Hanzai shakai-gaku kenkyû [Japanese Journal of Sociological Criminology], 33*, 122–135.

Miyazawa, S. (2013). Senshin-koku ni okeru hanzai hassei ritsu no jôkyô to nihon no jôkyô e no kokusai-teki kanshin [Crime Rates in Developed Countries and International Interest in Japan]. *Hanzai shakai-gaku kenkyû [Japanese Journal of Sociological Criminology], 38*, 7–35.

National Audit Office. (2012). *Comparing international criminal justice systems: Briefing for the house of commons justice committee*. Retrieved from https://www.nao.org.uk/wp-content/uploads/2012/03/NAO_Briefing_Comparing_International_Criminal_Justice.pdf

Oda, H. (2011). *Japanese law*. Oxford: Oxford University Press.

Office for National Statistics. (2016). *Crime and justice* Retrieved from https://www.ons.gov.uk/peoplepopulationandcommunity/crimeandjustice

Ohba, E. (2011). Nyûsu media ni okeru hanzai ni kansuru kenkyû dôkô: Hanzai nyûsu kenkyû no seika to kadai [Research Trends on Crime in News Media: Outcomes and Issues of Crime News Research]. *Hanzai shakai-gaku kenkyû [Japanese Journal of Sociological Criminology], 36*, 112–116.

Ohba, E. (2013). Hanzai nyûsu ni okeru hanzai no nami: Naze hanzai no genshô wa hitobito no wadai ni naranai no ka? [Crime Waves in Japanese News Media: Why is Declining Crime Not Newsworthy?]. *Hanzai shakai-gaku kenkyû [Japanese Journal of Sociological Criminology], 38*, 97–108.

Okuda, Y., Anderson, K., & Baum, H. (Eds.). (2013). *Glossary of Japanese criminal procedure in English, German, French and Spanish*. Tokyo: Akashi Shoten.

Osaki, T. (2016, May 24). Diet passes legislation to revamp Japan's criminal justice system. *The Japan Times*. Retrieved from http://www.japantimes.co.jp/news/2016/05/24/national/diet-passes-legislation-revamp-japans-secretive-judicial-system/

Padfield, N. (2003). Sentencing fundamentals and the impact of Europe. *Scottish Journal of Criminal Justice Studies, 9*, 30–40.

Padfield, N. (2005). Balancing rights in 'delayed' trials. *Archbold News, 9*, 7–9.

Padfield, N. (2010). Discretion and decision-making in public protection. In M. Nash & A. Williams (Eds.), *The handbook of public protection* (pp. 103–131). Cullompton: Willan.

Padfield, N. (2011). Time to bury the custody threshold? *Criminal Law Review, 8*, 593–612.

Padfield, N. (Ed.). (2012). *Who to release? Parole, fairness and criminal justice*. London: Routledge.

Padfield, N. (2013). Exploring the success of sentencing guidelines. In A. Ashworth & J. V. Roberts (Eds.), *Sentencing guidelines: Exploring the English model* (pp. 31–51). Oxford: Oxford University Press.

Padfield, N. (2014). Front door and back door sentencing. In G. Bruinsma & D. Weisburd (Eds.), *Encyclopedia of criminology and criminal justice* (pp. 1846–1855). New York: Springer.

Padfield, N. (2016a). The English jury: Issues, concerns and future directions. In A. Kapardis & D. P. Farrington (Eds.), *The psychology of crime, policing and the courts* (pp. 188–199). London/New York: Routledge.

Padfield, N. (2016b). Justifying indeterminate detention—On what grounds? *Criminal Law Review, 11*, 795–820.

Padfield, N. (2016c). Reflections on sentencing in England and Wales. In A. Kapardis & D. P. Farrington (Eds.), *The psychology of crime, policing and the courts* (pp. 231–257). London/New York: Routledge.

Pakes, F. (2012). Comparative criminology. In D. S. Clark (Ed.), *Comparative law and society* (pp. 61–76). Cheltenham/Northampton, MA: Edward Elgar.

Ramseyer, M., & Rasmusen, E. (2001). Why is the Japanese conviction rate so high? *Journal of Legal Studies, 30(1)*, 53–88.

Rasmusen, E., Raghav, M., & Ramseyer, M. (2009). Convictions versus conviction rates: The prosecutor's choice. *American Law and Economics Review, 11(1)*, 47–78.

Roberts, J. V. (2011). Punishing, more or less: Exploring aggravation and mitigation at sentencing. In J. V. Roberts (Ed.), *Mitigation and aggravation at sentencing* (pp. 1–20). Cambridge: Cambridge University Press.

Roberts, J. V. (2013). Sentencing guidelines in England and Wales: Recent developments and emerging issues. *Law and Contemporary Problems, 76(1)*, 1–25.

Roberts, J. V., & Ashworth, A. (2016). The evolution of sentencing policy and practice in England and Wales, 2003–2015. *Crime and Justice, 45*, 307–358.

Roberts, J. V., & Hough, M. (2011). Exploring public attitudes to sentencing factors in England and Wales. In J. V. Roberts (Ed.), *Mitigation and aggravation at sentencing* (pp. 168–187). Cambridge: Cambridge University Press.

Saikô Saiban-sho Jimu Sôkyoku [General Secretariat, Supreme Court]. (2012). *Saiban-in saiban jisshi jôkyô no kenshô hôkoku-sho [Verification Report on the Status of the Implementation of Jury Trials]*. Retrieved from http://www.saibanin.courts.go.jp/vcms_lf/hyousi_honbun.pdf

Sato, M. (2014). *The death penalty in Japan: Will the public tolerate abolition?* Wiesbaden: Springer.

Sentencing Council. (2012). *Drug offenses definitive guideline 2012*.

Sentencing Council. (2016). Retrieved from http://sentencingcouncil.org.uk/

Sher, E. M. (2011). Death penalty sentencing in Japan under the lay assessor system: Avoiding the avoidable through unanimity. *Pacific Rim Law and Policy Journal, 20(3)*, 635–658.

Shiroshita, Y. (2005). Raising the statutory penalty limits and legislative policy. *Hanzai shakaigaku kenkyû [Japanese Journal of Sociological Criminology], 30*, 7–19.

Shiroshita, Y. (2009). *Ryôkei riron no gendai-teki kadai [Recent Issues on Sentencing Theory]*. Tokyo: Seibundô.

Shiroshita, Y. (2010). Current trends and issues in Japanese sentencing. *Federal Sentencing Reporter, 22(4)*, 243–248.

Shiroshita, Y. (2015). Ryôkei handan ni okeru kô'i jijô to kô'i-sha jijô – shikei to muki no aida wo chûshin ni [Circumstances of the Offense and Circumstances of the Offender in Sentencing Judgments – Focussing on what lies 'Between Death Penalty and Life Imprisonment']. *Kikan keiji bengo [Criminal Attorneys' Quarterly], 83*, 127–134.

Sieber, U. (2004). *The punishment of serious crimes* (Vols. 1–2). Freiburg im Breisgau: Edition iuscrim.

Sieber, U., Jarvers, K., & Silverman, E., (Eds.). (2013). *National criminal law in a comparative legal context: Introduction to national systems* (Vols. 1.1 and 1.3). Berlin: Duncker & Humblot.

Smith, J. C. (1998). Is ignorance bliss? Could jury trial survive investigation? *Medicine, Science and the Law, 38*, 98–106.

Suzuki, Y. E. (2016). Sexual violence in Japan: Implications of the lay judge system on victims of sexual violence. *Journal of Law and Criminal Justice, 4(1)*, 75–81.

Thaman, S. C. (2012). Criminal courts and procedure. In D. S. Clark (Ed.), *Comparative law and society* (pp. 235–253). Cheltenham/Northampton, MA: Edward Elgar.

Thomas, D. (1982–2009). *Current sentencing practice.* London: Sweet & Maxwell.

TNS RMBB, & Office for National Statistics. (2016). *Crime in England and Wales: Year ending June 2016.* Retrieved from http://www.crimesurvey.co.uk

Tonry, M. (Ed.). (2010). *Why punish? How much? A reader on punishment.* Oxford: Oxford University Press.

Uga, K., Takahashi, S., & Ôhashi, Y. (Eds.). (2003). *Taiwa de manabu gyôsei-hô – Gyôsei-hô to rinsetsu-hô bun'ya to no taiwa [Learning administrative law through dialogues – conversations between administrative law and adjacent areas of law].* Tokyo: Yûhikaku.

van Zyl Smit, D., Weatherby, P., & Creighton, S. (2014). Whole life sentences and the tide of European human rights jurisprudence: What is to be done? *Human Rights Law Review, 14*, 59–84.

Vanoverbeke, D. (2015). *Juries in the Japanese legal system: The continuing struggle for citizen participation and democracy.* London/New York: Routledge.

Vanoverbeke, D. (2016). Le Juré Face au Juge: Une Analyse Socio-Juridique de la Domination aus sein du Jury Populaire. *Japon Pluriel, 11*, 47–57.

von Hirsch, A. (1976). *Doing justice.* New York: Hill and Wang.

Walker, N., & Padfield, N. (1999). *Sentencing: Theory, law and practice.* London: Butterworths.

Wilson, M. J., Fukurai, H., & Maruta, T. (2015). *Japan and civil jury trials: The convergence of forces.* Cheltenham: Edward Elgar.

Wood, J. (2009). Why public opinion of the criminal justice system is important. In J. Wood & T. A. Gannon (Eds.), *Public opinion and criminal justice* (pp. 33–47). Cullompton: Willan.

World Prison Brief & Birkbeck Institute for Criminal Policy Research. (2016). *World prison brief data.* Retrieved from http://www.prisonstudies.org

Chapter 12
Fire, Coerced Confession, and Wrongful Conviction: A Tale of Two Countries

Michael H. Fox

1 The Higashi-Sumiyoshi Case (Osaka)

> In the event of a fatal fire, the survivors will likely be charged with arson. (Interview Gerald Hurst, n.d.)

1.1 An Accidental Fire

On July 22, 1995, Tatsuhiro Boku, a 34-year-old electrician, filled his van at a gasoline stand before returning to his home in Osaka's Higashi-Sumiyoshi ward. Some 10 min later, he smelled smoke and noticed a small fire in the garage under the van. He searched for an extinguisher while his wife Keiko called the fire department. The two tried to extinguish the tiny fire with water. Suddenly, the tiny fire grew and spread, filling the house with smoke. The couple's 11-year-old daughter, who was in the first floor bath, was unable to escape. The official cause of death was tracheal scalding.

Both the police and fire departments carried out detailed investigations. The fire itself did not arouse the suspicion of the authorities, but the family circumstances certainly did. Police soon learned that the man and woman of the house, Tatsuhiro Boku and Keiko Aoki, did not share the same last name nor were they legally married. They had lived together for 6 years—a common law marriage—and their two children were from the Keiko's previous husband. (Note: "Boku" is a Korean name—the Japanese reading of the common surname name "Park.") Police also noted that Ms. Aoki had life insurance policies on both children.

M.H. Fox (✉)
Japan Innocence and Death Penalty Information Center, Hyogo University, Kakogawa, Japan
e-mail: jiadep.org@gmail.com

J. Liu, S. Miyazawa (eds.), *Crime and Justice in Contemporary Japan*,
Springer Series on Asian Criminology and Criminal Justice Research,
https://doi.org/10.1007/978-3-319-69359-0_12

Life insurance coverage for children is quite usual in Japan; most couples carry it as a matter of course. The conventional thinking is that children are an economic necessity and will work the rice fields when parents become infirm or incapacitated. Though most Japanese work in urban areas, and very few in farm, this agrarian consciousness still permeates society.

Premiums tend to be fairly low—not unusual for a society with advanced medicine and the world's longest life-span. The usual coverage for minors through major programs is 5 million yen ($45,000) which can be doubled to ten million yen ($90,000) for a nominal premium. The little girl who died was insured for 15 million yen ($120,000) and her brother for 20 million yen ($150,000) somewhat above the national norm.

1.1.1 The Interrogation

The investigation of the fire did not produce any suspicious findings. If it had, the police would have issued arrest warrants right away. Perhaps something about this case annoyed their conformist sensitivities, particularly the irregular family circumstances. At 7 a.m. on Sunday, September 10, some 6 weeks after the tragedy, a squad of detectives arrived at the couple's new domicile and requested both Boku and Aoki to appear for voluntary questioning.

Each was taken to a separate police station. The questionings soon became abusive and coercive—the detectives immediately demanded that each confess to arson, murder, and insurance fraud. When Boku refused, he was smacked, kicked, and choked. After many hours of resisting continued verbal and physical abuse, police lost patience with Boku and fabricated a story saying his 8-year-old stepson had already confessed to seeing him start the fire. He was reminded that Japan has a death penalty, and if cooperative, he would be spared from the noose. In a state of despair, Boku broke down and signed a confession admitting to the charges.

Aoki received much the same treatment. Though she was not physically assaulted, detectives laid pictures of her deceased daughter's dead body on a desk and screamed abuse. "You couldn't save your daughter so you in fact killed her." When she wouldn't comply, two detectives put their mouths to her ear and screamed "murderer" in tandem over and over. By 8 o'clock that evening, a psychologically broken Aoki signed a similar confession.

The next day, both were visited by lawyers. Both denied the charges, Aoki in tears.

1.1.2 Creating Evidence: The Reenactment

As the constitution of Japan prohibits conviction based solely on confession, prosecutors sought other evidence to cement the case. The police allege that on the day of the fire, Boku bought a simple plastic pump (see Fig. 12.1) which is commonly used to fill kerosene stoves in the winter. After returning home, he parked the van,

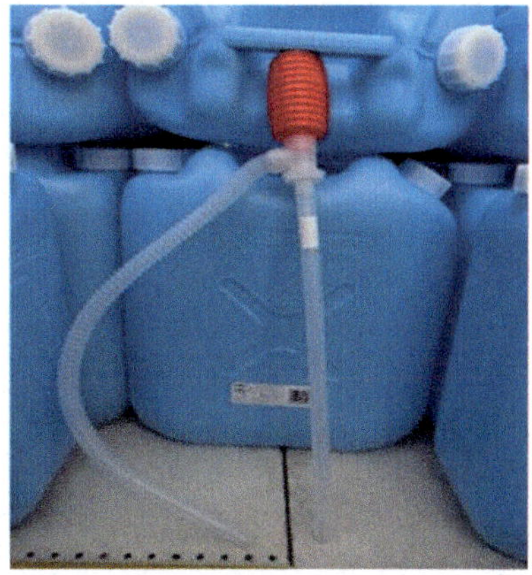

Fig. 12.1 Pump

Fig. 12.2 Bath heater

pumped out 6 or 7 L of gasoline from the tank, laid the pump under the van, and ignited the fire with a disposable tab lighter.

In order to support this story, the authorities commissioned the Scientific Criminal Investigation Laboratory, a governmental organization, to carry out a reenactment of the case. It procured a similar vehicle, built a garage to the same specification as the one in this incident, spread 7 L of gasoline on its floor, and set the entire thing ablaze. Unsurprisingly, the fire spread and the vehicle and garage burned. The experiment proved nothing (Fig. 12.2).

1.1.3 How Then Did the Fire Begin?

First off, a few words about traditional Japanese bath heaters. In older style Japanese home, baths are filled with cold water and then heated. The gas heater has a live flame and is installed outdoors adjacent to the home.

Such hot water heaters are found in traditional houses but are no longer installed in modern structures. The reason is twofold. First the chance of accident is quite high. Fill your bath, turn on the heater, fall asleep, and the bath will catch fire after a small amount of the water boils off.

Secondly, going outdoors to turn on the heater is meddlesome. The one I used for many years was on my second floor balcony. Going outside in the winter was uncomfortable, and heavy rain made usage difficult, sometimes impossible.

The danger of open flames in hot water heaters is well known in the USA. According to the building laws of most states, when installed in garages, gas water heaters must be set at least 24~36 in. above the floor (International Building Code, 2015). This is to protect against accidental oil and gas leakages from automobiles. In the Aoki home, the heater was originally installed outdoors—the garage was added on some years later.

It takes no great leap of imagination to surmise that this could have been an accidental fire. The van was parked in very close proximity to the bath heater. The heater has an open flame and was only 90 cm (35 in.) from the van's gas intake valve. The heater was lit shortly after the van was parked.

Shouldn't the police have noticed these details? From the time of the fire until the time of arrest, 6 weeks later, police investigators carried out extensive interviews with Honda, the manufacturer of the van, and Osaka Gas, the manufacturer of the heating unit and the natural gas provider. Honda insisted that an examination of the vehicle revealed no defects or any possible source of gas leakage. According to 2Attorney Masayuki Takeshita, the gas provider stated that it was impossible for such a fire to start due to the 90 cm distance between the flame and the vehicle (personal communication, May 11, 2008)!

1.1.4 Building a Defense

Japan is a leading modern industrialized country, constantly creating new technology. In some ways, it is behind the times. The USA is home to the National Association of Fire Investigators (NAFI) and the International Association of Arson Investigators (IAAI). Both of these bodies provide professional training and certification. Japan, on the other hand, has no such professional organization nor any licensed specialists in fire or arson investigation.

In order to build evidence, the defense first turned to Hideaki Mochizuki, a technical investigator who belongs to the Institution of Professional Engineers. He suggested the most probable cause of the fire was sparks from the air compressor igniting gasoline that had leaked from the fuel line. The tank was probably overfilled at the gas station, and a small quantity could have escaped from a crack in the vapor canister. The problem with the air compressor, made by a subsidiary manufacturer, was so widespread that Honda and other manufacturers issued a recall in 1991 (Mochizuki, 2001).

Defense attorneys also challenged other allegations made by the police. Boku confessed to purchasing the plastic kerosene pump, at a small hardware store he frequently used, the day of the fire. The owner of the small hardware store was called to the stand. Boku, a professional electrician, was a regular customer, and the owner knew him well. The owner testified that Boku did not stop in his store the day of the fire nor, for that matter, did he have any recollection of a customer ever requesting a kerosene pump in the midst of the sweltering Osaka summer (Himawari, n.d.).

After nearly 40 hearings apiece, in separate trials, the Osaka District Court issued judgment. On March 30, 1999, it sentenced Boku to life imprisonment. Some 6 weeks later, it sentenced Aoki to the same.

2 The Mark Kirk Case (Delaware)

On December 4, 1996, Mark Kirk (aged 35) and his girlfriend Darlene entertained some guests at their New Castle, Delaware, apartment. Delaware, the second smallest state, lies on the east coast, nestled next to the Atlantic Ocean. Though geographically small, it is an economic powerhouse. A tax haven to corporations, 50% of all publicly traded US companies are incorporated in Delaware.

Darlene was the mother to two sons, and Mark had moved in with her just 1 week before. The four friends had been drinking since early in the day. When Darlene began flirting with one of the guests, Mark became enraged. A vicious argument erupted and the guests left (Fox, 2016).

Mark and Darlene continued to argue and eventually agreed to a truce until the next day. In the early morning hours, while all were asleep, smoke began billowing from the kitchen. All four occupants managed to escape the apartment unharmed. The family in the apartment above was not so fortunate. A cruel act of fate, a father, and his two children ages 17 and 8, died in the blaze.

Kirk was told to appear at the police station the next day. He was interrogated by fire marshal Willard Preston. From the outset, Kirk adamantly denied the charge of arson. After many hours of pressure, he later admitted on video to deliberately starting the fire by pouring Captain Morgan's Spiced Rum onto one of the stove's electric burners. He was arrested and charged with three counts of murder.

2.1 *Junk Science*

There is one serious problem with this confession. Captain Morgan's Spiced Rum is entirely non-flammable. It is only 35% alcohol (70 proof). The remaining 65% is water, flavors, and other ingredients which retard burning. It is not like Bacardi 151, which is 75.5% alcohol and labeled "Danger: Flammable" (Lentini, 2006).

So how did the fire start? Several days before the blaze, a grease fire occurred on the same stove. Kirk cleaned the electric coil and then lifted up the stove top. He was shocked to see a pool of grease. Keeping the house clean and safe was not part of Darlene's agenda. The occupants agreed not to use the problematic burner until the apartment complex maintenance man was available for repair. A stroke of vicious irony, the maintenance man was the father who perished in the above apartment.

Grease fires usually occur when a stove is hot. So how could the fire start in the middle of the night? The partiers, smoking without lighters, were using the stove to light cigarettes. It is quite likely that the stove was left on before the angry couple turned off the lights and went to sleep.

While awaiting trial, a guard at the jail, a part-time firefighter who was called to the scene, offered Kirk an opinion. "I have never seen a fire spread so fast. It is hard to believe the building was constructed properly. A normal apartment should be better able to withstand a fire from a stove."

Kirk begged the guard to testify but he refused. "I have to think about my family" (Fox, 2016).

2.2 Further Evidence: Grease and Fire

Ten months after the fire, at the request of the prosecution, a technician examined the stove. The technician reported that there was no malfunction (Fox, 2016).

This finding was unsurprising. The National Fire Protection Association frequently reiterates that "the typical accidental cause of fires in the US is usually associated with kitchens and the result of fat, grease or oil" (Ahrens, 2013).

A perusal of archives from Delaware's largest newspaper, *The News Journal*, strongly confirms this fact. A simple web search turned up a shocking amount of articles caused by grease fires. In fact, a fire in the exact same apartment complex in the year 2000 was ruled an accident (Thompson, 2000)!

2.3 Death Aware in Delaware

Ineffective assistance of counsel is a serious problem in American trials. While it occurs in various degrees, the most heinous instance is when an innocent defendant is deemed guilty by counsel without even a perfunctory investigation. When attorneys believe a client is guilty, the triers of fact will certainly think the same. Before trial, one of Kirk's attorneys openly admitted his client's guilt. He commented to the press, "Kirk never intended to burn the building, but was trying to destroy the alcohol that fueled the couple's problems" (Hager, 1997).

Apparently, Kirk's lawyer's only goal was to spare their client from Delaware's well-used needle. A sentence of life, with or without parole, was the goal. In the 1990s, Delaware was one of the nation's leading per capita execution states. In fact, the second smallest state in the nation ranks as number three in gross per capita executions, just behind Oklahoma and Texas. With three executions alone in 1996, the year Kirk was arrested, his attorney's fear was not unfounded (Death Penalty Information Center, 2017).

At trial, the prosecution announced that it would seek death. In order to save their client, Kirk's attorneys opted for a bench trial—that is a trial by a judge alone—without a jury. Juries are easy to inflame, convention goes, especially with victim impact statements. Better to leave the verdict to an impassive judge.

Needless to say, how could the prosecution prove the impossible? What evidence could possibly prove how an inflammable liquid could be used to start a fire? The problem was easily solved. The state furnished a filmed burn test showing Captain Morgan's Spiced Rum erupting into a pyrotechnic flame when pooled upon a hot electric burner. Kirk's attorneys presented their own burn test in which the rum failed to ignite. In the end, the judge ruled that the two tests canceled each other out, and the confession carried weight.

The defense strategy worked. Kirk was spared the death penalty and sentenced to three consecutive life terms plus 23 years.

Could Kirk's attorneys have done more for their client? In fact, they could not have done any less. The obvious action would have been to contact the manufacturer of Captain Morgan's Spiced Rum and subpoena information about the product's flammability. But neither attorney bothered to do the obvious. And the reason they did not, quite simply, is that both thought Kirk guilty of the crime.

3 The Appeals

3.1 The Higashi-Sumiyoshi Case

Japan has a three-tier court system: district courts, high courts, and a supreme court. Upon being found guilty or innocent in the district court, both the defendant and the state have the right to appeal. The high court, consisting of three judges, then begins de novo review of the lower court's decision.

After the sentences of life imprisonment were imposed, the defense teams were fortified. Eight new attorneys joined the cases, meaning that both defendants would be separately represented by four to five attorneys each. And this would grow over time. Only one would receive any remuneration, all volunteered to represent Boku and Aoki pro bono. But pro bono is an understatement. Many dug into their own pockets to offer support, pay for evidence, and bring an expert witness to Japan.

In an opening statement before the appeals court, defense attorney Kazue Ogawa attacked the validity of the confessions:

> What would an ordinary middle class couple without financial difficulties have to gain from that amount of insurance money? How could they know that fire would spread and the smoke rise with the necessary precision to kill their daughter? If this was in fact a conspiracy, is it really possible that an ordinary couple could engineer a master crime in which the evidence points to an accident? A plan which specified details of how and when to call the fire department, what lies to feed the police, what belongings to remove, and where to live after the building was destroyed? (Ogawa, 2000)

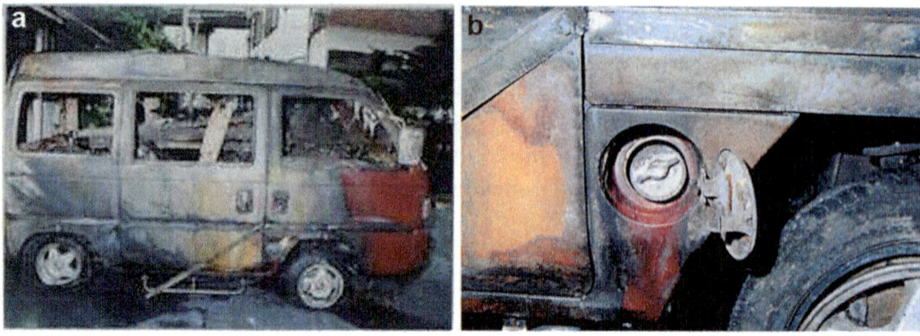

Fig. 12.3 (**a**, **b**) Boku's van and close-up of the gas intake valve

3.1.1 Enter the Expert

In 2004, the Higashi-Sumiyoshi defendants received a giant stroke of support. Peter Klaput, a professional arson investigator associated with the Cole Company in California, took interest in the case. A former police detective with FBI training, Klaput offered his services pro bono. He began examining pictures of the fire and offered an intriguing new analysis (Fig. 12.3).

To Klaput, the most telling picture, below, was the burn pattern around the gas intake valve. As can be seen in the picture, the original red paint below the valve remains clearly visible. This indicates that it did not burn. And the reason: it was wet.

Klaput is convinced that liquid gas was escaping from the intake valve. It comes as a surprise to the layman, but the hard fact is that liquid gasoline will not burn. What drives automobile engines are gas vapors, not liquids. Liquid gasoline is inflammable and will extinguish a fire if poured in extensive quantity.

Klaput came to Japan and examined the van firsthand. He had trouble removing the gas cap. Likewise, in the first stage of the police investigation, photographs show investigators using a large monkey wrench to remove the cap. Klaput believes that after the tank was filled, the attendant did not attach it properly, used improper force causing it to jam, and created a conduit for gas to leak.

Ambient conditions that day certainly exacerbated the consequences. July is a terribly hot month; the temperature that day was 33°C (91°F). Gas attendants usually overfill tanks. Moreover, the gasoline was being pumped from a cool underground tank and certainly expanded inside the hot automobile.

Klaput prepared an extensive report detailing his theory of the fire. He found Boku's confession to border on the absurd. Gas is not like kerosene but explodes when ignited. Had Boku used a tab lighter to start the fire, he would have suffered massive burn injuries.

The defense wanted Klaput to take the stand. His participation was summarily refused by the high court. The chief judge, near retirement age, and possibly brain dead (65), stated, "Well, what is he going to know about Japanese vehicles" (June 7, 2005). About half the vehicles Klaput examines in the states are Japanese (Personal communication, June 8, 2005).

Klaput also informed us of a PrimeTime Live special hosted by Dianne Sawyer on the dangers of accidental fires caused by gas spills and hot water heaters. New Orleans attorney Edward Downing, who appeared in the program, furnished us a copy (Sawyer, 1996). Despite protests of the prosecution, the documentary was accepted into evidence.

3.1.2 Decisions

The Osaka High Court decisions were issued in 2004. Despite much new evidence, Aoki's conviction was confirmed on November 2; Boku's was confirmed on December 20. The attorneys soon filed appeals with the supreme court.

The PrimeTime Live show would draw some attention from the Japanese media. In 2006, after receiving a letter from Aoki, a television program devoted entirely to wrongful convictions "The Scoop" (Za Sukoopu) decided to take on the case.

The show was very well done. A lot of money was put into the production—quite a surprise for a country with few documentaries and a plethora of brain-dead variety shows. Broadcast nationally, on May 4, 2006, it featured several burn tests, illustrating the easy ignitability of gas fumes in close proximity to a bath heater (Torigoe, 2006).

These reenactments were presented as new evidence to the supreme court. The supreme court turned down the appeal, and both Higashi-Sumiyoshi defendant's conviction were confirmed on November 7, 2006. Needless to say, The Scoop's coverage of the case impacted public opinion and drew attention to the case.

3.2 The Mark Kirk Case: A Study in Dysfunction

Delaware has a two-tier criminal court system: a superior court and the supreme court. After his direct appeal to the supreme court was rejected, the next step toward justice is a PCR (postconviction relief) appeal—a civil case. Defendants can bring up issues that were not addressed in the previous appeal, such as ineffective assistance of counsel. In a case such as Kirk's, with the defendant sentenced to life imprisonment, it is typical for the court to appoint counsel. When none was appointed, Kirk made an official request which was denied. A situation without rhyme or reason, Kirk was forced to become his own lawyer. His PCR appeals were rejected.

Ten years into his incarceration, Kirk wrote John Lentini, PhD, author of *Scientific Protocols for Fire Investigation* (Lentini, 2006), and considered the leading expert in the field. Lentini travels the country and lectures to all sort of audiences. He has spoken at the Innocence Network Conference and is sought after from both sides of the bench. Above all, he enjoys speaking in front of prosecutors, whom he refers to as "the gate keepers of our criminal justice system" (Personal communication, March 2013).

In 2006, Lentini conducted three tests to check the flammability of Captain Morgan's Spiced Rum. Despite his best effort, the rum would not ignite (Lentini, 2006).

With this new evidence, Kirk again requested that the state appoint PCR counsel. The request was again turned down. He drew up legal briefs and submitted this new evidence. It should have been a slam dunk; the Lentini tests unequivocally prove that the state's burn test was an utter fabrication. Needless to say, his PCR appeals were rejected. The courts found the new evidence to be "untimely and cumulative" (Fox, 2016).

After PCR appeals are exhausted, the next step toward exoneration is to seek relief in the federal courts. Once again it is routine for the courts to appoint legal counsel upon request of the inmate. The courts refused. Kirk directly contacted the Federal Public Defender in Delaware, enclosing copies of the Lentini tests. They also refused the case.

Once again Kirk was forced to file his own briefs. His appeals to all three tiers of the federal courts were summarily refused.

3.2.1 Poetic Justice?

Kirk did have several pyrrhic victories. In 2003, with a change to the definition of the state's felony murder rule, he made a timely pro se appeal which resulted in resentencing. He was resentenced to 46 years, a fair decrease from his first sentence of three life terms plus 23 years.

The Lentini tests did bring an unexpected result. Fifteen days after Kirk submitted this new evidence, J. Willard Preston, the fire marshal who both interrogated Kirk and fabricated the state's burn test, abruptly resigned on April 6, 2007. Fire commission members were startled. Preston gave no reason for the resignation (Sanginiti, 2007).

A second instant of poetic justice would soon follow. On November 12, 2008, Donald Roberts, one of Kirk's two prosecutors, was arrested. He was charged with drunk driving and public intoxication. He continued to drink and drive and was arrested again on December 4. In addition to DUI, this time, he was also charged with breaking and entering. He pleaded guilty and later resigned his position as prosecutor (Parra, 2008).

3.2.2 Would Death Be Better?

As mentioned above, Kirk's attorneys only goal was to spare their client from the needle. This they achieved, but, ironically, a sentence of death would have been better. Had Kirk received the death penalty, appointment of attorneys is mandatory. Death sentences play prominently in the media. And with the Lentini evidence, the media would have a heyday. The courts would certainly have granted a retrial.

And nobody understood this better than the prosecution. On the last day of his original trial, after the state asked for death, a special evening session was convened. Kirk, back at the jail, and already changed out of his court clothes, was suddenly called back to court. After demanding death, the prosecution requested a sentence of life imprisonment.

Interestingly enough, this episode was not transcribed, and no record exists. District Attorney Roberts complained that "Kirk is cunning enough to beat the system. We want to keep him inside. We therefore ask that he be sentenced to life without parole" (Fox, 2016).

3.3 *Why? An Attempt as Explanation*

3.3.1 The Higashi-Sumiyoshi Case

As mentioned above, Tatsuhiro Boku is a Korean resident of Japan. Like 600,000 others, he was born in Japan and speaks only Japanese. Yet he remains a citizen of South Korea. He can become a Japanese citizen, though it is a difficult and sometimes degrading process (Fukuoka, 2000).

Many Koreans face intense discrimination in Japan and use Japanese names to disguise their identity. Boku had never revealed his Korean identity to Aoki's father. In everyday life, he used a Japanese pseudonym. I asked defense attorney Tomoyo Saito if ethnic discrimination played some role in this case. "After the arrests, Aoki's father heard the name 'Boku' for the first time," she explained. When asked, "who is Boku?" a detective replied, "Oh, you didn't know your daughter was bedding down with a Korean?" (Tomoyo Saito, personal communication, June 8, 2001).

Quite clearly, cavorting outside the tribe is taboo in Japan, as it is throughout much of the world. But there is more to the story. Criminal justice authorities embrace "good girl vs bad girl" stereotypes. A much stricter demarcation attaches to the notion of "good mother vs unfit mothers." Motherhood is perhaps the most sacrosanct of all human institutions. Those who live outside convention are prone to social reproach, particularly for associating with bad men (Unfit Mothers, 2017). It is apparent that the forces of authority wanted to punish the couple, most of all, Aoki, for violating nativist lines—being a divorced mother— and cohabiting with a Korean.

3.3.2 Why? The Mark Kirk Case

The day after the fire, Kirk appeared at the police station for voluntary questioning. One thing struck him as very odd. The police knew Darlene by name and treated her quite convivially.

Kirk believes that she was the daughter of a police officer or someone well connected to the force. Supporting this contention is the curious fact that after

Mark's arrest, Darlene was being represented by legal counsel. This is most unusual—she was not charged as an accomplice or considered a suspect. And she was being represented by one of Delaware's most renown attorneys—Joe Hurley.[1] As shown below, Hurley is an attorney that the forces of law and order turn to in times of distress.

Why would Darlene need legal counsel? This story begins with a grease fire. The initial police investigation certainly discovered a grease buildup inside the stove. As mentioned above, Darlene was not one to put too much time into housekeeping.

Still, one has a legal duty to keep one's home safe and free from hazard. Leaving one's stove unattended and endangering others are a crime. Darlene could be charged with voluntary manslaughter. Regardless of the facts, no judge is going to hand out a suspended sentence for the deaths of a father and two children. In the end, Darlene was spared from prosecution, and Mark Kirk became the public enemy.

Adding fuel to this contention is his defense of another principle actor in this case. After prosecutor Donald Roberts was arrested and charged with multiple DUIs and breaking and entering, he needed legal counsel. He hired Joe Hurley (Duifoundation.org, 2008).

Yet another reason comes to mind. As mentioned above, a firefighter who arrived on the scene was aghast at the ferocity of the blaze. If indeed the apartment was not built according to code, somewhere, someone, would be guilty of fraud. Indeed more than someone. Perhaps even a large part of the building industry in this small state could come under the microscope. Conspiracy theories aside, the potential for a statewide scandal is quite palpable.

3.3.3 An Unusual Friendship

Though horrible miscarriages of justice, these cases do share one heartwarming story. I became involved with the Higashi-Sumiyoshi case at the start of the high court appeal back in 2001. After attending court, I wrote Boku a letter in Japanese. He replied in English. He admitted that this was his first ever letter in English and the first time that he had used the language since graduating from high school some 11 years before. The letter was somewhat difficult to read, but his writing abilities greatly improved over time.

I learned of the Mark Kirk case through the 2004 article authored by Kirk (Kirk, 2004). The case seemed eerily similar to the Higashi-Sumiyoshi case. I wrote Kirk, enclosed a donation, and requested that, in lieu of thanks, he send a letter to Boku.

The two began to correspond. Mark decided to study Japanese, ordered a textbook and a dictionary, and then subscribed to a Japanese learner's magazine. Boku wrote in English. The two exchanged many letters over the years. Two men wrongfully convicted of arson and murder due to coerced confessions—they see eye to

[1] I contacted Hurley seeking legal advice for Kirk. His secretary acknowledged his participation in the case. Hurley refused to speak to me (2009, September 26).

eye on many things. Unfortunately, once Boku's conviction was confirmed by the Japanese Supreme Court, he was transferred to a prison. Mail exchange with other prisoners became prohibited.

4 The Retrial

On July 7, 2009, the Higashi-Sumiyoshi defense teams filed for retrial with the Osaka District Court. The event drew fanfare—two attorneys and Boku's mother participated in a press conference. A favorite biblical adage of the Japan Federation of Bar Associations is that reopening a criminal case is about as easy as pulling a dromedary through the eye of the needle. At the time, no confirmed life imprisonment case had been reversed since 1986.

In order to reopen a closed case, new evidence must be submitted. The defense team submitted a new experiment performed by a professor at Hirosaki University. The prosecution did not present any new evidence. On March 7, 2012, the Osaka District Court granted retrials to both defendants. It was an amazing achievement. Simply put, the judges believed that the scientific evidence outweighed the confessions.

The prosecution immediately appealed. The high court reversed the district court's decision to temporarily release the defendants and began a de novo review of the district court's decision.

This time the prosecution did submit new evidence. It had the Scientific Criminal Investigation Laboratory, which carried out a new experiment. The defense was thrilled with the result. It acclaimed new evidence showing that the fire started spontaneously (Takeshita, 2013).

4.1 Osaka High Court: Decision

Kirk and Boku are now free to exchange letters again. On October 23, 2015, 3.5 years after the district court decided to reopen the case, the Osaka High Court rejected the prosecutorial appeal and ordered the case to be reopened. It also suspended the defendant's sentences and allowed provisional release. On October 26, Aoki and Boku walked out of their prisons after a 20-year nightmare.

With two courts granting retrials, a victory for the defense was almost assured. The defense teams began to prepare for court. Their jobs would be much easier than expected. Shortly after their release, the prosecution announced that they would not "risshou (立証)" the case. It is difficult to put this word into proper English. In short, they would not call any witnesses but would just make closing arguments.

On August 10, 2016, some 21 years after initial arrest, the Osaka District Court issued decisions of not guilty. The prosecution did not appeal, and the decisions were finalized. Boku and Aoki were completely exonerated.

5 Then and Now: If the Fires Had Occurred Today?

Two accidental fires, four deaths, and three wrongful convictions. Indeed the similarities between these cases are striking, even shocking. It is this author's opinion that had the fires and deaths occurred today, the American defendant would not be convicted and that the Japanese defendants would not even be prosecuted. Let us examine the reasons.

5.1 Confessions

Compared to 20 years ago, even mediocre defense attorneys are cognizant of the possibility of false confessions. A plethora of scholarship on false confessions has emerged, and new literature is coming out all the time. Recent statistics show that DNA evidence has contributed to 349 exonerations, of which 28% were accompanied by confessions (Innocence Project, 2017).

5.2 Fire Science-Growing Developments

Fire science and analysis has grown hugely over the last two decades. The National Fire Protection Association (NFPA) which is a nongovernmental trade association with over 65,000 members publishes "Guide for Fire and Explosion Investigations" (NFPA 921) considered by many to be the bible on the topic. Specific protocols for investigation are clearly detailed. Any criminal defense attorney in the present day could not ignore its contents. This guide has grown by leaps and bounds over the years. The guide specifies that fire "investigators must justify any claim that is made outside of the guide's parameters."

In 2006, noted fire investigator John Lentini, who performed burn tests in the Kirk case, established a new standard of analysis with the publication of *Scientific Protocols for Fire Investigation*. The book is now in its second edition, and a third edition is expected sometime soon (Lentini, 2006). Lentini debunked many accepted types of evidence and has explained the phenomena of "flashover" in which fires burn downward.

Over the last 20 years, membership in two professional organizations, the National Association of Fire Investigators (NAFI) and the International Association of Arson Investigators (IAAI), has grown tremendously. Both of these groups have branches in every state and the IAAI in many countries.

Thus said, defendants charged with arson, who are innocent, now have many more resources at their disposal. Only a truly ignorant defense attorney could be naïve to this development in fire science. But there is one more compelling incident regarding fire science and fantasy in the USA.

5.3 *Wrongfully Executed?*

On February 17, 2004, the state of Texas executed Cameron Todd Willingham. Willingham's three daughters died in a fire in December, 1991. He adamantly denied the charges but was convicted of murder by arson.

Various documentaries have been made about the case. Attorneys for Willingham are seeking to reopen the case. The state of Texas has been fighting tooth and nail to keep it sealed.

This case has grabbed national attention. The Willingham case is well known to the criminal bars throughout the entire country. In defending a case of arson and murder, two decades after Kirk was convicted, only the most incompetent or lazy attorney could accept prima facie evidence presented by the state as fact (Cameron Todd Willingham, 2017).

5.4 *Japan*

False confessions and wrongful convictions have a long history in Japan. The Matsukawa case of the 1940s, the Menda case of the 1950s, the Sayama and Nabari cases of the 1960s, and the Kabutoyama case of the 1970s are just a few to mention. In March 2014, former boxer and death row inmate Iwao Hakamada was paroled. Originally arrested in 1966, he was listed in the Guinness Book of Records as the world's longest incarcerated death row inmate (Jiadep Database, 2017). The defendants in all these cases gave confessions which were later discredited by the courts.

5.5 *Shibushi: A Case in Point*

Of the many cases of wrongful arrest that have surfaced in Japan in recent years, one particular incident has raised eyebrows and piqued public interest. In 2003, a local election was held in the rural coastal city of Shibushi, tucked away in the southern Kagoshima prefecture. Shibushi is best known for producing fresh bottled water. One of the candidates, without party affiliation, and who entered the race at a late time, defeated a long-standing LDP candidate (Nichibenren, 2008a).

Some weeks later, police and prosecutors launched an investigation into vote buying. The investigation turned from tide to tsunami, and 15 rural citizens, mostly senior citizens, were arrested. Though a non-violent crime, most were held in jail for 3–6 months. The candidate was incarcerated for 13 months, his elderly wife for 9 days.

Normally, such cases would not gain much public attention: a small election in a rural locale. The Shibushi case drew potent outside attention: *The New York Times*. On May 11, 2007, the *Times* published a stunning article on the case, outlining the allegations and displaying pictures of the arrested suspects—who appear as they are mundane, salt of the earth, rural senior citizens (Onishi, 2007). The Japanese media, always conscious of overseas attention, reexamined the case.

The Japan Federation of Bar Associations produced a DVD about the case in 2008. Perhaps the most damning caveat was the recreation of the interrogation of 55-year-old hotel/restaurant owner. After refusing to confess to buying votes with gifts, an interrogator wrote posters with imaginary messages from his father, "I don't remember raising such a lousy son," and from his grandchildren, "We hope you become an honest grandpa." He then grabbed the hotel owner's feet and forcefully trampled the posters (Nichibenren, 2008b).

This technique of extracting confession has a long history in Japan. In the sixteenth century, after Christianity was officially forbidden, suspected converts were made to trample pictures of crosses to ascertain their non-allegiance. The act is called fumie (literally "stepping picture"). Those who refused were summarily executed.

In the end, all 15 suspects of the Shibushi case were ultimately vindicated. A suit was brought against the state, and all received approximately $50,000 each (Jiken, 2017). In the end, the case demonstrated to the public the inner workings of police interrogation and the ease at which confessions can be coerced.

5.6 *Increasing Media Coverage*

Popular interest in interrogation and wrongful convictions has also spurred new publications. A quarterly magazine entirely devoted to wrongful convictions, Enzai File, began publication in March, 2008 (*enzai* means wrongful charge/conviction in Japanese). It is now in its 9th year, with 28 issues in print. Issue 16 covered the Higashi-Sumiyoshi case (Satomi, 2012).

Wrongful convictions have even made it to the movie screen. A motion picture entitled, "I just didn't do it" about a young man wrongfully charged for groping a woman on a crowded train was released in 2007 (Kameyama and Suo, 2007).

5.7 *A Mea Culpa Whistleblower*

Media coverage of wrongful convictions by Enzai File and The Scoop has certainly advanced public consciousness. Professional investigative journalism is a powerful tool. Yet, both Enzai File and The Scoop share the same focus, shining the light on injustice from outside the system.

It is unusual when the same light gets shown from the inside out. In 2012, a former prosecutor, Hiroshi Ichikawa, published a memoir. The book details his voyage from passing Japan's scrupulously difficult bar exam and entrance into the procuracy. At first, he had a real concern about defendants and the right of due process. This concern later degenerated, and Ichikawa would be removed from office for beating a suspect who refused to confess (Ichikawa, 2012).

Ichikawa managed to convict the suspect—the coerced confession was admitted in court. The defendant would later be exonerated on appeal, and Ichikawa was removed from his post as prosecutor.

Ichikawa went public and accepted responsibility about his antics. Apart from his book, he decided to show remorse in another traditional way. He apologized to the victim performing a *dogeza*, a full-frontal bow on his knees lowering his head to the ground.

The impact of a prosecutor revealing and apologizing for an egregious act of violence cannot be underestimated. Judges read newspapers and watch television much like anyone. If any had previous doubts about the use of pressure and violence in the interrogation room, those doubts were now dispelled.

5.8 US Scholarship

Enzai File, The Scoop, and Ichikawa's book have impacted public consciousness in Japan regarding the reality of police interrogation. But these works all have one common characteristic—Japanese authors writing about false confessions and wrongful convictions in Japan.

As stated above, conventional Japanese thought views the rights of the criminally accused as much better protected in the USA. Japan has many Miranda Associations which study this once hallow case. Part of the interest in Miranda stems from American movies and police dramas, as well as publications about American criminal cases.

It is easy to see how Japanese perceptions of American criminal justice have been shaped. Those who thought that coerced confession was more likely an indigenous practice, and less likely in a country that created Miranda rights, were stunningly surprised in 2009. "The Problems of False Confessions in the Post-DNA World," was published in Japanese translation (Drizin and Leo, 2009).

The two authors Steven A. Drizen and Richard Leo have stellar reputations. The book puts to rest the popular Japanese notion that the rights of the criminally accused are much better protected in the USA. Notice the use of the term, "much better protected." On the surface, they may be better protected than Japan. But in the final result, good interrogators in the USA are quite able to coerce false confessions from innocent suspects. Whether this work has impacted Japanese jurisprudence is, of course, a matter for conjecture. Needless to say, most judges are avid readers, and it can be surmised that the book is being read by the judiciary.

6 Saiban-in Seido: A Mixed Jury System

In 2009, Japan launched a new system of adjudicating criminal trials. Defendants charged with serious crimes would be tried by three professional judges and six citizens. This is called the "mixed jury system" (*saiban-in seido*). Japan did have jury trials from 1928 to 1943, but since then trials have all been adjudicated by judges only.

This system was introduced for various reasons. One of these was an angst about the guilty ratio in criminal trials. The figure, which has always been between 99.7 and 99.9%, has been a sore point in a country which is so sensitive to foreign eyes. Bringing citizens into the criminal adjudication process could defer criticism and foment legitimacy (Jones, 2008).

With this notion in mind, the first Japanese mixed jury trial began in 2009. It may be too early to assess how this system has impacted the adjudication of criminal justice. But it does appear that prosecutors are being somewhat more cautious about charging cases with insufficient evidence. One case in particular begs attention.

6.1 A Double Homicide

On June 19, 2009, an elderly couple in Kagoshima city was murdered. According to the autopsy, both the husband (age 91) and the wife (age 87) were bludgeoned to deaths with a shovel (Kagoshima kourei fuufu satsugai jiken, 2017).

The murder had all the signs of a crime of passion. Lacerations existed on the victims' faces and heads. Money and other valuables which were easily accessible were not taken. Robbery was not an apparent cause of the tragedy.

Ten days after the crime, police arrested and charged a 70-year-old former carpenter with the double murder.

From the outset, the suspect denied the charges. Of the 446 pieces of evidence submitted to the court, the prosecution insists 11 items, fingerprints, and DNA, which tie the defendant to the crime.

The defendant denied ever being in the victim's home. The defense, in perhaps a first ever for Japan, suggested that all evidence was planted. The prosecution demanded death.

What is most interesting about this case is the absence of a confession. Senior citizens will not put up much resistance to police pressure, and getting a signed confession would not be difficult. This could signal a change in attitude, a move toward prosecuting based on physical evidence and testimony.

The trial lasted 40 days, the longest mixed jury to date. On December 10, 2010, the Kagoshima district court issued a stunning verdict. It tossed out the defense's contention that the physical evidence was planted. But it excoriated the police investigation of the house, criticizing the paucity of photos taken at the crime scene, suggesting that things in the house could have been moved by a third party and that the motive of robbery was unjustifiable. The evidence presented by the prosecution was ruled circumstantial. The defendant was found not guilty (Kagoshima kourei fuufu satsugai jiken, 2017).

It was only the fifth time in the postwar period for a Japanese defendant to be found not guilty in a death penalty trial (Jiadep not guilty). Commenting on the case, former Tokyo High Court judge Hiroshi Kadono commented that, "under the mixed jury system, judges cannot simply try defendants in one breath. They must explain their thoughts clearly" (Mainichi Shinbun, 2010).

6.2 *Mark Kirk: Light on the Horizon?*

One would think that with scientific evidence of wrongful conviction, the mass media would take interest in Kirk's case. I have sent inquiries to every major American news show. These include *Dateline NBC*, *American Justice*, *20/20*, *Primetime: What Would You Do*?, etc. Not one has shown an iota of interest. The Kirk case leads to one gruesome factor about justice in the USA—if you are innocent—being sentenced to death is preferable to life imprisonment. Death penalty cases are guaranteed counsel through all level of appeals (with the exception of Alabama).

Capital cases attract both lawyers and the mass media. Nobody knows this better than Juan Melendez. On January 3, 2002, Melendez became the US's 99th death row exoneree. Melendez is an outspoken critic of the death penalty. Ironic as it is, he owes his freedom to capital punishment. "If I had been sentenced to life imprisonment, I would still be there" (Melendez, 2017).

6.3 *A Shimmer of Hope*

The Mid-Atlantic Innocence Project located at Georgetown University reviews cases of possible wrongful convictions in Washington D.C., Maryland, and Virginia. They have never taken on a case in Delaware. They are currently reviewing the Kirk case.

7 Summary

This paper has examined and compared two different cases of wrongful conviction in Japan and the USA. The defendants in both cases were charged with murder and arson, though no arson ever occurred. The Japanese defendants have been exonerated; the American remains imprisoned. False confessions were the central evidence in both cases.

Apart from coerced confessions, prosecutorial malfeasance is salient in both of these cases. The investigative authorities created crimes and prosecuted defendants they knew to be innocent. In the American case, they fabricated evidence as well. The defense attorneys were clearly ineffective.

In regard to the question of why these prosecutions occurred, this paper has boldly theorized that the Japanese defendants were arrested due to ethnic prejudice. The American defendant was most likely scapegoated to protect his female roommate from prosecution and perhaps to shield building and construction interests from investigation.

This paper has argued that had the fires occurred today, it is unlikely that the defendants would be convicted. This is due to a huge growth in conscientiousness among the general public, the bar, and the judiciary about interrogation practices and coerced confessions, on both sides of the pacific. And with the advent of the mixed jury system in Japan, this rise in conscientiousness has made it implausible for a prosecutor to seek conviction based on confession alone.

8 The End

Michael H. Fox is associate professor at Hyogo University. He is a webmaster of the Japan Innocence and Death Penalty Information Center (jiadep.org) and two other wrongful conviction websites,: the Worldwide Women's Criminal Justice Network (wcjn.org) and the Network for Innocent Arson Defendants (niad.info). Seaside walks and meditation help him maintain sanity.

References

Ahrens, M. (2013). *No. USS11*. Washington, DC: National Fire Protection Association.

Cameron Todd Willingham. (2017) in *Wikipedia*. Retrieved June 25, 2017 from https://en.wikipedia.org/wiki/Cameron_Todd_Willingham

Death Penalty Information Center. (2017). Available from http://www.deathpenaltyinfo.org/

Drizin, S., & Leo, R. (2009). *Naze mujitsu no hito ga jihaku suru no ka*. Tokyo: Nippon Hyouronsha.

Duifoundation.org. (2008, December 26). *Delaware prosecutor arrested again after DUI charge*. Retrieved June 25, 2017 from http://www.niad.info/Mark_Kirk.html

Fox, M. (2016). *The Mark Kirk story*. Justice: Denied!, 63, 3–5. Seattle: The Justice Institute.

Fukuoka, Y. (2000). *Lives of young Koreans in Japan*. Melbourne: Trans Pacific Press.

Hager, J. (1997, October 9). Murder, arson trial underway *The News Journal*. Retrieved June 25, 2017 from http://www.niad.info/Mark_Kirk.html

Himawari, T. (n.d.). *Higashi-Sumiyoshi Enzai Jiken wo shien suru kai*. Available at http://www.jca.apc.org/~hs_enzai/

Innocence Project. (2017). *DNA exonerations in the United States*. Available at https://www.innocenceproject.org/

Ichikawa, H. (2012). *Kenji Shikkaku*. Tokyo: Kodansha Gendai Shinsho.

International Building Code. (2015). *International Code Council*. Available at https://codes.iccsafe.org

Interview Gerald Hurst. (n.d.). Retrieved June 25, 2017 from http://www.pbs.org/wgbh/pages/frontline/death-by-fire/interviews/gerald-hurst.html

Jones, C. P. A. (2008). *Amerikajin bengoshi ga mita saibanin seido*. Tokyo: Heibonshashinsho.

Jiadep Database. (2017). Available at www.jiadep.org

Kameyama, A. (Producer), & Suo, M. (Director). (2007). *I just didn't do it. [Motion Picture]*. Tokyo: Toho Company.

Kagoshima kourei fuufu satsugai jiken. (2017). in *Wikipedia*. Retrieved June 25, 2017 from https://ja.wikipedia.org/wiki/鹿児島高齢夫婦殺害事件

Kirk, M. (2004). *Convicted of starting a deadly fire with an unburnable substance*. Justice:Denied!, 26, 8–10 Seattle: The Justice Institute.

Lentini, J. (2006). *Ignitability of Captain Morgan Rum on an electric range heating element*. Job #K103898 Florida: Applied Technical Services, Inc. Available at http://www.niad.info/Lentini_Tests.html

Shinbun, M.. (2010). *Kuro-zu appu 2010: Kagoshima fufu kyousatsu, muzai hanketsu*. Tokyo 2010/12/11

Melendez, J. (2017). Retrieved June 25, 2017 from https://www.journeyofhope.org/who-we-are/exonerated-from-death-row/juan-melendez/

Mochizuki, H. (2001, October). *Gijutsu-shi hoju iken-sho*. Unpublished manuscript.

Nichibenren. (2008a). *Enzai Shibushi jiken tsukurareru jihaku*. Tokyo: Gendai Jinbunsha.

Nichibenren. (2008b). *Tsukareru jihaku-Shibushi no higeki*. Tokyo: Seido Production.

Ogawa, K. (2000, October 10). Re: Lack of motivation for a criminal act. [Blog post]. Retrieved from http://www.jca.apc.org/~hs_enzai/aokikouhan01.html

Onishi, N. (2007, May 11). Pressed by police, even innocent confess in Japan. *New York Times*. Retrieved June 25, 2017 from http://www.nytimes.com

Parra, E. (2008, November 13). Delaware prosecutor arrested again after DUI charge. *The News Journal*. Retrieved June 25, 2017 from http://www.niad.info/Mark_Kirk.html

Sanginiti, T. (2007, April 6). State fire marshal abruptly resigns post. *The News Journal*. Retrieved June 25, 2017 from http://www.niad.info/Mark_Kirk.html

Satomi, S. (2012). *Higashi Sumiyoshi jiken no shinjitsu*. Enzai File No. 16. Tokyo: Nozominoki Shuppan.

Jiken S.. (2017). in *Wikipedia*. Retrieved June 25, 2017 from https://ja.wikipedia.org/wiki/志布志事

Sawyer, D. (1996, September 15). *Beware of gas fired water heaters*. [Television series episode]. *Primetime Live*. New York: ABC TV

Takeshita, M. (2013). *Boku-san, Aoki-san no mujitsu wo jisshou shita kensatsukan jiken*. Saishin Tsushin No. 106. Tokyo: Nichibenren.

Thompson D. (2000, April 2). Apartment fire displaces 36. *The News Journal*. Retrieved June 25, 2017 from http://www.niad.info/Mark_Kirk.html

Torigoe, S. (Writer) (2006, May 4). *Mama ha hanninjanai* [Television series episode]. *The Scoop*. Tokyo: TV Asahi.

Unfit Mothers. (2017). Retrieved from http://www.wcjn.org/Causes.html

Chapter 13
From Measuring Support for the Death Penalty to Justifying Its Retention: Japanese Public Opinion Surveys on Crime and Punishment, 1956–2014

Mai Sato

1 Introduction

The death penalty remains a controversial issue in Japan. While Japan has been a signatory to the International Covenant on Civil and Political Rights since 1979, the Japanese government has been reluctant to abolish the death penalty on the grounds that public opinion supported its retention. This claim rests on the results of surveys conducted every 5 years by the Japanese government. This article compares two of these surveys, from 1967 to 2014, showing how the nature of the questions has changed during this period, and reports on a secondary data analysis for the 1967 survey. First, the article argues that earlier surveys were more open and honest, and the later surveys are more geared to generating answers that support the government's position. Second, it argues that public opinion towards the death penalty is not as clear-cut as it seems. The rate of approval varies, and a more nuanced picture can be derived from both surveys. The article concludes that the public in fact would probably have been ready for abolition as long ago as 1967. While the government continues to cite public support for the death penalty as justification for retaining it, the strength of that support is ambiguous at best.

2 Public Judgement of a Secret System

The Japanese government's official justification for retaining the death penalty is that the public supports it. This justification is offered by many retentionist governments—often without providing any evidence of such support or citing a poll that

M. Sato (✉)
School of Law, University of Reading, Foxhill House, Whiteknights Road,
Reading RG6 7BA, UK
e-mail: m.sato@reading.ac.uk

J. Liu, S. Miyazawa (eds.), *Crime and Justice in Contemporary Japan*,
Springer Series on Asian Criminology and Criminal Justice Research,
https://doi.org/10.1007/978-3-319-69359-0_13

was conducted on an ad hoc basis. In contrast, the Japanese government takes the 'public opinion' argument seriously, carrying out its own survey approximately every 5 years. The results are then used as empirical evidence of how strongly the public wants to retain the death penalty. It could be argued that the Japanese government has made serious efforts to systematically measure and monitor public opinion in ways that other retentionist countries have not.

The government survey has been conducted since 1956, and the latest sweep was carried out at the end of 2014. To give a flavour of the commitment made by the Japanese government, every survey, including the latest, has been subcontracted to an independent market research company. Two-stage stratified random sampling is used to produce a nationally representative sample of Japanese men and women aged 20 and over. The results of the survey have been quoted by the government in every State Party Report submitted to the UN Human Rights Committee as a justification for Japan's inability to abolish the death penalty. In publishing the results of the 2014 survey—which showed that 80% of the public considered the death penalty to be 'unavoidable'—the then Minister of Justice stated at a press conference that she interprets it as evidence that the Japanese public continues to be in favour of the death penalty.[1] In sum, extensive efforts have been made to measure and monitor public opinion on the death penalty and to base government policy directly on the survey results.

Ironically, secrecy is a key feature of the Japanese death penalty system. In December 2007—after eight public opinion surveys had been conducted—the Japanese government began, for the first time, to announce the names of prisoners and the crimes they had committed after each execution. Before this, the number of executions was published in newspapers in just one sentence—for example, 'today, two people were executed'. The execution room was not made public until 2010, when the then Minster of Justice, as a one-off event, allowed camera crews to document what the room looks like when it is not in use. There is still no official information regarding the process of deciding which prisoners, and how many, are to be executed, the treatment of prisoners on death row, or the cost of executions. This situation has led scholars to state that 'the secrecy that surrounds capital punishment in Japan is taken to extremes not seen in other nations' (Johnson, 2006, p. 251) and that the public has only very 'abstract' ideas (Dando, 1996, p. 10) about the death penalty. The Japanese government has failed to reconcile the contradiction between the secrecy surrounding the death penalty and the delegation of responsibility to the general public to decide on its future use.

Even the public opinion survey itself is also not as public as it seems. First, at the same time as the publication of the 2014 survey report, minutes of the special Committee on Examining the Government Survey on the Death Penalty were published on the website of the Ministry of Justice.[2] While this was done to make the

---

[1] Minutes of the press conference are available from the Ministry of Justice website: http://www.moj.go.jp/hisho/kouhou/hisho08_00616.html (last accessed on 5 June 2015).

[2] The Committee minutes can be accessed from http://www.moj.go.jp/keiji1/keiji12_00098.html (last accessed on 5 June 2015).

Committee look transparent, no calls were made to submit evidence, and the Committee meeting was not announced in advance. The documents listed on the Committee website include a report which I co-authored with a United Kingdom (UK)-based nongovernmental organisation[3] and a report written by the Japan Federation of Bar Associations,[4] but none of the authors were asked to advise or appear before the Committee.

3 Japanese Attitudes Towards the Death Penalty[5]

Very few empirical studies have been conducted on Japanese attitudes towards the death penalty (a complete list is Alston, 1976; Kikuta, 1993; Tanioka, 2002; Shiho Kenshujo, 2007;[6] Hamai, 2008; Jiang, Pilot, & Saito, 2010; Sato, 2014). Alston's (1976) study is the most relevant for this article. He compared Japanese and American attitudes to the death penalty using the 1967 government survey in Japan and the 1972 US General Social Survey and argued that in both surveys, younger and more educated groups were less supportive of the death penalty. He also found no difference by sex for Japan, unlike in the USA, where there was a higher proportion of abolitionists among women. Tanioka (2002), using more recent data from the Japanese General Social Survey (a different survey from the 'government survey'), also confirmed that there seemed to be no clear difference between men and women in their support for the death penalty.[7] Higher educational background explained only a small difference in respondents' support for the death penalty, with educated females (16 years or more of education) showing less support for the death penalty than less educated females (12 years or less of education).[8]

Some studies focused on attitudinal indicators that correlate with death penalty attitudes. It has been argued that people who believe in the deterrence of the death

[3] The report is available from http://www.deathpenaltyproject.org/legal-resources/research-publications/the-death-penalty-in-japan/ (last accessed on 5 June 2015).

[4] This report can be accessed from http://www.moj.go.jp/content/001128770.pdf (last accessed on 5 June 2015).

[5] For a detailed review of studies of public attitudes to the death penalty in Japan and abroad, including the strengths and weaknesses of each study's methodology, see Sato (2014, Chap. 2).

[6] Shiho Kenshujo is a branch of the Supreme Court of Japan where lawyers, prosecutors and judges are trained and research is conducted on the work of judges and the courts. The survey used an almost identical question to that of the question used in the government survey and is not included in this section.

[7] Tanioka (2002) conducted a secondary analysis of the 2000 Japanese General Social Survey, which uses a representative sample of the Japanese public aged 20–89, obtained by two-stage stratified random sampling.

[8] Student surveys have also produced mixed results. Kikuta (1993) argued that male law students were more in favour of the death penalty than women, while others have found no difference (Jiang et al. 2010). In both student surveys, males were over-represented, as a small proportion of students of law in Japan are women. This characteristic of law students in Japan makes it problematic to use them as a convenience sample.

penalty are more likely to support the death penalty (Hamai, 2008; Jiang et al., 2010).[9] Jiang et al. (2010) argued that belief in deterrence was the strongest predictor of attitudes towards the death penalty, more so than beliefs in retribution, rehabilitation, the barbaric nature of execution, the prevalence of crime and the possibility of wrongful convictions.[10] Hamai (2008) noted other attitudinal correlates besides the belief in deterrence, though he did not specify whether they were stronger or weaker predictors. They include the belief that homeless people are to blame for their condition, worry about the decline in public safety, distrust of courts and politicians, and willingness to sacrifice privacy in order to fight crime.

Wording of the questionnaire also matters. When survey questions about death penalty retention were phrased differently from those in the government survey—more neutrally, according to the authors—the proportion of survey participants favouring retention declined (Hamai, 2008; Sato, 2014).[11] Furthermore, some studies measured the impact (or the assumed impact) of knowledge of and attitudes towards the death penalty. Kikuta (1993) compared first-year undergraduate law students (assumed to have no knowledge about the death penalty) with third-year undergraduate law students (assumed to be informed about the death penalty) and found that the third-year students were slightly more supportive of the death penalty. Even though the quality of the sample and the design of the survey were problematic, since it is not clear what kind of information the students were given (if any), the study was the first to explore the effect of knowledge on death penalty support in Japan. Sato (2014) further explored the impact of information and deliberation by conducting social experiments and found that death penalty attitudes are not fixed but fluid and that retentionists and abolitionists are not as different as often assumed.

This article uses the same data set used by Alston (1976) to analyse the 1967 government survey in more detail. Unlike Alston (1976), it does not provide a country comparison, but focuses on how the Japanese government survey has developed over the years, what is distinct about the 1967 survey and how the 2014 survey could be interpreted in light of the 1967 survey.

---

[9] Hamai (2008) conducted a survey of crime victimisation in 2006, using a random sample of the Japanese public ($N = 1208$). Jiang et al. (2010) used a convenience sample of 267 university law students surveyed in 2005.

[10] Belief in retribution positively predicted support for the death penalty, whereas belief in the barbarity of executions, the potential for rehabilitation and the occurrence of wrongful convictions all negatively predicted support.

[11] Hamai's (2008) and Sato's (2014) surveys each surveyed two samples, using the government survey questions with one sample and the authors' own questions with the other. The two studies also used a five-point scale for survey answers, in contrast to the binary option provided in recent government surveys.

Table 13.1 Government surveys

Year	Month	Name of survey
1956	April	Survey concerning the death penalty
1967	June	Survey concerning the death penalty
1975	May	Survey concerning crime and punishment
1980	June	Survey concerning crime and punishment
1989	June	Survey concerning crime and punishment
1994	September	Survey concerning the basic legal system
1999	September	Survey concerning the basic legal system
2004	December	Survey concerning the basic legal system
2009	December	Survey concerning the basic legal system
2014	December	Survey concerning the basic legal system

Source: Japanese Cabinet Office website

4 From Measuring Support for the Death Penalty to Justifying Its Retention

Table 13.1 lists all the government surveys on the death penalty in chronological order. These have used three different survey titles, each reflecting a somewhat different focus. The first two sweeps, in 1956 and 1967, focused exclusively on the death penalty. Beginning in the third sweep in 1975, although several questions on the death penalty were included, the survey focused more broadly on attitudes to crime and punishment. Beginning in 1994, sweeps further broadened the focus to attitudes towards the legal system.

As the title of the government surveys changed, so did the number of questions used to measure attitudes to the death penalty. In the 1967 survey, there were over 30 questions directly about or relating to the death penalty, whereas in recent sweeps, only six questions concerned the death penalty.

The 1956 and 1967 sweeps covered the following topics:

- Position on the death penalty (three questions)
- Position on immediate and long-term abolition and retention (two questions)
- Reasons for retention or abolition (two questions)
- Perception on deterrence (one question)
- Scenario-based position on the death penalty (13 questions)
- Possible alternative punishment to the death penalty (three questions)
- Process of sentencing and execution (three questions)
- Knowledge of the death penalty (two questions)
- Death penalty correlates—e.g. perception on crime rate (three questions)

The five sweeps conducted between 1994 and 2014 included the following types of death penalty questions:

- Position on the death penalty (one question)
- Position on immediate- and long-term abolition and retention (two questions)
- Reasons for retention or abolition (two questions)
- Perception on deterrence (one question)

In addition to the above, in the 2014 survey, a new question was added that asked respondents what their position on the death penalty would be if life imprisonment without parole were introduced.

The nature of the questions changed between the 1967 and the 2014 surveys, from measuring support for the death penalty to justifying its retention. For example, in the 1967 survey, there were three questions that asked in general terms about people's levels of support for abolition and retention. These questions—and many other questions in the 1967 survey—were framed in a way that tested the public's appetite for abolition. The 1967 survey asked:

- Do you think it is best not to execute, including those who have committed heinous crimes? (Options: best not to execute, do not agree, not sure)
- Do you agree with the view that the death penalty should be abolished in all circumstances? (Options: yes, no, not sure)
- Some countries have introduced a moratorium on the death penalty to test if heinous crimes increase and use the outcome as a basis for deciding whether to retain or abolish the death penalty. Do you agree with Japan abolishing the death penalty after such a measure has been introduced? (Options: yes, no, not sure)

By contrast, in the 2014 survey, only one question was related to the death penalty:

- I would like to ask you about Japan's punishment system. Which of the following opinions concerning the death penalty do you agree with? (Options: the death penalty should be abolished without conditions, the death penalty is unavoidable in some cases, not sure)

In the 2014 survey, the questions appeared more neutral, but the options were phrased to create a wide definition of retention ('the death penalty is unavoidable in some cases') and a narrow definition of abolition ('the death penalty should be abolished without conditions').

The enthusiasm for testing the public's attitudes towards abolition was also evident in other parts of the 1967 survey. It asked participants about their awareness of the abolitionist movement ('are you aware of the view to abolish the death penalty?'). The survey also asked 13 scenario-based questions, asking whether the death penalty should continue to apply to specific offences.[12] The survey was par-

[12] In Japan, 19 crimes are eligible for the death penalty. In practice, however, it is used for only a limited subset of these crimes, with almost all prisoners sentenced to death for one of three categories of offence: murder, robbery resulting in death or rape on occasion of robbery resulting in

ticularly concerned with political offences that do not involve loss of life, such as insurrection (Penal Code Article 77), inducement of foreign aggression (Penal Code Article 81) and participation in foreign military aggression against Japan (Penal Code Article 82). For these political offences, sub-questions are available only for those who answered that they should no longer be punishable by death, prompting them to give reasons—again highlighting the government's interest in attitudes towards abolition.

Thus, the survey changed over time regarding both the number and nature of questions on the death penalty, which suggests loss of enthusiasm for understanding public attitudes towards the death penalty in general and measuring support for abolition in particular.

5 Secondary Analysis of the 1967 Survey

5.1 Varying Degrees of Support

In this section, the focus is on secondary analysis of the 1967 survey. The sample is a probability sample of 2500 respondents with a response rate of 83%. As noted above, nearly half of the questions in the 1967 survey related to respondents' support for retention and abolition from various perspectives. Table 13.2 summarises the responses to all 16 questions, which were divided into general and offence-specific questions.

Support for retention varies enormously depending on the question asked. For the general questions, when respondents were asked about the possibility of a moratorium leading to future abolition, only 26% supported retention. When asked about immediate abolition, however, support for retention was much higher at 71% ('The death penalty should be abolished in all circumstances'). Views varied similarly for the scenario-based questions. First, the respondents were asked about their support for retention for homicide. Those who considered the death penalty should be applied to homicide were asked a series of sub-questions about various homicide scenarios. The highest support for retention was overturn of a train resulting in death (84%), and the lowest was for a fight resulting in death (31%). It is interesting that while both of these offences are homicides, the questions yielded very different results. Comparing the results for homicide scenarios (questions 5–12, Table 13.2) and non-homicide scenarios (questions 13–16) demonstrates that a loss of life does not necessarily equate to higher support for the death penalty. In other words, the retributive eye-for-an-eye notion is not strictly at play. The low levels of support for the death penalty for arson (43%) and insurrection (39%) indicate a gap with what the law is and what the public feels is appropriate.

---

death. For all offences, the death penalty is discretionary rather than mandatory; it is normally imposed only when a defendant is convicted of multiple killings.

Table 13.2 Results of the 1967 survey

Question	Responses (%)[a]		
	No	Yes	Don't know
General questions			
1. The death penalty should be abolished in all circumstances	71	16	14
2. The death penalty should be avoided even for people who commit heinous crimes	40	42	18
3. The death penalty can be abolished after a trial moratorium	26	49	25
Homicide-specific questions: Should the death penalty be retained for ...			
	Retain	*Abolish*	*Don't know*
4. ... homicide in general?[b]	70	17	14
5. ... homicide of a hostage?	63	8	28
6. ... overturn of a train, etc. resulting in death?	84	5	11
7. ... rape resulting in death?	82	6	13
8. ... robbery resulting in death?	80	6	14
9. ... homicide of a police officer?	60	25	16
10. ... homicide of a parent?	64	8	28
11. ... homicide of a politician?	49	18	33
12. ... fight resulting in death?	31	33	35
Non-homicide questions: Should the death penalty be retained for...			
13. ... destruction of property by explosives?	70	16	13
14. ... participation in foreign military aggression against Japan?	61	12	27
15. ... arson?	43	34	23
16. ... insurrection?	39	25	36

Source: 1967 government survey

[a]Not all rows add up to 100% due to the rounding of decimal points

[b]Questions 5–12 were asked as sub-questions to those who answered 'Retain' in question 4. Question 4: $N = 2500$. Questions 5–16: $N = 2081$

5.2 Crimes Punishable by Death Under the Penal Code

The scenario-based questions are tightly linked to crimes punishable by death under the Japanese penal code which has not changed since 1956 when the surveys began. The penal code prescribes a discretionary death penalty for offences that involve a loss of life and several that do not. In practice, however, its use is limited to homicides and almost always used for murder, robbery resulting in death or rape on occasion of robbery resulting in death. The range of scenario-based questions presented in the 1967 survey could be interpreted as the government testing the public's moral alignment to the criminal law for offences punishable by death. While it is difficult to establish a clear cut-off point for when a punishment no longer matches the offence in question, it is probably safe to say that offences such as a fight resulting in death (25% support for the death penalty), homicide of a politician (39%

support), insurrection (39% support) and arson (43% support) are not necessarily considered by public understanding to be punishable by death.

The scenario-based questions disappeared in subsequent sweeps. When the 1967 survey was administered, Japan had not ratified the International Covenant on Civil and Political Rights (ICCPR). After ratification in 1979, as a signatory to the ICCPR, the Japanese government assumed responsibility for reporting to, and receiving feedback from, the UN Human Rights Committee on Japan's progress in adopting the ICCPR. The Japanese government's policy and practice on the death penalty has been criticised in every Concluding Observations report published by the Committee. One criticism has consistently been raised: the lack of initiative shown by the Japanese government in reducing the number of offences punishable by death. The following quotes from the Committee's Concluding Observations depict their increasing frustration:

> The Committee is disturbed by the number and nature of crimes punishable by the death penalty under the Japanese Penal Code. (UN Human Rights Committee, 1993, para. 12)

> The Committee is gravely concerned that the number of crimes punishable by the death penalty has not been reduced, as was indicated by the delegation at the consideration of Japan's third periodic report. (UN Human Rights Committee, 1998, para. 20)

> While noting that, in practice, the death penalty is only imposed for offences involving murder, the Committee reiterates its concern that the number of crimes punishable by the death penalty has still not been reduced and that the number of executions has steadily increased in recent years. (UN Human Rights Committee, 2008, para. 16)

> The Committee remains concerned that several of the 19 capital offences do not comply with the Covenant's requirement of limiting capital punishment to the 'most serious crimes'. (UN Human Rights Committee, 2014, para. 13)

The result of the 1967 survey is evidence that punishment for some of the capital offences, which are still in the penal code of Japan, were already out of alignment with public opinion in the 1960s. By the time Japan ratified the Covenant, the government surveys had ceased to ask questions about specific capital offences. The findings from the 1967 survey were a missed opportunity for the Japanese government to honour its obligations under the Covenant. The government's supposed commitment to reflecting public opinion in its death penalty policy is not consistent with the facts.

5.3 Factors Differentiating Retentionists and Abolitionists

Using eight of the death penalty questions analysed above, a single scale ranging from 0 to 8 was created to measure the strength of support for retention (Cronbach alpha = 0.75).[13] General questions on the death penalty (questions 1–3 in Table 13.2),

[13] Binary variables were created for each question: 'retention' =2 and 'abolition' and 'don't knows' =1.

Table 13.3 Multiple linear regression predicting support for retention

		B	SE B	*β*
Constant		2.23	0.21	
Beliefs				
Deterrence (ref: false)				
True	**(0 = other, 1 = true)**	**1.48**	**0.10**	**0.32****
Don't know	(0 = other, 1 = don't know)	0.44	0.13	0.01
Remorse (ref: important)				
Irrelevant	**(0 = other, 1 = irrelevant)**	**1.02**	**0.14**	**0.18****
Don't know	**(0 = other, 1 = don't know)**	**−0.63**	**0.12**	**0.10****
Rehabilitation (ref: possible)				
Impossible	**(0 = other, 1 = impossible)**	**0.61**	**0.10**	**0.13****
Don't know	(0 = other, 1 = don't know)	−0.05	0.11	−0.01
Causes of crime (ref: society)				
Individual	(0 = other, 1 = individual)	0.06	0.10	0.01
Don't know	**(0 = other, 1 = don't know)**	**−0.27**	**0.10**	**−0.06***
Demographic factors				
Age	(1 = 20–29, 2 = 30–39, 3 = 40–49, 4 = 50–59, 5 = 60+)	0.05	0.03	0.03
Gender	**(0 = women, 1 = men)**	**0.36**	**0.08**	**0.08****
Education (ref: junior high school)				
University/college	(0 = other, 1 = university/college)	−0.10	0.15	−0.01
High school	(0 = other, 1 = high school)	0.10	0.15	0.02
Primary school	(0 = other, 1 = primary school)	−0.32	0.14	−0.04
Standard of living	**(1 = lowest, 5 = highest)**	**0.21**	**0.06**	**0.07****

$R^2 = 0.24$, $N = 2500$
$^*p < 0.05$, $^{**}p < 0.001$

a question on homicide (question 4) and non-homicide questions (questions 13–16) were used to create a scale. The scale was used as the dependent variable in a multiple linear regression testing the explanatory power of beliefs about (1) the causes of crime, (2) the deterrent power of the death penalty and (3) the capacity of people who have committed a heinous crime to show remorse and to rehabilitate (see Table 13.3).[14] The model controlled for demographic variables. The model showed explanatory power of $R^2 = 0.24$.

For demographic variables, age and education were not statistically significant, but gender and standard of living were. Men were more likely to support the death penalty, and higher standard of living also predicted support. For both

[14] The data for this secondary analysis, 'Opinion Poll on the Death Penalty', 1967, Miyake Ichiro, were provided by the Social Science Japan Data Archive, Center for Social Research and Data Archives, Institute of Social Science, University of Tokyo.

variables, even though they were both statistically significant at the 0.01 level, their standardised coefficients are small within the overall model.

For variables testing respondents' beliefs, causes of crime were measured by whether respondents considered society or the individual to be at fault for the crimes committed. Respondents who thought individuals are to be blamed for the crimes, compared with those who blamed society, did not predict respondents' support for the death penalty. Three variables did predict support for the death penalty: beliefs about the effect of the death penalty as a deterrent, beliefs about the importance of remorse and beliefs about the possibility of rehabilitation. Respondents who considered heinous crimes are likely to be deterred by the existence of the death penalty, compared with those who did not believe in the deterrent effect, were more likely to support retention. For those who believed in deterrence, their death penalty score was 1.48 points higher than those who did not believe in deterrence. This finding on deterrence is in line with that of Hamai (2008) and Jiang et al. (2010).

The remaining two variables that explained death penalty attitudes were belief in the importance of remorse and belief in the possibility of rehabilitation. The remorse variable was measured by a question that asked whether those who are sentenced to death should be executed immediately or whether there should be an observation period to see if they show remorse, in which case their sentence would be commuted to a lesser sentence like life imprisonment. Respondents who considered that remorse was irrelevant, in comparison to those who thought it was important, were more likely to support retention, resulting in a 1.02 point increase on the death penalty score. The rehabilitation variable measured the possibility of rehabilitation including those who committed heinous crimes. Respondents who believed offenders could not be rehabilitated, in comparison to those who thought they could be, were more likely to support the death penalty, resulting in a 0.61 point increase on the death penalty score.

Comparing remorse and rehabilitation variables, while both had a statistically significant effect in determining support for the death penalty, remorse was a slightly stronger predictor of death penalty support when comparing the standardised coefficients. Arguably, remorse and rehabilitation are intertwined concepts: the former could be a precondition for the latter. Remorse is often considered in sentencing to have a higher potential for rehabilitation (Proeve & Howells, 2006; Kleinke, Wallis, & Stalder, 1992; Eisenberg, Garvey, & Wells, 1997). My finding shows, however, for the general public, the theoretical foundations of rehabilitation (whether offenders feel remorseful) determine death penalty attitudes more than the practical aspect of rehabilitation (whether offenders can rehabilitate). This finding on the value attached to remorse over rehabilitation resonates with scholars such as Haley (1997) and Wagatsuma and Rosett (1986), who argued that enormous importance is placed in Japanese society on maintaining peace within the community and on the role of 'apology' and 'forgiveness'.

6 Differences Between the 1967 and 2014 Surveys

In this section, the results of the 1967 survey are analysed in light of the latest (2014) survey results. The 2014 results are taken from aggregated data published by the Cabinet Office. The 2014 survey used the same sampling methodology as the 1967 survey, albeit with a lower response rate (61%, resulting in a sample size of 1826).[15] Table 13.4 summarises responses to the questions that were present in both surveys.

The question of whether the death penalty has a deterrent effect has been asked consistently in the government surveys. From 1967 to 2014, the proportion of those answering 'yes' increased slightly (by 7 percentage points). As for the empirical validity of this claim, there is an increasing consensus within academia that it is virtually impossible to prove or disapprove it (see National Research Council, 2012). In any case, this is a matter of evidence and not a matter of opinion to be determined by public opinion. Hence, the government's inclusion of this question in all surveys for over 50 years is puzzling. The government so far has done nothing to address public misconceptions about deterrence, nor has any analysis been made to take into account those respondents who express support for the death penalty based on inaccurate beliefs. In addition to being silent about this public misconception, the Japanese government itself continues to offer the deterrent effect as a reason for

Table 13.4 Comparison of the 1967 and 2014 surveys

	1967	2014
Belief in the death penalty as a deterrent	52%	58%
Reasons for retention	*Rank*	*Rank*
- Serious crimes will increase if the death penalty is abolished	1	4
- Those who commit serious crimes should forfeit their lives	2	2
- It is necessary to deter offenders from committing further crimes	3	3
- It is necessary out of respect for the feelings of victims' families	4	1
Reasons for abolition	*Rank*	*Rank*
- Killing another human being is inhumane	1	4
- Even offenders who commit serious crimes have the potential to be rehabilitated	2	6
- It is better to keep prisoners alive and make them repent for their crimes	3	2
- Serious crimes will not increase even if the death penalty is abolished	4	5
- Miscarriages of justice in death penalty cases are irreversible	5	1
- Not even the state has the right to kill	N/A[a]	3
Response rate	83%	61%
Sample size	2500	1826

[a]This response was not an option in the 1967 survey

[15]The decline in response rates in recent years is not unique to the government survey; it is common to face-to-face surveys in general. An issue with the 2014 survey was the lack of corrections applied to the survey, resulting in over-representation of men and older people.

retaining the death penalty. For example, in the latest State Party Report to the Committee, the Japanese government explained, in addition to public opinion, that abolition is not possible because 'there is no end to atrocious crimes in Japan' (UN Human Rights Committee, 2012, para. 104).

Another question that was retained in the 2014 survey relates to reasons for retention and abolition. Respondents were given a choice between multiple reasons for retaining or abolishing the death penalty. While options offered in the survey remained almost unchanged between 1967 and 2014, respondents' choices have changed significantly. Potential reasons for retention included general and specific deterrence, retribution and the need to provide justice for victims' families. In the 1967 survey, the most popular reason for retention was general deterrence, followed by retribution. Concern for victims' families was ranked last. In the 2014 survey, the reverse was true: victims' families were ranked as the primary reason to keep the death penalty.

What changed? Miyazawa (2008a, 2008b) argued that the establishment in 2000 of the victims' rights group National Association of Crime Victims and Surviving Families (NAVS), and that group's increasing influence, combined with high-profile criminal cases in 2008, contributed to a punitive and victim-centred turn in penal politics. He argued that 2008 was an eventful year for the Japanese death penalty, as 15 executions were carried out, which is the highest yearly number in 39 years. In April 2008, a high court overturned the trial court's judgement of life imprisonment and sentenced a defendant to death (the Hikarishi case). The victim's husband is one of the co-founders of NAVS and had repeatedly appeared in the media urging a death sentence for the defendant and more power for crime victims.[16]

Survey respondents' choices of reasons for abolition also changed between 1967 and 2014. The most substantial change was the importance placed on the possibility of wrongful conviction. In 1967, this was the least popular option (see Table 13.4); in 2014, it was ranked first. This shift, too, may have been influenced by a recent miscarriages of justice case (Hakamada), where a retrial was ordered after a faulty police investigation. In the 2014 survey, concern about cruelty or human rights as a reason for abolition had dropped. While participants in the 1967 survey ranked 'killing another human being is inhumane' as the top reason for abolition, in the 2014 survey, abolitionists prioritised keeping prisoners alive and making them repent for their crimes (the second most popular option after wrongful convictions).

The main question—the relative levels of support for the death penalty in 1967 and 2014—is difficult to answer, due to changes in both the number and the wording of questions included in the sweeps, and thus it is not included in Table 13.4. As noted earlier, the government reported that 80% of respondents to the 2014 survey supported retention, but this figure was derived from a question that defined retention broadly and abolition narrowly. What is more, those who supported abolition at

[16] In June, the broadsheet Asahi newspaper called the then Minister of Justice a 'grim reaper' for authorising a record number of executions. NAVS complained about this, resulting in a formal apology from the newspaper, which stated that the article had been insensitive to victims' families.

some future point were included as retentionists; when that group is removed, just under half of survey respondents supported retention.[17] Support for retention declines further when we take into account answers to a new question added to the 2014 survey, introducing the possibility of life imprisonment without parole.[18] Arguably, respondents who (1) consider the death penalty to be unavoidable in some cases, (2) do not accept the possibility of future abolition and (3) oppose replacing the death penalty with life imprisonment without parole amount to 34% of all respondents. In other words, a closer examination of the latest government survey shows that notwithstanding the 80% support reported in headlines, the majority of the public do in fact accept future abolition, especially if alternative punishments are available.

This finding is not too far off from the findings from the 1967 survey analysed above. Support for retention varied from 26 to 70% depending on the questions asked (see Table 13.2). It is not possible to compare relevant figures in the 1967 and the 2014 surveys, but what is clear from both surveys is that expressions of support for abolition and retention can vary enormously depending on how the question is phrased. This is a methodological point as well as an important finding concerning the nature of public support. Neither 50 years ago nor now has the Japanese public supported the death penalty unconditionally, and support remains malleable and qualified. What seems to have changed in the last 50 years is the government's increasing reluctance to seriously measure attitudes towards abolition.

7 Conclusion

Many things have changed since the 1960s. Japan has undergone rapid economic growth and recessions. Annual recorded murder rates have halved since the 1960s and continue to decrease, dropping below 1000 in 2013.[19] Annual execution rates, which averaged in the double digits in the 1960s, decreased to an average of 5 in the last 10 years. Japan also ratified the ICCPR, but the Tokyo subway sarin attack of 1995 shocked the whole nation. Victims' rights group has gained enormous power, and the public is more involved in the criminal justice process with the introduction of the *saiban-in* (lay-judge) system. The government survey on the death penalty has also changed with time, from what appeared to be a genuine exploration of public acceptance of abolition to one that is used to justify retention. This is

[17] Out of the 80% that considered the death penalty to be unavoidable in some cases, 41% (or a third of the total sample) supported future abolition.

[18] Asked whether the death penalty should be abolished if life imprisonment without parole was introduced, 38% of respondents said it should be abolished, 52% said it should be retained, and 11% answered 'don't know'.

[19] Annual recorded murder figures show a steady decline since World War II. In 1967, the rate stood at 2111, and by 2013, it was at 938 (Ministry of Justice, 2014).

apparent from the number of questions asked and, more importantly, the nature of those questions.

Despite the differences between the 1967 and 2014 surveys, when results are analysed in detail, the similarities between them become clear. One similarity is that the public is not as committed to retention as is often reported. Support appears high in responses to some questions and much lower in others. Both responses are valid. The variation is simply a demonstration of how flexible and qualified public support is. The 1967 survey showed that the public considered capital punishment for some offences to be out of date and embraced the prospect of a moratorium. In the 2014 survey, many respondents also accepted the possibility of future abolition, combined with the introduction of life imprisonment without parole. Using survey responses as a social barometer is useful to inform policy and probably necessary in a democratic setting. However, the way in which the government has conducted death penalty surveys has distorted the nature of public opinion. If it was up to the public, the death penalty would have been abolished in 1967.

References

Alston, J. P. (1976). Japanese and American attitudes towards the abolition of capital punishment. *Criminology, 14*(2), 271–276.

Dando, S. (1996). Toward the abolition of the death penalty. *Indiana Law Journal, 72*, 7–19.

Eisenberg, T. G., Garvey, S. P., & Wells, M. T. (1997). But was he sorry?—The role of remorse in capital sentencing. *Cornell Law Review, 83*, 1599.

Haley, J. P. (1997). Apology and pardon: Learning from Japan. In A. Etzioni (Ed.), *Civic repentance*. New York: Lanham, Roman & Littlefield.

Hamai, K. (2008, June). *The death penalty in Japan* (pp. 44–50). Japan Echo.

Jiang, S., Pilot, R., & Saito, T. (2010). Why Japanese support the death penalty? *International Justice Review, 20*(3), 302–316.

Johnson, D. T. (2006). Where the state kills in secret: Capital punishment in Japan. *Punishment and Society, 8*(3), 251–285.

Kikuta, K. (1993). *Shikei to yoron [Death penalty and public opinion]*. Tokyo: Seibundo.

Kleinke, C. L., Wallis, R., & Stalder, K. (1992). Evaluation of a rapist as a function of expressed intent and remorse. *Journal of Social Psychology, 132*, 525–537.

Ministry of Justice (2014) *White Paper on Crime*. http://www.moj.go.jp/housouken/houso_hakusho2.html

Miyazawa, S. (2008a). Will penal populism in Japan decline? *Japanese Journal of Sociological Criminology, 33*, 122–135.

Miyazawa, S. (2008b). The politics of increasing punitiveness and the rising populism in Japanese criminal justice policy. *Punishment and Society, 10*(1), 44–77.

National Research Council. (2012). Deterrence and the death penalty committee on deterrence and the death penalty. In D. S. Nagin & J. V. Pepper (Eds.), *Committee on law and justice, division of behavioural and social sciences and education*. Washington, DC: The National Academies Press.

Proeve, M. J., & Howells, K. (2006). Effects of remorse and shame and criminal justice experience on judgements about a sex offender. *Psychology, Crime and Law, 12*, 145–161.

Sato. (2014). *The death penalty in Japan: Will the public tolerate abolition?* Berlin: Springer.

Shiho Kenshujo. (Ed.). (2007). *Keiryo ni kansuru kokumin to saibankan no ishiki ni tsuite no kenkyu: satsujinzai no jian wo sozai toshite [Public and the courts' attitudes towards sentencing: using murder as a case study]*. Tokyo: Hosokai.

Tanioka, I. (2002). Saibansho no hanketsu to shikeiseido saibansho e no shinraikan: hanzai no kyoakuka zoka wa hontoka [Court decisions, and trust in the death penalty system and the courts: Is there an increase and worsening of crimes?]. In N. Iwai & H. Sato (Eds.), *Nihonjin no sugata JGSS ni miru ishiki to kodo* (pp. 221–217). Tokyo: Yuhikaku.

UN Human Rights Committee. (1993). *Concluding observations of the UN human rights committee on Japan*. CCPR/C/79/Add.28.

UN Human Rights Committee. (1998). *Concluding observations of the UN human rights committee on Japan*. CCPR/C/79/Add.102.

UN Human Rights Committee. (2008). *Concluding observations of the UN human rights committee on Japan*. CCPR/C/JPN/CO/5.

UN Human Rights Committee. (2012). *State Party report to the UN human rights committee*. CCPR/C/JPN/6.

UN Human Rights Committee. (2014). *Concluding observations of the UN human rights committee on Japan*. CCPR/C/JPN/CO/6.

Wagatsuma, H., & Rosett, A. (1986). The implications of apology: Law and culture in Japan and the United States. *Law and Society Review, 20*, 461–498.

Chapter 14
Crime Victims' Protection Under the Free Speech Law in Japan

Yuichiro Tsuji

In 1997, a 14-year-old junior high school student killed his 11-year-old friend. He decapitated his friend and placed his head at the front gate of their school. Before the killer was arrested, he sent several letters to newspapers to publicize the murder. He was convicted in the juvenile court. Although Article 61 of the Juvenile Act prohibits the publication of a minor defendant's name in a newspaper or magazine, no civil or criminal sanctions are attached to such publications.

Under Japan's defamation law, matters relating to a crime are presumed to be of interest to the public. Accordingly, this falls within one of the three exceptions to defamation: public purpose, public matter, and proof. Privacy of the deceased is not protected under the privacy law in Japan. Thus, the name of crime victims may be published even though the Juvenile Act protects the names of a minor defendant by prohibiting their publication.

After getting out of Kanto Medical Reformatory in 2007, the convict in the 1997 decapitation published a book in 2015, describing the history of the case and his life after reform school. The father of the victim strongly opposed this publication, but failed to stop it. There is no way of ascertaining where the author lives now. Further, the Juvenile Act does not provide any recourse for the victim's family in the event that details of the crime are published by juvenile perpetrators. Some argue that the current provisions in the Juvenile Act are under inclusive and lament that the provisions do not adequately address issue arising from the burgeoning dimension of

Yuichiro Tsuji, Associate Professor of the Graduate School of Humanities and Social Science (legal major) at the University of Tsukuba; J.S.D University of California, Berkeley; LL.M. University of California, Berkeley; and Master of Law, Kyoto University. For a discussion on freedom of expression, Tsuji, Y. (2011). *Jouhouka Shakai No Hyougen No Jiyu* [The Freedom of Expression in the Information Oriented Society]. Nihon Hyoron Sha.

Y. Tsuji (✉)
Graduate School of Humanities and Social Science, University of Tsukuba, Tsukuba, Japan
e-mail: tsuji.yuichiro.gm@u.tsukuba.ac.jp

J. Liu, S. Miyazawa (eds.), *Crime and Justice in Contemporary Japan*,
Springer Series on Asian Criminology and Criminal Justice Research,
https://doi.org/10.1007/978-3-319-69359-0_14

Internet publication. Accordingly, new legislation may be necessary to protect and indemnify victims damaged by publications describing the crime.

To begin, this paper argues that the amount of damage awarded due to defamation or privacy infringement in Japan is so minimal that a publisher may still publish a book or article in the face of potential litigation. Even though publishers often lose defamation or privacy infringement lawsuits, their financial gains from publications likely outweigh those costs. Such outcomes reveal that the cost-benefit analysis simply does not err on the side of victims in defamation cases, and, even so, the financial awards in these cases fail to alleviate the grief and sorrow of the victim's families.

Next, this paper will review the applicability of the so-called Son of Sam law in *Simon & Schuster, Inc. v. Crime Victims Board.*[1] Then, the focus will shift to another case in 2013, in which a 21-year-old truck driver killed his 18-year-old ex-girlfriend after threatening to distribute sexual pictures taken during the relationship. Just before being arrested, he uploaded her private pictures online. Although the Stalker Control Act of 2000 and the Child Porn Act of 1999 had already been enacted before his arrest, the case prompted Parliament to enact a new, more relevant act, the Revenge Porn Act, in 2014, as such criminal publication of private material online has seriously affected its victims.

The defense asserted in these types of cases generally rests on an argument presented in a dissenting opinion in *Abrams v. United States*,[2] which asserted that free speech ensures a "marketplace of ideas" that encourages public discourse and promotes truthful revelations. It was Professor Yasuhiro Okudaira who imported this theory into Japan.

Finally, this paper will review if two recent cases have sufficiently challenged the marketplace of ideas concept. Typical free speech remedies in court include damages, injunctions, or the publication of an apology. Given the circumstances of this Internet era, injunctions may offer the most protection for privacy infringement; however, these protections may be inadequate, and, if so, additional laws may be necessary. With respect to this significant topic in constitutional law, this paper conducts its analysis using a comparative approach.

1 Defamation and Privacy Infringement in Japan

In Japan's Juvenile Act (*Shonen-hou*), Article 61 prohibits newspapers or other publications from publicizing any "article or photograph from which a person subject to a hearing and decision of a family court, or against whom public prosecution has been instituted for a crime committed while a Juvenile, could be identified based on name, age, occupation, residence, appearance, etc." (1948).

---

[1] Simon & Schuster, Inc. v. Members of New York State Crime Victims Board, 502 U.S. 105 (1991).

[2] Abrams v. United States, 250 U.S. 616 (1919).

In order to properly analyze the Juvenile Act and the publication of minors' crimes, this paper will provide a general overview of defamation and privacy infringement in Japan. The Japanese constitutional law protects freedom of expression under Article 21 of the Constitution, but also sets particular restrictions on certain expressions (1946). Courts have developed categories to distinguish protected speech from unprotected speech (Nonaka, Mutsuo, Kazuyuki, & Katsutoshi, 2012, p. 380). An example of unprotected speech is pornography; thus, if an article constitutes prohibited pornography, the article in question is outside of the protection. Article 175 of the Criminal Code establishes three different sanctions for such criminal publications: imprisonment with labor for not more than 2 years, a fine of not more than 2,500,000 yen, or a petty fine (1907).

Under Article 230 of the Criminal Code, defamation is defined as actions which cause a persons' social reputation to be degraded. Articles 230–232 protect the freedom of expression that is protected under Article 21 of the Constitution. According to these laws, when someone's social reputation is injured, the person asserting a defense of freedom of expression must establish, under Articles 230–232, the public purpose and public interest of the publication as well as proof that the publication is true. The Supreme Court in the 1969 *Yukan Wakayama Kisha* case[3] presented an additional factor relating to the defamation, holding that if the expresser has a reasonable ground upon which to mistakenly believe that it was true, then defamation cannot be established. This criminal law principle functions similarly in civil law liability under Article 709 of the Civil Code (1896). Japanese courts do not apply the actual malice principle established by the 1964 *New York v. Sullivan* case.[4]

In Japan, there are no criminal sanctions for privacy infringement. Article 13 of the Constitution protects personal rights and privacy within the realm of the "pursuit of happiness." The Tokyo District Court in the 1964 *Utage no ato* case[5] defined the right to be let alone, holding that private matters should not be publicized. The court explained to determine the applicability of such a right: first, the matter in question must be from one's private life or is something that people are likely to regard as private; second, the matter is such that an average reasonable person would not want it to be published; and, third, the matter must not have already been made public. In addition, the alleged victim must have felt genuine unease or distress related to the publication. This particular case was settled, without appeal to the Supreme Court; thus, the principles set forth in this district court principle prevail with respect to issues of privacy infringement by publication in books, magazines, and articles.

Importantly, if the person in the article consents to the publication of the article, then an infringement of privacy cannot be established. However, courts have determined that certain aspects of personal information, like criminal records, medical history, and physical characteristic attributions, such as fingerprints, are protected

---

[3] Saiko Saibansho [Sup. Ct] June 25, 1969, Showa 41(a) no.2472, 23(7) Saiko Saibansho Keiji Hanreishu [Keishu] 975.

[4] New York v. Sullivan, 376 U.S. 254 (1964).

[5] Tokyo Chiho Saibansho [Tokyo Dist.Ct.] Sep. 28, 1964, Showa 36 (wa) no. 1882, 385 Hanrei Jihou 12.

under the Constitution.[6] Then, in 2003, the Personal Information Act was established—providing a definition for personal information.

In the 1994 *Gyakuten* case,[7] the court reviewed the publication of nonfiction story regarding a criminal case in Okinawa. The court explained that when the author and publisher publish a book using a person's real name without consent, the court will review the person's circumstances, including the historical and social significance of the criminal case, the person's significance as a party in the case, the person's social activity, and the person's social influence, to determine if the purpose and significance of this person's identity necessitates the use of his or her real name. If the interest not to be publicized is superior to the interest to be publicized, the person seeking restitution may ask for emotional damages.

Notably, the judiciary has hesitated to use the term "privacy," as it has not appeared in statutes or the Japanese Constitution (Nonaka et al., 2012, pp. 275–278, 378–380). Even so, a plaintiff may seek damages or an injunction against the publication of an article. However, censorship by an administrative agency is strictly prohibited in Article 21 of the Constitution, and prior restraint also faces strict restrictions (Nonaka et al., 2012, pp. 356–360). This case is called *Sapporo Zeikan Jiken*.[8]

The 1984 *Hoppo Journal case*[9] examined the requirement of prior restraint to seek a court injunction when a candidate for governor of Hokkaido was severely criticized and brought a suit for injunction. In this case, the Supreme Court held that the candidate may ask of an injunction via his personal right under the Constitution, if (1) it is clear that the article in question lacks public purpose or is factually untrue and (2) the person in the article is likely to suffer significant and unrecoverable damage. The Supreme Court noted that when an injunction is considered, the author/publisher must be given an opportunity to rebut the allegations and evidence.

In the *Gyakuten* case in Okinawa, the plaintiff sought damages, not an injunction for the publication of a book (Isa, 2001). This is because the criminal case written about in this book occurred before Okinawa returned to governance by Japan in 1972. Thus, the crime was infamous only in Okinawa. However, the plaintiff had relocated to the Tokyo area and had a new job and family. In this case, the court held that even such criminal records may warrant protection.

In the 2002 *Ishi ni oyoku sakana* case,[10] the Supreme Court charted the requirements for a publication injunction. In this case, the author had written several

---

[6] Saiko Saibansho [Sup. Ct] Dec. 15, 1995, Heisei 2(a) no.848, 49(10) Saiko Saibansho Keiji Hanreishu [Keishu] 842.

[7] Saiko Saibansho [Sup. Ct] Feb. 8, 1994, Heisei 1(o) no.1649, 48(2) Saiko Saibansho Minji Hanreishu [Minshu] 149.

[8] Saiko Saibansho [Sup. Ct] Dec. 12, 1984, Showa 57 (gyo tsu) no.156, 38(12) Saiko Saibansho Minji Hanreishu [Minshu] 1308.

[9] Saiko Saibansho [Sup. Ct] June 11, 1984, Showa 56(o) no.609, 40(4) Saiko Saibansho Minji Hanreishu [Minshu] 872.

[10] Saiko Saibansho [Sup. Ct] Sep. 24, 2002, Heisei 13(o) no.851, 207 Saiko Saibansho Minji Hanreishu [Minshu] 243.

magazine stories that described, in detail, one female graduate student using unique facial features, the name of her university in Tokyo, and her family status and history. The author wanted to compile and publish the stories in a book. The Court approved an injunction—holding that her emotional distress would be amplified by increasing the number of readers, which may make it impossible for her to lead a normal life. Later, the expression to identify the character is modified. In regard to this case, Koji Sato pointed out that injunctions are only used in exceptional instances, and, in this case, the author recklessly described unique characteristics of the plaintiff without sincerely trying to keep her identity private (Sato, 2011, p. 268).

2 The Juvenile Act and Defamation and Privacy Rights

In the *Nagaragawa* case,[11] one of the most serious crimes committed by a minor in Japan, ten young people, including seven minors, committed serious crimes in Osaka, Aichi, and Gifu Prefectures. Their crimes, chronologically, included killing one person, abandoning a corpse, lynching one person in their group, and killing two people and injuring a third near the Nagaragawa River. A publisher, Shincho 45, published an article with the presumed names of the criminals—such that those who knew these individuals may have easily determined who they were.

In this case, the Supreme Court[12] offered two distinct holdings. First, it held that the article did not violate Article 61 of the Juvenile Act—stating that the article included private information, which would allow only people who already knew these individuals to recognize and identify the subjects of the article. The Court explained that the standard for violating Article 61 is that the article must be written in such a way that anyone in the general population could presume the identities of the subjects of the article and the general public could not make such a presumption in this case.

Second, the Court vacated and remanded the case to decide if the publisher was civilly liable for defamation and privacy infringement. For defamation, the courts review the facts case-by-case, determining whether there is justifiable cause. When courts review the public purpose, public matters, and proof of truth and reasonable ground to mistakenly believe it to be true, privacy is balanced considering the interest to publicize and not to be publicized.

The Court offered additional factors relevant to the matter, including the scope of private information communicated, extent of concrete damage, purpose and significance of the article, social circumstances at the time of publication, and necessity of the publication. The Supreme Court remanded the case to the Nagoya High Court to

[11] Saiko Saibansho [Sup. Ct] March 10, 2011, Heisei 17(a) no.2358, 303 Saiko Saibansho Keij Hanreishu [Keishu] 133.

[12] Saiko Saibansho [Sup. Ct] March 14, 2003, Heisei 12(ju) no.1335, 57(3) Saiko Saibansho Minji Hanreishu [Minshu] 229.

review these factors. The Nagoya High Court[13] found that the fact that the convicted was a minor at the time did not outweigh the public interest, defamation was not established, and no privacy infringement existed because the interest to publicize was superior to the interest of the convicted.

These cases call into question the purpose of the Juvenile Act. Essentially, the Act is based on a presumption that young people who have committed crimes will recover well in society. However, if the court sentences the minor to death, there is no reason to protect that minor because he or she will not have an opportunity to recover in society. In similar other cases, some media have released the names of defendants sentenced to death, and other media did not. For example, in 1999, in Hikarishi city in Yamaguchi Prefecture, an 18-year-old killed a 23-year-old housewife and sexually violated her corpse and killed an 11-month-old girl. During the criminal trial, the defendant pled insanity, but the Supreme Court found him guilty and sentenced him to death. Some news outlets and journals released his name.

There is no statute prohibiting publication of an adult defendant's real name in Japan. When an adult commits a crime, the name of the victim and defendant are publicized. These matters are presumed to be of public interest. When a minor commits a crime, only the victim's name is released, unless he or she is a minor, as the Juvenile Act protects minor's names. Presently, it is very easy to track and identify the information of minors using an Internet search, even though the Juvenile Act prohibits journals or magazines from publicizing. Thus, Shigenori Matsui argues that the Juvenile Act is useless and unconstitutional (Matsui, 2000).

3 Zekka Case

The Zekka book aptly demonstrates why the Juvenile Act is problematic (Shonen, 2015). Before analyzing this book, however, we need to review the author's crimes. As a 14-year-old, the convict decapitated an 11-year-old boy in 1997. He then wrote letters to the newspapers regarding these killings, revealing that before this murder, he had killed another younger child and injured a few more (Hardung, 2000).

Under the Criminal Code, a person under 14 years old is not criminally responsible, and the previous Juvenile Act provided that a minor under 16 years old could not be prosecuted (Art. 41, 1907)—meaning that minors between 14 and 16 years old were not punishable by criminal sanctions. Instead, family court charged the juveniles as delinquent. It has been a tough movement for the Juvenile Act amendment (Kuzuno, 2005).

In 2001, the Juvenile Act was amended to state that that crimes committed by minors over 14 years old are eligible for criminal sanctions. The 2014 amendment to the Juvenile Act modified the youngest age for reformatory school from 14 years old to 12 years old. Furthermore, the amendment permits courts may render sentence

[13] Nagoya Koto Saibansho [Nagoya High. Ct], May 12, 2004, Heisei 15(ne) no.275, 1870 Hanrei Jihou 29.

of up to a maximum of 15 years for minor crimes and, for major crimes, like murder, the court may impose a maximum of 20 years in prison.

The convict was released from Kanto Medical Reformatory in 2007, and, then, as a 32-year-old, he publicized a book in 2015, titled *Moto Shounen A* (former boy A), which described his crimes and the subsequent interrogations. He titled the book as such because, following the murder, the convict was referred to in the newspapers as "boy A." Though one publisher refused to publish his book, he found one who would. Even before the *Zekka* case, his parents had written and published a book in 2001, titled *Bearing This Boy A* with names "Parents of Shonen A," not real ones as authors. The parents of the murdered boy brought a tort action for this publication. The Kobe District Court[14] granted an award for damages including 43,939,700 yen for the loss, 4,263,270 yen for funeral cost, and 25,000,000 yen for mental suffering consolation.

Regarding the Zekka book, the father of the victim again alleged that the publication of this book caused further emotional damages and, therefore, should have been approved for publication by the victims' families. The families had received letters from the convict every year, but declined them after the book was published. The Zekka author offered the families part of the profits from the book, but they rejected the offer because the book was published without their consent. It was only after publication that the victims' families were made aware of its publication, and, at that point, they argued that the book should be returned to the publisher.

The Zekka author created a website and established email subscriptions for his articles. Initially, his website crashed due to the overwhelming Internet traffic. Later, however, the Internet service provider canceled service to his website.

The *Zekka* case might have followed one precedent, the *Nagayama* case[15] which is a precedent for victim's families under similar circumstances. This case involved a 19-year-old boy who stole a pistol and killed four people during escape in 1968. In 1983, the Supreme Court sentenced him to death—establishing the standard for rendering the death penalty. Before his arrest and prosecution, he could not read or write well—thus, he learned these skills in prison. He wrote a book *Muchi no namida* (Tears of Ignorance) with his real name as an author, which was highly admired and even received an award in 1983. The profits he received from the book he sent to his victims' families, though some rejected it. So, instead, he used the money to establish the Nagayama Foundation to support abused children (Nagayama, 1999).

[14] Kobe Chihou Saibansho [Kobe Dist. Ct], March 11, 1999, Heisei 10(wa) no.1779, 1677 Hanrei Jihou 110.

[15] Saiko Saibansho [Sup. Ct] July 8, 1983, Showa 56(a) no.1505, 37(6) Saiko Saibansho Keiji Hanreishu [Keishu] 609.

4 New Legislation for the Internet Era

4.1 Defamation or Privacy Infringement

Today the Internet allows anyone to send or receive information quickly, cheaply, and across national borders. Anyone can read and judge the information's quality by themselves, as the government is strictly prohibited to censor matters online. In the marketplace of ideas, expressed by Justice Holmes in his dissenting opinion in *Abrams v. United States*,[16] "we the people" are able to more easily determine the truth on our own by having access to a greater amount and diversity of information. However, it is not clear if the Internet has achieved this optimistic notion regarding the marketplace of ideas (Tsuji, 2002, p. 887). The value of the freedom of expression was imported into Japan by Yasuhiro Okudaira (1988). As a strong advocate for free speech, he emphasized self-realization and self-governance in the right of free expression.

The Japanese constitutional law does not allocate special legal status to the media (Nonaka et al., 2012, p. 400). Traditionally, average people do not have access to large media; thus, those researching Japanese public law have advocated for the right to receive information (Nonaka et al., 2012, p. 363).

Even in marketplace of ideas, unprotected speech exists and is categorized by the following definition and analysis. Defamation is a type of unprotect speech that is defined as speech that degrades the social reputation of an individual person. Hate speech regarding a certain group or ethnic community, therefore, does not constitute defamation. Regarding pornography, the Supreme Court, in the *Lady Chatterley's Lover* case,[17] defined it as expression or speech that harms a reasonable person's sense of shame, rouses or stimulates the reasonable viewer's sexual desire, and is counter to an appropriate sexual moral sense. Thus, by definition, unprotected speech is clarified in marketplace of ideas.

The Zekka book was not defamatory, as it did not damage a certain person's reputation; rather, its publication caused suffering to the victims' families. This book might be helpful to consider a serious crime in the future. Around the same time, the judge, Yasuhiro Igaki, who heard this case in the Kobe family court, contributed to an article that included private matters that were not even published in Zekka (Igaki, 2015, p. 138). The hearing of the family court for juvenile case was not open to the public. Thus, Igaki was chastised by the family court director, as the director insisted that hearings in family court should be classified. The *Zekka* and *Nagaragawa* cases may illustrate the limit to the marketplace of ideas because although one may find truth with a greater array of information, you also promote emotional damage to victims' families.

---

[16] Abrams, *supra* note 2.

[17] *Hoppo Journal* case, *supra* note 9.

4.2 *Cost and Benefit of Publication in the* Zekka *and* Nagaragawa *Cases*

The remedies for defamation, under Article 723 of the Civil Code, include damages, injunctions, or court orders to publicly apologize. The *Zekka* and *Nagaragawa* cases show that injunctions are more appropriate for victims' families, but injunctions must prevail over the prohibition of prior restraint of the freedom of expression under Article 21 of the Constitution. The *Nagaragawa* case illustrates only the reason why the Juvenile Act has been criticized as overprotective, as the name of victim was publicized, but, in keeping with the Juvenile Act, the name of the minor defendant was not.

The publisher of the Zekka book expected to sell one million copies; however, only 100,000 were sold—likely because it was published by an alias because the Juvenile Act prevented publication of the defendant's name before he committed the crimes when he was 14 years old. When considering the publication of this or similar books, one must consider how much attention these scandalous cases attract. Accordingly, injunctions against publication must pass the requirements set out in *Hoppo Journal* case[18]: the person must demonstrate that they will suffer grievous, unrecoverable damage, the purpose for publications must not be a matter of public interest, and the publisher/author is given an opportunity to rebut.

In these scandalous cases, large media are eager to publicize articles even though they include real names of minor defendants and/or constitute defamation or privacy infringement. It comes down to a question of profits—the more people who purchase that article, the greater the publishers' profits. Even when the subjects of these defamatory articles are high-profile public officials or famous actors, the emotional damage awards granted for defamation are minimal. This is because damage is estimated by the harm, not the profits gained (Tsukuda, 2005, p. 215; Yamada, 2012, p. 2). Some courts[19] have increased damage awards for famous people to prevent reckless publication.

Thus, even when a publisher knows that it is likely to lose in prospective defamation or infringement of privacy litigation, article profits may prevail. Meanwhile, the magazine or newspaper will argue in court that the article in question relates to a public matter and its publication is motivated by some public purpose, not by profit.

Once a plaintiff proves that his or her social reputation has been degraded, unlike the actual malice principle, the publisher or speaker has the burden to prove that the article is a public matter and has a public purpose and that the material was true or at least that they mistakenly but reasonably believed it to be true. In 1981, the Court

[18] *Hoppo Journal* case, *supra* note 9.

[19] Tokyo Chiho Saibansho [Tokyo Dist.Ct.] March 27, 2001, Heisei 12 (wa) no. 5109, 1754 Hanrei Jihou 93. Tokyo Koto Saibansho [Tokyo High.Ct.] Oct. 30, 2003, Heisei 15 (ne) no. 2728, D-1 Law.com (No. 28091823).

in the *Gekkan pen* case[20] held that when the plaintiff is a private citizen, not a public official or candidate, but still has a strong influence on society, the article regarding the plaintiff may, in some cases, be a public matter.

In the *Ishini oyogu sakana* case,[21] the Court granted injunction to publication. The literary world announced that the author and her work, the *Ishini oyogu sakana*, are protected under Article 21 of the Constitution. In this case, the author described one female graduate student with a unique scar on her face and her families (Yu, 2002). It was so clear to find out her student identity by reading this book. The Court noted that the more people read this description, the more serious emotional damage would be caused. In a sense, author gained public attention by this injunction. It might be unclear that the author needs to write her facial character in detail.

Today, some courts award higher damages to famous people, but these increases have not been the trend when it comes to defamation litigation for the general population. The actual malice principle from *New York v. Sullivan* has not taken a prevailing position in the studies of free expression in Japan (Matsui, 2000). With respect to the actual malice principle, when the plaintiff is a public official, he or she has to prove that the publisher/author had malicious intent when publishing the material. Koji Sato believes that, especially in injunction cases, like *Hoppo Journal*, the actual malice principle should be applied (Sato, 2011, p. 266). Urabe and Matsui argue that actual malice principle applies to public officials in Japan. Ashibe introduced only actual malice principle into Japanese studies (Urabe, 2016, p. 173; Matsui, 2007, p. 462; Ashibe, 2000, p. 477, 506).

4.3 *Injunction and Free Speech in the Internet Era*

Preventive approaches, like injunctions, lead to serious concerns over censorship or prior restraint under the Constitution. Censorship was defined in the *Sapporo Zeikan* case.[22] The Court explained it as the review of publication content and prohibition of publication by an administrative agency. The Court said prohibited censorship

> as a special quality, the prohibition of publication of what are judged inappropriate, after the administrative authorities as the main organ, for the purpose of prohibition of publication as a whole or a part, covering the matters of expression of substance of thought, etc., conduct the comprehensive and general examination of the above specific matters of expression prior to its publication.

The definition of censorship is still controversial, and Tomatsu argues that *Hoppo Journal* infringes on the superior status of free expression (Nonaka et al., 2012, p. 357, 376; Sato, 2011, pp. 256–259). In the *Hoppo Journal* case,[23] the court

[20] Saiko Saibansho [Sup. Ct] April 16, 1981, Showa 55(a) no.273, 35(3) Saiko Saibansho Keiji Hanreishu [Keishu] 84.

[21] *Ishini oyogu sakana* case, *supra* note 10.

[22] *Sapporo Zeikan* case, *supra* note 8.

[23] *Hoppo Journal* case, *supra* note 9.

balanced the interests of the sender and receiver of the information to determine whether an injunction was appropriate (Tomatsu, 2015, p. 239).

The Japanese Internet Service Provider Act (ISP Act) of 2001 followed this approach. When requested to by the receiver, an Internet service provider (ISP) initially determines if the posted content on a website violates the receiver's rights related to defamation or infringement of privacy. The receiver may request for the information to be deleted (ISP Act, 2001, Art. 3) or for the identity of the sender be released to move forward with litigation (ISP Act, 2001, Art. 4). If the material clearly infringes on the rights of the receiver, ISP may delete it. In the majority of messages posted on websites, ISP may not be able to definitively know whether something clearly infringes on the right of others. In such instances, the ISP may first ask the sender if the ISP may delete it for 7 days. When no response arrives to the ISP in 7 days, the ISP takes no responsibility even though it deletes the message in question. If neither party can determine if the material does violate the receiver's rights, the court ultimately decides. When the identification of a sender is requested, first, the ISP will ask whether the sender wants to be identified or not. If the message by the sender clearly infringes on the receiver's right, and there is reasonable reason to identify the sender for suit for damage, the ISP may identify the sender. An ISP takes responsibility for not disclosing the identity of the sender only when the ISP's action is grossly negligent or intentional.

This ISP law and the *Hoppo Journal* decision propose concrete rules for the marketplace of ideas. Legislation is one of several approaches for dealing with defamation and privacy infringement; the other approach is available in court decisions that evaluate the amount of damages and apply the actual malice principle.

4.4 Son of Sam Law in Japan

It is unclear whether the Son of Sam law, a New York state law, is helpful or not in Japan. In the related US case, the defendant published a book about his crime and profited greatly from it. Under New York law (N.Y. Exec. Law § 632a(1), 1982), a crime victim's committee decided to transfer the profit to the victims' families.

The Supreme Court, in *Simon & Schuster, Inc. v. Crime Victims Board*, invalidated this state law, stating that though compensation from the defendant to the victims' families is a compelling interest, it is unconstitutional because under state law, any financial benefit of a person "accused or convicted of a crime" for production of a book or other article transfers to the New York State Crime Victims Board.[24] The Board allocates funds from an escrow account to any victims who obtained civil judgments against the accused or convicted within 5 years. The state law defines "person convicted of a crime" as "any person who has voluntarily and intelligently admitted the commission of a crime for which such person is not prosecuted" (N. Y. Exec. Law § 632-1(10)(b), 632-a(11), 1991).

[24] *Simon & Schuster*, *supra* note 1, at 110.

By striking down the application of the Son of Sam law, the US Supreme Court explained that the law "singles out speech on a particular subject for a financial burden that it places on no other speech and no other income and, thus, is presumptively inconsistent with the Amendment".[25]

The Court noted that "in order to justify the differential treatment imposed by the law, the State must show that its regulation is necessary to serve a compelling state interest and is narrowly drawn to achieve that end".[26]

> The State has a compelling interest in compensating victims from the fruits of crime. … The Board cannot explain why the State should have any greater interest in compensating victims from the proceeds of criminals' 'storytelling' than from any of their other assets, nor offer any justification for a distinction between this expressive activity and any other activity in connection with its interest in transferring the fruits of crime from criminals to their victims.[27]

> The law is significantly overinclusive, since it applies to works on any subject provided that they express the author's thoughts or recollections about his crime, however tangentially or incidentally, and since its broad definition of 'person convicted of a crime' enables the Board to escrow the income of an author who admits in his work to having committed a crime, whether or not he was ever actually accused or convicted. These two provisions combine to encompass a wide range of existing and potential works that do not enable a criminal to profit from his crime while a victim remains uncompensated.[28]

The Supreme Court used strict scrutiny and recognized a compelling governmental interest, finding that the means to achieve the purpose was overbroad. It noted that the government singling out certain methods of financial gain and applying uniform restrictions, such as general tax on any book, would be regarded as censorship (Farber, 2010, p. 24). Is this US Supreme Court decision applicable or helpful in today's publication issues in Japan?

In Japan, it is possible to bring a suit for emotional damages arising from a publication under general tort law or would the principle of free expression prevent it. If a statute prohibits publication beforehand, it would be considered censorship, which is prohibited by Constitution.

Differential treatment needs constitutional justification even in Japan under Article 14 of the Constitution. Thus, the *Simon & Schuster* decision reveals how difficult it is to clarify scope within which financial profits can be transferred to victim's families.

There are several ways the Son of Sam law can be applied to the *Zekka* case in Japan. First, the greater concern in Japan might be that the purpose of this litigation is not financial compensation. As the *Simon & Schuster* case describes, it is difficult to define financial benefit of the convicted author, and monetary transfer does not alleviate the grief and suffering of victims' families; in fact, sometimes it could generate a sense of unease or discomfort as in the *Zekka* case. In the Japanese legal

---

[25] *Id.* at 107.

[26] *Id.* at 115.

[27] *Id.* at 121.

[28] *Id.*

system, in order to move forward with such a law, the Diet would need to pass a statute under Article 41 of the Constitution. As of now, the Diet has not reached a consensus that economic interest should transfer from convicted authors to victims' families.

Second, although not applicable to defamation or privacy infringement suits, in Japan, criminal procedure was amended in 2008, to allow the families of victims of serious crimes, such as murder, rape, and human trafficking, to participate in criminal trial proceeding (Code of Criminal Procedure, 1948, Art. 290–292; Johnson and Satoru, 2015). These families are therefore represented in the trial and have the opportunity to hear the case (Johnson and Satoru, 2015; Ii, 2012).

Third, in defamatory suits in Japan, many victims' families prefer not to be compensated because they care more about winning the suit on principle. In such instances, they may be more motivated by the impact the publication would have on their social reputation or by the sense of closure they may feel—such motivations are not typically seen outside this particular type of litigation.

4.5 Consent of the Convicted

When the subject of the publication consents, this prevents them from suing for defamation of privacy infringement. However, it may be difficult to determine if the person gave sufficient consent relevant to the article or information posted. In the *Hikari city* case, a journalist visited and interviewed a convicted inmate several times and also exchanged letters. She collected and published material from the interviews and letter using the convict's name. Lawyers for the convict sought an injunction and damages for publication. In 2013, the Hiroshima High Court[29] denied both the defamation and privacy infringement allegations. In 2014, the Supreme Court[30] denied the appeal. The Hiroshima High Court noted that the convict's name is publicly available on the Internet, and the convict gave the author consent.

Regarding revenge pornography, consent is a tricky matter as the pictures are generally taken with consent by close partners in a relationship. This consent is usually only available to the partner with whom the pictures are shared. In these instances, there is no written contract to prohibit disclosure in general and to delete after the relationship ends. The party may bring a suit against the other under general tort law as there is no special statute allowing party to request that the data—stored on a smartphone or computer—be deleted. Once the pictures are distributed to the general public, it is very difficult to delete them all, which causes more suffering to victim's families.

In Japan, apologies from the convicted are often effective for avoiding civil suits from the victim's families (Hardung, 2000, pp. 152–153). Unlike apology by court

[29] Hiroshima Koto Saibansho [Hiroshima High. Ct], May 30, 2013, Heisei 24(ne) no.354, 2202 Hanrei Jihou 28.

[30] Saiko Saibansho [Sup. Ct] Sep.25, 2014, Heisei 25(o) no.1765, D-1 Law.com (No. 28224039).

order under Article 723 of the Civil Code, apology letters from the convicted or the parents of the convicted offer forms of communication with the victim's family that are not legally forced. Furthermore, courts are likely to consider a convict's voluntary apology when sentencing juvenile or other general criminal cases.

4.6 Revenge Porn Act in Japan

In 2014, the US Supreme Court[31] reviewed federal law requiring persons held guilty for possession of child pornography to make full restitution to the victims of the child pornography in *Paroline v. United States*. The Court held that the state is required to prove a casual or proximate relationship for restitution of all the losses described. There are no counterparts in the Japanese law. The *Paroline* case demonstrated that even when the victims' suffering is serious and such a remedy is expected, the court cannot uphold the law if it targets any financial profit of the convicted as it might infringe on the convict's due process of law (2014: Roberts, dissent).

In Japan, several cases have encouraged the legislature to pass a statute to regulate a certain field. Before the Revenge Porn Act was passed in 2014, there were two related statutes, one regulating stalking (Stalker Control Act, 2016) and the other child pornography (Child Pornography Act, 1999). Due to the fact that the Internet has increased access to individual's information, including pictures, names, addresses, and family composition, stalking and child pornography cause greater harm. In 2017, the Supreme Court[32] held that parties may request Google, Inc. to delete search outcome URLs when inputting a person's name. When determining whether the deletion is necessary, the Court considered the factual character and content, the scope and concrete damage by the distributed URL, the article's purpose and significance, social circumstances, and later social life change. When the person's lost interest is superior to the interest to publicize, the party may request deletion of the URL of the searched information. In this case, the Court did not mention the "right to be forgotten," and the party requesting deletion had been convicted under the Child Pornography Act 5 years earlier. The Supreme Court held that, in this case, his crime related to a public matter and, therefore, denied his deletion request.

One case prompted the legislature to pass a statute. A high school girl was stalked by her ex-boyfriend. He snuck into her house and killed her. Just before he was arrested, he distributed sexual pictures, which were taken while they were in a relationship. In general, privacy of the deceased is not protected under the privacy law in Japan. Thus, the name of the victim could be published as the publishers could choose whether or not they wanted to publish the minor victim's name. So, for a time, before the ISP deleted the search URL, pictures were available to anyone.

---

[31] Paroline v. United States, 134 S.Ct.1710 (2014).

[32] Saiko Saibansho [Sup. Ct] Jan 31, 2017, Heisei 28(kyo) no.45, 1669 Saibansho Jihou 1.

In this case, her family hesitated to complain to the Ministry of Justice for an infringement of the Child Pornography Act for their daughter. Her families wanted a more serious sanction, and, in the high court's review, they added a complaint for child pornography infringement. However, the sentence for this particular crime was minimal. Following this case, the Revenge Porn Act was enacted to provide that the ISP Act shorten the 7-day wait time to 2 days for matters involving revenge porn (ISP Act, 2001, Art. 4).

These cases show that in the Internet era, when similar cases reveal gaps in the law, the legislature will pass specific statute to rectify that particular issue.

4.7 Victims Suffering from Publication by the Convicted

The Crime Victim Support Act of 2001 was modified to create the Basic Act on Crime Victims in 2004 (Miyazawa, 2014, p. 71). In the Civil Code, victims or their families may bring a tort action under Article 709 of the Civil Code. The statute of limitation is 3 years from the time the victim became aware of the damage and defendant or 20 years from the tort action (Civil Code, 1896, Art. 724). This Act is not generally applicable for damage caused by publication of a crime; instead, it covers only serious physical danger or death of victim, not defamation or privacy infringement.

The ISP Act permits deletion of posted images and requests for identification of a sender and applies tort law general damage principles. ISP responsibility is exempted in part only when the active ISP takes action without any gross negligence or intention. Usually, the convicted do not have to be financially solvent for civil action damages, and ISPs are exempt from monetary damages. As discussed above, however, victim's families may prefer deletion and injunction of posted messages or articles over damages.

Another problem victims and their families face are the excessive interviews of participants, family members, and neighbors by the media. Oftentimes, disheartened victim's families are targeted for popular interviews (Okudaira, 1997). Interview might be so heated and cause secondary emotional damage that victim's families might break up and need financial support later.

5 Conclusion

The Juvenile Act's purpose is based on the presumption that young criminals will recover from criminal ways and grow up to be contributing members of society. In the *Nagaragawa* case, one journal publicized a presumed name, and the convicted brought a suit for defamation and privacy infringement. The Court developed factors in several cases for determining whether there was a privacy infringement, including scope of the private information communicated, extent of concrete damage, purpose and significance of article, social circumstances at the time of publication, and necessity of the publication.

The Zekka author committed a serious crime when he was 14 years old. Article 61 of the Juvenile Act prohibits publication of identified persons, but provides no civil, criminal, or administrative sanctions for publication. But today, such a prohibition is futile because using Internet search engines it is easy to identify such persons. Furthermore, when juveniles are sentenced to death, the media may release names because there is no longer a concern about hindering their future life in society.

In the *Zekka* case, after reformatory school, the convicted published one book describing his crimes, interrogations, and life in reformatory school without permission of victim's families. This book resulted in a significant financial gain for the convict. He did not use real name as an author. The Zekka book was not at all defamatory, so it was difficult for victims' families to request an injunction against publication under the Civil Code. And, as in most cases, the damage award is so minimal that publishers are encouraged to publish and sell even in the face of potential litigation. To curb these behaviors, court may apply the actual malice doctrine or raise the damage award for cases involving famous people.

The *Hoppo Journal* case set out standards for seeking publication injunctions. When reviewing an injunction request, the court must provide the author/publisher an opportunity to rebut the plaintiff's evidence. The *Simon & Schuster* decision in the United States illustrated the difficulties surrounding the transfer of convicts' financial profits from crime-related publications to victims' families. The ability to tell one's story is protected under the US Constitution, and, although the Court acknowledged that compensating the victims was a compelling interest, the means for this compensation was not narrowly tailored to the goal.

Although it may be possible for the Japanese Diet to pass a similar statute covering all the Japanese territory, it seems that the consensus for transferring financial profits from convicts to victims has not yet been reached. In Japan, victims' families often do not feel comfortable accepting money from the convicted.

Consent involves with a sanction or damage to both of the convicted and victims for publication or uploading pictures. Consent extinguishes any argument for defamation and privacy infringement; although, it is possible to argue that distributing data to other people is outside of the scope of consent. In such cases, the applicable injunction proceeding is based on the general Civil Code and the analysis in the *Hoppo Journal* case.

There is no comprehensive statute covering expression on the Internet. The only relevant statutes have been passed on the Diet after several similar cases expose legal gaps in particular domains. For example, there are statutes supporting victims for serious crime, but not for defamation and privacy infringement. The Revenge Porn Act was passed after the Child Pornography Act and the Stalker Control Act.

The marketplace of ideas first arose with respect to the freedom of expression in a famous US case in 1919 and was imported into the Japanese constitutional law. It thinks that we are able to easily determine the truth on our own by having access to a greater amount and diversity of information. It is a general principle that lacks concrete guidelines necessary for specific cases in today's Internet era. In Japan, the marketplace of ideas works in principle, and, when it fails, the government offers specific rules prepared especially for concrete disputes among conflicting constitutional interests.

References

Ashibe, N. (2000). *Kenpougaku III* [Constitutional theory III]. Yuhikaku.

Farber, D. (2010). *The first amendment* (3rd ed.). Foundation Press.

Hardung, J. (2000). The proposed revision to Japan's Juvenile law: If punishment is their answer, they are asking the wrong question. *Pacific Rim Law & Policy Journal, 9*(139), 143–145.

Igaki, Y. (2015). *Moto Sohunen A Zekka Ni Kakanakatta Sinjistu.* Bungei Shunju.

Ii, T. (2012). Saiban-in trials: An observation of the Aomori District Court. In T. Ginsburg & H. Schiber (Eds.), *The Japanese legal system: An era of transition 113 (The Robbins Collection).*

Isa C. (2001). *Gyakuten.* Iwanami Shoten.

ISP Act of 2001. *Purobaida sekinin seigen hou* [Japanese Act on the Limitation of Liability for Damages of Specified Telecommunications Service Providers and the Right to Demand Disclosure of Identification Information of the Senders], Law No. 137.

Johnson, D. T., & Satoru, S. (2015). Judging Japan's new criminal trials: Early returns from 2009. In L. Wolf, L. Nottage, & K. Anderson (Eds.), *Who rules Japan.* Edward Elgar Publishing.

Kuzuno, H. (2005). Juvenile diversion and the get-tough movement in Japan. *Ritsumekan Law Review, 22*, 1–21.

Matsui, S. (2000). *Shounen Jiken No Jitsumei Houduoha Yurusarenainoka* [Should Be Minor Named in News]. Nihonhyouronsha.

Matsui, S. (2007). *Nihon Koku Kenpo* [Japanese Constitution] (3rd ed.). Yuhikaku.

Miyazawa, S. (2014). Citizen participation in criminal trials in Japan: The saiban-in system and victim participation in japan in international perspectives. *International Journal of Law, Crime, & Justice, 42*(2), 71–82. https://doi.org/10.1016/j.ijlcj.2014.03.002.

N.Y. Exec.Law § 632a(1) (McKinney 1982).

Nagayama, N. (1999). *Muchi no namida* [tears of ignorance]. Kawaide shobou.

Nonaka, T., Mutsuo, N., Kazuyuki, T., & Katsutoshi, T. (2012). *Japan constitutional law 1* (3rd ed.). Tokyo: Yuhikaku.

Okudaira, Y. (1988). *Naze Hyougen No Jiyuka* [Why freedom expression matters]. Tokyo: Tokyo University Press.

Okudaira, Y. (1997). *Ja-Narizumu to Hou* [Journalism and Law]. Shinseisha.

Parents of Shonen A. (2001). *Shounen A No Fubo, Konoko Wo Unde* [Give birth this boy]. Bungei Shunju.

Sato, K. (2011). *Kenpo* [Constitution]. Seibundo.

Shonen A. (2015). *Zekka.* Ohtashuppan.

Tomatsu, H. (2015). *KENPO* [Constitution]. Koubundo.

Tsuji, Y. (2002). Constitutional analysis about internet service provider's responsibility in Japan. *Law and Political Association, 53*(4), 887.

Tsukuda, K. (2005). *Meiyokison No Houritsu Jitumu* [Legal practice of defamation]. Koubundou.

Urabe, N. (2016). *Kenpo Gaku Kyusitsu* [Class for Constitution]. Nihon hyoronsha.

Yamada, R. (2012). *Kisha Tokidoki Gakusha No Kenpo Ron* [Constitutional studies of the reporter sometimes scholar]. Nihon Hyoronsha.

Yu M. (2002). *Ishi ni oyoku sakana* [Fish swimming in stone]. Shinchosha.

Statutes

Basic Act on Crime Victims of 2004. Hanzai higaisha tou kihon hou [Basic Act on Crime Victims, Act No. 161 of December 8, 2004], Law Act No. 161.
Crime Victim Support Act of 1980. Hanzai higaisha tou yufukin no sikyutou ni yoru hanzai higaisha touno sienni kansuru houritsu [The Act on Support for Crime Victims, etc. Such as Payment of Crime Victims Benefit], Law Act No. 36.
Child Pornography Act of 1999. Jidō poruno kinshi-ho [Japanese Act on Punishment of Activities Relating to Child Prostitution and Child Pornography, and the Protection of Children], Law No. 52.
Keihou [Japanese Penal Code], Law No. 45 (1907), Art. 175.
Keihou [Japanese Penal Code], Law No. 45 (1907), Art. 230–232.
Keihou [Japanese Penal Code], Law No. 45 (1907), Art. 41.
Keiji soshou hou [Japanese Code of Criminal Procedure], Law No. 131 (1948), Art. 290–292.
Personal Information Protection Act of 2003. Kojin jouhou hogo hou [Japanese Act on the Protection of Personal Information], Law No. 57.
Minpou [Japanese Civil Code], Law No. 89 (1896), Art. 709.
Minpou [Japanese Civil Code], Law No. 89 (1896), Art. 723.
Minpou [Japanese Civil Code], Law No. 89 (1896), Art. 724.
Nihonkoku Kenpo [Japanese Constitution], Art. 21.
Nihonkoku Kenpo [Japanese Constitution], Art. 13.
Nihonkoku Kenpo [Japanese Constitution], Art. 14.
Nihonkoku Kenpo [Japanese Constitution], Art. 41.
Revenge Porn Act of 2014. Watakushigoto-sei-teki gazō kiroku no teikyō-tō ni yoru higai no bōshi ni kansuru hou [Japanese Act on the Prevention of Damage Caused by The Provision of Private Affairs Sexual Image Recording], Law No. 126.
Juvenile Act of 1948. Shounen hou, Law No. 168.
Stalker Control Act of 2016. Sutōkā koui touno kisei ni kansuru hōritsu, Law No. 102.

Judicial Decision

Japan

Hiroshima Koto Saibansho [Hiroshima High. Ct], May 30, 2013, Heisei 24(ne) no.354, 2202 Hanrei Jihou 28.
Kobe Chihou Saibansho [Kobe Dist. Ct], March 11, 1999, Heisei 10(wa) no.1779, 1677 Hanrei Jihou 110.
Nagoya Koto Saibansho [Nagoya High. Ct], May 12, 2004, Heisei 15(ne) no.275, 1870 Hanrei Jihou 29.
Saiko Saibansho [Sup. Ct] March 13, 1957, Showa 28(a) no.1713, 11(3) Saiko Saibansho Keij Hanreishu [Keishu] 997.
Saiko Saibansho [Sup. Ct] June 25, 1969, Showa 41(a) no.2472, 23(7) Saiko Saibansho Keiji Hanreishu [Keishu] 975.
Saiko Saibansho [Sup. Ct] April 16, 1981, Showa 55(a) no.273, 35(3) Saiko Saibansho Keiji Hanreishu [Keishu] 84.
Saiko Saibansho [Sup. Ct] July 8, 1983, Showa 56(a) no.1505, 37(6) Saiko Saibansho Keiji Hanreishu [Keishu] 609.
Saiko Saibansho [Sup. Ct] June 11, 1984a, Showa 56(o) no.609, 40(4) Saiko Saibansho Minji Hanreishu [Minshu] 872.

Saiko Saibansho [Sup. Ct] Dec. 12, 1984b, Showa 57 (gyo tsu) no.156, 38(12) Saiko Saibansho Minji Hanreishu [Minshu] 1308.
Saiko Saibansho [Sup. Ct] Feb. 8, 1994, Heisei 1(o) no.1649, 48(2) Saiko Saibansho Minji Hanreishu [Minshu] 149.
Saiko Saibansho [Sup. Ct] Dec. 15, 1995, Heisei 2(a) no.848, 49(10) Saiko Saibansho Keiji Hanreishu [Keishu] 842.
Saiko Saibansho [Sup. Ct] Sep. 24, 2002, Heisei 13(o) no.851, 207 Saiko Saibansho Minji Hanreishu [Minshu] 243.
Saiko Saibansho [Sup. Ct] March 14, 2003, Heisei 12(ju) no.1335, 57(3) Saiko Saibansho Minji Hanreishu [Minshu] 229.
Saiko Saibansho [Sup. Ct] March 10, 2011, Heisei 17(a) no.2358, 303 Saiko Saibansho Keij Hanreishu [Keishu] 133.
Saiko Saibansho [Sup. Ct] Jan 31, 2017, Heisei 28(kyo) no.45, 1669 Saibansho Jihou 1.
Saiko Saibansho [Sup. Ct] Sep.25, 2014, Heisei 25(o) no.1765, D-1 Law.com (No. 28224039).
Tokyo Chiho Saibansho [Tokyo Dist.Ct.] Sep. 28, 1964, Showa 36 (wa) no. 1882, 385 Hanrei Jihou 12.
Tokyo Koto Saibansho [Tokyo High.Ct.] Oct. 30, 2003, Heisei 15 (ne) no. 2728, D-1 Law.com(No. 28091823).
Tokyo Chiho Saibansho [Tokyo Dist.Ct.] March 27, 2001, Heisei 12 (wa) no. 5109, 1754 Hanrei Jihou 93.

U.S.

Abrams v. United States, 250 U.S. 616 (1919).
New York v. Sullivan, 376 U.S. 254 (1964).
Paroline v. United States, 134 S.Ct.1710 (2014).
Simon & Schuster, Inc. v. Members of New York State Crime Victims Board, 502 U.S. 105 (1991).

Part IV
Lay Judges' System

Chapter 15
The Impact of Previous Sentencing Trends on Lay Judges' Sentencing Decisions

Masahiko Saeki and Eiichiro Watamura

1 Introduction

The Lay Judge system (*Saiban-in Seido*) has been in effect in Japan since 2009. Under this system, certain serious cases are heard and judged by a panel of professional judges and lay judges. Generally, the panel consists of three professional judges and six lay judges (Article 2(2), Act on Criminal Trials with Participation of *Saiban-in*: ACTPS). The panel of professional judges and lay judges decides whether the defendant is guilty or not guilty, and if the defendant is found to be guilty, then the panel determines an appropriate punishment for the convicted defendant (Article 6(1), ACTPS).

The panel makes decisions using a special majority rule. Under this rule, majority votes must include at least one vote from both a professional judge and a lay judge (Article 67(1), ACTPS). When it comes to determining an appropriate punishment, it is plausible that there are two or more different opinions and that none of them satisfy the requirement of the special majority rule. In this case, the number of votes for the most unfavorable outcome for the accused will be added to the number

While drafting the scenario for the mock trial video that was used in the experiment introduced in this chapter, Mr. Hiroshi Kawatsu (attorney-at-law) provided many useful comments based on his experience and knowledge. The authors would like to thank him for his helpful and important comments.

The translation of Japanese law into English here is not an official legal translation. The Ministry of Justice's database that compiles translation of Japanese law was consulted. For the Web page of that database, see http://www.japaneselawtranslation.go.jp/?re=01 [Accessed 10 March 2017].

M. Saeki (✉)
Graduate School of Social Sciences, Chiba University, Chiba, Japan
e-mail: m-saeki@chiba-u.jp

E. Watamura
Graduate School of Human Sciences, Osaka University, Osaka, Japan

J. Liu, S. Miyazawa (eds.), *Crime and Justice in Contemporary Japan*,
Springer Series on Asian Criminology and Criminal Justice Research,
https://doi.org/10.1007/978-3-319-69359-0_15

of votes for the second most unfavorable until a majority is attained with support of at least both one professional judge and one lay judge. The panel's decision will be that of the opinion most favorable to the accused among votes by the majority group (Article 67(2), ACTPS).[1]

This chapter zeros in on the impact of information about prior sentencing trends on sentencing decisions by lay judges. In the next section, practices and arguments about sentencing decisions are described. Subsequently, a research question is identified, and results of an original psychological experiment are presented. Finally, interpretation of the results, limitations of the experiment, and future tasks are discussed.

2 Practices and Issues of Sentencing in Japan[2]

2.1 Sentencing Practices by Professional Judges in Japan

Before the introduction of the Lay Judge system, sentences were rendered only by professional judges. To make issues of sentencing practices under the Lay Judge system clear, the sentencing practices of professional judges are summarized below.

Ranges of statutory penalties in the Japanese Penal Code are very broad. For example, in homicide cases, the defendant can be punished by the death penalty or imprisonment with work for life or for a definite term of not less than 5 years (Article 199, Penal Code). In addition, when some circumstances about mitigation or aggravation are established, the range can be broadened. Although there is much discretion by the professional judge to decide an appropriate punishment, there is no formal provision that guides judicial decision-making. Therefore, professional judges have to choose a particular punishment among many options without any clear stipulation of law. However, it is said that professional judges manage this difficult task with the aid of a kind of practical "sentencing standard (*Ryokei-Souba*)."[3] This sentencing standard is the subjective sense that tells professional judges a certain range of punishment appropriate for the case with which they are confronted. With the help of this subjective sense, professional judges can narrow down the options of the punishment for the defendant within the broad range of statutory penalties. This sense is said to be shared by professional judges with a certain amount of experience (Harada, 2008). This experience-based sense of sentencing standard is considered to be effective in achieving equal treatment among similar cases (Endo, 2011; Harada, 2011). Namely, when professional judges are confronted with similar cases, they will consider a nearly identical appropriate range of

[1] For a more detailed explanation about the Japanese lay judge system, see Anderson and Nolan (2004), and Ikeda et al. (2016).

[2] As for a general explanation on sentencing in Japan, see Shiroshita (2010), which was consulted to write this section.

[3] To translate the word *Ryokei-Souba*, Shiroshita (2010) was consulted.

punishments through this shared sense, and they will choose a punishment within this range, which is narrower than the range of statutory penalty.

The limited range of appropriate punishment is derived primarily from the information about the circumstances of the crime, and this range determines the outline of a final output on sentencing. To decide one definite punishment within this range, professional judges consider more specific information on the case that is not categorized as the circumstances of the crime. For example, they take into consideration whether the defendant is regretful, what his or her surrounding conditions are, whether they have any supporters, whether or not the defendant settled with the victim, and so on.[4]

2.2 Issues Regarding Sentencing Practices Under the Lay Judge System in Japan

As can be easily imagined, it is almost impossible for lay judges to follow the professional judges' way of sentencing, because they do not have a subjective sense of sentencing standard. Without any aid to reach a decision on punishment, it would be hard for lay judges to decide a punishment for the convicted defendant. Therefore, the Supreme Court of Japan created a database of past sentencing decisions. Outcomes of trials and some relevant features of crimes are compiled in the database. This database was launched on 1 April 2008, and it compiles information about the cases where judgments of conviction have been delivered in first instance courts since that date. This database also has a search function. Concrete search conditions depend on the type of crimes, but the search conditions are primarily related with culpabilities of criminal acts (Aoki, 2013). There are two display formats for the search results. One is Case List (*Jirei Ichiranhyo*), which is the list of the cases that satisfy designated search conditions. The other form is Frequency Distribution Graph (*Ryokei Bunpu Graph*), which shows the frequency distribution of sentencing outcomes of past cases that satisfy designated search conditions. It is thought that lay judges would try to find the most similar case among the list if they pay much attention to a Case List. Due to this problem, some professional judges express their reluctance to rely heavily on a Case List (Ito & Maeda, 2010). On the other hand, they think that a Frequency Distribution Graph is helpful for lay judges without any experience of sentencing decisions (Ito & Maeda, 2010). Therefore, it is presumed that lay judges mainly refer to Frequency Distribution Graphs to grasp previous sentencing trends. In this way, the database and its retrieved information can ensure meaningful participation for lay judges in sentencing decision-making processes. However, if previous sentencing trends exclusively determine sentencing decisions of the cases confronting lay judges and professional judges, there would be no use for lay judges' participation in criminal trials. Therefore, it is emphasized

[4] However, in practice, some factors that are not categorized as the circumstances of the crime have a significant impact on sentencing decisions (Endo, 2011).

that the database is intended to help lay judges to formulate their sentencing opinions and that it is not a binding standard (Harada, 2011).[5]

In contrast, others argue that prior sentencing trends should be treated as more than a mere point of reference to ensure fair treatment among similar cases (Sakamaki, 2006). They emphasize that punishment should be proportional to the seriousness of criminal acts, and therefore punishment should be equal among the cases with similarly severe criminal acts. Since items for search conditions of the database are chosen to reflect basic factors categorized in terms of the circumstances of the crime, prior sentencing trends shown by the database are thought to reflect rough ranges of appropriate punishments that are proportionate to the seriousness of criminal acts (Aoki, 2013). Therefore, it is proposed that such trends should be valued beyond mere points of reference. After the commencement of the Lay Judge system, the Legal Training and Research Institute (*Shihokenshujyo*) of the Supreme Court of Japan published their draft plans on how to conduct sentencing deliberation by professional judges and lay judges (Shihokenshujyo, 2012). It expresses the stance described above.[6] In addition, on 24 July 2014, the Supreme Court of Japan established that prior sentencing trends should be respected and that if punishments diverging from the trends are to be handed down to the convicted defendant, they must explain the rationale behind the divergence (Judgment by the Supreme Court of Japan, 24 July 2014, 68 Saiko Saibansho Keiji Hanreishu [Keishu] 925 (1st petty bench)).

In this way, the judicial attitude toward sentencing trends seems to be changing somewhat.[7] At first, judicial personnel emphasized at least outwardly that previous sentencing trends would help lay judges to formulate sentencing opinions and that they are not binding standards. However, as it is crystallized in the abovementioned judgment of the Supreme Court of Japan, the emphasis is now on that previous sentencing trends should be respected to grasp an appropriate range of punishments to ensure equality of punishment among cases with similar seriousness of criminal acts. Although it is difficult to evince empirically,[8] the use of materials regarding sentencing trends in the deliberation among lay judges and professional judges may also change to reflect this attitude change of the judiciary.

[5] It is reported that top court officials in Japan said "they should not hesitate in showing material on past sentences as long as they emphasize that it is only meant for reference and not binding criteria" (Fukue & Kato, 2009).

[6] Aoki (2013) describes Shihokenshujyo (2012) as the de facto official opinion of the Supreme Court of Japan.

[7] As for the judicial attitude on previous sentencing trends in the context of the lay judge system, see also Koike (2016).

[8] First, confidentiality requirements (Articles 9(2), 70(1), and 108, ACTPS) may prevent disclosure of information inside deliberation rooms. Second, currently researchers do not have any method to contact experienced lay judges systematically.

2.3 Research Question

As described just above, it is thought that many lay judges refer to materials about previous sentencing trends. However, there are different evaluations on these materials. On the one hand, it is argued that previous sentencing trends should only be used to help lay judges formulate their sentencing opinions and should not have any binding impact on their decisions. If previous sentencing trends had any binding impact on their decisions, the values of the Lay Judge system might be impaired. On the other hand, it is argued that previous sentencing trends should be esteemed and therefore have meaning beyond being a point of reference. The Supreme Court of Japan seems to show their preference for the latter camp by requiring rational reasons when sentencing outside of trends (Judgments by the Supreme Court of Japan, 24 July 2014, 68 Saiko Saibansho Keiji Hanreishu [Keishu] 925 (1st petty bench)). In this way, the issue on how to use materials about previous sentencing trends could be related to the issues regarding the extent to which citizen participation can be achieved under the Lay Judge system. Therefore, it is important to explore the impact of previous sentencing trends on lay judges' sentencing decisions.

This chapter focuses on the issue of when previous sentencing trends should be shown to lay judges. The database can be used not only by judges but also by public prosecutors and defense lawyers. For example, public prosecutors and defense lawyers can use materials derived from the database when they make closing arguments. For this reason, lay judges can be shown some materials on previous sentencing trends before they start to deliberate. Although it is possible for them to know some aspects of previous sentencing trends before the initiation of deliberations, the timing on the use of previous sentencing trends in deliberation processes is the focus of this chapter. Since professional judges seem to prefer Frequency Distribution Graphs to Case Lists (see Sect. 2.2), the experiment described below focuses on the impact of Frequency Distribution Graphs on lay judges' sentencing decisions.

There are two major ways to use Frequency Distribution Graphs in terms of when lay judges and professional judges refer to those materials. One way to refer to Frequency Distribution Graphs is by talking about concrete punishments only after referring to Frequency Distribution Graphs to know previous sentencing trends for similar cases.[9] The other way is to talk about concrete punishments even before referring to Frequency Distribution Graphs. It is thought that lay judges may stick to extreme opinions even after they are shown previous sentencing trends if they have an opportunity to express their opinions on possible punishments before they refer to Frequency Distribution Graphs (Ito & Maeda, 2010). Conversely, if they are shown Frequency Distribution Graphs before they express their opinions about concrete punishments, lay judges might think that their participation is less necessary

[9] This way seems common in actual practices (see Nagoya Chiho Saibansho Keiji Practice Kento Iinkai, 2016).

because previous sentencing trends could be perceived to be what determine the outline of sentencing.[10]

3 The Experimental Study

3.1 Procedure

To explore the impact of Frequency Distribution Graphs on lay judges' sentencing decisions, a mock trial experiment was conducted in October 2013. Participants were 133 undergraduate students enrolled in an introductory psychology course at a university in Tokyo. Participants were asked to watch a video about a fictional criminal trial. In the fictional case, the defendant was prosecuted for injury causing death (Article 205, Penal Code). The defendant and his attorneys claimed that his deed was committed in self-defense. In the fictional case, the incident was triggered by a fight between the defendant and the victim. However, the story is constructed so that almost all people think that the defendant's deed is not committed in self-defense to ensure that enough data can be collected on sentencing decisions.

The experiment was conducted according to the following procedure. First, participants completed a *pre-movie questionnaire* that inquired about their basic demographics and attitudes toward punishments. Second, they were asked to watch the movie about the fictional trial on the guilt phase (*guilt-phase movie*) while imagining themselves as an actual lay judge who is appointed for this fictional case. Third, they completed a *post-guilt-phase questionnaire*. At this point, the first manipulation was conducted. About half of the participants were asked to decide whether the defendant was guilty or not guilty. The remaining participants were asked only to guess the other hypothetical lay judges' decision on whether the defendant was guilty or not guilty.[11] Fourth, they watched the movie about the trial on the sentencing phase (*sentencing-phase movie*). Fifth, they completed a *post-sentencing-phase questionnaire*. In this questionnaire, all participants were asked to decide whether the defendant was guilty or not guilty. After that, they were asked to evaluate how much weight several sentencing factors should be given in determining an appropriate punishment for the convicted defendant. Then, the second manipulation was conducted. About half of the participants were asked to determine an appropriate punishment for the convicted defendant. The remaining participants were asked to

[10] Taguchi (2013) compiles impressions from 14 experienced lay judges. Although it is not guaranteed that these 14 experienced lay judges are representative, this book is important for providing a first glimpse into actual lay judges' impressions. Taguchi (2013) introduces experienced lay judges' impressions that citizen participation would not be useful if the punishment was decided based on prior sentencing trends.

[11] However, this manipulation is not related to the topic of this chapter. Therefore, the analyses on this first manipulation are not reported in this chapter. For the analyses on this manipulation, see Saeki (2017).

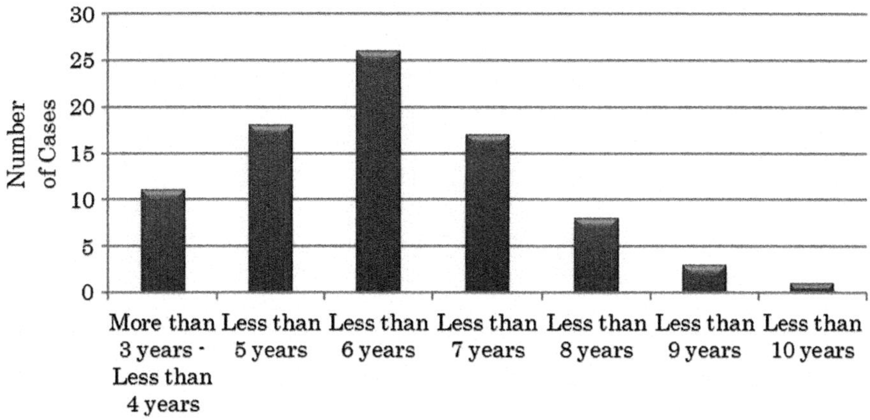

Fig. 15.1 The fictional Frequency Distribution Graph (Words in the figure were originally in Japanese. To put this figure on this chapter, those words were translated from Japanese to English)

guess other hypothetical lay judges' sentencing decision. That is, they were not asked to state their sentencing decisions in this *post-sentencing-phase questionnaire*.[12] Sixth, they were shown a fictional Frequency Distribution Graph about recent sentencing outcomes in similar cases (Fig. 15.1), and seventh, they completed a *post-graph questionnaire*. In the *post-graph questionnaire,* all participants were required to determine an appropriate punishment for the defendant. Finally, participants exchanged their questionnaires in groups of two or three and evaluated each other's responses to the questionnaires.

As for the second manipulation, about one half of participants were asked to state their own concrete sentencing opinions before they referred to the fictional Frequency Distribution Graph. They were required to express their concrete sentencing opinions again after they referred to fictional Frequency Distribution Graph. This first condition is called the *opinion first condition*. The other half of participants were not asked to state their own concrete sentencing opinion before they referred to the fictional Frequency Distribution Graph. They were required only to guess other hypothetical lay judges' sentencing decision in the *post-sentencing-phase questionnaire*.[13] After they were shown the fictional Frequency Distribution Graph, they had an opportunity to express their own concrete sentencing opinions. This second condition is called the *graph first condition*.

It can be hypothesized that participants tend to stick to their prior sentencing decisions even after they refer to the fictional Frequency Distribution Graph in the *opinion first condition* (Ito & Maeda, 2010). To explore this possibility, the participants in the *opinion first condition* were asked to state their own concrete sentencing

[12] Both first and second factors were manipulated by randomly assigning various sets of questionnaires to the participants.

[13] This question was introduced to make the burden of the experimental task equal between the two conditions.

opinions before they referred to the fictional Frequency Distribution Graph. However, if they only wrote their opinions in the *post-sentencing-phase questionnaire*, it would not be enough for them to commit to their own opinions. After all, writing down an opinion is a private behavior. To make participants in the *opinion first condition* commit to their sentencing opinions written down in the *post-sentencing-phase questionnaire*, participants were told in advance that they would be required to exchange their own questionnaires with other participants and that all responses would be evaluated by other participants. In doing so, their answers to the *post-sentencing-phase questionnaire* became public ex post facto.

3.2 Data

Some participants were excluded from the analyses for several reasons. First, two participants were excluded because they didn't give a correct answer to the question regarding what the contested issue was in the fictional trial.[14] Second, 28 participants who answered that they were not able to concentrate for the duration of the experiment were also excluded. Because the *guilt-phase movie* is approximately 30 min, and the *sentencing-phase movie* is about 10 min, it was not guaranteed that all participants concentrated on the experiment. Therefore, at the end of the experiment, the participants were asked whether they thought they were able to concentrate or not. Third, four participants whose questionnaires had a blank answer on more than one page in a row were excluded. Fourth, since the main purpose of this experiment was to explore the impact of commitment to their own sentencing opinions, the participants who did not find the defendant guilty in the *post-sentencing-phase questionnaire* were excluded. Only eight participants answered that the defendant was not guilty, and one participant failed to answer to this question.[15] Since there was a significant overlap of participants in these four exclusion categories, the analyses below are based on 94 participants' responses.[16,17]

[14] This question was asked in the *post-guilt-phase questionnaire*. In the fictional trial video that was shown to the participants, whether the defendant's act is self-defense or not is contested. The participants were asked to choose the issue of the fictional trial among three options, and only two participants were not able to answer to this question correctly.

[15] In this experiment, the first manipulation that was done during the *post-guilt-phase questionnaire* created two conditions, and the second manipulation, which was done during the *post-sentencing-phase questionnaire*, also created two conditions. Therefore, in total there are four conditions in the experiment. Since only a few participants did not find the defendant guilty, no statistically significant relationship between the rate of finding the defendant guilty in the *post-sentencing-phase questionnaire* and the four conditions was detected using Fisher's exact test ($p = 0.552$).

[16] Due to the existence of missing data, some analyses were conducted based on a sample of fewer than 94 participants.

[17] It is arguable whether the participants who admitted that they did not concentrate on the experimental task or whose questionnaires had a blank answer on more than one page should be excluded from the analysis. The participants who admitted their lack of concentration might concentrate on the task enough, but their assessment criteria might be too high. The participants who did not fill

3.3 Results

3.3.1 Subjective Impressions on the Frequency Distribution Graph

If lay judges tend to abide by their opinions when they state their concrete sentencing opinions before referring to a Frequency Distribution Graph, it is possible that they give less weight to the graph than when stating concrete sentencing opinions only after referring to the graph. To assess the participants' impressions of the fictional Frequency Distribution Graph in the experiment, they were asked to answer two questions about the graph in the *post-graph questionnaire*. The first question was "To what extent did you consult the Frequency Distribution Graph that was shown?", and the second question was "To what extent did you think the Frequency Distribution Graph that was shown should be respected?" These questions were answered on a five-point scale.[18]

As for the question on the degree of consultation, there was no statistically significant difference between the *opinion first condition* and the *graph first condition* based on the one-way ANOVA ($F(1, 91) = 0.382$, $p = 0.538$).[19] In both conditions, the means were below the midpoint of the scale (*opinion first condition*, $M = 2.53$, SD = 1.334, and *graph first condition*, $M = 2.36$, SD = 1.382), and the differences between the means and the midpoint of the scale were statistically significant (*opinion first condition*, $t(42) = -2.287$, $p = 0.027$, and *graph first condition*, $t(49) = -3.276$, $p = 0.002$). Therefore, in both conditions, the participants tended to consult the Frequency Distribution Graph that was shown.

Conversely, as for the answers to the question about the degree of respect for the graph, the difference between the *opinion first condition* and the *graph first condition* was statistically significant based on the one-way ANOVA ($F(1, 91) = 4.279$,

---

in more than one page of the questionnaire might be fully involved with the task during the other parts of the questionnaire. Therefore, the analyses were also conducted including those participants. It became apparent that this inclusion did not affect the basic findings shown below. However, where slight differences between the analyses with and without those participants were found, these are also reported at the appropriate places.

[18] With regard to the first question, "one" means that they consulted the graph, "three" means that it is difficult to say whether they consulted the graph or not, and "five" means that they did not consult the graph. For the second question, "one" means that they thought the graph should be respected, "three" means that it is difficult to say whether they thought the graph should be respected or not, and "five" means that they thought the graph should not be respected.

[19] As mentioned, there were two manipulations in the experiment, and this chapter focuses on only second manipulation. However, it is possible that the first manipulation affected the answers to the question. For this reason, a two-way ANOVA was also conducted, and the result of this analysis was very similar to that of the one-way ANOVA. Neither the two main effects nor the interaction was statistically significant (main effect of the first manipulation, $F(1, 89) = 2.033$, $p = 0.157$; main effect of the second manipulation, $F(1, 89) = 0.365$, $p = 0.547$; interaction, $F(1, 89) = 0.440$, $p = 0.509$).

As for the remaining results of the one-way ANOVA, which are introduced below in this chapter, there was no difference between the one-way and two-way ANOVA in terms of the main effect of the second manipulation. Therefore, only the results of the one-way ANOVA are shown below.

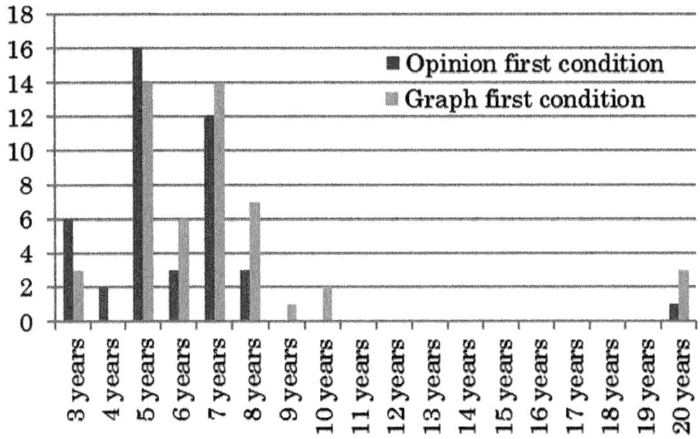

Fig. 15.2 Distributions of sentencing decisions in the *post-graph questionnaire*

$p = 0.041$).[20] The participants in the *graph first condition* thought more strongly than the participants in the *opinion first condition* that the graph should be respected. The mean of the *graph first condition* on this question was below the midpoint of the scale ($M = 2.64$, SD = 1.120), and the difference between the mean and the midpoint of the scale was statistically significant ($t(49) = -2.272$, $p = 0.028$). In contrast, the mean of the *opinion first condition* was slightly higher than the midpoint of the scale ($M = 3.14$, SD = 1.207), and the difference between the mean and the midpoint of the scale was not statistically significant ($t(42) = 0.758$, $p = 0.453$). In the *graph first condition*, the participants indicated that the Frequency Distribution Graph should be respected. Contrarily, the average opinion of the participants in the *opinion first condition* is that it is difficult to say whether the graph should be respected or not.

3.3.2 Sentencing Decisions

Figure 15.2 shows the distributions of the participants' sentencing opinions in the *post-graph questionnaire*. In both conditions, their sentencing opinions were concentrated between 5 and 7 years of incarceration.[21] Although it is thought that lay judges may adhere to their extreme opinions if they express concrete sentencing opinions before referring to a Frequency Distribution Graph (Ito & Maeda, 2010), there were fewer extreme sentencing opinions in the *opinion first condition* than in the *graph first condition*. Since the number of the participants who expressed

[20] When the participants who admitted that they did not concentrate on the experimental task or whose questionnaires had a blank answer on more than one page are included in the analysis, the difference between *opinion first condition* and *graph first condition* is statistically significant at 0.10 level of significance ($F(1, 119) = 3.234$, $p = 0.075$).

[21] In this chapter, incarceration means imprisonment with required labor, not imprisonment without work.

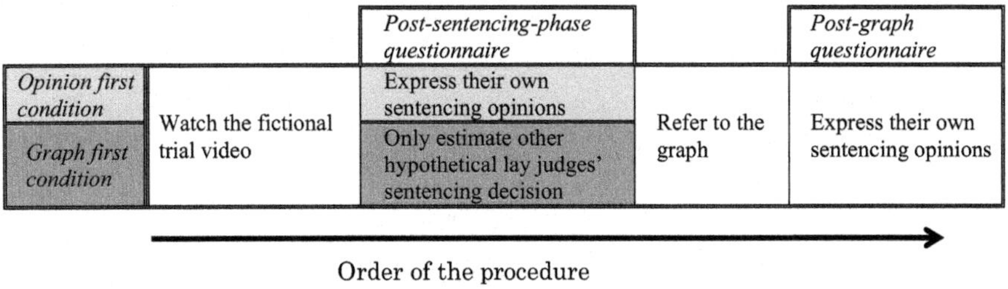

Fig. 15.3 Basic structure of the second manipulation

extremely heavy sentencing opinions was scarce, it was difficult to conduct any reliable statistical test. However, the number of participants who thought 20 years of incarceration would be an appropriate sentence for the defendant was fewer in the *opinion first condition* ($n = 1$) than in the *graph first condition* ($n = 3$). It is fair to conclude that the hypothesis that lay judges are more likely to maintain extreme sentencing opinions if they can express their concrete sentencing opinions before referring to a Frequency Distribution Graph is not supported by this experiment. One possible force that converges sentencing opinions could be the public prosecutor's opinion. In the *sentencing-phase movie*, the prosecutor demanded 7 years of incarceration for the defendant. When lay judges formulate their sentencing opinions, the sentencing opinions of public prosecutors could function as an anchor.

The next question is about the participants' opinion changes after referring to the graph. Did the participants change their sentencing opinions because of the reference to the graph? If they did, how did they change their opinions? If lay judges tend to adhere to their original sentencing opinions, it was hypothesized that the participants in the *opinion first condition* would be unlikely to change their sentencing opinions and would be likely to adhere to their already expressed sentencing opinions even after referring to the graph. According to the analyses on their subjective impressions of the Frequency Distribution Graph (Sect. 3.3.1), the participants in the *opinion first condition* were less likely to think that the graph should be respected than the participants in the *graph first condition*. Therefore, it seems rational to hypothesize that the participants in the *opinion first condition* would be more likely to disregard the graph and to adhere to the sentencing decisions that they expressed before referring to the graph.

Before testing this hypothesis, the limitation of the experiment should be noted. As explained (Sect. 3.1), the participants in the *graph first condition* were not required to express their concrete sentencing opinions before referring to the graph. They were required only to estimate the other hypothetical lay judges' sentencing decision (for the experimental design regarding this, see Fig. 15.3). For this reason, the sentencing opinions that the participants in the *graph first condition* considered before referring to the graph were not observed. Given this research design, it is impossible to compare the opinion change in the *opinion first condition* with the *graph first condition* in a rigorous manner.

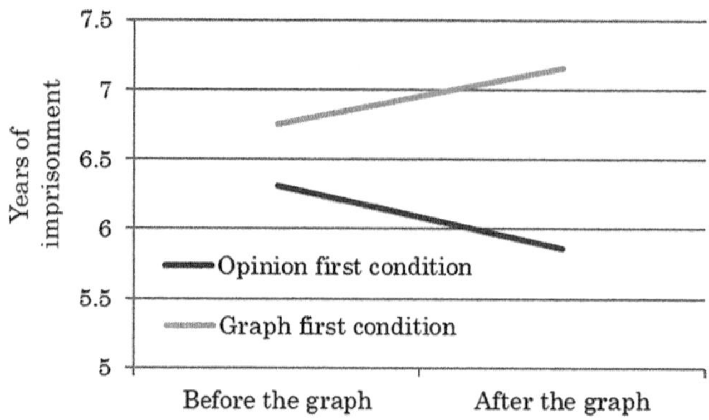

Fig. 15.4 Sentencing decisions/estimations before and after referring to the graph

Despite this limitation, analyzing the data is meaningful to gain some insights into this issue.[22] Figure 15.4 shows the changes in the averages about sentencing opinions and/or estimations. According to the one-way ANOVA, it can be seen that the difference between the mean of sentencing decisions before referring to the graph in the *opinion first conditions* and the mean of estimations on other hypothetical lay judges' sentencing decisions before referring to the graph in the *graph first condition* was not statistically significant ($F(1, 90) = 0.576$, $p = 0.450$). Contrarily, the difference between the averages of sentencing decisions after referring to the graph in the two conditions was statistically significant at 0.10 level of significance ($F(1, 91) = 3.772$, $p = 0.055$).[23]

Although it is hypothesized that lay judges adhere to the sentencing decisions that they expressed before referring to the graph, the participants in the *opinion first condition* seemed to decrease the length of time of incarceration after referring to the graph so that their sentencing opinions were closer to the mode of the fictional

[22]As shown in Fig. 15.2, a few outliers are present for answers about appropriate punishments. Therefore, the analysis excluding outliers was also conducted. Outliers were defined as more than M + 2SD (there were no responses below M − 2SD). To identify the outliers, the calculation was conducted using all participants' valid answers. For answers to the questions about sentencing decisions/estimations both in the *post-sentencing-phase questionnaire* and in the *post-graph questionnaire*, outliers were defined as 14 years of incarceration and longer. In addition, nonparametric analyses were also conducted while including these outliers because there is the matter of arbitrariness about exclusion of outliers. These additional analyses did not yield the results that contradicted this chapter's conclusions. Since the results of the analyses without the outliers are quite similar with the results of the nonparametric analyses, the latter results are also reported where slight differences between the parametric analyses with outliers and these two additional analyses were found.

[23]As to this difference, the nonparametric analysis (Mann-Whitney U test) yielded the similar result at 0.05 level of significance ($p = 0.014$). Contrarily, when the participants who admitted that they did not concentrate on the experimental task or whose questionnaires had a blank answer on more than one page were included in the analysis, the difference between the two conditions was not statistically significant ($F(1, 119) = 2.747$, $p = 0.100$). Therefore, it should be noted that this result is not stable.

Frequency Distribution Graph (Fig. 15.1), which was less than 6 years of incarceration. Based on a paired *t*-test, we can see that the difference between sentencing decisions in the *opinion first condition* before and after referring to the graph was statistically significant at 0.10 level of significance ($t(41) = 1.991, p = 0.053$).[24]

Since sentencing opinions before referring to the graph in the *graph first condition* were not observed due to the design of the experiment, the opinion change in the *graph first condition* could not be estimated. This limitation prevents the evaluation of an opinion change in the *opinion first condition* in comparison with the *graph first condition*. However, three findings can be derived from the analyses described above. First, even the participants in the *opinion first condition* changed their opinions after referring to the fictional Frequency Distribution Graph. Second, they seem to change their previous opinions so that their sentencing opinions approached the mode of the graph. Lastly, although this result is not stable, the mean of final sentencing decisions after referring to the graph in the *opinion first condition* was closer to the mode of the graph than that of the *graph first condition*.

4 Discussion

Although it is thought that lay judges adhere to the concrete sentencing opinions that they express before referring to a Frequency Distribution Graph (Ito & Maeda, 2010), this experiment does not support this concern. The participants were less likely to think that the graph should be respected if they had an opportunity to express their concrete sentencing opinions before referring to the graph. However, even if they expressed their sentencing opinions before referring to the graph, they were willing to change their sentencing opinions so that their opinions were more congruent with the previous sentencing trends that were reflected in the graph. In addition, it is plausible that the participants who expressed their opinions before referring to the graph rendered sentencing decisions that were closer to the mode of the graph than the participants who did not express their opinions before referring to the graph.

These results are partially inconsistent. If the participants in the *opinion first condition* tended not to respect the Frequency Distribution Graph, the mean of their final sentencing decisions should be more distant from the mode of the graph than that of the *graph first condition*. Despite this possible hypothesis, the experiment shows the opposite results. Although the participants in the *opinion first condition* were less likely to think that the Frequency Distribution Graph should be respected, they seemed to be more affected by the graph than the participants in the *graph first condition*. How can these inconsistent findings be interpreted consistently? One

[24] When the participants who admitted that they did not concentrate on the experimental task or whose questionnaires had a blank answer on more than one page were included in the analysis, the difference between sentencing decisions in the *opinion first condition* before and after referring to the graph was statistically significant at 0.05 level of significance ($t(53) = 2.614, p = 0.012$).

possible interpretation is that the participants in the *opinion first condition* felt forced to change their opinions when they were asked to make a sentencing decision again in the *post-graph questionnaire*. Despite already having expressed their sentencing opinions, they were shown the previous sentencing trends and asked to make a sentencing decision again. It is possible that they thought that they were being persuaded to change their sentencing opinions to reach the decisions that are more congruent with previous trends. Conversely, the participants in the *graph first condition* were asked to state their sentencing opinions only once, after referring to the graph. Therefore, they were free from a feeling of obligation that the participants in the *opinion first condition* might have experienced. Indeed, the participants in the *graph first condition* might have felt pressure to use the fictional graph to formulate their sentencing opinions like the participants in the *opinion first condition*. However, they should have felt less pressure to *change* their own opinions based on the fictional graph than the participants in the *opinion first condition*.

In the setting of this experiment, this feeling of obligation might have been induced by the experimenters. This means that the participants in the *opinion first condition* might think that the experimenters tried to persuade them to change their sentencing opinions by showing them the previous sentencing trend. In an actual trial setting, this feeling may come from professional judges. If lay judges are shown a Frequency Distribution Graph, they may feel that they should obey this trend and think that professional judges want them to state sentencing opinions that are congruent with the trend.[25] According to the results of the experiment, lay judges will obey the previous sentencing trends, rather than adhering to their original opinions by resisting the pressure from the graph and professional judges.

If this inference indicated by the results of the experiment is true, the remaining issue is about lay judges' evaluation of participation in criminal trials. If they feel that they are being persuaded to change their sentencing opinions when they refer to a Frequency Distribution Graph, they may not be satisfied with their experience as a lay judge, and they may evaluate the meaning of citizen participation negatively. Such negative evaluation by experienced lay judges will hamper promotion of the citizens' understanding of and enhancement of their trust in the judicial system (see Article 1, ACTPS). Considering that discussing concrete sentencing options mainly after referring to a Frequency Distribution Graph is likely to be a current common practice (see Nagoya Chiho Saibansho Keiji Practice Kento Iinkai, 2016), the current practice of sentencing deliberations that is similar with the *graph first condition* may contribute to keeping lay judges' subjective experience in a good state or enhancing it. However, this tentative conclusion is based on the inference from the results of the experiment that was shown above. In the experiment, participants'

[25] It is emphasized that professional judges do not show a Frequency Distribution Graph but that professional and lay judges construct a search condition for the case in cooperation and derive previous sentencing trends according to that search condition (Shihokenshujyo, 2012). If such collaboration is materialized in actual deliberations and lay judges can indeed understand the purpose of such collaboration, they may not feel any pressure from professional judges.

impressions of their experience as lay judges were not directly observed.[26] The Supreme Court of Japan has indicated the importance of previous sentencing trends clearly (Sect. 2.2). Given this situation surrounding the Lay Judge system, it is crucial to explore the impact of previous sentencing trends not only on sentencing decisions but also on lay judges' subjective evaluation of their involvement in criminal trials.[27]

Lastly, three main limitations of the experiment are discussed. First, the sample size may have been too small. In addition, all the participants in the experiment were undergraduate students from one university. It is necessary to replicate these findings with more diverse samples.

Second, the manipulation may not have been strong enough. This experiment was conducted in a relatively large class of an introductory psychology course for undergraduate students. Such a situation made it difficult to design the experiment so that the participants in the *opinion first condition* stated their own sentencing opinions clearly in front of other people before referring to the fictional Frequency Distribution Graph. As indicated above (Sect. 3.1), to solve this problem, participants were told that they would be exchanging their questionnaires and that other participants would review their responses. Although this declaration might clarify that their answers would be public, it was only ex post facto. Therefore, the stimulus might have been too weak to detect the impact of their commitment to previously expressed sentencing opinions in the *opinion first condition.*

Third, as mentioned, the design of the experiment did not allow for comparison of opinion changes between the *opinion first condition* and the *graph first condition.* Given the nature of the hypothesis, it is difficult to achieve this comparison in a rigorous manner. However, to derive more conclusive findings, a more creative experimental approach is needed.

[26] In addition, even if there is no opportunity to express their own sentencing opinions before referring to the graph like the *graph first condition*, they can feel the pressure to *change* their sentencing opinions when they are asked to reconsider sentencing opinions that are expressed after referring to the graph. Since such a dynamic was not replicated in the simple experiment, this task should be explored in the future.

[27] It should be noted that this chapter does not intend to claim that the subjective satisfaction of experienced lay judges outweighs preservation of equality of punishment among cases with similar seriousness of criminal acts. Shihokenshujyo (2012) states that previous sentencing trends should be shown to lay judges even if lay judges do not want to refer to them. Behind this statement, there seems to be a value judgment that it is important to ensure equality of punishment at the expense of having some negative effects on lay judges' evaluations about their experience and the lay judge system as a whole. This chapter intends to provide basic findings to evaluate the lay judge system, especially the materials about previous sentencing trends, not to conduct normative evaluation itself. In addition, professional judges seek to explain how lay judges should make sentencing decisions and try to make them accept such a way of thinking (e.g., Shihokenshujyo, 2012). If this persuasion succeeds, lay judges may accept the importance of previous sentencing trends and still evaluate their participation in criminal trials positively. This possibility remains to be explored.

Acknowledgement This work was supported by Grants-in-Aid for Scientific Research (KAKENHI) of Japan Society for the Promotion of Science (JSPS), grant numbers 24101502 and 26101701.

References

Anderson, K., & Nolan, M. (2004). Lay participation in the Japanese justice system: A few preliminary thoughts regarding the lay assessor system (*saiban-in seido*) from domestic historical and international psychological perspectives. *Vanderbilt Journal of Transnational Law, 37*, 935–992.

Aoki, T. (2013). *Legal reform on criminal procedure and the lay judge system [Keiji Shiho Kaikaku to Saiban-in Seido]*. Tokyo: Nippon Hyoron Sha.

Endo, K. (2011). General examination on the process of sentencing decision [Ryokei Handan Katei no Soronteki Kento]. In Osaka Keiji Jitsumu Kenkyukai (Ed.), *A treatise on sentencing law and practice in Japanese criminal cases [Ryokei Jitsumu Taikei]* (Vol. 1, pp. 1–204). Tokyo: Hanrei Times.

Fukue, N., & Kato, M. (2009, May 14). Determining sentences seen as lay judges' hardest task. *The Japan Times*.

Harada, K. (2008). *The practice of sentencing in Japan [Ryokei Handanno Jissai]* (3rd ed.). Tokyo: Tachibana-Shobo.

Harada, K. (2011). *Saiban-in trials and sentencing law [Saiban-in Saiban to Ryokei Ho]*. Tokyo: Seibundoh.

Ikeda, O., Goda, Y., & Ando, A. (2016). *Commentary on the act about the lay judge system [Kaisetsu Saiban-in Ho]* (3rd ed.). Tokyo: Koubundou.

Ito, M., & Maeda, I. (2010). The way to conduct the sentencing deliberation with lay judges [Saiban-in tono Ryokeihyogi no Arikata]. In Harada Kunio Hanji Taikankinenronbunshu Kankokai (Ed.), *Criminal trials in a new era [Atarashii Jidai no Keijisaiban]* (pp. 371–382). Tokyo: Hanrei Times.

Koike, S. (2016). The theory of sentencing [Ryokei Ron]. In A. Yamaguchi & K. Kai (Eds.), *Basic theory and current issues of criminal law in Japan and China: Report on the symposium about criminal law in Japan and China [Nicchu Keijiho no Kisoriron to Sentanmondai: Nicchu Keijiho Symposium Hokokusho]* (pp. 43–68). Tokyo: Seibundoh.

Nagoya Chiho Saibansho Keiji Practice Kento Iinkai. (2016). A standard picture on how to conduct a sentencing deliberation [Ryokei Hyogi no Hyojyunteki Shinko Image]. *Hanrei Times, 1423*, 5–14.

Saeki, M. (2017). Bifurcation of the trial and the sentencing decision [Tetsuduki Nibun to Ryokei]. In K. Ageishi, H. Otsuka, K. Musashi, & M. Hirayama (Eds.), *The legal process in contemporary Japan: A Festschrift in honor of professor Setsuo Miyazawa's 70th birthday [Gendai Nihon no Ho-Katei: Miyazawa Setsuo Sensei Kokikinen Ronbunshu]* (Vol. 2, pp. 259–277). Tokyo: Shinzansha.

Sakamaki, T. (2006). Criminal trial in the 21th century: Practical issues on Saibanin (Lay person's participation in the judicial panel) trial [21-seiki no Keijisaiban: Saiban-in Seido Unyojyo no Kadai to Tenbo]. *Law Journal of the Legal Training and Research Institute [Shihokenshujyo Ronshu], 115*, 99–122.

Shihokenshujyo. (2012). *On the way to conduct the sentencing deliberation in the lay judge system [Saiban-in Saiban niokeru Ryokei Hyogi no Arikata nitsuite]*. Tokyo: Hosokai.

Shiroshita, Y. (2010). Current trends and issues in Japanese sentencing. *Federal Sentencing Reporter, 22*, 243–248.

Taguchi, M. (2013). *Inside the minds of lay judges [Saibanin no Atamano Naka]*. Tokyo: Gendaijinbun-sha.

Chapter 16
To Be Suspended or Not to Be?: The Effects of Emotions and Personality Variables on Lay People's Judgment of Suspension of Punishment

Masahiro Fujita

1 Background

Deciding punishment for the accused is one of the most important processes in criminal trials. Of course, fact-finding and deciding guiltiness are the most important parts of criminal trials, but once after the accused is found guilty, the next focus moves on to the sentencing of the case. In reality, the defendants admit his or her guilt in the major part of the criminal cases; the substantive decision-makings which should be made in criminal trials are sentencing. The sentencing is very significant in the case.

In many countries with petty jury system, jurors do not decide the punishment, while professional judges choose sentencing. On the other hand, in some mixed jury systems like Japan (Foote, 2014), where criminal trial panels consist both of lay participants and professional judges, civic participants to the justice system decide the punishment. As a whole of criminal trial procedures, both professional judges and lay participants can be decision-makers of the severity of punishment, which should be imposed on the culprit.

To decide punishment, decision-makers would refer to similar precedents of the case, sentencing standards which have been established through criminal trials, the fact of the case, and situation of the accused including repentance and objective circumstances. In doing so, they make efforts to decide the punishment which balances with other cases and the conducts which were made by the culprit.

Sometimes, it is said that those punishments are decided under the influence of emotions. Humans are animals of emotions. And theoretically, legal blame is based on moral blame which roots in moral outrage. It is natural that some emotions, like anger, could be involved in the judgment of punishment. In modern thinkings,

M. Fujita (✉)
Faculty of Sociology, Kansai University, Suita 564-8680, Osaka, Japan
e-mail: m.fujita@kansai-u.ac.jp

J. Liu, S. Miyazawa (eds.), *Crime and Justice in Contemporary Japan*,
Springer Series on Asian Criminology and Criminal Justice Research,
https://doi.org/10.1007/978-3-319-69359-0_16

significance has been put on human reason. We tend to think that judging based on reason is desirable while judging affected by emotion is not preferable.

But recently, many thinkers in the field have shown importance of emotion in judgment (Haidt, 2007). Especially, our emotions play important roles in deciding what conducts are immoral and morally desirable (Haidt, Koller, & Dias, 1993). In Haidt's argument, disgust is an important emotion in deciding what behavior is to be considered as immoral (Haidt, McCauley, & Rozin, 1994; Schnall, Haidt, Clore, & Jordan, 2008). And our judgment on morality of conducts is preceding reasonable inference. And even in criminal laws, emotions are important (Kahan & Nussbaum, 1996). Anger on those who violate equality of humans and empathy for others are proper emotions for fundamentals of law (Nussbaum, 2006). To investigate how we integrate those emotions in legal judgment, including punishment, is one of the important issues in the field of law and society.

Also, it is said that sympathy to the peer people is important in moral judgment (Smith, 2010). Moral cognition has motivating power because it is a sort of emotional reaction to the actions. Sympathy is experiencing the same emotions which are felt by other people. As the competence of feeling the same emotions is experienced by others, Davis (1980) pointed out four dimensions of empathy, that is, perspective-taking, empathic concern, fantasy, and personal distress. The Davis's four dimensions of empathy should be understood as the concept of "experiencing emotions of others" has four facets. The first dimension is to take other's places when we see other's situation. This is rather cognitive competence than emotional ability. The second dimension is to care about other's feeling with sound interest in others. The third dimension is fantasy, that is, the ability to imagine something we don't experience. The fourth dimension is extracted from the question items which are asking negative feelings. We tend to refer to negative feelings of others when we discuss about empathy, because we often think someone is empathic when the person feel the same negative feelings which are experienced by significant others. Davis composed personality scales for measuring those four facets of empathy.

2 Deciding Punishments

Choosing punishments is composed of some processes. Those processes are choosing the sorts of punishment, severity of punishment, and, when possible, if the punishments should be suspended or not. The first process is to select one form of punishment from which the law allows decision-makers. The forms of punishment would be fines, definite term imprisonment, life imprisonment, and death penalty, if the law permits. Then if the decision-makers choose definite term imprisonment, they have to choose the length of the imprisonment. Or if they chose fines, they need to decide the amount of fines within the range the law specifies. If the length of the imprisonment or the amount of fine is light enough, the decision-makers can suspend the punishment.

It is said that civic participants make decisions to suspend the punishments easily, putting the defendant on probation, compared to professional judges, under the effects of emotions. But there have been rarely studied effects of emotional or other subjective factors on suspending decisions or decisions on definite term imprisonment or life imprisonment. Prior studies showed severity of punishments overall, but not specifically on decisions of suspension or definite/life imprisonment decisions.

In this study, the author explored the effects of emotions, that is, disgust, anger, and empathy, on the decisions of punishment. Those decisions are decisions of suspension, definite term or life imprisonment, and years of imprisonment. The years of imprisonment are contained to assess the linear effects of those emotions on the decisions of punishments. In that sense, years of imprisonment were included partly to see the difference of findings of prior studies.

Adding to it, with measuring attitudes toward rules and crimes, the author intended to control the effects of those attitudes by throwing those variables into analyses. The author expected that the recognition of importance of social rules, including law, imposes severer punishment on the accused.

3 Method

3.1 Participants and Procedure

The author conducted group questionnaire surveys with participation by university undergraduate students. The surveys were conducted in July 2013. The participants were the students who attended two different classes at the Faculty of Sociology, Kansai University. One was an introductory psychology class for freshmen, and another was an upper-level social psychology class for students from sophomores to seniors.

The number of responders overall was 308. 251 out of 308 participants were students who majored psychology, 38 majored sociology, 8 majored mass media, and 9 majored social system design. Two respondents did not answer their major. Their ages varied from 18 to 24. Their mean age was 18.92, and the standard deviation of the age was 1.07. The number of male respondents was 96 (31.7%), while the number of female respondents was 210 (68.18%).

These surveys were carried out as students' experience participating in a real psychological research. Before starting, the author explained the objective of this study and how to answer the questions. Answering the questionnaire was encouraged, but it was not compelled. They were not rewarded monetary or extra course credit for responding the questionnaire. After the respondents finished the questionnaire, the author explained the details of this study. The details included the objective, research design, and personality measures. The explanation included the relationships between the question items and the objectives of this study.

3.2 *The Questionnaire*

The questionnaires were printed on paper and compiled as booklets. The questionnaire included a scenario of a fictitious criminal case, questions on punishment of the case, questions assessing some attitudes of the respondents, and demographic variables. All questions measuring attitudes were answered in 5-point Likert scales. The scale ranged from 1 (not at all agree) to 5 (strongly agree).

3.2.1 The Instruction

The first page of this questionnaire was dedicated to instruction for respondents. In the instruction, it is explained that this questionnaire is to ask respondents to think about punishments. And the instruction read: there were no correct answers for the questions, and respondents would never be identified after finishing the questionnaire. After that, the instruction gave practical information on answering each question.

3.2.2 The Scenario

Right after the instruction, a summary of a criminal case was presented. This case was a fictitious criminal case based on a real case. To sum up, this case was on a murder without precedent plan (voluntary manslaughter) and abandoning the corpse under circumstances of caregiver fatigue. The accused was 62 years old and a daughter of the 98-year-old victim. The victim had raised the accused with sufficient affection and material environment. After fracture of the femur, the victim was bedridden all the time and needed full-time care at home. The accused took care of the victim for 7 years, resulting in a situation of caregiver fatigue. The accused despair of her and the victim's future, and one day the accused chocked the victim spasmodically and abandoned the victim's dead body. The instructions appeared in the questionnaire requested the participants to take all the facts written in the scenario true, and the accused should be guilty about this case.

3.2.3 Judgments of Punishment

In this set of questions, the respondents were asked which kind of punishment should be imposed on the accused. The choices were definite term imprisonment, life imprisonment (literally infinite imprisonment), and death penalty. When the respondent chose definite term imprisonment, there was a scale to choose the length of imprisonment, ranging from 1.5 to 20 years. This was a single Likert scale based on horizontal line marked at regular intervals with numerical anchor stimuli. After that, when the participants chose 3 years or less definite term imprisonment, they were asked whether they would like to suspend the punishment. In Japanese criminal law, imprisonment can be suspended only at the case when the imprisonment is 3 years or less. When the participant decided to suspend the imprisonment, they chose the length of the term of suspension, from 1 to 5 years on a discrete scale.

3.2.4 Emotions on the Murder Case

The author assessed respondents' emotion when they read the case and know the behavior of the accused. The questions were "the behavior of the accused is disgusting" and "the behavior of the accused is not forgivable." The former question measured the extent of respondents' disgust, and the latter assessed anger of the participants.

3.2.5 Attitudes Toward Social Rules

We assessed respondents' social attitudes toward social rules. The questions were "social rules like law is important" and "(a person who conducted) a very cruel crime should be punished severely." The former question asked the extent to put significance on formal social rules, and the latter assessed strictness for a person who committed a crime.

3.2.6 Davis's (1980) Four-Faceted Emotional Scale

To assess respondents' tendency of empathy, the author included the empathy scale taken from Davis (1980). This set of questionnaires was composed of 29 question items. Those items were classified into four categories, that is, empathic concern, perspective-taking, personal distress, and fantasy imagination. Every question item was related to each facet of empathy. In drawing up the questionnaire, the question items for these four dimensions were randomly rearranged. In the actual study, a Japanese version of Davis's scale was employed, which was confirmed empirically in its validity and reliability (Tobari, 2003).

3.2.7 Demographic Variables

This section included questions on respondents' major in their university, age, sex, and school year.

4 Results

4.1 Analyses

To assess which factors determine the judgment on the punishment and suspension, the author conducted logistic regressions and a multiple regression. In the next sections, I present the results of those regression analyses.

4.2 Factors That Affect Suspension

Table 16.1 showed the result of logistic analysis on the factors which affect participants' judgment on punish suspension. For this analysis, a number of respondents were reduced to 132, because the participants who could make this decision were limited to those who chose punishment of definite term imprisonment for 3 years or below. Missing values were omitted listwise.

In this analysis, the categories on the dependent variable were set as suspended being zero and "not suspended" being one. And so the positive coefficients show inclination to "not suspended," while negative coefficients show tendency toward suspension. The independent variables are emotions, attitudes toward rules, demographic variables, and scales for empathy.

From this result, the factors that affect decision on suspension are emotions of disgust and outrage, attitudes toward social rule, and fantasy imagination. Coefficients for attitudes toward social rules and fantasy imagination were negative, so those independent variables had effects to incline to suspend the punishment.

Table 16.1 Predictors of suspension

	Suspension		
Variable	*B*		Exp (*B*)
Disgust	0.59*		1.81
Outrage	0.76†		2.14
Social rule is important	−1.1*		0.33
Cruel crimes should be punished severely	0.22		1.25
Gender	−0.26		0.77
Age	−0.05		0.95
Perspective-taking	−0.02		0.98
Empathic concern	0.06		1.06
Fantasy imagination	−0.21**		0.81
Personal distress	−0.06		0.94
−2LogLikelihood		73.00	
Nagelkerke's pseudo R^2		0.39	

Note. Suspend = 0, not suspend = 1, $N = 132$
$^{**}p < 0.01$, $^{*}p < 0.05$, $^{\dagger}p < 1$

Table 16.2 Predictors of decision on definite or life imprisonment

	Imprisonment		
Variable	*B*		Exp (*B*)
Disgust	0.57*		1.77
Outrage	0.95**		2.57
Social rule is important	−0.90*		0.41
Cruel crimes should be punished severely	0.40		1.50
Gender	−0.38		0.68
Age	0.09		1.09
Perspective-taking	0.12†		1.13
Empathic concern	−0.04		0.96
Fantasy imagination	−0.04		0.96
Personal distress	0.06		1.07
−2LogLikelihood		126.46	
Nagelkerke's pseudo R^2		0.27	

Note. Definite imprisonment = 0, life imprisonment = 1, $N = 297$
$^{**}p < 0.01$, $^{*}p < 0.05$, $^{\dagger}p < 0.1$

4.3 *Factors That Affect Definite Term or Life Imprisonment*

Table 16.2 showed the result of logistic analysis on the factors which affect participants' judgment on decision for choosing definite term imprisonment or life imprisonment. The number of respondents who were included in this analysis was 297, because almost all of the participants selected imprisonment, besides 1 respondent who voted for death penalty. The other ten respondents were excluded from this analysis because they had one or more missing values in their answers.

In this analysis, the categories on dependent variable were set as definite term imprisonment being zero and life imprisonment being one. And so the positive coefficients show tendency to life imprisonment, and negative coefficients show inclination to definite term imprisonment. The independent variables are the same as shown in Table 16.1.

From this result, the factors that affect decision on whether the imprisonment should be definite or indefinite are emotion of disgust, outrage, and attitudes toward social rule. And perspective-taking had an effect to move the decision toward life imprisonment. Other empathy scales have effects on this choice. Coefficients for attitudes toward social rules were negative, so attitudes toward social rules had effects to incline to definite term imprisonment.

4.4 *Factors That Affect Years of Imprisonment*

Table 16.3 showed the result of multiple regression analysis on the factors which affect years of imprisonment. The number of respondents who were included in this analysis was 273, because the participants who were included were those who

Table 16.3 Predictors of years of imprisonment

Variable	Years of imprisonment		
	B		*β*
Disgust	0.29		0.07
Outrage	1.04***		0.25
Social rule is important	0.97*		0.14
Cruel crimes should be punished severely	−0.48		−0.10
Gender	0.45		0.05
Age	−0.19		−0.05
Perspective-taking	0.01		0.01
Empathic concern	0.03		0.04
Fantasy imagination	−0.14		−0.10
Personal distress	0.05		0.05
Adjusted R^2		0.09	
F		3.75***	

Note. $N = 273$
$^{***}p < 0.001$, $^{*}p < 0.05$

selected definite term imprisonment. In this analysis, positive coefficients show tendency to make longer the life imprisonment, and negative coefficients show inclination to definite term imprisonment. The independent variables are the same as shown in Table 16.1.

From this result, the factors that affect decision on the years of imprisonment are emotion of outrage and attitudes toward social rules. No empathy scale has effects on this choice nor disgust. Both of the significant coefficients were positive, so those independent variables had effects to make longer the term of imprisonment.

5 Discussion

5.1 *Decision-Making for Suspension*

5.1.1 Disgust

On the decision of suspension, emotion of disgust worked as a key emotion in choosing punishment, that is, suspension and term of imprisonment. If the respondents feel more disgust, the probability that the accused is not suspended raised 1.805 times, and the probability of life imprisonment increased 1.766 times. On the other hand, disgust had no significant effect on the years of imprisonment.

According to the argument of Nussbaum (2006), the emotion like disgust is not democratic because emotions like that assume hierarchic relationships among humans. But in the series of studies conducted by Haidt, hierarchy and disgust are important sources of morality (Haidt et al., 1993; Haidt et al., 1994; Haidt, 2007; Schnall et al., 2008). On our results, the author cannot help acknowledging Haidt's theory, even if we think about and make judgments on legal matters. In the setting of this study, the respondents primed legal, formal social rules, and they made judgment on this scenario as a matter of legal concern. But in that setting, the participants' feeling of disgust may have an effect on their judgments.

5.1.2 Outrage

The other important emotion we dealt here was anger on illegal behavior. On the decision of suspension, emotion of anger worked as a key emotion in choosing punishment, that is, suspension and term of imprisonment. If the respondents feel more anger, the probability that the accused is not suspended raised 2.14 times, and the probability of life imprisonment increased 2.57 times. And also, outrage had significant effect on years of imprisonment. When the outrage got increased 1 point in the 5-point Likert scale, the year of imprisonment raised 1.04 years. To sum up, outrage had consistent effects on punishment in the direction of making punishments harsher.

Granted those results, outrage is a significant emotion in decision-making of severity of punishment. In civil jury, outrage did not have a direct effect on the amount of damage awarded, even if it has a relationship with the defendants' blameworthiness (Ogloff, 2002). But in this study, in a decision of criminal punishment, anger has direct effect of this result to confirm the prior studies (Feather & Souter, 2002).

5.1.3 Feeling of Importance of Social Rule

The author expected that the recognition of importance of social rules, including law, imposes severer punishment on the accused. Regarding years of imprisonment, the expectation was fulfilled. When the respondents increased 1 point on the scale for the recognition of importance of social rules, the period of imprisonment raised .97 years. But this study showed that recognition of importance of social rules had inclination to suspend the imprisonment, definite term imprisonment. It is a little bit hard to understand those seemingly inconsistent results. One possibility may be that the respondents included in the analysis shown in Table 16.3 were the rest of the respondents excluded being low scorers of the recognition of importance of social rules. Given that, comparing Tables 16.2 and 16.3, high scorers of the recognition of importance of social rules may feel less disgust on crimes and less severe on deciding punishments.

5.1.4 Empathy

Contrary to the author's advance expectation, four facets of empathy scales did not have so much with judgments of the punishments. On the decision of suspension, imagination had an effect on the decision. Concerning Table 16.2, perspective-taking had an effect on decisions of definite/life imprisonment. None of the four facets of empathy had effects on years of imprisonment. The result in the first table may come from a feature of the scenario used in this study, which was a caregiver fatigue case. The accused was in a situation which arose sympathy of those who have rich imaginations. And perspective-taking had marginally significant effect on the decision of life imprisonment. Perspective-taking is a more cognitive aspect in empathy rather than emotional, so when the participants can show the competence of perspective-taking, they tend to take the significance of the result of this case into their consideration, as they chose the punishment. From the result shown in the second table, the respondents with higher perspective-taking decided to favor life imprisonment more. This result shows that those who are perspective-taking tended to think of the significance of the results of the crime.

5.2 Limitation

5.2.1 External Validity

Major part of the limitation of this survey comes from samples and circumstances of the study. This study was conducted as a group questionnaire survey on a fictitious criminal case with student participants; external validity might be lower than studies with jury-eligible people and real criminal trials. Participants read the scenario and imagine how the case should be and judged punishment which was imposed on an imaginary person. So, there is some room for emerging different findings under more authentic circumstances. But the author thinks major results of this study could be applied to judgments made under more authentic situations. Emotions of disgust and anger will play important roles in judgments of punishment in real criminal trials, and they will have similar inclination of effect on the severity of punishment, when we take the findings in prior studies into our consideration.

5.2.2 Measurement

Another limitation of this study may come from the form of measurement. In this study, I employed questionnaire survey. Questionnaire surveys have some advantages compared to experimental study. Questionnaire surveys are easy to conduct, because questionnaire surveys do not need any complex or expensive machines, and respondents do not need to get accustomed to specific tasks which may be required to do during experiments.

Because the respondents can answer the questions with their answers that can be described with the respondents' conscious minds, questionnaire surveys cannot measure implicit attitudes of the respondents in principle. And the respondents may alter their answers to meet the author's expectation, because when respondents are aware of the expectation of the conductor of the study, they might want to act as desirable participants

(Kintz, Delprato, Mettee, Persons, & Schappe, 1965). Even I expect that their responses on emotions and empathy were not remote from what they really feel, but due to limitation of the form of measurement, I cannot argue if it is true until I employ the measurement method which will not be distracted by conscious process held by respondents.

5.3 Implications and Future Direction

5.3.1 Emotions and Punishment

Kant argued in his *The Metaphysics of Morals* (Kant, 1996) that the punishments should be based on pure retributivism, and punishment should not be based on other reasons, because no one should be objective. Granted that moral blaming is fundamentally emotional (Haidt, 2008; Nussbaum, 2006; Smith, 2010), the sense of blaming can emerge from our emotions. From the results of this study, emotions of disgust and anger really have effects on severity of punishment, so reasonably expressed blameworthiness can be based on emotional, intuitional, and unconscious judgment of our human nature.

The judges may justify their decisions in their sentencing, which should be declared in the law courts. Even civic participants decide punishments; professional judges attend the judicial panels which determine the final punishment which should be imposed on the accused. The reasons for choosing particular punishment will be shown in the written documents that are declared in the law court by the judges. The reasons in the documents are full of very reasonable and coolheaded logics.

But before reaching those logics, civic participants and maybe the judges went through the process of intuitive judgment that is affected by their sentiments (Wrightsman, 1999). In this study, disgust, anger, and attitudes toward social rules are the subjective factors which have influence on decisions of punishments.

On the other hand, we are inclined to think that empathy with the accused lighten the punishment, while empathy with the victim may make the punishments severer. In this study, I found that imagination can relate negatively on the decision of suspension. And four facets of empathy showed different results for judging punishment. From those results, the problem is not so simple as what we assume. We need to investigate the role of empathy, carefully employing the scales reflecting the four dimensions.

5.3.2 Future Directions

In this study, the author investigated with student participants. If possible, more authentic circumstances and compared results obtained by this study will increase external validity of this series of studies. And in this study, only the main effects of each emotion and scale of empathy were investigated. Deeper relationship among those emotions and maybe more significant emotions can be involved in this study.

Adding to it, the relationships with reasonable inference and those emotions can be explored to understand the whole picture of the factors of judgment of punishment.

Acknowledgments This study is a part of the results of Foreign Residency Research Program as an academic research of Kansai University in the academic year 2013. Major parts of the analysis were done during the residency period, when the author has been a visiting scholar at the Center for the Study of Law and Society of the University of California, Berkeley. This paper is to be presented at the 50th annual conference of the Law and Society Association at the Hilton Minneapolis, Minneapolis, Minnesota, USA, from May 27 to June 1, 2014. Round-trip travel expenses between Berkeley and Minneapolis were disbursed by the accompanied grant of the Foreign Residency Research Program of Kansai University.

References

Davis, M. H. (1980). A multidimensional approach to individual differences in empathy. *JSAS Catalog of Selected Documents in Psychology, 10*, 85.

Feather, N. T., & Souter, J. (2002). Reactions to mandatory sentences in relation to the ethnic identity and criminal history of the offender. *Law and Human Behavior, 26*(4), 417–438.

Foote, D. H. (2014). Citizen participation: Appraising the saiban'in system. *Michigan State International Law Review, 22*(3), 755–775.

Haidt, J. (2007). The new synthesis in moral psychology. *Science, 316*(5827), 998–1002.

Haidt, J. (2008). Morality. *Perspectives on Psychological Science, 3*(1), 65.

Haidt, J., Koller, S. H., & Dias, M. G. (1993). Affect, culture, and morality, or is it wrong to eat your dog? *Journal of Personality and Social Psychology, 65*(4), 613–628.

Haidt, J., McCauley, C., & Rozin, P. (1994). Individual differences in sensitivity to disgust: A scale sampling seven domains of disgust elicitors. *Personality and Individual Differences, 16*(5), 701–713. https://doi.org/10.1016/0191-8869(94)90212-7.

Kahan, D. M., & Nussbaum, M. C. (1996). Two conceptions of emotion in criminal law. *Columbia Law Review, 96*, 269–374.

Kant, I. (1996). *The metaphysics of morals*. Cambridge/New York: Cambridge University Press.

Kintz, B. L., Delprato, D. J., Mettee, D. R., Persons, C. E., & Schappe, R. H. (1965). The experimenter effect. *Psychological Bulletin, 63*(4), 223.

Nussbaum, M. C. (2006). *Hiding from humanity: Disgust, shame, and the law*. Princeton, NJ: Princeton University Press.

Ogloff, J. R. P. (Ed.). (2002). *Taking psychology and law into the twenty-first century*. New York: Kluwer Academic/Plenum.

Schnall, S., Haidt, J., Clore, G. L., & Jordan, A. H. (2008). Disgust as embodied moral judgment. *Personality and Social Psychology Bulletin, 34*(8), 1096–1109. https://doi.org/10.1177/0146167208317771.

Smith, A. (2010). *The theory of moral sentiments*. Penguin. (Original work published 1759).

Tobari, M. (2003). Seinenki no kyoukansei no hattatsu: Tajigen-teki shiten ni yoru kentou. [The development of empathy in adolescence: Investigation from multidimensional view]. *Japanese Journal of Developmental Psychology, 14*(2), 136–148. [In Japanese with English title and abstract].

Wrightsman, L. S. (1999). *Judicial decision making: Is psychology relevant?* New York: Kluwer Academic/Plenum.

Chapter 17
A Future Prospect of Criminal Justice Policy for Sex Crimes in Japan- the Roles of the Lay Judge System There

Mari Hirayama

1 Introduction

Japanese society has been often criticized for its lenient policy on sex crimes. Especially as regards child pornography issues, for a long time Japan remained the only nation among OECD (Organization for Economic Co-operation and Development) countries which did not punish the mere possession of child pornography. This policy has been of course widely criticized, and Japan has finally decided to revise its Act on Punishment of Activities Relating to Child Prostitution and Child Pornoraphy, and the Protection of Children (originally enacted on November 1, 1999), which was enacted on July 15, 2014, and now prohibits the mere possession of child pornography (Watanabe, 2015: 34). The law, however, placed "more than 1 year" moratorium period before its enactment, as much confusion and chaos especially among those who possess possible child pornography are likely to happen (so a revised law was enacted from July 15, 2015). These responses for the legislation of child pornography are surely outdated compared to other countries.

Professor of Criminal Procedure and Crime Policy at Hakuoh University, Faculty of Law, Tochigi, Japan. This paper is based on my presentation at the 6th Conference of the Asian Criminological Society in Osaka in June 2014. This paper is also part of the research supported by Grant-in-Aid for Young Scientists (B) "Research on Sex Crime and Lay Judge Trials: Issues in Trials, Impacts on Sentencing, Corrections and the Criminal Justice Policy for Sex Crime" (4/2011–3/2014).
I would like to show my sincere gratitude to Professor Jianhong Liu and Professor Setsuo Miyazawa for providing me this great opportunity.

M. Hirayama (✉)
Faculty of Law, Professor of Criminal Procedure and Crime Policy at Hakuoh University, Tochigi, Japan
e-mail: ma07@fc.hakuoh.ac.jp

J. Liu, S. Miyazawa (eds.), *Crime and Justice in Contemporary Japan*, Springer Series on Asian Criminology and Criminal Justice Research, https://doi.org/10.1007/978-3-319-69359-0_17

Also, groping in crowded trains (known as "Chikan") in Japan is infamous globally.[1] To the dismay of many victims' advocates, penal punishment and sentencing for sex crimes in Japan had been often criticized as too lenient (Nagata, 2013). Unfortunately, it can be said that Japan, as a society, seems to have quite a tolerance for problems of sexual deviancy.

On the other hand, what about policy for victims of sex crimes? If the society is lenient for sexual deviancies, does it also mean that the society does not blame victims? You may already know the answer, and the answer is "no." In Japan, the culture of "shame"[2] is still strong, and this "shame" is unfortunately put on victims' sides too, especially in sex crime cases.[3] Are these two tendencies contradicting from each other? Absolutely not; it makes sense that a society with lenient attitudes toward sex crimes is harsh on victims of sex crime.

Recently, however, light has been shed on this dark alley, and it has much to do with the introduction of 裁判員制度: *Saiban-in Seido* (the Lay Judge System), in which six lay people join a panel with three professional judges to try very serious felony cases. Because of the input of lay people's opinions, the sentencing for sex crime cases has increased in severity, and the general public now seems to pay much more attentions to sex crime issues—regarding both offenders and victims. And this tendency has given a significant impact to amend the Penal Code regarding sex crime. On June 8, 2017, the Lower Congress passed the Amended Penal Code to change the punishment for rape from "no less than 3 years" to "no less than 5 years."

In this chapter, I discuss the future prospect of criminal justice policy for sex crimes in Japan. In doing so, I focus on this role of the lay judge system. This is because, as I have just stated, this new system seems to be the starting point from which to discuss so many issues regarding sex crimes.

---

[1] Not only Japan but also some other countries have problems of crowded trains; however, it seems the groping problem is most serious in Japan. This chapter does not aim to find out why, but it is an interesting and important topic. Though groping is a very serious issue in Japanese society, there are not many academic publications on groping. One of the first comprehensive academic publications on Chikanis Akiyoshi Saito, *Otoko Ga Chikan Ni Naru Riyuu* [The Reason Why Men Become Gropers], East Press Publication, 2017.

[2] The famous crime theory, shaming and reintegration, by John Braithwaite may mean to mainly apply to wrongdoers though. *See* John Braithwaite's *Crime, Shame and Reintegration*, Cambridge University Press 1989. On the other hand, some people also feel "shame" to become victims, as they blame themselves for not being able to avoid the victimization. These unreasonable responses are commonly seen among victims of sex crime. And these tendencies are especially strong in Japan.

[3] At the ACS conference in Osaka, I had quite an interesting conversation with students who were from Taiwan. Their research interests were in support system for victims of sexual harassment. They found the warning signs (posters) at railway stations for groping problems in Japan were wired, as many posters said something like "If you see groping problems, please take courage to say something and save the victim." They told me that many posters in their country (Taiwan) said like "If you are victimized of groping, please ask for the help." The Japanese version may sound more supportive to victims, but, in fact, it may be an evidence that victims of groping in Japan have much more difficulties to speak up, so the passengers are expected to save the victims.

2 Sex Crimes Tried in Lay Judge Trials

2.1 *Why Focusing on Sex Crime Cases?*

The Japanese criminal justice system introduced a new style for trying serious cases—the lay judge system—on May 21, 2009. This new system targets only very serious criminal cases (see Table 17.1). The lay judge system deals with crimes that carry death penalty sentences or indefinite imprisonment. And if a perpetrator intentionally commits a crime which results in the death of a victim, such a case is also tried by a lay judge trial. There are approximately 1000–2000 of such cases a year, which is about 2% of all criminal trials at the district courts. And unlike the jury system in Western countries, defendants cannot choose whether their cases go to lay judge trials or bench trials (judge-only trials). Being tried by his or her peers at trials is not a defendant's right in the Lay Judge System.

There are many reasons and justifications why this new system targets only very limited crime cases. The most persuadable explanation is that the more severe the case, the more interest the public have.

So what percentages of these cases are sex crime cases? As you can see in Table 17.1, around 20% of all lay judge trials are sex crime cases every year. Sex crime is not the minority in crimes tried by lay judge trials. Please also note that not every sex crime is categorized as "crime tried by lay judge trials." Rape and indecent assault which do not resulted in "injury or death" of victims are tried by bench trials, not lay judge trials.

As you can easily imagine, the lay judge system has changed criminal trials greatly, and lay people now may not feel OK to say " Oh no, criminal trials are none of our business." The Lay Judge System is expected to provide an opportunity for the general public to become more interested in issues in the criminal justice system, both victims' issues and offenders' issues. The biggest concern is whether or not sentencing has changed because of lay inputs. Unlike jury systems in many countries, a mixed panel of three professional judges and six lay people decide not only fact finding but also sentencing.[4]

2.2 *Impact on Sentencing for Sex Crime Cases*

Let me compare sentencing patterns in lay judge trials and bench trials on sex crime cases (see Table 17.2). Do inputs of lay people change sentencing patterns? According to the annual report on the lay judge system by the General Secretariat of Supreme Court of Japan (The General Secretariat of Supreme Court of Japan, 2010), there are some gaps in sentencing in some crimes. They compare the sentencing pattern between bench trials and lay judge trials for some period after the

[4]For details of the lay judge system, please visit the website of the Japanese Ministry of Justice, http://www.moj.go.jp/ENGLISH/issues/issues03.html (last visited 1/31/2012).

Table 17.1 Number of defendants referred to prosecutor's office for the crime which shall be tried by lay judge trials

		2009	2010	2011	2012	2013	2014	2015	2016
Total Number	11,503	1,196	1,797	1,785	1,457	1,465	1,393	1,333	1,077
Robbery causing Injury	2,680	295	468	411	329	342	321	290	224
Homicide	2,467	270	350	371	313	303	302	303	255
Arson with Premises	1,135	98	179	167	128	141	136	162	124
Battery Resulted in Death	1,003	70	141	169	146	136	131	107	103
Drug Smuggling	880	90	153	173	105	105	129	58	67
Indecent Assault Causing Death or Injury	867	58	105	105	109	133	131	111	115
Rape Causing Injury or Death	851	88	111	137	124	121	91	104	75
Robbery in the Scene of Rape	449	61	99	83	59	57	36	34	20
Robbery Causing Death	289	51	43	37	37	37	27	35	22
Uttering Counterfeited Currencies	201	34	60	30	34	12	4	20	7
Dangerous Driving Causing Death	177	13	17	20	27	21	23	28	28
Counterfeited Currencies	106	14	18	20	19	17	4	8	6
Gang Rape Causing Injury or Death	73	13	2	17	6	9	17	8	1
Violation of Firearms and Swords Control Act sing Death	70	13	5	3	4	10	10	15	10
Abandonment by a Person who is responsible for Protection causing Death	55	7	9	12	4	5	7	5	6
Illegal Arrest and Confinement resulted in Death	54	4	18	21	1	4	3	2	1
Violation of Organized Crime Punishment Act	47	6	5	-	-	3	14	18	1
Violation of Special Act of the Narcotics	27	1	5	3	2	1	1	11	3
Violation of Explosives Control Act	16	6	-	-	5	2	-	2	1
Abduction for Ransom	9	-	3	-		1	1	-	3
Violation of the Concerning Special Provisions for the Narcotics and Psychotropic Control Act,	9	1	3	1	2	2	-	-	^
Receiving Ransom	3	-	-	-	-	-	-	2	1
Others	35	3	3	5	2	3	5	10	4
% of Sex Crime Cases	19.47%	18.39%	17.64%	19.16%	20.45%	21.84%	19.74%	18.75%	19.59%

Sex crime are highlighted

Based on Saiban in saiban no jissi jyokyo ni tsuite, seido siko-Heisei 29 nen 9gatsu, sokuho chi (The Report on the status of the Lay System, since the system started to September 2017, preliminary figures), at 1.by the Supreme http://www.saibanin.courts.go.jp/vcms_lf/h29_9_saibaninsokuhou.pdf

introduction of the lay judge system: bench trials (April 1, 2008–March 31, 2011) versus lay judge trials (May 21, 2009–March 31, 2011). Certain serious crime cases in Table 17.1 which prosecuted after May 21, 2009 are tried by lay judge trials; therefore, there is some overlap during this period.

As you can see in Table 17.2, the mode-the most frequent sentence in "rape causing injury or death" and "indecent assault causing death or injury" cases have moved toward harshness.

Table 17.2 Comparisons of "the most frequent sentence" for sex crimes: the bench trials and lay judge trials w/ S means the sentence was suspended.

Rape Causing Injury or Death Case

Sentencing	Bench Trial	Lay Judge Trial
Less than 3yrs(w/ S)	12	3
Less than 3yrs	9	2
Less than 5yrs	72	18
Less than 7yrs	41	37
Less than 9yrs	17	19
Less than 11yrs	13	13
Less than 13yrs	8	9
Less than 15yrs	7	3
Less than 17yrs	5	0
Less than 19yrs	6	4
Less than 21yrs	4	2
Less than 23yrs	3	0
Less than 25yrs	2	1
Less than 27yrs	0	1
Less than 29yrs	1	0
Less than 30yrs	0	0
Indefinite Sentence	2	0
Death Penalty	0	0
Total:	202	112

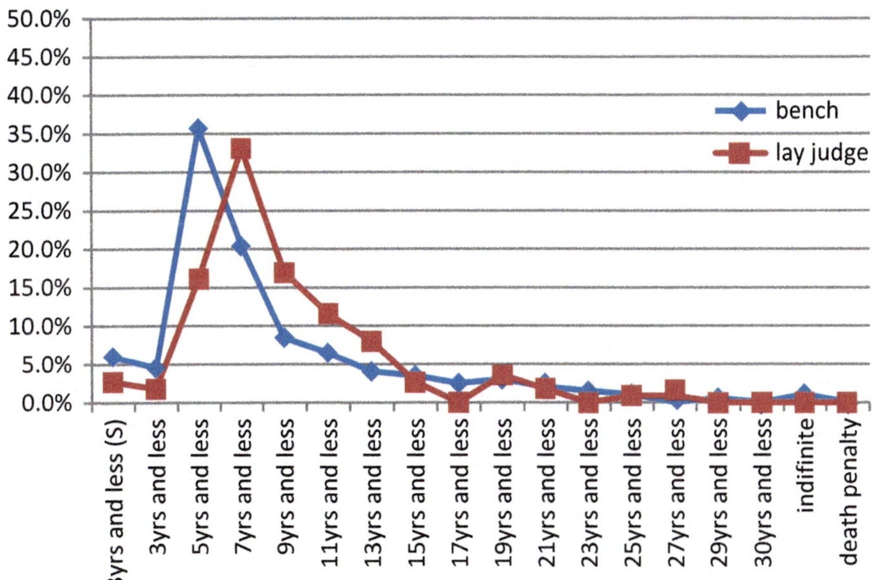

(continued)

Table 17.2 (continued)

Indecent Assault Causing Injury or Death Cases

Sentencing	Bench Trial	Lay Judge Trial
Less than 3yrs(w/ S)	61	41
Less than 3yrs	32	12
Less than 5yrs	25	28
Less than 7yrs	11	12
Less than 9yrs	5	5
Less than 11yrs	3	1
Less than 13yrs	2	0
Less than 15yrs	0	0
Less than 17yrs	0	0
Less than 19yrs	0	0
Less than 21yrs	0	0
Less than 23yrs	0	0
Less than 25yrs	0	0
Less than 27yrs	0	0
Less than 29yrs	0	0
Less than 30yrs	0	0
Indefinite Sentence	0	0
Death Penalty	0	0
Total:	139	99

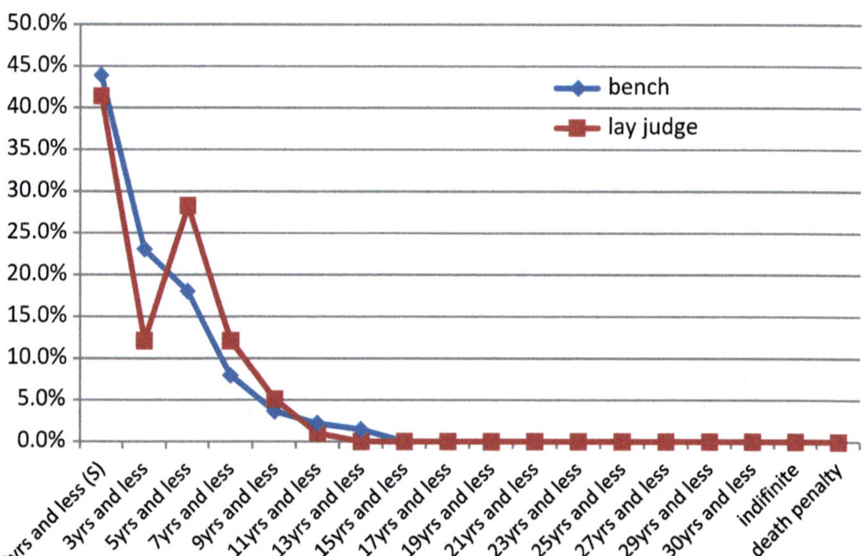

Source: The General Secretariat of the Supreme Court of Japan (2010), Heisei 21 Nen Ni Okeru Saiban In Saiban No Jissi Jyokyo Toh Ni Kansuru Shiryo [The Report on the Status on the Lay Judge System in 2009] http://www.courts.go.jp/saikosai/vcms_lf/80804004.pdf (last visited 3/31/2017)

2.3 Impact on Sentencing-the Ratio of Sentence/Sentence Asked

Before the introduction of the system, one of the biggest concerns was whether Japanese people would corporate with this new system or not. Many polls showed negative results, which meant many Japanese people were reluctant to serve as lay judges. Contrary to these concerns, lay people have been quite cooperative and participatory. When courts summon prospective lay judges, most district courts have a high rate of turnout. The average rate of all district courts was 83.9% (The General Secretariat of the Supreme Court of Japan, 2010).

Also, on the contrary to my concern—citizens may not agree to talk before the press after their giving verdicts as they do not want to talk about their feelings in the public—many lay judges have actually agreed to answer questions by press, and some of them even agree to release their names and their faces in newspapers. In May 2010, exactly 1 year after the introduction of the system, the Shinbun Kyokai (the newspaper association in Japan) reported that lay judges had agreed to participate in press conferences in 95% of all lay judge trials (Ji-ji Tsushinsya, 2010).

Another big concern for the *Saiban-in* system was whether or not lay people can try cases rationally. Some people concern about emotional factors that can impact lay judge decisions. The victims' participation system (Code of Criminal Procedure Article 316–33 to 316–39), in which crime victims, including bereaved families, can participate in criminal trials and even demand sentencing, was introduced 6 months before the introduction of the *Saiban-in* system (December 1st, 2008). How victims' participation can impact lay judges when they deliberate sentencing has been also a big concern.[5] However, in most cases, there have not been seen great changes especially in sentencing between "before and after" of introduction of these new two systems.

But when we carefully examine the sentencing pattern after the introduction of the lay judge system carefully, we can see bipolarization. At one end, there are homicide cases that are related to family issues. In these cases, the defendants tend to get more lenient sentences compared with those before. The other side are, as I already discussed above- sex crime cases. In sex crime cases tried by lay judge trials, sentencing has been increasing after the introduction of the lay judge system.

[5] I should also add that, as the criminal procedure in Japan is not divided into fact-finding phase and sentencing phase (the same panel, either in lay judge trials or bench trials, decide both fact finding and sentencing in consecutive process), there is a risk where victim inputs can influence fact-finding decision. See Mari Hirayama, "How Criminal Trials in Japan Will be Changed?-Impacts by the Victims Participation System and the Lay Judge System" [Keiji Saiban Ha Donoyouni Kawarunoka-Higaisyasanka Seido To Saiban In Seido no Impact], *Aoyama Gakuin Law Review, Vol. 51 No.1/2,* (2009), pp. 585–606.

Therefore, it is quite important to discuss the impact of the lay judge system on the criminal justice system for sex offenders.[6]

I have collected and analyzed all sex crime cases tried by lay judge trials in Japan ($N = 208$) for 2 years since the Lay Judge System started (from May 21, 2009, to May 20, 2011). In some cases there was more than one defendant, so there were 212 defendants for sex crimes tried during these 2 years. Out of these 212 defendants, 177 defendants received sentences without suspension and 2 of them received 30 years' sentences where indefinite sentence was asked by the prosecutors, so I excluded these 2 defendants. I calculated the sentencing ratio (sentence/sentence asked by prosecutors) for these 175 defendants.

The average sentencing ratio in all cases is 75.95% (until the end of January 2010). On the other hand, the sentencing ratio for sex crimes, for the 2 years examined, is 82.17%, which is more than 5% higher than average. If we focus only on "rape resulting in injury" cases, the ratio goes up even higher to 86.54%. It is quite clear that input of lay people has made sentencing for sex crimes be raised (Hirayama, 2013).

3 Why There HasBeen a Gap, Especially in Sex Crime Cases?

So a question arises about why there has been such a gap between lay people and professional judges (bench trials before the introduction of the lay judge system) on what they think proper sentences should be for sex crime cases.

A male-dominated culture in legal profession, especially among professional judges, has played a big role in Japan. Under this culture, a "blaming victims" theory often shows up which results in underestimating the sufferings of victims and eventually leads to imbalanced and lenient sentencing guidelines for sex crimes (Hirayama 2012). These sentencing guidelines have become precedents, and professional judges may have felt huge reluctance to divert from them.

When the courts hand down the verdict and sentencing (to clarify, in Japanese criminal trials, the same panel—either of professional judges only or with lay judges—decide both verdict and sentencing, and the courts hand down the verdict and the sentencing at the same time), the courts also mention the reasons why their deliberation reached to that sentence (量刑の理由). And, in many trials, presiding judges often make some comments then, partly explaining the reason for the sentencing in an open court and in front of defendants. It is quite interesting to review these comments delivered by presiding judges. Let me introduce some remarks by

[6] As for the research discussing the sex crime cases tried by lay judge trials, *see* Mari Hirayama, "Saiban-in Saiban to Sei Hanzai" [the Lay Judge Trials and Sex Crime], *Ritsumeikan Law Review*, 323/328, pp. 668–691 (2010), and Sawako Hirai, "Sei Bouryoku Hanzai to Saiban-in Saiban-2009 nen no Jirei kara" [Sexually Violent Crime and the Lay Judge Trials- Cases tried in 2009]," *Seinan Univ. Law Review*, (2010) pp. 225–243.

presiding judges in sex crime trials, mentioning about the change in sentencing for sex crime cases.

> "It is necessary to change the sentencing for sex crime" (on February 18, 2010, at the Tokushima District Court, rape causing injury case, 10 years imprisonment/12 years asked (ratio is 83.5%).
>
> "The sentencing for sex crime so far have been lenient, in terms of opinions of the public" (on March 2, 2010, Tokyo District Court, rape causing injury case, 6 years/7 years (86%).
>
> "Judging from recent legislations and tough-on-crime trends, we should well reflect what lay citizens want for punishment. We have explored a new approach for sentencing for sexual crimes". (April 23, 2010, Osaka District Court, indecent assault causing injury case, 6 years/8 years (67%))

When we review these comments, an important question we might want to ask to those judges may be, "If you think that way, why haven't you handed tougher sentence in sex crime cases so far?

These comments I introduced above seemed to expect (or should I say take advantage of) inputs of lay judges in order to give harsher punishment in sex crime cases.

Also, "*Jidan*" (settlement out of court) plays an important role in sex crime cases in Japan. It is not difficult to imagine that the reasons why sex crime victims agree to sign *Jidan* are not because they forgive offenders.[7] Some victims have no choice but to sign *Jidan* because they fear a second rape (second victimization) at trials. Others may desperately need compensation from offenders because they had to quit their jobs because of the suffering from victimization and would rather avoid the risk of lesser or no compensation.

These "hidden but real reasons" for victims' accepting *Jidan* have not, however, been seemed to be considered carefully by professional judges in some cases. In Japan, there are no sentencing guideline to decide sentence ,[8] which means the court can have quite a huge discretion to consider or not to consider various circumstances and information regarding the crime. Professional judges, however, have quite automatically interpreted victims' accepting of *Jidan* as a sign for forgiveness from victims, which often eventually lead to lenient sentences for offenders. Again, the male-dominated culture of professional judges plays a huge role here.

---

[7] There are very few researches on *"Jidan" in sex crime cases. See, for example, Akita Kazue, Tatoe Jidan demo Yurusarenai. Teikyo Dai Rugby Buin Rape Jiken [Even if a Jidan is Settled, the Offender must not be Forgiven. A Rape Committed by Students in Teikyo University Rugby Sport Team],* Monthly Magazine POST, Vol. 30 No. 8 (1998), pp. 46–47.

[8] One exception is death penalty cases. When the court decides to send a defendant to death row, the court considers "Nagayama Criteria." These criteria were used in Nagayama case in 1968, where a 19-year-old man killed four people. The Nagayama Criteria plays a significant role for courts to choose the death penalty or indefinite sentence; however, they are not sentencing guideline. As for the Nagayama Criteria, *see* Daniel A. Metraux, "The Nagayama Criteria for assessing the Death Penalty in Japan: Reflections of a Case Suspect", *Southeast Review of Asian Studies*, Volume 31 (2009), pp. 282–289.

On the other hand, lay judges apparently do not put much weight on *Jidan*. It seems that they still try to see sufferings of victims in cases where *Jidan* is established.

4 The Impacts of the Lay Judge System on Law Reform

4.1 The Birth of the Special Commission of Ministry of Justice to Discuss Punishment for Sex Crime

I have discussed that there have been big changes in sentencing for sex crime cases tried by lay judge trials.

The lay judge system has been a kind of an alert to the general public who have now started to notice many issues regarding sex crimes. The inputs of lay people can be expected to impact some legal reform of sex crime issues. This timing was also overlapped with the appointment of the 94th Minister of Justice, Ms. Midori Matsushima who had shown enthusiastic support for victims' advocates and legal reform on sex crimes (Sankei Newspaper, 2014). Matsushima decided to establish, in October 2014, a special committee to discuss the penal reform of sex crimes. This committee met 12 times and gave some advices in the Final Report on Punishment for Sex Crimes (hereinafter, the Final Report) in August 2015.[9] There are many important issues in the Report. Most of these issues had been discussed for a long time without ever reaching the point of actual reform. The lay judge system seems to be one of the important factors to cast a stone to this silent lake.

4.2 The Launch of Amended Penal Code Regarding Sex Crime

On June 8, 2017, the Lower Congress passed「刑法の一部を改正する法律」(the Law to Amend a Part of the Penal Code; hereinafter, the Amended Penal Code) which not only amend some provisions regarding sex crime but also establish some new sex crime categories. After the Final Report was issued, on March 7, 2017, the Cabinet decided to deliberate the Bill of the Amended Penal Code; therefore, it had been expected that the Amended Penal Code was past at the Congress earlier. There had been, however, another significant (and very controversial) debates regarding legislation of crime and punishment in Japan at the time, which is the Anti- Conspiracy Law. The Bill of the Anti-Conspiracy Law, on the other hand, was decided by the Cabinet to deliberate, on May 22, which was 2 weeks later than the Amended Penal Code. The gravity, however, was put on the debates for the

[9] http://www.moj.go.jp/keiji1/keiji12_00090.htm. (last visitd 7/31/2017)

Anti-Conspiracy Law both by politicians and the public,[10] and there was quite a good amount of risk that the Amended Penal Code wouldn't pass during the session.

The Amended Penal Code has changed the provision regarding the sex crime greatly. It was actually the first amendment on *actus reus* of sex crime in 110 years after the enactment of the Penal Code in 1907.[11] The Amended Penal Code was enacted on July 13, 2017.

Below are some of the amendments of provisions for sex crime.[12]

4.2.1 Crime of Rape Changed into "Crime of Coerced Intercourse"

One of the major changes this time is, under the Amended Penal Code, "Crime of Rape (強姦罪)" which is now changed into "Crime of Coerced Intercourse (強制性交等罪)." Before the amendment, Crime of Rape, Article 177, stated as follows[13]:

Article 177 (Crime of Rape). A person who, through assault or intimidation, forcibly commits sexual intercourse with a female of not less than 13 years of age commits the crime of rape and shall be punished by imprisonment with work for a definite term of not less than 3 years. The same shall apply to a person who commits sexual intercourse with a female under 13 years of age (underline added by the author).

As you can see, before the amendment, the victims of rape always had to be "female," and "male" had been excluded from the category of victims of rape. This gender discrimination, of course, has been criticized by many scholars and gender equality advocates. Under the new provision, "Crime of Coerced Intercourse" states as follows:

Article 177 (Crime of Coerced Intercourse). A person who, through assault or intimidation, forcibly commits sexual intercourse, anal intercourse, or oral intercourse (hereinafter, intercourse or alike) with **a person** of not less than 13 years of age commits the crime of coerced intercourse or alike and shall be punished by

---

[10] As for the controversial debate regarding the legislation at the Congress and among the public, see Tomohiro Osaki "Conspiracy Law ramrodded through Diet as opposition reckons with ruling camp tactics", *The Japan Times*, June 15, 2017.

[11] In December 2004, the Amended Penal Code 2004 was enacted. In that amendment, new sex crime provision for "gang rape" (Penal Code 178–2; punishable no less than 4 years of imprisonment with work) was added. The amendment 2017, however, is the first reform to change *actus reus* of sex crime.

[12] For these amendments, *see* Takako Maesawa, "Overview of the Bill to Amend Penal Code Regarding Sex Crime" [Seihanzai Kitei Ni Kakaru Keiho Kaisei An No Gaiyo], National Diet Library Research and Information No. 962 (May 2017), pp. 1–13. Available at http://dl.ndl.go.jp/view/download/digidepo_10350891_po_0962.pdf?contentNo=1 (last visited 6/30/2017).

[13] For the English translation of the Japanese Penal Code, I referred to the website "Japanese Law Translation" by the Ministry of Justice at http://www.japaneselawtranslation.go.jp/law/detail/?id=1960&re=02&vm=04 (last visited 6/31/2017).

imprisonment with work for a definite term of not less than 5 years. The same shall apply to a person who commits sexual intercourse with **a person** under 13 years of age(emphasis and underline added by the author).

As you can see here, under the Amended Penal Code, now male can be also victims of rape, which is a big change in sex crime provisions. There have been no sex crime lay judge trials where victims are male so far (indecent assault (Penal Code 176) has stated victims as both female and male, and indecent assault causing death or injury (Penal Code 181 (1)) cases are included for category for crime tried by the lay judge trials (see Table 17.1). Therefore, there could have been the indecent assault causing death or injury cases where the victims were male, so that tried by the lay judge trials in these 8 years). But still, the increased attention to sex crime issues in general after the introduction of the Lay Judge System has been one of the major triggers to make this big change happen.

4.2.2 Increased Punishment for Some of Sex Crime

The Amended Penal Code increased the punishment for "crime of coerced intercourse" from "no less than 3 years" to "no less than 5 years" (see the two Provisions I stated above). The punishment for "rape" had been criticized as "too lenient" by feminists and victim advocates. One of their critiques was that, as the punishment for "robbery" is "no less than 5 years," they claimed that it was unreasonable to provide less punishment for rape than that of robbery. Also, the minimum punishment for "coerced intercourse or alike causing death or injury" (Penal Code 181 (2)) is also increased, from "no less than 5 years or up to indefinite sentence" into "no less than 6 years or up to indefinite sentence).

As you can see from Table 17.1, "crime of coerced intercourse or alike" (used to be named as rape) is not tried by the lay judge trials, but "crime of coerced intercourse or alike causing death or injury" (used to be named as rape causing injury or death) is. Therefore, focusing on this increase of minimum punishment will impact sentencing trend in sex crime lay judge trials will be significant.

4.2.3 Sex Crime Against Children by Their Custodians

Another big change by the amendment this time is the establishment of new category of sex crime. Under the Amended Penal Code, Article 179 states as follows:

Article 179 Intercourse and Indecency by Custodians

1. A person who commits indecency against a child under 18 years old, who is under the custody of that person, commits the crime of indecent behavior by the custodians and shall be punishable no less than 6 months and no more than 10 years of imprisonment with work.

2. A person who commits intercourse with a child under 18 years old, who is under the custody of that person, commits the crime of coerced intercourse by the custodians and shall be punishable no less than 5 years of imprisonment with work.

The big difference between these new crime and "coerced intercourse" is whether the crime requires "assault and intimidation" to be established. In Japan, the courts have interpreted these requirements quite strictly, which has made difficult for the victims if the courts do not think "she fought back strongly enough." On the other hand, however, when a person who is a custodian over a child, and if that person commits these sexual behaviors by taking advantage of that position, the prosecution does not need to prove that the perpetrator used "assault and intimidation," which is a big relief for victims. There have been, of course, many discussions to introduce these new categories of crime (Abe, 2006), even before the introduction of the lay judge system; however, the lay judge inputs have increased the public attention, and the legal reform is realized.

4.2.4 Complaints from Victims Are Not Required for Prosecutors to Indict the Sex Crime

Rape and indecent assault used to require "complaints" (告訴) from victims for the prosecutors to indict these crimes. When victims somehow get some injury because of these crimes (or in the worst case, death), the prosecutor does not need their complaints though (which means, as you can see from Table 17.1, sex crimes tried by the lay judge trials do not require victims' complaints to be indicted). The reasoning for that is to protect victims' privacy; however, at the same time, it put much burden on victims, as they themselves have to make the decision to send the perpetrators to the court or not.

The Amended Penal Code abolished these special provisions. This amendment can be evaluated either way.

On the one side, it can be good as victims will not have to face with the big decision. But on the other side, victims of sex crime now have to face with the fear that even though they do not want to have any involvement with the criminal justice system, their cases can be prosecuted, and they may have to testify at trials. There are several protection methods (using partitions around a witness stand, video-linked system, and so on) when they testify at open court. But there are no evidence laws or regulations to restrict the defense lawyers to ask questions such as their past sexual experience or sexual orientations. We need to introduce the law like "rape shield law" which is enacted in the USA or some other Western countries. Now the Amended Penal Code may coerce more victims to testify at trials; therefore, we need some laws to protect victims from being hurt more.

5 Conclusion

The lay judge trial law was expecting the review for the reform after 3 years since the enactment.[14] Therefore, right after the system started, the Ministry of Justice established the Special Review Committee for the lay judge system, consisting of 11 experts in the field of lay judge system.[15] The Final Report was issued by the Special Review Committee for the lay judge system in June 2013 (hereinafter the Lay Judge Final Report).[16] The Committee also discussed whether sex crime cases should be excluded from the lay judge system, and their final advisement was "There were no active opinions to exclude sex crimes."[17] Their advisement was integrated into the Reformed Lay Judge Act enacted in June 2015 (hereinafter, the Reformed Act). Under the Reformed Act, of course, sex crimes remain as crimes tried by lay judge trials.

As discussed in this chapter, I strongly support trying sex crime in trials with lay participation. Lay involvement in issues of sex crimes—an untouchable and taboo topic for a long time—can be important for both offenders and victims.

The Reformed Act also put forward the supplementary provision, 3 years after its enforcement of the Reformed Law, to review the lay judge system, which might be reformed again around 2020. At that time, again, sex crimes may be targeted for exclusion from lay judge system. However, with new movements of penal law reform regarding sex crimes, the discussion may be very different at that time. We need to keep our eyes on that.

References

Abe, Y. (2006). Waga kuni ni okeru jido gyakutai no shomondai: niche bei ni okeru jido gyakutai no teigi nit suite [Issues in Child Abuse in Japan: The Definition of Child Abuse in Japan and the US]. *Joruna1 of International Buddhist University*, *44*, 71–88.

Hirayama, M. (2012). Gender to saiban in seido: seihanzai saibanin saiban no kadai [Gender and the lay judge system]. In The Japanese Assocaition of Gender and the Law (Ed.), *Gender and law: Freeing from violence* (pp. 107–122). Tokyo: Kajyo Shuppan Publication.

Hirayama, M. (2013). Saiban in seido no eikyo, kadai, tenbo: seido shiko go 2nen kan no seihanzai saiban in saiban no kento wo tsujite tou [Impacts, Issues and prospects of the lay judge system: through reviewing sex crime cases tried by lay judge trials for 2 years since it's introduction]. *Japanese Journal of Law and Society*, *79*, 85–105.

Ji-ji Tsushinsya. (2010, May 21). In *95% of All Trials, Lay Judges have attended post-verdicts press conferences.*

[14] Supplementary Provision 9.

[15] http://www.moj.go.jp/shingi1/keiji_kentoukai_saibaninseido_top.html. (last visited 7/31/2017)

[16] http://www.moj.go.jp/content/000112006.pdf. (last visited 7/31/2017)

[17] Id. pp. 4–5.

Nagata, M. (2013). Beikoku karano tayori seihanzai, houritsu to keibatsu no nitibei hikaku: genbatuka wo susumetekita America Nihon ha? [Letter from the US, sex crime, comparision on law and punishment in Japan and the US: US has been promoting tough on sex crime in the US. how about Japan]. *Newsletter by the Support and Education Center for Safety and Health for Women*, *38*, 30–38.

Sankei Newspaper. (2014, September 27). *Midori Matshusima. Considering harsher punishment on sex crime: Interviewing Minister of Justice*.

The General Secretariat of the Supreme Court of Japan. (2010). *Heisei 21 Nen Ni Okeru Saiban In Saiban No Jissi Jyokyo Toh Ni Kansuru Shiryo* (The Report on the Status on the Lay Judge System in 2009). http://www.courts.go.jp/saikosai/vcms_lf/80804004.pdf. Last visited 31 March 2017.

Watanabe, T. (2015). Jidoh poruno no keiji kisei: kaisei no keii to ronten [Regulatigehng child pornography by criminal law: The process and issues of revisement]. *Criminal Law Journal*, *43*, 35–44.

Part V
Juvenile Justice and Support System in Japan

Chapter 18
The Juvenile Justice System of Japan: An Overview

Marika Dawkins and Camille Gibson

This chapter offers a brief profile of Japan and its policies influencing the juvenile justice system. Second, recent trends and patterns in juvenile delinquency are described. Third, the role of various agencies, including the family court, is presented. The characteristics of juvenile offenders are described. Lastly, the chapter concludes with a discussion on the quality of Japan's juvenile data, how the community responds to juvenile delinquency, the unique structure of its juvenile justice system, and how current trends may shed light on future developments.

1 Profile of Japan

Japan is located in East Asia between the north Pacific Ocean and the Sea of Japan, which is east of the Korean Peninsula. The country gained independence on May 3, 1947, nearly 2 years after the end of World War II. It is about 377,915 square kilometers, which is somewhat smaller than the US state of California (Central Intelligence Agency, 2017). The climate varies between the south and the north—the north is

---

Marika Dawkins is a faculty member at the University of Texas Rio Grande Valley. She is one of the United States' few holders of a doctorate in Juvenile Justice. Her research has largely been about the effectiveness of various justice policies.
Camille Gibson is a faculty member at Prairie View A&M University in the College of Juvenile Justice & Psychology. She is a native of Jamaica. Her research interests include schools and delinquency; youth gangs; and youth violence.

M. Dawkins (✉)
University of Texas Rio Grande Valley, Edinburg, TX, USA
e-mail: marika.dawkins@utrgv.edu

C. Gibson (✉)
Prairie View A&M University, Prairie View, TX, USA
e-mail: cbgibson@pvamu.edu

J. Liu, S. Miyazawa (eds.), *Crime and Justice in Contemporary Japan*, Springer Series on Asian Criminology and Criminal Justice Research, https://doi.org/10.1007/978-3-319-69359-0_18

generally cool temperate while the south tends to be tropical. The country is largely mountainous and rugged. It has a population of more than 126 million, with 98.5% being Japanese, 0.5% Koreans, and 0.6% classified as others (Central Intelligence Agency, 2017; July 2016 estimates). Over 93% of its population is considered urban, and approximately 22% of its population is under the age of 24 (roughly 13% of its population is 14 or younger). The population is mostly homogeneous and dwells in densely populated areas. The country is divided into 47 prefectures, each with its own local elected government. While the official language is Japanese, English is taught in schools and citizens are expected to learn it as a foreign language. The government is based on a parliamentary constitutional monarchy, and the Emperor is regarded as the head of state, which is hereditary. Japan has a prime minister (Shinzo Abe has been the prime minister since 2012) who is generally the leader of the majority party and who appoints a cabinet as part of governing the country. Given that an Emperor is the head of state, the local government may not be fully autonomous.

Japan is one of the safest nations in the world (Chung, 2016). Police brutality and corruption are virtually nonexistent among its 245,000 officers which are divided into group-oriented units called Kidotai (Terrill, 2009). The officers are based in local police boxes called kobans. Indeed, the culture's strong group orientation is believed to be a key factor in keeping behaviors in check. Given Japan's successes, it is necessary to further examine its policies that may influence the justice system and to gain a better understanding of how the system operates. Therefore, in the next section, policies and legislations enacted in Japan are reviewed broadly to provide an understanding of the structure of the Japanese juvenile justice system and the sphere of its influences.

2 Policies and Legislations

After Japan's defeat in World War II, the collapse of its imperial regime and loss of its empire, the criminal justice system became more democratized (Minoru, 2015) or western. The exposure to the western legal system was during the United States' occupation of Japan from 1945 to 1952, in the aftermath of World War II. Previous legal influences included socialism, Romano-Germanic, and French (Terrill, 2009). A new constitution was enacted in 1946; the new penal code was revised in 1947; and in 1948 a new Code for Criminal Procedures was put into place (Minoru, 2015). The new code was designed based on the American system of due process. There are two primary legislations that address the treatment of juveniles. Yoshinaka (1997) described them as the 1947 Child Welfare Law (also known as Jido-Fukushi-Ho) and the 1949 Juvenile Law (also known as Shonen-Ho). The Shonen-Ho is considered to be the foundation of the Japanese's juvenile justice system as it is concerned with both justice and welfare. The Shonen-Ho is linked to juvenile justice legislation in the United States. On the other hand, Yoshinaka (1997) suggested that the Jido-Fukushi-Ho, which emphasizes only the welfare aspect of caring for children, is ineffective and plays very little role in how juveniles are treated because of the dominance of Shonen-Ho.

Kuzuno (2006) noted that there was an increase in the wave of juvenile delinquency in Japan following World War II, which led to concerns. A new constitution was enacted that focused on children's rights and education. A new juvenile law, modeled after the US standard Juvenile Act of 1943, was passed in 1948 "replacing" the previous 1922 law. The new law focused mainly on using the educative function to address the seriousness of juvenile offenses. It should also be noted that it was after the United States established a juvenile court in Cook County, Chicago, Illinois, in 1899 that Japan enacted the 1922 Juvenile Law. For more than two decades, the Minister of Justice was responsible for and managed the juvenile court. This changed after World War II. While various researchers have referenced different time periods when legislations were enacted to address juvenile delinquency, it is evident that a number of changes took place after World War II as Japan attempted to confront challenges related to crime and delinquency. After World War II, most juvenile offenses were property crimes for subsistence which fit the country's relational approach to juvenile offending but which may seem an ill-fit for certain modern offending trends which include more horrific offenses (Masato Takahash- attorney, see Ito, 2015).

In terms of delinquency prevention, Japanese communities tend to have a chonaikai, a neighborhood association with a crime prevention unit called a bohan kai. These groups will monitor their communities for youth status offenses and attempt to address them. They will communicate with schools and law enforcement as necessary. The police will then determine if the offense is furyo koi shonen (misbehavior) or guhan shonen (criminal-like). Ellis and Kyo (2017) describe this process as net widening which occurs in Japan without the collection of data to assess its real impact. They believe that the process unfairly targets working class youth.

Overall, Japan tends to take a conservative approach to reforms and is slow to change (Chung, 2016). For example, Chung claimed that there were changes to the justice system in the late 1980s and those changes were largely insignificant. Recent evidence suggests that Japan is taking a gradually more punitive approach. For example, Miyazawa (2008) examined newspaper reports and found some increase in the severity of punishment (also referred to as genbatsuka). Such an increase or changes in punishment appear to be supported by the law and citizens. The "get-tough" approach is generally embraced by proponents of law and order.

Like other developed nations, youth offending is a common Japanese concern. "Historically, Japanese law has contained exemptions or reductions in punishment for young offenders" (Elrod & Yokoyama, 2006, p. 217). For example, the Criminal Code of One Hundred Articles passed in 1742 suggested that individuals under 15 years of age should receive less severe punishments (Elrod & Yokoyama, 2006). There were exemptions or reductions in punishments for juveniles beginning in the latter part of the seventieth century (Minoru, 2015). The Ministry of Justice in Japan noted that a majority of crimes are committed by a small number of offenders (recidivists), and the prison rate appears to be increasing as of 2004. The year 2002 had the highest number of cases (violations of the penal code) in Japan's postwar history, and the clearance rate was also low, which led to major concerns for the country (Ministry of Justice, 2015). Nevertheless, in comparison with its western and developed counterparts, Japan has a lower crime rate overall.

3 Trends and Patterns in Juvenile Delinquency

Historical peaks in youth offending in Japan include 1951, given the rise in poverty, postwar; 1964, reflecting postwar baby boomers; and 1981, which saw an increase in property crimes, drug use, school dropouts, and reckless driving car gangs (bosozoku) (Terrill, 2009). An overview of recent trends and patterns in juvenile delinquency is necessary to contextualize the challenges confronting the Japanese juvenile justice system. Approximately 10% of Japan's population is reportedly between 10 and 19 years of age (Chung, 2016). There are approximately two million criminal cases per year in Japan, but half are linked to traffic incidences (Chung, 2016). Of the remaining cases, juvenile offenders below the age of 20 represented half of the other cases. Based on the Ministry of Justice (2015) statistical data, the number of reported cases (see Table 18.1) of juveniles being detained and/or placed in classification homes (custody) has been decreasing since 2004.

Despite these trends, a few horrific cases in recent years have shocked the delicate Japanese conscience into a desire for more punitive approaches. There was the murder of Ryota Uemura, a 13-year-old whose tortured and naked body was found by the Tama River in February 2015. An 18-year-old was found to be responsible for the murder, with two 17-year-old accessories. Uemura had previously been bullied

Table 18.1 Juveniles detained and held in classification homes

Year	Detained[a]	Classification homes[b]	Sum of detained and classification
2000	22,525	6052	28,577
2001	22,978	6008	28,986
2002	22,767	5962	28,729
2003	23,063	5823	28,886
2004	21,031	5300	26,331
2005	19,626	4878	24,504
2006	18,171	4482	22,653
2007	15,800	4074	19,874
2008	15,098	3971	19,069
2009	14,565	3962	18,527
2010	13,639	3619	17,258
2011	13,189	3486	16,675
2012	12,547	3498	16,045
2013	11,491	3193	14,684
2014	10,194	2872	13,066

[a]Detained—includes juveniles who are newly committed in classification homes (detention)
[b]Classification homes—represent juveniles in custody

by his killer. Also in 2015, a 15-year-old boy in Yokohama was taken into custody for the killing of his grandmother and mother after a talk about his studies. In 2014, a 19-year-old in Nagoya killed a 77-year-old man to fulfill what she described as a long-time desire to kill someone. The girl was also suspected of poisoning a high school peer. In 2004, an 11-year-old girl in Sasebo killed her classmate with a knife. She was detained in a state facility for 4 years. In 1997, in Kobe, a 14-year-old, Shinichirou Azuma who called himself "Seito Sakakibara" (Apostle Devil Rose), killed two children, Ayaka Yamashita, 10 years old, and Jun Hase, 11 years old. They were bludgeoned with a pipe and strangled, plus three others were injured. Hase's severed head was left by the school gate with a note stuffed in his mouth taunting the police. Azuma had a history of violence toward people and cruelty to animals. He was eventually detained in the juvenile justice system for a little over 6 years. It was this case that led to the age of responsibility being lowered from 16 to 14 years old in 2000. Other reactions have included legislative efforts to drop the age of majority from 20 to 18 years old. More punitiveness has been restrained by the perception that maladjusted youngsters are not totally culpable as they reflect the failings of their social context.

Such horrific cases led a majority of the population to believe that juvenile offending is increasing when in actuality, it has been declining. In 2012, the delinquency rate was 6.7 per 1000 (Ellis & Kyo, 2017). There were 203,684 arrests of minors in 2003 but 90,413 by 2013. There were 96 minors involved in homicides in 2003 but 55 in 2013 (Ito, 2015). The overall decreasing delinquency seems to be related to Japan's decreasing birth rate. Some experts believe that those who do offend might be reacting negatively to the enormous academic pressure to achieve in Japan (BBC, 2001). Japan's children have long been academic leaders in achievement scores, and adults have been known to work themselves to death, such that some companies have started to turn off company lights at 10 p.m. to encourage their workers to go home. Midnight trains in the cities tend to be packed with workers. Stressed-out people might experience frustration and dissatisfaction, commonly referred to as mukatsuku. This can erupt into sudden self- or other harmful conduct called kireru (referred to as someone having "snapped" in the United States). Relatedly, the calls for a more punitive juvenile justice might reflect an increasing diversity in Japan's population that makes life less familiar to its aging citizens and informal social controls less powerful (this is called the nihonjinron view) (Yoder, 2011). Curiously, while youth offending has been declining, offending by those over 65 years of age has been increasing.

What has been increasing among the youth are instances of school bullying (ijime). This has been associated with increases in youth suicides (Victim's Justice, 2015) and dropping out (tokokyohi). Yoder (2011) concluded that student bullying seems to be a learned behavior given the teachers' bullying of students to conform. At risk are students who may differ in given foreign ways, a physical disability, being a slow learner, a loner or loner-nerd (otaku), etc. School for too many is a place of dread. Unconnected youth can then fall prey to youth motorcycle gangs (bosozoku) or crime syndicate gangs like the Yakuza.

4 The Japanese Juvenile Justice System

The premise of the Japanese juvenile justice system rests on the notion that for juveniles to become successful adults, they should be given both education and protection (Hartjen, 2008). Based on Article 3 of the Japanese Juvenile Law, a juvenile is referred to as an individual ranging from 14 to 19 years of age and who has committed a criminal act. Also according to Japanese law, delinquency covers three different behaviors: (1) offenses committed by juveniles who are 14 years and older (defined as juvenile delinquents/offenders), (2) juveniles who are younger than 14 years of age and have committed an illegal act (defined as juveniles below 14), and (3) juveniles who are more inclined to violate the law and/or commit an offense based on their living environment, personalities, and/or inability to follow instructions (defined as predelinquents) (Ministry of Justice, 2015). Consider, for example, the findings of Kumagami and Matsuura (2009) who found that in a study of 428 cases in family court, juveniles from severe environmental circumstances were more likely to have a pervasive developmental disorder than youth in the general population. Juveniles with this disorder had significantly higher rates of sex-related offenses, thus emphasizing the relationship between context and juvenile outcomes.

Both the implementation and philosophy of the original Juvenile Act placed emphasis on diverting juveniles from the criminal justice system and rehabilitating them (Ryan, 2005).

Therefore, the Japanese juvenile justice model includes an aspect of informality where decision-making is based on the family court, but there are various actors—probation officers, judges, police, welfare workers, and public prosecutors (bengoshi)—involved in the process. The structure of the Japanese juvenile justice system therefore allows for the processing of various offenders (see Fig. 18.1). For example, if a juvenile committed a less severe offense which may be punishable with a fine, the judicial police official sends the case to the family court. In the event of a severe offense, the official may send the case to a public prosecutor. Juveniles younger than 14 (predelinquents) are subject to the Child Welfare Law. The police may investigate a situation or event if they suspect that a juvenile younger than 14 has committed an illegal act. Based on the investigation, the police are expected to send the case to a child consultation center director. For serious offenses, the director is expected to send the case to the family court. The identity of juvenile defendants must be kept out of the media per Article 61 of the law.

Punishment is not allowed for persons under 14 per Article 41 given an assumption of a lack of criminal capacity, that is, an inability to distinguish right from wrong. For those 14–20 years old, punishment must be a very rare response and is limited to those who are at least 16 years old. Overall, rehabilitation is the system's central goal. Researchers Ellis and Kyo (2017) concluded that Japan has retained its *parens patriae*-like orientation because unlike the United States, the philosophy has not been challenged in Japan as in the United States with *US v. Gault* in 1967 which severely weakened it by extending to juveniles a number of legal rights. Further, the

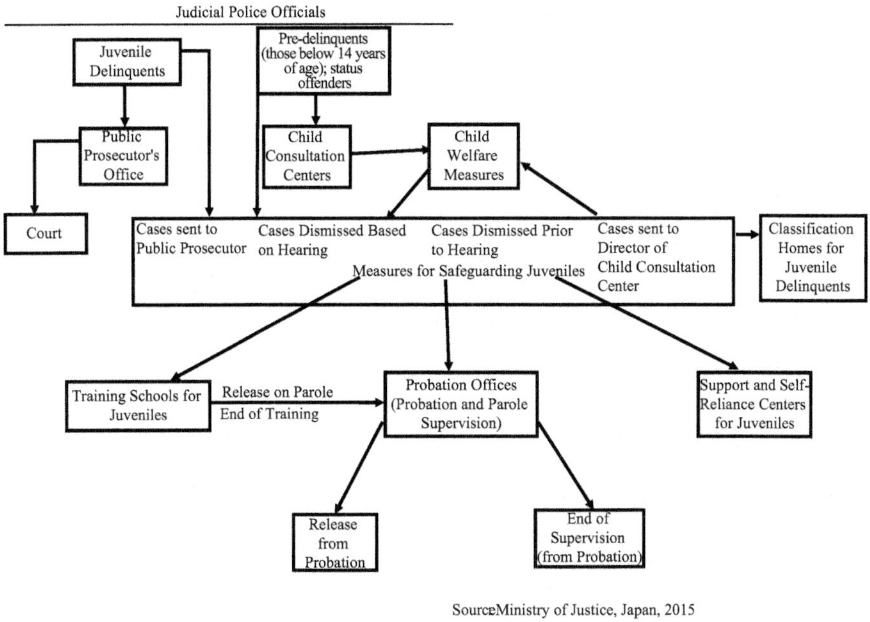

Fig. 18.1 An overview of the Japanese juvenile justice system

Japanese have frowned at efforts to have the police attempt to profile likely predelinquent youth based on their record of status-type offenses (Terrill, 2009).

5 The Family Court Procedures

Judicial power is established by the supreme court and other courts, according to the Japanese constitution (Elrod & Yokoyama, 2006). Within this framework, the family court plays a crucial role in juvenile justice. A number of cases referred to it are summary judgment cases or kanisochi which are dispensed without a hearing (Ellis & Kyo, 2017). While there is one primary family court, there are various branches in each of Japan's prefectures (similar to districts). The family court may send juveniles to a classification home for an evaluation, protection, and observation. The Juvenile Classification Home Act (Act no. 59 of 2014—full effect on July 1, 2015) covered the administration and management of juvenile classification homes.

In cases where juveniles are committed to classification homes, they are evaluated based on the expertise of the specific home (in other words, the juvenile is evaluated based on the specific home's knowledge of pedagogy, medicine, sociology, psychology, and other factors) that may aid the family court's hearing. Findings from the classification home are then shared with the probation office and/or training school as a guide for a juvenile's treatment following the hearing and any ruling regarding protective measures for the juvenile (Ministry of Justice, 2015). It should also be noted that the family court first investigates the cases assigned to it before sending juveniles to classification homes.

6 Family Court Hearings

Japan has 50 family courts (Terrill, 2009). The number of cases sent to family court is relatively small; for example, there were 343 cases in 2013 (Ellis & Kyo, 2017). After an investigation, the family court usually issues a ruling for when a hearing will begin. Generally, only one judge will preside over a hearing in the family court. However, there are cases in which several judges are expected to hear and make decisions. These cases are usually based on legal statutes or when a panel has issued a certain ruling. While guardians and/or juveniles can name an assistant, they are required to get the family court's permission to name an individual in place of the attorney as the assistant (Ministry of Justice, 2015). Juvenile hearings are generally private, but victims may be able to observe hearings if the court grants them permission following their requests to such hearings, provided that the victim's observation will not adversely impact the juvenile's development.

For serious offenses, the family court must allow a public prosecutor to participate in the process which could include a hearing to help determine the facts of the case. Juveniles may be able to have an attorney to aid their cases or the court may assign an attorney, if they do not have one. If the family court finds that protective measures are needed, the juvenile may be placed on probation and assigned a probation officer. The court may suggest short-term probation, depending on the delinquency level. Generally, juveniles on probation are assigned a probation officer who offers guidance, instructions, supervision, and assistance that should promote their rehabilitation prior to the termination of probation or until age 20. In 2001, Japan had less than 1000 probation officers but 50,000 volunteer probation officers each with about four youth on a caseload (BBC, 2001).

In some cases, it is not possible to offer juveniles protective measures given the nature and seriousness of their offenses. Consequently, the family court may decide to refer the case to the director of a child consultation center, if appropriate, or refer the case to a public prosecutor. Generally, when the case is referred to a public prosecutor, the case is considered punishable by either imprisonment (that is, imprisonment without or with work) or death (Ministry of Justice, 2015). Serious offenses committed by juvenile offenders, who are at least 16 years of age, that have led to a victim's death are referred to a public prosecutor by the family court. More generally, the family court is expected to assign juveniles to probation and send them to a foster home (if juveniles are under 18 years old), a self-reliance support center, or training school (juveniles should be at least 12 years old) for less severe offenses.

An attorney for the juvenile and/or the juvenile him/herself may appeal a ruling that requires protective measures within a specified timeframe, typically 2 weeks, if there are any errors in the facts, violation of regulations, or other occurrences that might be considered unsuitable. As noted by the Ministry of Justice (2015), a public prosecutor, who participated in the hearing, may ask a high court to review the case within specified timeframe. Why are these judges so particularly child welfare oriented? Their training differs from that in many other countries. After law school and passage of the bar examination, there is a year and a half of training at the Legal Training and Research Institute. Thereafter, persons apply for a position as either a public procurator or a judge (Terrill, 2009).

For children sent to foster homes and self-reliance support centers, the Child Welfare Law is used as a guide. Based on this act, these homes and support centers are generally open and offer children the essential tools they need to become developmentally sound individuals. In contrast, those juveniles sent to training schools and/or placed on parole are considered to be "in custody." The Ministry of Justice (2015) noted that there were 52 training schools for juveniles in Japan. Juveniles may remain in a training school until age 20, although in some cases they may remain in training schools until age 26. For example, the training school superintendent may extend a juvenile's commitment until he/she is 23 years old, or the family court may extend a juvenile's commitment until 26 years old for medical reasons. More generally, juveniles may be released prior to the termination of their commitment or after the termination of their commitment, according to a parole board's ruling.

Of the 343 cases sent to family court in 2013, 30 (8.7%) were addressed without a hearing. Of the 313 going through a hearing, 123 (39%) received probation; 94 (30%) were held in a training school; 41 (13%) were placed in a social welfare institution; 27 (9%) were served by a social welfare agency; and 28 (9%) had no further action (Ellis & Kyo, 2017). For juveniles, the Bureau of Corrections (within the Ministry of Justice) has juvenile prisons, juvenile training schools, and juvenile classification homes (for mental and/or physical treatment) available. The programming for reform tends to involve individually tailored education, socialization to conform to group norms, and reintegration preparation (Reformatory sets mock law trials, 2010). For foreign-born juveniles, there is a special emphasis on learning Japanese ways of being as a part of the reintegration process (Osaki, 2014). A comparable Rehabilitation Bureau (also under the Ministry of Justice) oversees the release and supervision of inmates.

In practice, the Japanese juvenile justice system generally operates on reintegrative shaming and restorative justice principles (Sakiyama, Lu, & Lang, 2011). The underlying premise of reintegrative shaming rests on the notion that disapproval (also referred to as shame) along with forgiveness, respect, and acceptance by society may lead to a lower crime rate if the disapproval of crime is communicated effectively. The restorative justice aspects reflect the Japanese emphasis on apologies and redemption minus the guilt.

The system has long been criticized as discounting victims in its efforts to rehabilitate offenders and to protect offenders' rights. For example, despite the heinous nature of some offenses, the identity of offenders is protected, and victims' families were not privy to family court proceedings until as late as 2008. Now, victims and their families may make impact statements and have the right to have hearing outcomes explained to them.

7 Conclusion

In many ways, the Japanese juvenile justice system is quite similar to the American juvenile justice system. Both systems aim to balance competing goals—welfare (protection and sound development of juveniles) and punishment (accountability for violation of the penal code)—although the challenge is perhaps more stark in the United States where juvenile offending is more common than in Japan. While it is evident that some features of Japan's juvenile justice system are similar to the United States, it is important not to broadly generalize in this regard as Japan's system is rather uniquely reflective of Japan's cultural influences. Japan remains a largely homogenous society, and it does not share some of the challenges that a more diverse country, like the United States, encounters with regard to crime and delinquency as there are varying community challenges across the United States. In many delinquencies, root causes and challenges, coupled with Japan's culture, are unique, which makes it an important country to review and highlight its similarities to the United States where possible.

Empirical studies on crime and punishment in Japan appear to be limited (Sakiyama, Lu, & Lang, 2011), but in cases where there have been increases in crime and delinquency, both the public and the law appear to be more supportive of more punitive measures or seek ways to address crime-related issues. For example, comprehensive reform measures were introduced in 2012 as part of the government's efforts to address recidivism (Ministry of Justice, 2015). Youth are assumed to be at risk for deviance given increasing academic pressures that eventually forces some youngsters out of conventional competitiveness. For these socially isolated youngsters, deviance can become an attractive option. The Japanese government is aware of research evidence that indicates that youth are less likely to recidivate if they are employed and supported by their families (The Daily Yomiuri, 2011). Additionally, within the system's residential facilities, there has been an increased care in monitoring the safety of the youngsters after a Hiroshima Juvenile Reformatory staff abuse scandal. Overall, Japan's juvenile justice orientation remains one of treatment.

References

BBC. (2001). Japanese Juvenile Justice. *BBC World Service transcript*. Retrieved from http://www.bbc.co.uk/worldservice/people/highlights/010223_japan.shtml

Central Intelligence Agency. (2017). *The world factbook: Japan*. Retrieved from https://www.cia.gov/library/publications/the-world-factbook/geos/ja.html

Chung, J. J. (2016). The politics of criminal and juvenile justice policies in Japan. *Crime, Law and Social Change, 66*, 359–374.

Ellis, T., & Kyo, A. (2017). Reassessing juvenile justice in Japan: Net widening or diversion? *The Asia-Pacific Journal, 15*(9), 1–17.

Elrod, P., & Yokoyama, M. (2006). Juvenile justice in Japan. In P. C. Friday & X. Ren (Eds.), *Delinquency and juvenile justice systems in the non-Western world* (pp. 211–228). Monsey, NY: Criminal Justice Press.

Hartjen, C. A. (2008). *Youth, crime, and justice*. Piscataway, NJ: Rutgers University Press.

Ito, M. (2015, May 23). Shifting the scales of justice. *The Japan Times*. Retrieved from http://www.japantimes.co.jp/news/2015/05/23/national/social-issues/shifting-scales-juvenile-justice/

Kumagami, T., & Matsuura, N. (2009). Prevalence of pervasive developmental disorder in juvenile court cases in Japan. *The Journal of Forensic Psychiatry and Psychology, 20*, 974–987.

Kuzuno, H. (2006). Juvenile diversion and the get-tough movement in Japan. *Ritsumeikan Law Review, 22*, 1–21.

Ministry of Justice. (2015). *White paper on crime*. Tokyo, Research and Training Institute. Retrieved from http://hakusyo1.moj.go.jp/en/64/nfm/n_64_2_3_1_0_0.html

Minoru, Y. (2015). Juvenile justice and juvenile crime: An overview of Japan. In J. A. Winterdyk (Ed.), *Juvenile justice: International perspectives, models, and trends* (pp. 179–208). Boca Raton, FL: CRC Press/Taylor & Francis Group.

Miyazawa, S. (2008). The politics of increasing punitiveness and the rising populism in Japanese criminal justice policy. *Punishment and Society, 10*, 47–77.

Osaki, T. (2014, January 9). Foreign delinquency presents special challenges. *The Japan Times* n.p.

Reformatory sets mock lay trials. (2010, May 16). *The Daily Yomiuri (Tokyo)*. p. 3.

Ryan, T. (2005). Creating 'problem kids': Juvenile crime in Japan and revisions to the juvenile act. *Journal of Japanese Law/Zeitschrift fur Japanisches Recht, 19*, 153–188. Retrieved from https://sydney.edu.au/law/anjel/documents/ZJapanR/ZJapanR19_11_Ryan.pdf

Sakiyama, M., Lu, H., & Liang, B. (2011). Reintegrative shaming and juvenile delinquency in Japan. *Asian Criminology, 6*, 161–175.

Terrill, R. J. (2009). *World criminal justice systems: A survey* (7th ed.). New Providence, NJ: Matthew Bender &.

The Daily Yomiuri. (2011, November 13). *Employment called key to curbing recidivism among young offenders*, p. 3.

Victim's Justice. (2015, July 15). *The Economist*. n.p.

Yoder, R. S. (2011). *Deviance and inequality in Japan: Japanese youth and foreign migrants*. Bristol: The Policy Press.

Yoshinaka, N. (1997). Historical analysis of the juvenile justice system in Japan. *The Hiroshima Law Journal, 20*, 292–302.

Chapter 19
Empirical Research on Sociocultural Transition in Children in a Children's Self-Reliance Support Facility and the Effect of Support

Takaharu Ohara

1 Introduction

In Japan, there are Juvenile Training Schools (*Shonen-in*) for delinquent youths, which provide education under the jurisdiction of the Ministry of Justice, as well as Children's Self-Reliance Support Facilities (*Jido-jiritsu Shien Shisetsu*) under the jurisdiction of the Health, Labor, and Welfare Ministry. There are 52 Juvenile Training Schools and 58 Children's Self-Reliance Support Facilities in Japan (Ministry of Health, Labour and Welfare, 2009). As of 2011, there were 3486 youths in Juvenile Training Schools (Ministry of Justice, 2011) and 1544 in Children's Self-Reliance Support Facilities (Ministry of Health, Labour and Welfare, 2009). In cases of serious delinquency, youths go to Juvenile Training Schools, whereas in cases largely related to home environmental factors, youths are admitted to Children's Self-Reliance Support Facilities. Even though the two facilities seem to have similarities, they provide different support systems. This report focuses on Children's Self-Reliance Support Facilities, which developed their own system of support.

According to the Child Welfare Act, Children's Self-Reliance Support Facilities are defined as:

> facilities intended for admitting children who have committed, or are likely to commit, delinquencies and other children in need of daily life guidance due to their family environment or other environmental reasons, or having those children commute there from their guardians, and providing necessary guidance to these children in accordance with their individual circumstances and supporting their self-reliance. It is also intended to provide consultation and other assistance to those who have left.

T. Ohara (✉)
Self-Reliance Support Facilities, National Musashino Gakuin, Saitama, Japan
e-mail: oharatakaharu@gmail.com

J. Liu, S. Miyazawa (eds.), *Crime and Justice in Contemporary Japan*,
Springer Series on Asian Criminology and Criminal Justice Research,
https://doi.org/10.1007/978-3-319-69359-0_19

The Child Welfare Law Article 36 requires that prefectural governments have these facilities.

The history of Children's Self-Reliance Support Facilities is over 100 years long. They began with the name *Kankain* (reform schools) (1990–1993), which was then changed to *Shonen Kyougo In* (Juvenile Education and Protection Center) (1900–1933), and then *Kyougo In* (Education and Protection Center) (1947–1997).

Changes in laws, particularly the revision of the Child Welfare Act of 1997, expanded admission to include not only "delinquent youths" but also "those who need life guidance, because of their home environment and/or other reasons."

As juvenile delinquency is often described as reflecting the times, the characteristics of the youths in Children's Self-Reliance Support Facilities changed alongside Japanese society, as has their placement in the law. However, despite a history of more than 100 years, there is not enough empirical data on the characteristics of youths admitted to Children's Self-Reliance Support Facilities. Based on the following three findings, this study reveals the sociocultural transition (three decades) of youths in Children's Self-Reliance Support Facilities and the effect of the support provided by the facilities.

2 History and Challenges of Children's Self-Reliance Support Facilities

2.1 Historical Changes in Children's Self-Reliance Support Facilities

The history of changes in the treatment of juvenile delinquency can be traced back to the *Kanka Law Act* enacted in 1900. Before then, the treatment of juvenile delinquency was carried out under the *Kangokusoku* (Regulations for Prisons), which was anything but educational and positioned as part of criminal policy (National Children's Self-reliance Support Facility Council, 1999). The *Kanka-ho* was established to influence youths aged 8–15 years who had lost their caregivers, committed a delinquency, and had delinquent companionship; in other words, it was founded to provide a positive influence by admitting delinquents to a facility to improve their emotional and behavioral problems. By this law, *Kankain* were established throughout the nation, and the national reformatory (*Kokuritsu Kankain*) was founded in 1919.

In 1933, *Shonen Kyougo-ho* (the Juvenile Education and Protection Act) was established to institutionalize youths aged less than 14 years who committed or were likely to commit delinquent acts. *Shonen Kyougo In* (Juvenile Education and Protection Centers) can be characterized as follows:

1. They were appointed by the Shonen Kyougo Committee for delinquency prevention, early detection, and probation supervision.
2. They introduced temporary protection, as necessary, before putting youths on probation.

3. They established juvenile detention centers for the scientific examination of youths.
4. They opened doorways for discharged youths to obtain an academic certificate equivalent to Jinjo Elementary School education (elementary school in the old education system).
5. They were forbidden to publish the names of youths on juvenile probation in newspapers.
6. They enabled that juvenile detention centers could receive a government subsidy.
7. They appointed the nationwide Shonen Kyougo Committee (National Children's Self-reliance Support Facility Council, 1999).

As a result, *Kanka In* was renamed *Shonen Kyougo In*.

Subsequently, upon Japan's defeat in World War II, there were homeless children and orphans throughout the country, which was when the measurement proved most useful. In 1947, the Child Welfare Act was enacted, and *Shonen Kyougo In* was renamed *Kyougo In*. Specifically, pursuant to the fundamental principle of the Child Welfare Act, which strives to guarantee the welfare of children and provide for the *Kyougo* and the particular care and protection of certain youth instead of their parents, these child welfare facilities provided the appropriate environment for children. *Kyougo* staff members spend daily life with them to improve their lives through guidance, so that these children could become healthy members of society in the future (Ministry of Health and Welfare Children's Bureau, 1959). The age for admission was less than 18 years.

With the revision of the Child Welfare Act of 1997, *Kyougo In* changed its name to Children's Self-Reliance Support Facilities. The following revisions were made:

1. The socially negative (stigmatizing) name was no longer used.
2. To meet additional needs that arose because of a lack of child-rearing capacity, the definition of targeted youths was extended from "children who committed or are likely to commit delinquencies" to "other children in need of daily life guidance in their family environment or other environmental reasons," and support was provided after discharge to assist the children's independence.
3. In addition to the existing forms of admission, a commute system was adopted to alter the closed facility, which was isolated from society (until now only admission).
4. The facilities now conduct normal school education (public education) for admitted children (Kobayashi, 2004).

2.2 Challenges

Thus, Children's Self-Reliance Support Facilities today have a long history and tradition among other child welfare facilities. However, there is little data or information regarding the characteristics of children in the different times of their operation. Therefore, the following problems emerge:

1. There is not enough empirical data on admitted children depicting their presenting status.
2. There is not enough empirical data for presenting the status of admitted children, their transition between being admitted and discharged, and their prognosis.
3. In connection with the above, the presenting status of youths from the perspectives of legal, social, and cultural transitions has not been revealed.

3 Objectives

The purpose of this study is to reveal the presenting status of admitted children based on empirical data. Therefore, in this study, we targeted children in the Children's Self-Reliance Support Facility and extracted the necessary information from their records. We tried to objectively measure their attributes, transition, and delinquency, as well as changes in their family relationships.

4 Methods

4.1 Subject and Period

In this study, the subjects included the records of children (only males) in a particular Children's Self-Reliance Support Facility and their lives. The period of study is 30 years, from 1980 to 2010. The records include information on admitted children such as their history and family background. Welfare officers at the Child Guidance Center are required to create a record of each child. An analysis of these records enables an understanding of the presenting status of the children before they were admitted. The life records capture staff reports on the children's presenting status after admission, thus providing information on the children from their admission to discharge as well as their prognosis.

4.2 Extraction Items

Basic attributes included: (1) age at the time of admission; (2) reason for referral; (3) types of delinquency, which became the reason for admission; (4) how many times they changed facilities; (5) parents' ages; (6) family background (number of siblings); (7) history and type(s) of abuse; and (8) age at the time of the first admission for the first delinquency.

Attributes after admission included: (1) age at the time of admission; (2) intelligence quotient; (3) academic scores during admission and at discharge (for Japanese, Social Study, Math, Science, Music, Art, Physical Education, Technological Arts,

Home Economics, and Foreign Language); (4) ADL (basic lifestyle, autonomy, responsibility, perseverance, ingenuity, emotional stability, tolerance, cooperation, fairness, and public morality), emotions, behavior, and relationships measured at the time of admission and discharge; (5) social resources (number of contact situations with family, etc.); (6) types of delinquency during admission; and (7) career or further education after discharge.

4.3 *Input Method, Analysis Method, and Perspectives*

For input, we created a manual that specified the extraction criteria for each item and carried out in multiple people. For selection criteria, we reviewed the standards until researchers met a 100% rate of consistency.

For the analysis, we divided the time into decades, namely, the 1980s, 1990s, and 2000s, and conducted simple counting using SPSS.

4.4 *Ethical Considerations*

The subjects of this study were the records of children in the past. Therefore, it is difficult to directly obtain the consent of the children or parents. Instead, we explained the purpose, significance, research method, and ethical considerations of this study to the principal of the facility and obtained consent. The subject facility and the admitted children remained anonymous, and data has been encrypted.

In addition, the study was certified by the "Ethics Committee for Research on Human Subjects" at Sophia's University. Furthermore, the study was part of the facility's projects.

5 Results

The subjects were the cases of 483 children admitted to the Children's Self-Reliance Support Facility between 1980 and 2010 (252 cases in the 1980s, 147 in the 1990s, and 84 in the 2000s). There were some missing values for some extracted items; however, as they are valuable data, we decided to use them effectively.

5.1 *Basic Attributes*

The average ages of the placements were 13.4 years (SD = 1.6) for the 1980s, 13.9 years (SD = 1.6) for the 1990s, and 14.3 years (SD = 1.6) for the 2000s. Respectively, the ages of onset were 9.8 years (SD = 2.9), 9.9 years (SD = 2.8), and

Table 19.1 Characteristics of children

	1980s			1990s			2000s		
	N	*M*	SD	*N*	*M*	SD	*N*	*M*	SD
Age of placement	252	13.4	1.6	147	13.9	1.6	84	14.3	1.6
Age of first juvenile delinquency	238	9.8	2.9	143	9.9	2.8	75	9.6	3.3
Period of placement	244	583	384	144	582	472	79	489	392
IQ	234	91.1	14.8	139	87.4	12.8	74	85.9	14.5
Age of placement-age of first juvenile delinquency	237	3.7	2.6	143	4.0	2.8	75	4.6	3.1

9.6 years (SD = 3.3), and the periods of admission were 583 days (SD = 384), 582 days (SD = 472), and 489 days (SD = 391). Finally, their IQs were 91.9 (SD = 14.8), 87.4 (SD = 12.8), and 85.9 (SD = 14.5), respectively. The value obtained by subtracting the initial delinquency age from the age at the time of admission was 3.7 years (SD = 2.6), 4.0 years (SD = 2.8), and 4.6 years (SD = 3.1) (Table 19.1).

5.2 *Types of Delinquency (Before Admission)*

For the types of delinquency for which the children were admitted, we conducted simple counting for each decade (Table 19.2). It should be noted that the types of delinquency were not once-off events. The children were admitted after repeating multiple types of delinquencies.

In the 1980s, 134 youths committed bicycle and motor bicycle theft (53.6%), 171 theft (68.4%), 60 threatened others (24.0%), 168 went missing from home (67.2%), 65 were involved in drug abuse (26.1%), 92 smoked (36.8%), and 95 took money from home (38.0%).

In the 1990s, 7 children committed snatching (4.8%), 7 fraud (4.8%), 35 threatened others (24.1%), 88 demonstrated nighttime wandering (61.1%), 76 demonstrated delinquent companionship (52.1%), committed arson (8.3%), 22 played with fire (15.1%), 13 drank alcohol (8.9%), 29 demonstrated reckless driving (19.9%), 36 damaged property (24.7%), 27 were bullied (18.5%), and 119 neglected their schoolwork (81.5%).

In the 2000s, 50 children committed shoplifting (60.2%), 18 domestic violence (21.7%), 24 school violence (28.9%), 25 other types of violence (30.1%), 5 molested children (6.0%), 4 molested someone of the same age or older (4.8%), 4 had sexual problems with others of the same sex (10.8%), 20 displayed behaviors related to sexual problems (24.1%), and 14 hazer (16.9%).

Table 19.2 Characteristics of juvenile delinquency

		1980s	1990s	2000s
Shoplifting	*N*	122	79	50
	%	48.8	54.1	60.2
Snatcher	*N*	6	7	2
	%	2.4	4.8	2.4
Make off with a bicycle and bike	*N*	134	67	34
	%	53.6	45.9	41.0
Theft (others)	*N*	171	78	27
	%	68.4	53.4	32.5
DV	*N*	35	23	18
	%	14.0	15.8	21.7
School violence	*N*	36	26	24
	%	14.4	17.8	28.9
Violence of others	*N*	43	29	25
	%	17.2	19.9	30.1
Fraud	*N*	5	7	1
	%	2.1	4.8	1.2
Blackmail	*N*	60	35	9
	%	24.0	24.1	10.8
Runaway and sleepover	*N*	168	90	44
	%	67.2	62.5	53.0
Nighttime wandering	*N*	131	88	41
	%	52.8	61.1	49.4
Consort with a rogue	*N*	114	76	28
	%	45.6	52.1	33.7
Arson	*N*	9	12	3
	%	3.6	8.3	3.6
Play with fire	*N*	17	22	8
	%	6.8	15.1	9.8
Drug	*N*	65	32	2
	%	26.1	21.9	2.4
Smoking	*N*	92	62	28
	%	36.8	42.5	33.7
Drinking	*N*	7	13	6
	%	2.8	8.9	7.2
Indecent assault of juniority opposite sex	*N*	7	2	5
	%	2.8	1.4	6.0
Indecent assault of the same age	*N*	3	4	4
	%	1.2	2.7	4.8
Sexual problem of same sex	*N*	1	5	9
	%	0.4	3.4	10.8
Sexual problem	*N*	13	18	20
	%	5.2	12.3	24.1

(continued)

Table 19.2 (continued)

		1980s	1990s	2000s
Take out of money in my house	*N*	95	54	28
	%	38.0	37.0	33.7
Biker-gang	*N*	32	29	7
	%	12.7	19.9	8.4
Damage to property	*N*	31	36	16
	%	12.8	24.7	19.3
Bully	*N*	23	21	14
	%	9.2	14.4	16.9
Bullied	*N*	30	27	13
	%	12.0	18.5	15.7
Cutting of school	*N*	184	119	56
	%	73.6	81.5	68.3

5.3 *Parental Factors (Before Admission)*

We added the total of parents' conditions described in the records of the children. We conducted simple counting for each decade. The overall results are shown in Table 19.3. In 1980, compared to other decades, there was no single major factor.

For the 1980s, 147 parents demonstrated a lack of parenting skills (59.5%), 123 had difficulties parenting (50.2%), and 119 had marital problems (48.0%), which is a marked majority.

For the 1990s, 5 parents were teenagers (3.4%), 76 had marital problems (51.7%), 46 had livelihood protection (31.3%), 68 experienced parent-child conflict (46.3%), 24 parents had prison records (16.3%), and 81 had parenting difficulties (55.1%).

For the 2000s, 13 parents had mental disorders (15.9%), 8 parents were suspected of mental disorders (9.8%), 35 parents were emotionally unstable (42.7%), 60 parents had intellectual disabilities (73.2%), 24 parents had addiction problems (drugs, alcohol) (29.3%), 6 parents were of foreign nationality (7.3%), 26 had Domestic Violence (DV;31.7%), 41 had economic problems (50.0%), and 26 had livelihood protection (31.7%).

6 Discussion

This study revealed the basic attributes and characteristics of delinquency, as well as parental factors based on the records of children in the Children's Self-Reliance Support Facility between the 1980s and 2000s. The subjects were 483 male children (252 cases in the 1980s, 147 in the 1990s, and 84 in the 2000s). First, we consider the basic attributes.

Table 19.3 Characteristics of parent

		1980s	1990s	2000s
Parental mental disorder	*N*	15	8	13
	%	6.2	5.5	15.9
Parental suspicion of mental disorder	*N*	12	9	8
	%	4.9	6.2	9.8
Parental emotional instability	*N*	57	50	35
	%	23.1	34.0	42.7
Parental intellectual disability	*N*	15	9	3
	%	6.0	6.1	3.7
Parental inexperience	*N*	147	91	60
	%	59.5	61.9	73.2
Underage parent	*N*	4	5	2
	%	1.6	3.4	2.4
Dependence (alcohol, drug)	*N*	41	27	24
	%	16.5	18.4	29.3
Marital discord	*N*	119	76	38
	%	48.0	51.7	46.3
Parental foreign nationality	*N*	6	3	6
	%	2.4	2.0	7.3
DV	*N*	48	29	26
	%	19.2	19.7	31.7
Economic poverty	*N*	102	64	41
	%	41.1	43.5	50.0
Livelihood protection	*N*	56	46	26
	%	22.7	31.3	31.7
Parent-child conflict	*N*	60	68	24
	%	24.3	46.3	29.3
Parental prison records	*N*	28	24	11
	%	11.4	16.3	13.4
Parenting difficulty	*N*	123	81	45
	%	50.2	55.1	54.2

6.1 Basic Attributes

The ages of placement tended to increase from 13.4 years in the 1980s to 14.3 years in the 2000s. On the other hand, the admission periods gradually decreased from 583 days in the 1980s, 582 days in the 1990s, to 489 days in the 2000s. In other words, as time progressed since the 1980s, therapeutic education was completed and the children were discharged within shorter periods.

However, this does not necessarily mean that more effective treatment education was adopted during this time. Rather, in the institutional system, most children are discharged when they complete compulsory education.

In addition, as the admission age increases, it is necessary to consider that it may be associated with the age of the initial delinquency. The onset ages for each decade were between 9 and 10 years, except in 2000, when it was comparatively lower. Therefore, as time progressed, the periods from the initial delinquency age to admission lengthened. This means that the result indicating an increasing admission age is not because thc initial delinquency age increased; rather, new admissions are getting younger, and society treats these children instead. As background, this is influenced more by the judgment of caseworkers at the Child Guidance Center than by the Child Self-Reliance Support Facility. This must be considered from multiple perspectives; for example, it may be too difficult for caseworkers at the Child Guidance Center to deal with delinquency while they are occupied daily with reports of abuse. Even though they try to achieve adjustment to the environment, it depends on whether the children will be ultimately admitted to the institution.

Furthermore, for the actual measurement, it is necessary to provide early effective support between the initial delinquency and admission (3.7 years in the 1980s to 4.6 years in the 2000s).

6.2 Types of Delinquency and Parental Factors

Yamaguchi (1999) named types of delinquency from 1971 to 1989 as "types of delinquency related to parenting problems." In the 1970s, a number of heinous and violent delinquencies were evident; however, these decreased after peaking in 1983. They were replaced by "minor delinquencies" or "impulsive delinquencies" such as dumping bicycles and shoplifting (Yamaguchi, 1999). A state of anomie can be pointed out as the background to these shifts.

In this study, delinquencies characterizing the 1980s were bicycle and motor bicycle theft, theft, and drug abuse, somewhat similar to Yamaguchi (1999) "impulsive delinquency," or as presented in the third peak of juvenile delinquency as a "play delinquency" (Muramatsu,2002).

In this regard, parental factors in the 1980s were not as major as in the other two decades. In other words, compared to other decades, a state of anomie in the period was presented as delinquency, more than was parental factors. However, considering the home environment such as whether abuse was present may reveal the characteristics of the Children's Self-Reliance Support Facility; therefore, there is a need for further consideration in the future.

Second, delinquencies characterizing the 1990s were nighttime wandering, delinquent companionship, and reckless driving. Yamaguchi (1999) named these characteristics "delinquencies related to parenting problems," pointing out the major changes in parenting and children's growth, and the delinquency of children who could only find their place in virtual reality.

Muramatsu (2002) considers the characteristics of delinquency after 1997 as "new types of delinquency." Citing previous studies by Shimizu (1999), he pointed out that recent types of delinquency are characterized as a momentary instantaneous manifestation of personal feelings such as "it is disgusting" and "pissing off."

In this study, major delinquencies among children in the facility were as follows: 88 children displayed nighttime wondering (61.1%), 76 delinquent companionship (52.1%), 35 threatening behaviors (24.1%), 29 reckless driving (19.9%), and 36 damaged property (24.7%). Extending the play types of delinquency, these can be characterized as seeking stimulation as a group.

For the 2000s, many children were admitted to the facility for shoplifting, violence at home, and behaviors related to sexual problems. In addition, the major parental factors were as follows: 36 parents were immature or lacked parenting skills (73.2%), 35 were emotionally unstable (42.7%), and 24 had problems with addiction (drugs and alcohol) (29.3%). Many of the parents also experienced abuse; thus, this generation seemed to differ in terms of merely displaying delinquent behavior. More juvenile youths were admitted to the facility, because of developmental problems or difficulties controlling their effects and behaviors. In other words, these children displayed "emotional behavioral delinquency."

7 Summary and Future Challenges

This study revealed the characteristics of children admitted to Children's Self-Reliance Support Facilities, which traditionally provided therapeutic education for delinquent youths in Japan. Especially for the three decades between the 1980s and the 2010s, the characteristics of delinquency and parental factors were the focus of attention. However, there are future challenges.

First, the data used in this study are based on the records of children at the Child Guidance Center, and the information is limited to what we could understand from the context provided in the reports. In addition, the period is limited to the 30 years between 1980 and 2010, which is restrictive. It is planned to supplement the data with information from the 1950s to the 1970s.

Second, the simple counting method was used as the method of analysis in this study. Therefore, in the future, it is necessary to add statistical tests to present empirical data. The focus of the study was the characteristics of each decade; therefore, more analysis of correlations between the factors is needed.

Finally, in the discussion, there is a need to further consider mutual correlation among (1) data in the relation to social background and (2) types of delinquency, family background, and abuse.

References

Kobayashi, H. (2004). *Educational security of institutionalized children*. Kyoto: Minerva Shobo.

Ministry of Health and Welfare Children's Bureau. (1959). Kyogo in management guidelines-basic administration version, Japan Child Welfare Association.

Ministry of Health, Labour and Welfare. (2009). *Survey for children admitted to foster homes*. http://www.mhlw.go.jp/toukei/saikin/hw/jidouyougo/19/,2014/10/19

Ministry of Justice. (2011). White paper on crime 2011. http://hakusyo1.moj.go.jp/en/60/nfm/mokuji.html, 2014/10/19

Muramatsu, T. (2002). Juvenile delinquency: Recent trends, clinical. *Psychology, 8*(2), 154–162.

Shimizu, K. (1999). *The world of modern juvenile delinquency*. Yuhikaku.

Yamaguchi, S. (1999). *Children's self-reliance support management handbook; overcoming delinquency and the philosophy and practice of children's independence*. Sangaku Shuppan.

National Children's Self-reliance Support Facility Council (1999). *Children's self-reliance support management handbook; overcoming delinquency and the philosphy and practice of children's independence*. Sangaku Shuppan.

Index

J. Liu, S. Miyazawa (eds.), *Crime and Justice in Contemporary Japan*, Springer Series on Asian Criminology and Criminal Justice Research, https://doi.org/10.1007/978-3-319-69359-0

C